Welcome to the

✳ **Dreamhouse**

CONSOLE-ING PASSIONS

Television and Cultural Power

Edited by Lynn Spigel

Welcome to the

Dreamhouse

Popular Media and Postwar Suburbs

Lynn Spigel

DUKE UNIVERSITY PRESS * Durham and London * 2001

© 2001 Duke University Press
All rights reserved
Printed in the United States of
America on acid-free paper ∞
Designed by Amy Ruth Buchanan
Typeset in Sabon by Tseng
Information Systems, Inc.
Library of Congress Cataloging-in-
Publication Data appear on the last
printed page of this book.

With love to my mother,

Roslyn Spigel,

1922–1999

Contents

Acknowledgments

✱ Thank you to my friends and colleagues for their wisdom and guidance. Charlotte Brunsdon, Julie D'Acci, Michael Curtin, and George Lipsitz read various essays and inspired me with their own work. My dear friends Margie Solovay and Chris Berry always deserve very special thanks. Victoria Johnson, Anna Everett, Steven Classen, Chris Anderson, Ellen Seiter, David Morley, Horace Newcomb, Moya Luckett, Constance Penley, Henry Jenkins, Herman Gray, Nick Browne, Jan Olsson, Mimi White, William Forman, and Mary Beth Haralovich all offered much appreciated support. I'm also grateful to USC friends and colleagues Marita Sturken, Dana Polan, Tania Modleski, Marsha Kinder, Barbara Corday, Michael Renov, Tara McPherson, Alison Trope, and Doug Thomas for their ideas and collaboration over the years. Heather Osborne, Innis Barton, and Liza Trevino provided valuable help with research. I am also grateful to the people at the Wisconsin Center State Historical Archives, the John Fitzgerald Kennedy Library, the USC Doheny Cinema Library, the UCLA Film and Television Archive, the Museum of Television and Radio, the Smithsonian Institution, and the Museum of Modern Art Library and Archive. Finally, I am especially thankful to Jeffrey Sconce for his kindness, intelligence, and humor while I put this collection together.

ship practices, profit incentives, and other political-economic demands all constrain ideals of democratic participation and free speech. However, by attending to the surrounding historical contexts into which media are placed, and by looking at the way they are received or rejected by their publics, we might better understand their wider social and cultural significance. Rather than asking how media have devasted family life or how they have destroyed public culture, we should begin by asking why people have been so invested in perceiving their private lives as separate from their public worlds, and why media have been so central to that set of cultural beliefs.

The essays in this book are based on interpretative method, using archival research and, in two cases, participant observation and interviews. Following the work of Hayden White, Dominick LaCapra, Michel de Certeau and many others, I believe that history is fundamentally an interpretative project.[28] History is a kind of knowledge based not only on the historian's subjective determinations regarding evidence but also on conventions of writing that govern other kinds of textual production. But while I agree with critical historiographers who argue that historical writing is a mode of literary (or mix of literary and scientific) production, I still think that historical arguments need to be researched and judged on supporting evidence. In other words, I believe that historical interpretation is best when based on extensive empirical data. By this I am not suggesting that the "quantity" of facts alone makes or breaks an argument. (A call for empirical evidence is not the same as faith in the philosophical tenants of empiricism.) For in the end, it is the quality questions we pose about our findings that matter. It is the process of interpretation—and the ways in which we use evidence to produce an argument—that is at stake.

In fact, in many cases it is the very absence of evidence that should make us wonder about past events and how to understand them. As Carlo Ginzburg has argued, history is a process of conjecture, more akin to hunting than to science. In a brilliant essay on this subject, Ginzburg shows how three figures of modernity—the art historian/connoisseur Giovanni Morelli, the psychoanalyst Sigmund Freud, and Sir Arthur Conan Doyle's fictional detective Sherlock Holmes—reconstruct past events by following a trail of meanings, by tracing a set of seemingly incidental symptoms. Analyzing their methods of artistic attribution, psychoanalysis, and detection, Ginzburg argues that historical knowledge is based on this kind of semiotic work. Historians look for traces of the past; they search for "clues" to a reality that remains opaque and ultimately unknowable in any absolute way. And following the trail of Morrelli, Freud, and Holmes, Ginzburg claims that it is often the seemingly incidental details that provide the most important clues to past events.[29]

Many of the questions I pose are about elusive and ephemeral realities, about unrecorded histories (or histories of women, children, and people of color whose acts and beliefs don't typically wind up in the archival record). In addition, many of these essays are based on sources that exist in incomplete or partial form. (For example, because it was often shot live, early television programming exists only in cases where people at the time recorded and saved it on kinescope.) Insofar as many of the objects I look at are artifacts of material culture (magazines, television shows, fanzines, toys, etc.) I do my research in flea markets, thrift stores, collector's homes, and by watching television, as much as I use libraries, museums, and archives. From this point of view, it isn't only some pre-ordained method and theory but also the kinds of objects we study and places we actually practice our research that govern the ways we interpret the past. Because my research often takes place in retail spaces as much as it occurs in government or university archives, the divide between what is generally considered high versus low knowledge (or perhaps scholarship versus shopping) is central to the kinds of interpretations I make. In general, my interest has been to scandalize these divisions in the process of research, to demonstrate how scholars must engage fully not only with sources from established archives but also with popular media itself.

Too often studies of popular media are based on one or two examples, or else on a scientific sampling of texts, as if the whole of popular media were so banal and so redundant that each text always said the same thing. It is this bias that governs much of social scientific method (especially traditional content analysis), which starts out by assuming that the purpose is to demonstrate general principles (how many acts of violence or how many negative representations of women are there, for example, in soap operas or sitcoms?). It would be impossible to imagine that the same researcher would come up with a scientific "representative" sample of, for instance, Faulkner or Picasso and then proceed to count the negative portrayals of women in those stories or on those canvases. The works of the "masters" are somehow deemed important for their variation, singularity, and nuance, while the works of popular media are considered wholly repetitive and "typical." However, as Janice Radway has shown in *Reading the Romance,* the people who read and watch popular media often find great differences among texts, and they select them accordingly.[30] The focus on quantity and regularity in media studies obscures the vast differences within popular media—both the texts and their interpretations by audiences.

I am more interested in understanding contradictions and alterity in culture than I am in discovering regularities and covering laws. This focus on the particular, however, does not mean a neglect of the general. Rather, I explore relationships between the particular and the general in ways that force a reevaluation of each. Why do certain examples seem to defy the general logic of the culture? How do seemingly aberrant and marginal activities or thoughts suddenly become "normal" things to do or say? What are the conditions of possibility—the generative mechanisms—through which particular things happen or by which specific statements are made? From this point of view, individual cases are not a set of fetish facts or mere anecdotal flourish with no relation to more abstract thought and generalization. Instead, the individual example becomes the ground for a theorization of language and culture that is capable of understanding things that do not fit into reigning epistemologies or social practices (as well as things that do). From this point of view, these essays rely on the anthropological ideal of "thick description" as I attempt to understand the varied meanings of cultural forms and their social contexts.

Many of these essays are based on documents that historians typically consider "bad evidence." Why study mass media to understand culture when mass media present clearly biased views generated by the culture industry—not by people? For one thing, all documents are "biased" in some way. Nothing is written without some intent, some set of power relations between those who record their history and those who don't, some internal enunciative logic. Court documents are filled with power relations and biased accounts; census reports are filled with ideologies about what constitutes a household or what is worth measuring. Oral history accounts are replete with power relations between the interviewer, interviewee, and the historian's imagined reader. Diaries are not simply the "horse's mouth"; they are based on literary conventions for autobiography formed in women's culture. As so many historians admit, there is no source that is not without its own conditions of power and its own conventions of representation through which it speaks to its imagined publics.

From this point of view, it is always a matter of how the historian uses the source—what questions she asks of it and what answers she assumes it can provide. Clearly, the documents I use here—women's magazines, advertisements, television shows, films, books—do not reflect their society directly. I look at mass media as evidence not for what people do, think, or feel but for evidence of what they read, watch, and say. From this perspective, media products form an intertextual network—a set of related texts—through which people encounter statements about and images of their social world. These statements and images form a horizon of expectations about that world. For example, in my work on early television I am interested in the ways popular media spoke of the new medium and how the media devised rules for watching TV. In my work on television and art I am interested in the way television directed the public to think about the arts in America and the ways in which these expectations coincided with concerns in the art world itself. Or, in my essay on Barbie I am interested in how people generate their own artistic and autobiographical statements out of the raw materials provided by commercial culture to the degree that they transform Barbie into an art object and source of collective memory. By looking at mass media as something other than simply "bad evidence" we might begin to understand the role commercial culture plays in people's everyday lives.

As I stated early on, many of these essays explore visual media and commercial culture in relation to practices of everyday life in the postwar suburb. While people obviously consume mass media in places other than suburbia, and while the suburb is itself a nineteenth-century invention, my focus here is on the rise of a new kind of mass-produced suburb in postwar America and its cultural dominance as a postwar landscape. By looking at visual media culture (especially television) and suburbia in connection with one another I am interested in how the two mutually reinforce each other as social practices and cultural fantasies. Television and suburbs are both engineered spaces, designed and planned by people who are engaged in giving material reality to wider cultural belief systems. In addition, media and suburbs are sites where meanings are produced and created; they are spaces (whether material or electronic) in which people make sense of their social relationships to each other, their communities, their nation, and the world at large. The simultaneous rise of the mass-produced suburb and a ubiquitous place called Televisionland raises a set of questions that scholars have only recently begun to ask.

Emerging scholarship on the postwar suburb and consumer culture has attempted to get past a long tradition of scholarly dismissals and aversions that imagine the suburb and television in purely negative terms as inauthentic, alienating, and decidedly of "low" cultural worth. As John Hartley has suggested, "scholars rarely venture into suburbia except to pathologize it."[31] This kind of pathologization, he argues, is based on an overassessment of the achievements of the enlightenment public sphere, which in turn proceeds on a binary logic that values cities over suburbs by simultaneously imagining them as masculine versus feminine, participatory versus passive, productive versus consumer-oriented, and so forth. In adopting this binary—and often misogynist—logic, twentieth-century social critics have foreclosed a broader and more thoughtful understanding of the kinds of things that are taking place inside the postmodern, mediated world of suburbia. Ultimately, in Hartley's view, we need to understand suburbanization and mass media as the nodal points of a new "postmodern public sphere" in which "the classical functions of teaching, dramatizing and participating in the public sphere . . . are increasingly functions of popular media" and people "are political animals not in the urban forum but on the suburban couch; citizen readers, citizens of media."[32]

I agree with Hartley that we need to understand the new kinds of knowledge, participation, and social communication that goes on in the media/suburb, and that we should do this without the cultural pessimism and gender biases of so much social theory. There are, however, some problems entailed in thinking about the media/suburb as a postmodern public sphere, especially in the United States where the suburb has been predicated on racial segregation. Red-lining (or zoning) practices of the Federal Housing Administration ensured that the new suburban communities of the 1950s would zone out people of color, a practice that, when coupled with prejudicial realtor and bank loan policies as well as the devastating effects of urban renewal, resulted in long-term social injustices. As George Lipsitz points out, these kinds of housing policies were part of a "possessive investment in whiteness" that hasn't been easy to reverse. Despite the Civil Rights movement and fair housing legislation of the 1960s, "from 1960–1977 4 million whites moved out of central cities, while the number of whites living in suburbs increased by twenty-two million." And "during the same years, the inner city black population grew by 6 million, but the number of blacks living in suburbs increased only by

500,000."[33] Moreover, suburban migration among African Americans is primarily a middle-class phenomenon. For reasons such as these, it seems misleading to think about suburbia as a public sphere—at least in the ideal sense as a space of participatory democracy for all.

Thus, although I want to move away from the kind of pathologizing rhetoric that impedes our ability to understand suburbia and postwar media culture, I do not consider suburbs and media as some kind of new postmodern public sphere. This kind of terminology confuses too many issues. Instead, I think of the suburb and media culture (especially television and new electronic media) as historical constructs that negotiate the contradictory—yet mutually dependent—values of privacy and publicity. Why and how do people imagine their social relationships through the media? Why has television created imaginary spaces and narrative universes that obsessively rehearse and restage private life in the suburb? How does media establish rules and conventions for what is public and what is private? Or, to what degree have media obliterated these distinctions altogether? To be sure, at this historical moment when the Internet poses endless fears about privacy, surveillance, and the future of family life, these questions are as pertinent today as they are to the early postwar period I discuss in these essays.

This book is divided into five sections, each of which traces a specific set of historical cases within larger concerns. The essays were written during the course of the 1990s, and in this sense present an implicit history of my own engagements with the issues discussed therein. Each section contains one previously published essay and one new essay written for this volume. Although topically they do not address the same subject, they do collectively map out a series of broader dialogues about media, art, and culture in relation to questions of gender, space, and public and private life.

The first section, "TV Households," looks at the introduction of television and portable technologies in the 1950s and 1960s. The first essay, "The Suburban Home Companion: Television and the Neighborhood Ideal in Postwar America," deals with my early work on television's installation in American homes in the 1950s, particularly with regard to the rise of mass-produced suburbs. This essay examines early television's relationship to changes in public and private culture during a time when more and more white American families were moving out of cities and into suburbia. The second essay, "Portable TV: Studies in Domestic Space Travel," is a follow-up study that looks at the introduction of portable televisions in the 1960s and considers the culture's fascination with mobility more generally. This essay suggests that the nuclear family ideals of 1950s America had, by the 1960s, transformed, and that these transformations bear important relations to changes in the way television was marketed, represented, and conceptualized in American culture. In both essays I am particularly interested in how the rise of television and satellite technologies coincided with larger changes in the structures of American communities—especially the rise of postwar suburbs and the new ideals for everyday life and gender roles within the home.

The second section, "White Flight," represents my interests in the cultural history of the space race and its relationship to social space more generally. My work on postwar suburbia increasingly led me to wonder about how and why those suburban dreams so quickly turned to nightmarish visions of "split level traps" (as one popular book of the 1960s called them). I began to think of this critique of suburbia in relation to another kind of space—that is, outer space. I wondered how the wide-scale disappointment with suburbs related to the new utopian project of the space race, and I began to think about a host of images—in magazines, on television, in films, and in advertisements—that depicted outer space as a new frontier that promised something more progressive than the suburban lifestyles of Eisenhower America.

The first essay in this section, "From Domestic Space to Outer Space: The 1960s Fantastic Family Sitcom," explores the cultural fascination with outer space and the genre of the "fantastic" that began to infiltrate popular images of family life. The essay considers how both documentary and fictional representations of space travel repeatedly used family melodrama and images of family life to convey scientific information about the National Aeronautics and Space Administration (NASA). Looking at how suburbia itself began to be imagined through the iconography of outer space (for example, spaceship-styled architecture or *Jetson*-style furniture), the essay focuses on the rise of the "fantastic family sitcom," a hybrid genre that mixed family comedy with science fiction and horror. I explore how the fantastic "defamiliarized" the tried-and-true conventions of the 1950s family sitcoms by, for example, turning June Cleaver housewives into witches (*Bewitched*), genies (*I Dream of Jeannie*), or robots (*My Living Doll*).

In the course of writing this essay, it became clear that the space race was also largely about the politics of race, as images of space travel almost always relied on the portrayal of happy, white astronaut couples and their suburban families. I began to wonder what African Americans had to say about NASA. Looking through the black press, and through President Kennedy's and NASA's public relations files on the space race, I found an intense cultural debate that revolves around the racism of space travel. Moreover, whereas mainstream media represented outer space as a final frontier for the white suburban family, the African American press typically spoke of the space race as a waste of tax dollars that might better be spent on inner cities. "Outer Space and Inner Cities: African American Responses to NASA" considers how the African American press discussed the space race in relationship to wider issues of social space, especially the plight of inner cities, urban renewal, and racist housing policies that enforced suburban segregation.

Section three, "Baby Boom Kids," contains two essays about postwar childhood that speak directly to proponents of "family values." The first essay was written in the early 1990s in response to my frustration with broadcast policy debates that revolved around the figure of the innocent child. One day, in the midst of various congressional debates about broadcast censorship, Al Sikes, then Chair of the Federal Communications Commission (FCC), presented a public lecture at my university. I was the only woman in the room. Sikes engaged us in a heated debate about the need for a ratings system, claiming that programs like *Married with Wives* (he had the title wrong) were trash. My frustration didn't end with his obvious lack of any knowledge about what was actually on television. Instead, my annoyance only multiplied when I raised my hand to make some comments. Before I said a word, Sikes looked at me and said (something along the order of) "I have talked to feminists before." After I made some comments about the problems with ratings systems, he asked me if I had any children. Now I was clearly the outcast in the room—a barren feminist who had no right to speak.

The essays in this section deal with the way the innocent child has been used by people like Sikes to bolster their political positions. "Seducing the Innocent: Childhood and Television in Postwar America" explores debates about children's television in the 1950s, concentrating on the way middle-class taste standards and sentimental views about childhood innocence governed the assumptions about what constituted appropriate children's entertainment (assumptions that children themselves didn't necessarily agree with). "Innocence Abroad: The Geopolitics of Childhood in Postwar Kid Strips" deals with the way images of childhood innocence were related to cold war politics. It looks at the rise of two postwar kid strips—*Dennis the Menace* and *Peanuts*—in relation to images of children from other nations, and it considers how the kid strips were used to bolster the idea that America was a superior nation because it was the only place where childhood still existed. In this sense, both essays attempt to consider family-values rhetoric in relation to cold war nationalism and public policy.

Section four, "Living Room to Gallery," focuses on the cultural transactions between the private space of the home and the more public world of "high" art. In different ways, I question how cultural categories like "high" and "low" are formulated and how domesticity plays a role in this process. "High Culture in Low Places: Television and Modern Art, 1950–1970" examines the role television played in defining the American vernacular after World War II. I am especially interested in how television served to popularize modern painting and how it contributed to the nationalist goal of creating a uniquely American image—distinct from European painting, especially that of Paris. I am also interested in how television served to valorize commercial and advertising art as a truly American and democratic form.

The next essay in section four had a rather unexpected scholarly trajectory. "Barbies without Ken: Femininity, Feminism, and the Art-Culture System" is about Barbie dolls, but not in the ways that I would have predicted when I first started collecting them in 1989. The essay looks at Barbie collectors and their display cultures at conventions, in club meetings, in collectors' magazines, and in museums. Drawing on insights from critical anthropology, it combines my own participant observation in collectors' culture with my interests in the way collectors remake Barbie into an object of craft culture, or alternatively, an object of high art (so high in fact that she has been on exhibit in leading art museums). I further relate this process of cultural reevaluation to the way collectors have reevaluated Barbie's feminine status. That is, they have taken a doll who is widely criticized for her impossible proportions and unyielding whiteness and made her into an icon of feminism. Many collectors see Barbie as a prototype for the women's movement, arguing that she was an astronaut, a doctor, and a president long before any real women had a place in these professions. At the same time, some collectors appropriate her through a queer sensibility, displaying her as a camp object and using her as a narrative vehicle for coming-out stories and homoerotic fantasies. These practices, I show, are ultimately also incorporated back into the corporate logic of Mattel, which now holds Barbie art expositions and markets dolls aimed at collectors' sensibilities.

The final section, "Rewind and Fast Forward," considers issues of nostalgia and popular memory in relation to the 1950s and 1960s suburb. "From the Dark Ages to the Golden Age: Women's Memories and Television Reruns" was written in response to my own classroom situations. After teaching television history for several years I noticed that many of my students seemed to think that television sitcoms from the 1950s reflected that era, and that sitcoms of today reflect a more progressive culture, especially for women. The essay is an attempt to understand why my students think television is a source for women's history and why they are so invested in believing in television's narratives of women's progress. The final essay, "Yesterday's Future, Tomorrow's Home," considers the way contemporary images of the future are laced with nostalgia, not for the 1950s per se but for the 1950s vision of the future. The essay looks at recent images of futuristic homes and new domestic technologies. It considers these images in relationship to Hollywood time-travel films such as *Pleasantville* that "go back to the future" of the 1950s past and replay the history of television and suburbs. The essay ultimately considers how our visions of the future and our visions of the past are connected, and how both are laced with the social concerns and needs of the present. Overall, then, the final section attempts to understand how memory and nostalgia not only take us back to the past but also how they serve to narrate the present.

Taken together, then, all of the essays relate media to their social contexts of everyday life. Thinking about suburban domesticity in terms of the language and images used to describe it is, I believe, a necessary step in understanding the way people have conceptualized and also lived their social relationships. Criticism of the suburbs has generally been divided between the culturalists interested in "belief systems" and the structuralists interested in economic and political policy. More recently, the field of critical geography and suburban history has complicated this culture/structure split. Historians such as Margaret Marsh and Elizabeth Wilson, and critics such as Mike Davis, have provided ways to see the connections among language systems, media images, and the institutional policies that affect urban and suburban design.[34] Images of suburban families after World War II were deeply implicated in the housing and neighborhood planning policies of postwar social life. The metaphors used to describe suburbia were not just secondary reflections of these institutional policies, they also helped to create a language for domestic and suburban space—a spatial language in which people lived their lives and through which new designs for living were also formulated. A good (if somewhat idiosyncratic) example of this reciprocal relationship between media and social space is the recent construction of a precise replica of the Simpson's TV home in a Las Vegas, Nevada, neighborhood. Even more pervasively, planned communities such as Disney's Celebration, Florida, or new urban communities such as Seaside, Florida, suggest the integral connections between media images of ideal towns and the actual built environment. With this in mind, *Welcome to the Dreamhouse* considers the media to be central to the social relationships in the everyday landscapes of postwar society.

I write about the history of commercial media because I believe that people should understand that media do in fact have a history, and in many cases media have numerous histories through which they were imagined and used by different groups. By understanding this simple point —that media have a history—we might also begin to devise alternative ways to think about and use them.

Despite my interest in alternatives, I am sure it will become evident that history—as I deploy it here—is not a predictive science. Insofar as these essays assume that subjectivity is itself historical, there is no reason to believe in the persistence of our vision. Rather than thinking of history as a kind of projection machine that allows us to see into the future, I am more interested in historical work that denaturalizes the present.

Our contemporary ideas about media, family, and public life are part of a set of belief systems that also have a history. Exploring that history allows us to see media culture as contingent, contradictory, and always formed through power struggles among different social groups. When viewed against their historical backdrop, our commonsense ideas about media, family, and public life seem less commonsensical. While there is always a danger in projecting our own contemporary logic onto the past (a danger referred to as "presentism"), this does not mean that historians can or should think about the past without reference to the here and now. Indeed, historical thought is formed through contemporary systems of knowledge and structures of feeling. To be sure, however, the best scholarship searches for evidence and interpretive frameworks that can challenge our contemporary assumptions and attitudes, not merely reinforce them. The point is not to impose our will on the past but rather to understand the past in all its difference and complexity.

Welcome to the Dreamhouse is thus inspired not only by a historian's interest in the past but also the concerns of the moment. While I don't come up with visions for a better future, I hope these essays will demonstrate that media and cultural practices are formed through historical struggles and, therefore, are always open to positive change.

Notes

1 *Look,* 27 May 1969, pp. 32–34.

2 "The New Boundaries of Home," *House and Garden,* February 1965, p. 87.

3 Judith Stacey, *In the Name of the Family: Rethinking Family Values in the Postmodern Age* (Boston: Beacon, 1996), p. 101.

4 Jürgen Habermas, *The Structural Transformation of the Public Sphere,* trans. Thomas Burger (Cambridge: MIT Press, 1989).

5 For a discussion of the potential of the public sphere model in relation to television, see, for example, Tamar Liebes and James Curan, *Media, Ritual, and Identity* (London: Routledge, 1998), pp. 153–219; and Jostein Gripsrud, ed., *Television and Common Knowledge* (London: Routledge, 1999). Central issues that inform such debates include questions regarding consensus of opinion among divided publics and the concept of rational debate itself (and the underlying ideologies of Western reason).

6 Nancy Fraser, "Rethinking the Public Sphere: A Contribution to the Critique of Actually Existing Democracy," in *Habermas and the Public Sphere,* ed. Craig Calhoun (Cambridge: MIT Press, 1992), pp. 109–42; in the same volume, see also Mary P. Ryan, "Gender and Public Access: Women's Politics in Nineteenth-Century America," pp. 259–88.

7 See, for example, Paolo Carpignano et al., "Chatter in the Age of Electronic Reproduction: Talk Television and the 'Public Mind,' " in *The Phantom Public Sphere,* ed. Bruce Robbins (Minneapolis: University of Minnesota Press, 1993), pp. 93–120; and Sonia Livingstone and Peter Lunt, *Talk on Television: Audience Participation and Public Debate* (London: Routledge, 1994). Discussions of television as spaces for public dialogue aren't necessarily attached to the theoretical project of Habermas. For example, Horace Newcomb and Paul M. Hirsch offer an alternative model of television as "cultural forum," one that is influenced by anthro-

pological paradigms of ritual theory. See Newcomb and Hirsch, "Television as a Cultural Forum," in *Television: The Critical View*, ed. Horace Newcomb (New York: Oxford University Press, 1994), pp. 503–15.

8 John Hartley, "The Sexualization of Suburbia," in *Visions of Suburbia*, ed. Roger Silverstone (London: Routledge, 1997), pp. 180–216.

9 Lizabeth Cohen, *Making a New Deal: Industrial Workers in Chicago, 1919–1939* (Cambridge, Eng.: Cambridge University Press, 1990), chapter 3.

10 Ibid.; Hamid Naficy, *The Making of Exile Cultures: Iranian Television in Los Angeles* (Minneapolis: University of Minnesota Press, 1993).

11 See, for example, Steven G. Jones, ed., *Virtual Culture: Identity and Communication in Cybersociety* (London: Sage, 1997); Beth E. Kolko, Lisa Nakamura, and Gilbert B. Rodman, eds., *Race in Cyberspace* (New York: Routledge, 2000); and Ella Shohat, "By the Bitstream of Babylon: Cyberfrontiers and Disasporic Vistas," in *Home, Exile, Homeland: Film, Media, and the Politics of Place*, ed. Hamid Naficy (New York: Routledge, 1998), pp. 213–32.

12 For more on amateur art in the 1950s, see Karal Ann Marling, *As Seen on TV: The Visual Culture of Everyday Life in the 1950s* (Cambridge: Harvard University Press, 1994), chapter 2.

13 Doreen Massey, *Space, Place, and Gender* (Minneapolis: University of Minnesota Press, 1994); Elizabeth Wilson, *The Sphinx in the City: Urban Life, the Control of Disorder, and Women* (Berkeley: University of California Press, 1991).

14 Andreas Huyssen, *After the Great Divide: Modernism, Mass Culture, Postmodernism* (Bloomington: Indiana University Press, 1986), pp. 44–62; Lucy R. Lippard, *The Pink Glass Swan: Selected Feminist Essays on Art* (New York: New Press, 1995); Christopher Reed, ed., *Not at Home: The Suppression of Domesticity in Modern Art and Architecture* (New York: Thames and Hudson, 1996); Penny Sparke, *As Long as It's Pink: The Sexual Politics of Taste* (London: Pandora, 1995); Cecile Whiting, *The Taste for Pop: Pop Art, Gender, and Consumer Culture* (Cambridge, Eng.: Cambridge University Press, 1997).

15 Beatriz Colomina, *Privacy and Publicity: Modern Architecture as Mass Media* (Cambridge: MIT Press, 1996).

16 Raymond Williams, *Television: Technology and Cultural Form* (New York: Schocken, 1975); Paddy Scannel, *Radio, Television, and Modern Life* (Oxford: Blackwell, 1996); Carolyn Marvin, *When Old Technologies Were New: Thinking about Electric Communication in the Late Nineteenth Century* (New York: Oxford University Press, 1988); Joshua Meyrowitz, *No Sense of Place: The Impact of Electronic Media on Social Behavior* (New York: Oxford University Press, 1985); Cecelia Tichi, *Electronic Hearth: Creating an American Television Culture* (New York: Oxford University Press, 1991); Anna McCarthy, *Ambient Television* (Durham, N.C.: Duke University Press, forthcoming 2001); Lynn Spigel, *Make Room for TV: Television and the Family Ideal in Postwar America* (Chicago: University of Chicago Press, 1992).

17 David Morley, *Family Television: Cultural Power and Domestic Leisure* (London: Comedia, 1986) and *Television Audiences and Cultural Studies* (London: Rout-

ledge, 1992); Ann Gray, *Video Playtime: The Gendering of Leisure Technology* (London: Routledge, 1992); Odina Fachel Leal, "Popular Taste and Erudite Repetoire: The Place and Space of Television in Brazil," *Cultural Studies* 4:1 (1990): 19–29; Roger Silverstone, *Television and Everyday Life* (London: Routledge, 1994); Andrea Press, *Women Watching Television: Gender, Class, and Generation in the American Television Experience* (Philadelphia: University of Pennsylvania Press, 1991); James Lull, ed., *World Families Watch Television* (Newberry Park, Calif.: Sage, 1988) and *Inside Family Viewing: Ethnographic Research on Television's Audiences* (New York: Routledge, 1990); Ellen Seiter, *Television and New Media Audiences* (London: Oxford University Press, 1999).

18 For Jean Baudrillard, see especially "The Ecstasy of Communication," in *The Anti-Aesthetic: Essays on Postmodern Culture,* ed. Hal Foster (Port Townsend, Wash.: Bay Press, 1983); Margaret Morse, *Virtualities: Television, Media Art, and Cyberculture* (Bloomington: Indiana University Press, 1998); McKenzie Wark, *Virtual Geographies: Living with Global Media Events* (Bloomington: Indiana University Press, 1994).

19 Carolyn Marvin, *When Old Technologies Were New;* Jeffrey Sconce, *Haunted Media: Electronic Presence from Telegraphy to Television* (Durham, N.C.: Duke University Press, 2000); Susan Douglas, *Listening In: Radio and the American Imagination* (New York: Times Books, 1991); William Uricchio, "Storage, Simultaneity, and the Technologies of Modernity," paper delivered at Technologies of the Moving Image Conference, Stockholm University, Stockholm, Sweden, December 1998.

20 David Morley and Kevin Robbins, *Spaces of Identity* (London: Routledge, 1996); Naficy, *Home, Exile, Homeland;* Marie Gillespie, *Television, Ethnicity, and Cultural Change* (London: Routledge, 1995); Purnima Mankekar, "National Texts and Gendered Lives: An Ethnography of Television Viewers in a North Indian City," *American Ethnologist* 20:3 (1993): 543–63.

21 For a discussion of this issue along with an extensive bibliography on feminist television studies, see Charlotte Brunsdon, Julie D'Acci, and Lynn Spigel, eds., *Feminist Television Criticism: A Reader* (London: Oxford University Press, 1997); for new work on these issues, see Mary Beth Haralovich and Lauren Rabinovitz, eds., *Television, History, and American Culture: Feminist Critical Essays* (Durham, N.C.: Duke University Press, 1999).

22 Lisa Lewis, *Gender Politics and MTV: Voicing the Difference* (Philadelphia: Temple University Press, 1990); Moya Luckett, "Girl Watchers: Patty Duke and Teen TV," in *The Revolution Wasn't Televised: Sixties Television and Social Conflict,* ed. Lynn Spigel and Michael Curtin (New York: Routledge, 1997), pp. 95–117; Moya Luckett, "Sensuous Women and Single Girls: Reclaiming the Female Body on 1960s Television," in *Swinging Single: Representing Sexuality in the 1960s,* ed. Hilary Radner and Moya Luckett (Minneapolis: University of Minnesota Press, 1999); Mary Kearney, "Girls, Girls, Girls: Gender and Generation in Contemporary Discourses of Female Adolescence," Ph.D. diss., University of Southern California, 1998.

23 Serafina Bathrick, *"The Mary Tyler Moore Show:* Women at Home and at Work,"
    in *MTM: Quality Television,* ed. Jane Feuer, Paul Kerr, and Tise Vahimigi (Bloom-
    ington: Indiana University Press, 1984), pp. 99–131; Ella Taylor, *Prime-Time Fami-
    lies: Television Culture in Postwar America* (Berkeley: University of California
    Press, 1989); Judith Mayne, *"L.A. Law* and Prime-Time Feminism," *Discourse*
    10:2 (1988): 30–47; Julie D'Acci, *Defining Women: The Case of Cagney and Lacey*
    (Chapel Hill: University of North Carolina Press, 1994); Margaret J. Heide, *Tele-
    vision, Culture, and Women's Lives: "thirtysomething" and the Contradictions of
    Gender* (Philadelphia: University of Pennsylvania Press, 1995); Prabha Krishnan
    and Anita Dighe, *Affirmation and Denial: Construction of Femininity on Indian Tele-
    vision* (New Delhi: Sage, 1990); Lauren Rabinovitz, "Sitcoms and Single Moms:
    Representations of Feminism on American TV," *Cinema Journal* 29:1 (1989): 3–
    9. Many of these studies also focus on television's representation of feminism and
    "new women." For more examples, see the bibliography in Brunsdon et al., *Femi-
    nist Television Criticism.*

24 Herman Gray, *Watching Race: Television and the Struggle for "Blackness"* (Min-
    neapolis: University of Minnesota Press, 1995); George Lipsitz, "The Meaning of
    Memory: Family, Class, and Ethnicity in Early Network Television Programs," in
    Private Screenings: Television and the Female Consumer, ed. Lynn Spigel and Denise
    Mann (Minneapolis: University of Minnesota Press, 1992), pp. 71–108; Aniko
    Bodroghkozy, "Is This What You Mean by Color TV?": Race, Gender, and Con-
    tested Meanings in NBC's *Julia,"* in *Private Screenings,* pp. 143–68; Wanamena
    Lubiano, "Black Minstrals, Welfare Queens, and State Minstrals: Ideological War
    by Narrative Means," in *Race-ing Justice, En-Gendering Power: Essays on Anita
    Hill, Clarence Thomas, and the Construction of Social Reality,* ed. Toni Morrison
    (New York: Pantheon, 1992), pp. 323–63; Tricia Rose, "Never Trust a Big Butt
    and a Smile," *Camera Obscura* 23 (1990): 108–31; Kathleen Rowe, "Roseanne: Un-
    ruly Woman as Domestic Goddess," *Screen* 31:4 (1990): 408–19; Jaqueline Bobo
    and Ellen Seiter, "Black Feminism and Media Criticism: *The Women of Brewster
    Place,"* *Screen* 32:3 (1991): 172–81; Sasha Torres, ed., *Living Color: Race and Tele-
    vision in the United States* (Durham, N.C.: Duke University Press, 1998).

25 Williams, *Television, Technology, and Cultural Form;* Nick Browne, "The Political
    Economy of the Television (Super) Text," in *American Television: New Directions
    in History and Theory,* ed. Nick Browne (Chur, Switzerland: Harwood, 1994), pp.
    69–95; Jane Feuer, "The Concept of Live Television: Ontology as Ideology," in
    Regarding Television, ed. E. Ann Kaplan (Frederick, Md.: University Publications
    of America, 1983), pp. 12–22; Tania Modleski, *Loving with a Vengeance: Mass-
    Produced Fantasies for Women* (London: Methuen, 1984); Newcomb and Hirsch,
    "Television as a Cultural Forum."

26 Modleski, *Loving with a Vengeance;* Nina Liebman, *Living Room Lectures: The
    Fifties Family in Film and Television* (Austin: University of Texas Press, 1995);
    Laura Mulvey, "Melodrama In and Out of the Home," in *High Theory/Low Cul-
    ture: Analyzing Popular Television and Film,* ed. Colin McCabe (New York: St.
    Martin's Press, 1986), pp. 80–100; Lynne Joyrich, "All That Television Allows:

TV Melodrama, Postmodernism and Consumer Culture," *Camera Obscura* 16 (1988): 129–54; Robert C. Allen, ed., *To Be Continued: Soap Operas Around the World* (New York: Routledge, 1995); Christine Geraghty, *Women and Soap Opera: A Study of Prime Time Soaps* (Oxford: Polity, 1991); Ien Ang, *Watching Dallas: Soap Opera and the Melodramatic Imagination*, trans. Della Douling (London: Methuen, 1985); Jane Feuer, *Seeing Through the Eighties: Television and Reaganism* (Durham, N.C.: Duke University Press, 1995); Purnima Mankekar, "Television Tales and a Woman's Rage: A Nationalist Recasting of Draupadi's Disrobing," *Public Culture* 5:3 (1993): 469–92; Laura Stempel Mumford, *Love and Ideology in the Afternoon: Soap Opera, Women, and Television Genre* (Bloomington: Indiana University Press, 1995). For more references, see the bibliography in Brunsdon et al., *Feminist Television Criticism*.

27 Two recent contributions to this interdisciplinary project—Silverstone, ed., *Visions of Suburbia* and Linda McDowell, ed., *Undoing Place? A Geographical Reader* (London: Arnold, 1997)—are of special note here, not only because they deal with subject matter germane to my interests but also because they seem to me exemplary of the kind of results that are possible when multiple systems of knowledge, focusing on both structural and cultural causes, are used simultaneously to explore issues of space, place, and cultural identity.

28 Hayden White, *Tropics of Discourse: Essays in Cultural Criticism* (Baltimore: Johns Hopkins University Press, 1978); Dominick LaCapra, *History and Criticism* (Ithaca: Cornell University Press, 1987); and Michel de Certeau, *The Writing of History*, trans. Tom Conley (New York: Columbia University Press, 1988) and his "History: Science and Fiction," in *Heterologies: Discourse on the Other*, trans. Brian Massumi (Minneapolis: University of Minnesota Press, 1986), pp. 199–221.

29 Carlo Ginzburg, "Morelli, Freud, and Sherlock Holmes: Clues and Scientific Method," *History Workshop* 9 (spring 1980): 5–36.

30 Janice A. Radway, *Reading the Romance: Women, Patriarchy, and Popular Literature* (Chapel Hill, N.C.: University of North Carolina Press, 1984).

31 Hartley, "The Sexualization of Suburbia," p. 186.

32 Ibid., p. 180. Note that Hartley is not blindly celebrating this new postmodern public sphere, nor is he necessarily celebrating the suburb and media. His point is that we need to understand how knowledge circulates and how publics are formed in these new configurations of physical and electronic space.

33 George Lipsitz cites these statistics in *The Possessive Investment in Whiteness: How White People Profit from Identity Politics* (Philadelphia: Temple University Press, 1998), p. 7.

34 Margaret Marsh, *Suburban Lives* (New Brunswick, N.J.: Rutgers University Press, 1990); Wilson, *The Sphinx in the City*; Mike Davis, *City of Quartz: Excavating the Future in Los Angeles* (New York: Vintage, 1990).

Part I: TV Households

The Suburban Home Companion:
Television and the Neighborhood Ideal
in Postwar America

✱ In December 1949, the popular radio comedy *Easy Aces* made its television debut on the DuMont network. The episode was comprised entirely of Goodman Ace and his wife Jane sitting in their living room, watching TV. The interest stemmed solely from the couple's witty commentary on the program they watched. Aside from that, there was no plot. This was television, pure and simple. It was just the sense of being with the Aces, of watching them watch, and of watching TV with them, that gave this program its peculiar appeal.

The fantasy of social experience that *Easy Aces* provided is a heightened instance of a more general set of cultural meanings and practices surrounding television's arrival in postwar America. It is a truism among cultural historians and media scholars that television's growth after World War II was part of a general return to family values. Less attention has been devoted to the question of another, at times contradictory, ideal in postwar ideology—that of neighborhood bonding and community participation. During the 1950s, millions of Americans—particularly young, white couples of the middle class—responded to a severe housing shortage in the cities by fleeing to new mass-produced suburbs. In both scholarly studies and popular literature from the period, suburbia emerges as a conformist-oriented society where belonging to the neighborhood network was just as important as the return to family life. Indeed, the new domesticity was not simply experienced as a retreat from the public

sphere, it also gave people a sense of belonging to the community. By purchasing their detached suburban homes, the young couples of the middle
class participated in the construction of a new community of values; in
magazines, in films, and on the airwaves they became the cultural representatives of the "good life." Furthermore, the rapid growth of family-
based community organizations like the PTA suggests that these neosub-
urbanites did not barricade their doors, nor did they simply "drop out."
Instead, these people secured a position of meaning in the *public* sphere
through their new-found social identities as *private* landowners.

In this sense, the fascination with family life was not merely a nostalgic
return to the Victorian cult of domesticity. Rather, the central preoccupation in the new suburban culture was the construction of a particular
discursive space through which the family could mediate the contradictory
impulses for a private haven on the one hand, and community participation on the other. By lining up individual housing units on connecting
plots of land, the suburban tract was itself the ideal articulation of this discursive space; the dual goals of separation from and integration into the
larger community was the basis of tract design. Moreover, as I have shown
elsewhere, the domestic architecture of the period mediated the twin
goals of separation from and integration into the outside world.[1] Apply-
ing principles of modernist architecture to the mass-produced housing of
middle-class America, housing experts of the period agreed that the modern home should blur distinctions between inside and outside spaces. As
Katherine Morrow Ford and Thomas Creighton claimed in *The American
House Today* (1951), "the most noticeable innovation in domestic architecture in the past decade or two has been the increasingly close relationship
of indoors to outdoors."[2] By far, the central design element used to create an illusion of the outside world was the picture window or "window
wall" (what we now call sliding-glass doors), which became increasingly
popular in the postwar period. As Daniel Boorstin has argued, the widespread dissemination of large plate-glass windows for both domestic and
commercial use "leveled the environment" by encouraging the "removal
of sharp distinctions between indoors and outdoors" and thus created an
"ambiguity" between public and private space.[3] This kind of spatial ambiguity was a reigning aesthetic in postwar home magazines, which repeatedly suggested that windows and window walls would establish a continuity of interior and exterior worlds. As the editors of *Sunset* remarked in
1946, "Of all improved materials, glass made the greatest change in the

Western home. To those who found that open porches around the house or . . . even [the] large window did not bring in enough of the outdoors, the answer was glass—the invisible separation between indoors and out."[4]

Given its ability to merge private with public spaces, television was the ideal companion for these suburban homes. In 1946, Thomas Hutchinson, an early experimenter in television programming, published a popular book designed to introduce television to the general public, *Here Is Television, Your Window on the World*.[5] As I have shown elsewhere, commentators in the popular press used this window metaphor over and over again, claiming that television would let people imaginatively travel to distant places while remaining in the comfort of their homes.[6]

Indeed, the integration of television into postwar culture both precipitated and was symptomatic of a profound reorganization of social space. Leisure time was significantly altered as spectator amusements—including movies, sports, and concert attendance—were increasingly incorporated into the home. While in 1950 only 9 percent of all American homes had a television set, by the end of the decade that figure rose to nearly 90 percent, and the average American watched about five hours of television per day.[7] Television's privatization of spectator amusements and its possible disintegration of the public sphere were constant topics of debate in popular media of the period. Television was caught in a contradictory movement between private and public worlds, and it often became a rhetorical figure for that contradiction. In the following pages, I examine the way postwar culture balanced these contradictory ideals of privatization and community involvement through its fascination with the new electrical space that television provided.

Postwar America witnessed a significant shift in traditional notions of neighborhood. Mass-produced suburbs like Levittown, New York, and Park Forest, Illinois, replaced previous forms of public space with a newly defined aesthetic of prefabrication. At the center of suburban space was the young, upwardly mobile middle-class family; the suburban community was, in its spatial articulations, designed to correspond with and reproduce patterns of nuclear family life. Playgrounds, yards, schools, churches, and synagogues provided town centers for community involvement based on discrete stages of family development. Older people, gay and lesbian people, homeless people, unmarried people, and people of color were simply written out of these community spaces, and were relegated back to the cities. The construction and "red-lining" policies of the Federal Housing Administration gave an official stamp of approval to these exclusionary practices by ensuring that homes were built for nuclear families and that "undesirables" would be "zoned" out of the neighborhoods. Suburban space was thus designed to purify communal spaces, to sweep away urban clutter, while at the same time preserving the populist ideal of neighborliness that carried Americans through the Depression.

Although the attempt to zone out "undesirables" was never totally successful, this antiseptic model of space was the reigning aesthetic at the heart of the postwar suburb. Not coincidentally, it had also been central to utopian ideals for electrical communication since the mid-1800s. As James Carey and John Quirk have shown, American intellectuals of the nineteenth century foresaw an "electrical revolution" in which the grime and noise of industrialization would be purified through electrical power.[8] Electricity, it was assumed, would replace the pollution caused by factory machines with a new, cleaner environment. Through their ability to merge remote spaces, electrical communications like the telephone and telegraph would add to this sanitized environment by allowing people to occupy faraway places while remaining in the familiar and safe locales of the office or the home. Ultimately, this new electrical environment was linked to larger concerns about social decadence in the cities. In both intellectual and popular culture, electricity became a rhetorical figure through which people imagined ways to cleanse urban space of social pollutants; immigrants and class conflict might vanish through the magical powers of electricity. As Carolyn Marvin has suggested, nineteenth-century thinkers hoped that electrical communications would defuse the threat of cultural difference by limiting experiences and placing social encounters into safe, familiar, and predictable contexts. In 1846, for example, *Mercury* published the utopian fantasies of one Professor Alonzo Jackman, who imagined a transcontinental telegraph line through which "all the inhabitants of the earth would be brought into one intellectual neighborhood and be at the same time perfectly freed from those contaminations which might under other circumstances be received." Moreover, as Marvin suggests, this xenophobic fantasy extended to the more everyday, local uses of communication technology: "With longdistance communication, those who were suspect and unwelcome even in one's neighborhood could be banished in the name of progress." Through telecommunications it was possible to make one's family and neighborhood into the "stable center of the universe," eliminating the need even to consider cultural differences in the outside world.[9]

Although Marvin is writing about nineteenth-century communication technology, the utopian fantasy that she describes is also part and parcel of the twentieth-century imagination. Indeed, the connections between electrical communications and the purification of social space sound like a prototype for the mass-produced suburbs. Throughout the twentieth century, these connections would be forged by utility companies and electrical manufacturers who hoped to persuade the public of the link between electricity and a cleaner social environment. Then, too, the dream of filtering social differences through the magical power of the "ether" was a reigning fantasy in the popular press when radio was introduced in the early 1920s. As Susan Douglas has shown, popular critics praised radio's ability to join the nation together into a homogeneous community where class divisions were blurred by a unifying voice. This democratic utopia was, however, imbricated in the more exclusionary hope that radio would "insulate its listeners from heterogeneous crowds of unknown, different, and potentially unrestrained individuals."[10] Thus, broadcasting, like the telephone and telegraph before it, was seen as an instrument of social sanitation.

In the postwar era, the fantasy of antiseptic electrical space was transposed onto television. Numerous commentators extolled the virtues of television's antiseptic spaces, showing how the medium would allow people to travel from their homes while remaining untouched by the actual social contexts to which they imaginatively ventured. Television was particularly hailed for its ability to keep youngsters out of sinful public spaces, away from the countless contaminations of everyday life. At a time when juvenile delinquency was considered a number-one social disease, audience research showed that parents believed television would keep their children off the streets.[11] A mother from a Southern California survey claimed, "Our boy was always watching television, so we got him a set just to keep him home." Another mother from an Atlanta study stated, "We are closer together. . . . Don and her boyfriend sit here instead of going out, now."[12] Women's home magazines promoted and reinforced these attitudes by showing parents how television could limit and purify their children's experiences. *House Beautiful* told parents that if they built a TV fun room for their teenage daughters they would find "peace of mind because teenagers are away from [the] house but still at home."[13] Television thus promised to keep children away from unsupervised, heterogeneous spaces.

But television technology promised more than just familial bliss and "wholesome" heterosexuality. Like its predecessors, it offered the possibility of an intellectual neighborhood, purified of social unrest and human misunderstanding. As NBC's president Sylvester "Pat" Weaver declared, television would make the "entire world into a small town, instantly available, with the leading actors on the world stage known on sight or by voice to all within it." Television, in Weaver's view, would encourage world peace by presenting diverse people with homogeneous forms of knowledge and modes of experience. Television, he argued, created "a situation new in human history in that children can no longer be raised within a family or group belief that narrows the horizons of the child to any belief pattern. There can no longer be a We-Group, They-Group under this condition. Children cannot be brought up to laugh at strangers, to hate foreigners, to live as man has always lived before." But for Weaver, this democratic utopian world was in fact a very small town, a place where different cultural practices were homogenized and channeled through a medium whose messages were truly American. As he continued, "It [is] most important for us in our stewardship of broadcasting to remain within the 'area of American agreement,' with all the implications of that statement, including however some acknowledgement in our programming of the American heritage of dissent." Thus, in Weaver's view, broadcasting would be a cultural filter that purified the essence of an "American" experience, relegating social and ideological differences (what he must have meant by the "American heritage of dissent") to a kind of programming ghetto. Moreover, he went on to say that "those families who do not wish to participate fully in the American area of agreement" would simply have to screen out undesirable programming content by overseeing their children's use of television.[14]

The strange mix of democracy and cultural hegemony that ran through Weaver's prose was symptomatic of a more general set of contradictions at the heart of utopian dreams for the new antiseptic electrical space. Some social critics even suggested that television's ability to sanitize social space would be desirable to the very people who were considered dirty and diseased. They applauded television for its ability to enhance the lives of disenfranchised groups by bringing them into contact with the public spaces in which they were typically unwelcome. In a 1951 study of Atlanta viewers, Raymond Stewart found that television "has a very special meaning for invalids, or for Southern Negroes who are similarly barred from public entertainments."[15] One black respondent in the study claimed:

> It [television] permits us to see things in an uncompromising manner. Ordinarily to see these things would require that we be segregated and occupy the least desirable seats or vantage point. With television we're on the level with everyone else. Before television, radio provided the little bit of equality we were able to get. We never wanted to see any show or athletic event bad enough to be segregated in attending it.[16]

Rather than blaming the social system that produced this kind of degradation for African Americans, social scientists such as Stewart celebrated the technological solution. Television, or more specifically, the private form of reception that it offered, was applauded for its ability to dress the wounds of an ailing social system. As sociologist David Riesman claimed, "The social worker may feel it is extravagant for a slum family to buy a TV set on time, and fail to appreciate that the set is exactly the compensation for substandard housing the family can best appreciate—and in the case of Negroes or poorly dressed people, or the sick, an escape from being embarrassed in public amusement places."[17] Riesman thus evoked images of social disease to suggest that disempowered groups willed their own exclusion from the public sphere through the miraculous benefits of television.

Although social critics hailed television's ability to merge public and private domains, this utopian fantasy of space-binding revealed a dystopian underside. Here, television's antiseptic spaces were themselves subject to pollution as new social diseases spread through the wires and into the citizen's home. Metaphors of disease were continually used to discuss television's unwelcome presence in domestic life. In 1951, *American Mercury* asked if television "would make us sick . . . or just what?" Meanwhile, psychologists considered television's relation to the human psyche. Eugene Glynn, for example, claimed that certain types of adult psychoses could be relieved by watching television, but that "those traits that sick adults now satisfy by television can be presumed to be those traits which children, exposed to television from childhood . . . may be expected to develop."[18] More generally, magazine writers worried about the unhealthy psychological and physical effects that television might have on children. Indeed, even if television was hailed by some as a way to keep children out of dangerous public spaces, others saw the electrical environment as a threatening extension of the public sphere.[19] Most typically, television was said to cause passive and addictive behavior that would in turn disrupt good habits of nutrition, hygiene, social behavior, and education.[20]

Metaphors of disease went beyond these hyperbolic debates on human contamination to the more mundane considerations of set repair. Discussions of technology went hand in hand with a medical discourse that attributed to television a biological (rather than technological) logic. A 1953 Zenith ad declared, "We test TV blood pressure so you'll have a better picture." In that same year *American Home* suggested that readers "learn to diagnose and cure common TV troubles," listing symptoms, causes, treatments, and ways to "examine" the set. Thus the television set was itself represented as a human body, capable of being returned to "health" through proper medical procedures.[21]

Anxieties about television's contaminating effects were based on a larger set of confusions about the spaces that broadcast technology brought to the home. Even before television's innovation in the postwar period, popular media expressed uncertainty about the distinction between real and electrical space and suggested that electrical pollutants might infiltrate the physical environment. *Murder by Television,* a decidedly B film of 1935, considered the problems entailed when the boundaries between the television universe and the real world collapsed. The film featured Bela Lugosi in a nightmarish tale about a mad corporate scientist who transmits death rays over electrical wires. In an early scene, Professor Houghland, the benevolent inventor of television, goes on the air to broadcast pictures from around the world. But as he marvels at the medium's ability to bring faraway places into the home, his evil competitor, Dr. Scofield, kills him by sending "radiated waves" through the telephone wires and into the physical space of the television studio where the unfortunate Professor Houghland dies an agonizing death.

While less extreme in their representation of threatening technology, film comedies of the thirties and forties contained humorous scenes that depicted confusion over boundaries between electrical and real space. In the farcical *International House* (1933), for example, businessmen from around the globe meet at a Chinese hotel to witness a demonstration of the first fully operating television set. When Dr. Wong presents his rather primitive contraption to the conventioneers, television is shown to be a two-way communication system that not only features entertainment but can also respond to its audiences. After a spectator (played by W. C. Fields) ridicules the televised performance of crooner Rudy Vallee, Vallee stops singing, looks into the television camera, and tells Fields, "Don't interrupt my number. Hold your tongue and sit down." Later, when watching a naval battle on Wong's interactive television set, Fields even shoots down one of the ships in the scene. Similarly, in the popular film comedy serial *The Naggers,* Mrs. Nagger and her mother-in-law confuse the boundaries between real and electrical space in a scene that works as a humorous speculation about television ("The Naggers Go Ritzy," 1932). After the Naggers move into a new luxury apartment, Mr. Nagger discovers that there is a hole in the wall adjacent to his neighbor's apartment. To camouflage the hole, he places a radio in front of it. When Mrs. Nagger turns on the radio, she peers through the speaker in the receiver, noticing a man in the next apartment. Fooled into thinking that the radio receiver is really a television, she instructs her mother-in-law to look into the set. A commercial for mineral water comes on the air, claiming, "The Cascade Spring Company eliminates the middle-man. You get your water direct from the spring into your home." Meanwhile, Mrs. Nagger and her mother-in-law gaze into the radio speaker hoping to see a televised image. Instead, they find themselves drenched by a stream of water. Since a prior scene in the film shows that the next-door neighbor is actually squirting water at the Naggers through the hole in the adjacent wall, the joke is on the technically illiterate women who can't distinguish between electrical and real space.[22]

By the late 1940s, the confusion between spatial boundaries at the heart of these cinematic jokes was less pronounced. People were learning ways to incorporate television's spectacles within the contours of their homes. As I have shown elsewhere, postwar home magazines and handbooks on interior decor presented an endless stream of advice on how to make the home into a comfortable theater.[23] In 1949, for example, *House Beautiful* advised its readers that "conventional living room groupings need to be slightly altered because televiewers look in the same direction and not at each other." *Good Housekeeping* seconded the motion in 1951 when it claimed that "television is theatre; and to succeed, theatre requires a comfortably placed audience with a clear view of the stage."[24] Advertisements for television sets variously referred to the "chairside theater," the "video theater," the "family theater," and so forth. Taken to its logical extreme, this theatricalization of the home transformed domestic space into a private pleasure dome. In 1951, *American Home* displayed "A Room that Does Everything," which included a television set, radio, phonograph, movie projector, movie screen, loudspeakers, and even a barbecue pit. As the magazine said of the proud owners of this total theater, "The Lanzes do all those things in *The Room*."[25] In fact, the ideal home theater was precisely "the room" that one need never leave, a perfectly controlled environment of wall-to-wall mechanized pleasures.

But more than just offering family fun, these new home theaters provided postwar Americans with a way to mediate relations between public and private spheres. By turning one's home into a theater, it was possible to make outside spaces part of a safe and predictable experience. In other words, the theatricalization of the home allowed people to draw a line between the public and the private sphere—or, in more theatrical terms, a line between the proscenium space where the spectacle takes place and the reception space where the audience observes the scene.

Indeed, as Lawrence Levine has shown, the construction of that division was central to the formation of twentieth-century theaters.[26] Whereas theater audiences in the early 1800s tended to participate in the show through hissing, singing, and other forms of interaction, by the turn of the century theaters increasingly attempted to keep audiences detached from the performance. The silent, well-mannered audience became a mandate of "good taste," and people were instructed to behave in this manner in legitimate theaters and, later, in nickelodeons and movie palaces. In practice, the genteel experiences that theaters encouraged often seem to have had the somewhat less "tasteful" effect of permitting what George Lipsitz (following John Kasson) has called a kind of "privacy in public."[27] Within the safely controlled environment of the nickelodeon, audiences—especially youth audiences—engaged in illicit flirtation. At a time of huge population increases in urban centers, theaters and other forms of public amusements (most notably, as Kasson has shown, the amusement park) offered people the fantastic possibility of being alone while in the midst of a crowd. Theaters thus helped construct imaginary separations between people by making individual contemplation of mass spectacles possible.

In the postwar era, this theatrical experience was being reformulated in terms of the television experience. People were shown how to construct an exhibition space that replicated the general design of the theater.

However, in this case the relationship between public/spectacle and private/spectator was inverted. The spectator was now physically isolated from the crowd, and the fantasy was now one of imaginary unity with "absent" others. This inversion gave rise to a set of contradictions that weren't easily solved. According to popular wisdom, television had to re-create the sense of social proximity that the public theater offered; it had to make the viewer feel as if he or she were taking part in a public event. At the same time, however, it had to maintain the necessary distance between the public sphere and private individual on which middle-class ideals of reception were based.

The impossibility of maintaining these competing ideals gave rise to a series of debates, as people weighed the ultimate merits of bringing theatrical experiences indoors. Even if television promised the fantastic possibility of social interconnection through electrical means, this new form of social life wasn't always seen as an improvement over real community experiences. The inclusion of public spectacles in domestic space always carried with it the unpleasant possibility that the social ills of the outside world would invade the private home. The more that the home included aspects of the public sphere, the more it was seen as subject to unwelcome intrusions.

This was especially true in the early years of innovation when the purchase of a television set quite literally decreased privacy in the home. Numerous social scientific studies showed that people who owned television receivers were inundated with guests who came to watch the new set.[28] But this increased social life was not always seen as a positive effect by the families surveyed. As one woman in a Southern California study complained, "Sometimes I get tired of the house being used as a semi-private theater. I have almost turned the set off when some people visit us."[29] Popular media were also critical of the new "TV parties." In 1953, *Esquire* published a cartoon that highlighted the problem entailed by making one's home into a TV theater. The sketch shows a living room with chairs lined up in front of a television set in movie theater fashion. The residents of this home theater, dressed in pajamas and bathrobes with hair uncombed and feet unshod, are taken by surprise when the neighbors drop in—a bit too soon—to watch a wrestling match on television. Speaking in the voice of the intruders, the caption reads, "We decided to come over early and make sure we get good seats for tonight's fight." In that same year, a cartoon in *TV Guide* suggested a remedy for the troublesome neighbors—a hand-held mechanical device known as "Fritzy." The caption read, "If your neighbor won't buy his own set, try 'Fritzy.' One squeeze puts your set on the fritz." [30]

Such popular anxieties are better understood when we recognize the changing structure of social relationships encountered by the new suburban middle class. These people often left their families and life-long friends in the city to find instant neighborhoods in preplanned communities. Blocks composed of total strangers represented friendships only at the abstract level of demographic similarities in age, income, family size, and occupation. This homogeneity quickly became a central cause for anxiety in the suburban nightmares described by sociologists and popular critics. In *The Organization Man* (1957), William Whyte argued that a sense of community was especially important for the newcomers who experienced a feeling of "rootlessness" when they left their old neighborhoods for new suburban homes. As Whyte showed, the developers of the mass-produced suburbs tried to smooth the tensions caused by this sense of rootlessness by promising increased community life in their advertisements. For example, Park Forest, a Chicago suburb, assured consumers that "Coffeepots bubble all day long in Park Forest. This sign of friendliness tells you how much neighbors enjoy each other's company—feel glad that they can share their daily joys—yes, and troubles, too." [31] But when newcomers arrived in their suburban communities they were likely to find something different from the ideal that the magazines and advertisements suggested. Tiny homes were typically sandwiched together so that the Smiths' picture window looked not onto rambling green acres but rather into the Joneses' living room—a dilemma commonly referred to as the "goldfish bowl" effect. In addition to this sense of claustrophobia, the neighborhood ideal brought with it an enormous amount of pressure to conform to the group. As Harry Henderson suggested in his study of Levittown, New York (1953), the residents of this mass-produced suburb were under constant "pressure to 'keep up with the Joneses'," a situation that led to a "kind of superconformity" in which everyone desired the same luxury goods and consumer lifestyles. In his popular critique of the new suburbia, aptly titled *The Crack in the Picture Window* (1956), John Keats considered the tedium of this superconformity, describing the life of Mary and John Drone who lived among a mob of equally unappealing neighbors. And in *The Split-Level Trap* (1960), Richard Gordon and others used eight case studies to paint an unsettling picture of the anxieties of social dislocation experienced in a suburban town they called "Disturbia." [32]

These nightmarish visions of the preplanned community served as an impetus for the arrival of a surrogate community on television. Television provided an illusion of the ideal neighborhood—the way it was supposed to be. Just when people had left their life-long companions in the city, television sitcoms pictured romanticized versions of neighbor and family bonding. When promoting the early domestic comedy *Ethel and Albert,* NBC told viewers to tune into "a delightful situation comedy that is returning this weekend. . . . Yes, this Saturday night, *Ethel and Albert* come into view once again to keep you laughing at the typical foibles of the kind of people who might be living right next door to you." The idea that television families were neighbors was also found in critical commentary. In 1953, *Saturday Review* claimed, "The first thing you notice about these sketches [*The Goldbergs, The Adventures of Ozzie and Harriet, Ethel and Albert,* and the live *Honeymooners* skits] is that they are incidents; they are told as they might be told when neighbors visit (in the Midwest sense of the word) on the front porch or the back fence." Indeed, because many of the comedies had been on radio in the thirties and forties, the characters and stars must have seemed like old friends to many viewers. Then, too, several of the most popular sitcoms were set in urban and ethnic locales, presenting viewers with a nostalgic vision of neighborhood experiences among immigrant families.[33] Even the sitcoms set in suburban towns externalized the private world by including neighbor characters who functioned as life-long friends to the principal characters.[34] The opening credits of fifties sitcoms further encouraged audiences to perceive television's families as neighbors, linked through electrical wires to their own homes. Typically, the credit sequences depicted families exiting their front doors (*Donna Reed, Leave It to Beaver, Make Room for Daddy, Ozzie and Harriet*) or greeting viewers in a neighborly fashion by leaning out their windows (*The Goldbergs*), and the programs often used establishing shots of the surrounding neighborhoods (*Father Knows Best, Ozzie and Harriet, Leave It to Beaver, Make Room for Daddy, The Goldbergs*).

Early television's most popular situation comedy, *I Love Lucy,* is a perfect—and typical—example of the importance attached to the theme of neighborhood bonding in the programs. The primary characters, Lucy and Ricky Ricardo, and their downstairs landlords, Ethel and Fred Mertz, were constantly together, and the more mature Mertzes served a quasi-parental role so that neighbors appeared as a family unit. In 1956, when the Ricardos moved from their Manhattan apartment to an idyllic Connecticut suburb, Lucy and Ricky reenacted the painful separation anxieties that many viewers must have experienced over the previous decade. In an episode entitled "Lucy Wants to Move to the Country," Lucy has misgivings about leaving the Mertzes behind, and the Ricardos decide to break their contract on their new home. But at the episode's end, they realize that the fresh air and beauty of suburban life will compensate for their friendships in the city. After learning their "lesson," the Ricardos are rewarded in a subsequent episode ("Lucy Gets Chummy with the Neighbors") when they meet their new next-door neighbors, Ralph and Betty Ramsey, who were regularly featured in following programs. While the inclusion of these neighbor characters provided an instant remedy for the painful move to the suburbs, the series went on to present even more potent cures. The next episode, "Lucy Raises Chickens," brings Ethel and Fred back into the fold when the older couple sell their Manhattan apartment to become chicken farmers in the Connecticut suburb—and of course, the Mertzes rent the house next door to the Ricardos. Thus, according to this fantasy scenario, the move from the city would not be painful because it was possible to maintain traditional friendships in the new suburban world.

The burgeoning television culture extended these metaphors of neighborhood bonding by consistently blurring the lines between electrical and real space. Television families were typically presented as "real families" who just happened to live their lives on TV. Ricky and Lucy, Ozzie and Harriet, Jane and Goodman Ace, George and Gracie, and a host of others crossed the boundaries between fiction and reality on a weekly basis. Promotional and critical discourses further encouraged audiences to think that television characters lived the life of the stars who played them. For example, when writing about *The Adventures of Ozzie and Harriet,* a critic for a 1953 issue of *Time* claimed that the "Nelson children apparently accept their double life as completely natural." In that same year, the *Saturday Review* commented, "The Nelsons are apparently living their lives in weekly installments on the air. . . ." In a 1952 interview with the Nelsons, *Newsweek* explained how "Ricky Nelson kicks his shoes off during the filming, just as he does at home, and both boys work in front of the cameras in their regular clothes. In fact, says Harriet, they don't even know the cameras are there." Even those sitcoms that did not include real-life families were publicized in this fashion. In 1954, *Newsweek* assured its readers that Danny Thomas was a "two-family man," and that "Danny's TV family acts like . . . Danny's own family." One photograph showed Danny in a family portrait with his television cast while another depicted Danny at his swimming pool with his real family. The reviewer even suggested that Danny Williams (the character) resembled Danny Thomas (the star) more than Gracie Allen resembled herself on *The George Burns and Gracie Allen Show*.[35]

These televised neighbors seemed to suture the "crack" in the picture window. They helped ease what must have been for many Americans a painful transition from the city to the suburb. But more than simply supplying a tonic for displaced suburbanites, television promised something better: it promised modes of spectator pleasure premised on the sense of an illusory—rather than a real—community of friends. It held out a new possibility for being alone in the home, away from the troublesome busy-body neighbors in the next house. But it also maintained ideals of community togetherness and social interconnection by placing the community *at a fictional distance*. Television allowed people to enter into an imaginary social life, one that was shared not in the neighborhood networks of bridge clubs and mahjong gatherings but on the national networks of CBS, NBC, and ABC.

Perhaps this was best suggested by Motorola television in a 1951 advertisement. The sketch at the top of the ad shows a businessman on his way home from work who meets a friend while waiting at a bus stop. Learning that his friend's TV set is on the blink, the businessman invites the friend home for an evening of television on his "dependable" Motorola console. A large photograph farther down on the page shows a social scene where two couples, gathered around the television set, share in the joys of a TV party.[36] Thus, according to the narrative sequence of events, television promises to increase social contacts. What is most significant about this advertisement, however, is that the representation of the TV party suggests something slightly different from the story told by the ad's narrative structure. In fact, the couples in the room do not appear to relate to one another; rather they interact *with and through* the television set. The picture emanating from the screen includes a third couple, the television stars George Burns and Gracie Allen. The couple on the left of the frame stare at the screen, gesturing toward George and Gracie as if they were involved in conversation with the celebrities. While the husband

Real-life couples meet TV couples in this 1951 ad for Motorola TV sets.
(Copyright, Motorola Corp.)

on the right of the frame stares at the television set, his wife looks at the
man gesturing toward George and Gracie. In short, the social relationship between couples in the room appears to depend on the presence of
an illusion. Moreover, the illusion itself seems to come alive insofar as
the televised couple, George and Gracie, appear to be interacting with the
real couples in the room. Television thus promises a new kind of social
experience, one that replicates the logic of real friendship (as told by the
sequence of events in the advertisement's narrative) but that transforms it
into an imaginary social relationship shared between the home audience
and the television image (as represented in the social scene). In this advertisement as elsewhere, it is this idea of simulated social life that is shown
to be the crux of pleasure in television.

Indeed, television—at its most ideal—promised to bring to audiences
not merely an illusion of reality as in the cinema but a sense of "being
there," a kind of *hyperrealism*. Television producers and executives devised schemes by which to merge public and private worlds into a new
electrical neighborhood. One of the central architects of this new electrical space was NBC's Pat Weaver, who saw television as an extension of
traditional community experiences. As he claimed, "In our entertainment,

we . . . start with television as a communications medium, not bringing shows into the living room of the nation, but taking people from their living rooms to other places—theaters, arenas, ball parks, movie houses, skating rinks, and so forth."[37] Implementing these ideals in 1949, Weaver conceived *The Saturday Night Review,* a three-hour program designed to "present a panorama of Americans at play on Saturday night." The program took the segmented format of variety acts and film features, but it presented the segments as a community experience shared by people just like the viewers at home. As *Variety* explained, "For a film, the cameras may depict a family going to their neighborhood theatre and dissolve from there into the feature."[38] Thus, television would mediate the cultural transition from public to private entertainment by presenting an imaginary night at the movies.

While Weaver's plan was the most elaborate, the basic idea was employed by various other programs, particularly by television shows aimed at women. In 1952, New York's local station, WOR, aired *TV Dinner Date,* a variety program that was designed to give "viewers a solid two-and-a-half hours of a 'night out at home.' "[39] CBS even promised female viewers an imaginary date in its fifteen-minute program *The Continental.* Sponsored by Cameo Hosiery, the show began by telling women, "And now it's time for your date with the Continental." Host Renza Cesana (who *Variety* described as Carl Brisson, Ezio Pinza, and Charles Boyer all rolled into one) used a vampirelike Transylvanian accent to court women in the late-night hours. Cesana addressed his romantic dialogue to an off-camera character as he navigated his way through his lushly furnished den, a situation designed to create the illusion that Cesana's date for the night was the home viewer.[40] Meanwhile, during daytime hours, numerous programs were set in public spaces such as hotels or cafes with the intention of making women feel as if they were part of the outside world. One of the first network shows, *Shoppers Matinee,* used a subjective camera that was intended to take "the place of the woman shopper, making the home viewer feel as if she were in the store in person."[41] In 1952, CBS introduced the daytime show *Everywhere I Go,* boasting of its "studio without walls" that was designed to "create the illusion of taking viewers to the actual scene" of presentation. One segment, for example, used rear-screen projection to depict hostess Jane Edwards and her nine-year-old daughter against a backdrop of their actual living room.[42] More generally, locally produced "Mr. and Mrs." shows invited female viewers into the homes of local celebrities, providing women with opportunities imaginatively to convene in familiar family settings with stars that exuded the warmth and intimacy of the people next door.

Television's promise of social interconnection has provided numerous postwar intellectuals—from Marshall McLuhan to Joshua Meyrowitz—with their own utopian fantasies. Meyrowitz is particularly interesting in this context because he has claimed that television helped to foster women's liberation in the 1960s by bringing traditionally male spaces into the home, thus allowing women to "observe and experience the larger world, including all male interactions and behaviors." "Television's first and strongest impact," he concludes, "is on the perception that women have of the public male world and the place, or lack of place, they have in it. Television is an especially potent force for integrating women because television brings the public domain to women. . . ."[43] But Meyrowitz bases this claim on an essentialist notion of space. In other words, he assumes that public space is male and private space is female. However, public spaces like the office or the theater are not simply male; instead they are organized according to categories of sexual difference. In these spaces certain social positions and subjectivities are produced according to the placement of furniture, the organization of entrances and exits, the separation of washrooms, the construction of partial walls, and so forth. Thus, television's incorporation of the public sphere into the home did not bring "male" space into female space; instead it transposed one system of sexually organized space onto another.

Not surprisingly in this regard, postwar media often suggested that television would increase women's social isolation from public life by reinforcing spatial hierarchies that had already defined their everyday experiences in patriarchal cultures. The new family theaters were typically shown to limit opportunities for social encounters that women traditionally had at movie theaters and other forms of public entertainment. In 1951, a cartoon in *Better Homes and Gardens* stated the problem in humorous terms. On his way home from work, a husband imagines a night of watching boxing on TV while his kitchen-bound wife, taking her freshly baked pie from the oven, dreams of a night out at the movies.[44] Colgate dental cream used this dilemma of female isolation as a way to sell its product. A 1952 advertisement that ran in *Ladies' Home Journal* showed a young woman sitting at home watching a love scene on her television set, complaining to her sister, "All I do is sit and view. You have dates any time

In this 1951 *Better Homes and Gardens* cartoon, private
and public amusements are divided along gender lines.
(Copyright, Merideth Corp.)

you want them, Sis! All I get is what TV has to offer." [45] Of course, after she
purchased the Colgate dental cream, she found her handsome dream date.
Thus, as the Colgate company so well understood, the imaginary universe
that television offered posed its own set of female troubles. Even if television programs promised to transport women into the outside world, it
seems likely that women were critical of this, that they understood that
television's electrical space would never adequately connect them to the
public sphere.

In 1955, the working-class comedy *The Honeymooners* dramatized this
problem in the first episode of the series "TV or Not TV." [46] The narrative
was structured on the contradiction between television's utopian promise
of increased social life and the dystopian outcome of domestic seclusion.
In an early scene, Alice Kramden begs her husband Ralph to buy a television set:

> I . . . want a television set. Now look around you, Ralph. We don't
> have any electric appliances. Do you know what our electric bill was
> last month? Thirty-nine cents! We haven't blown a fuse, Ralph, in ten
> years. . . . I want a television set and I'm going to get a television set. I

have lived in this place for fourteen years without a stick of furniture being changed. Not one. I am sick and tired of this. . . . And what do you care about it? You're out all day long. And at night what are you doing? Spending money playing pool, spending money bowling, or paying dues to that crazy lodge you belong to. And I'm left here to look at that icebox, that stove, that sink, and these four walls. Well I don't want to look at that icebox, that stove, that sink, and these four walls. I want to look at Liberace!

Significantly, in this exchange, Alice relates her spatial confinement in the home to her more general exclusion from the modern world of electrical technologies (as exemplified by her low utility bills). But her wish to interconnect with television's electrical spaces soon becomes a nightmare because the purchase of the set further engenders her domestic isolation. When her husband Ralph and neighbor Ed Norton chip in for a new TV console, the men agree to place the set in the Kramden's two-room apartment where Norton is given visitation privileges. Thus, the installation of the set also means the intrusion of a neighbor into the home on a nightly basis, an intrusion that serves to take away rather than to multiply the spaces that Alice can occupy. In order to avoid the men who watch TV in the central living space of the apartment, Alice retreats to her bedroom, a prisoner in a house taken over by television.

Social scientific studies from the period show that the anxieties expressed in popular representations were also voiced by women of the period. One woman in a Southern California study confessed that all her husband "wants to do is to sit and watch television—I would like to go out more often." Another woman complained, "I would like to go for a drive in the evening, but my husband has been out all day and would prefer to watch a wrestling match on television."[47]

A nationwide survey suggested that this sense of domestic confinement was even experienced by teenagers. As one respondent complained, "Instead of taking us out on date nights, the free-loading fellas park in our homes and stare at the boxing on TV." For reasons such as these, 80 percent of the girls admitted they would rather go to a B movie than stay home and watch television.[48]

If television was considered to be a source of problems for women, it also became a central trope for the crisis of masculinity in postwar culture. According to popular wisdom, television threatened to contaminate masculinity, to make men sick with the "disease" of femininity. As other scholars have observed, this fear of feminization has characterized the debates on mass culture since the nineteenth century. Culture critics have continually paired mass culture with patriarchal assumptions about femininity. Mass amusements are typically thought to encourage passivity, and they have often been represented in terms of penetration, consumption, and escape. As Andreas Huyssen has argued, this link between women and mass culture has, since the nineteenth century, served to valorize the dichotomy between "low" and "high" art (or modernism). Mass culture, Huyssen claims, "is somehow associated with women while real, authentic culture remains the prerogative of men."[49] The case of broadcasting is especially interesting because the threat of feminization was particularly aimed at men. Broadcasting quite literally was shown to disrupt the normative structures of patriarchal (high) culture and to turn "real men" into passive homebodies.

In the early 1940s, this connection between broadcast technology and emasculation came to a dramatic pitch when Philip Wylie wrote his bitter attack on American women, *Generation of Vipers*. In this widely read book, Wylie maintained that American society was suffering from an ailment that he called "momism." American women, according to Wylie, had become overbearing, domineering mothers who turned their sons and husbands into weak-kneed fools. The book was replete with imagery of apocalypse through technology, imagery that Wylie tied to the figure of the woman. As he saw it, an unholy alliance between women and big business had turned the world into an industrial nightmare where men were slaves both to the machines of production in the factory and to the machines of reproduction—that is, women—in the home.

In his most bitter chapter, titled "Common Women," Wylie argued that women had somehow gained control of the airwaves. Women, he suggested, made radio listening into a passive activity that threatened manhood, and in fact, civilization. As Wylie wrote,

> The radio is mom's final tool, for it stamps everyone who listens to it with the matriarchal brand—its superstitions, prejudices, devotional rules, taboos, musts, and all other qualifications needful to its maintenance. Just as Goebbels has revealed what can be done with such a mass-stamping of the public psyche in his nation, so our land is a living representation of the same fact worked out in matriarchal sen-

timentality, goo, slop, hidden cruelty, and the foreshadow of national
death. . . .[50]

In the annotated notes of the 1955 edition, Wylie updated these fears,
claiming that television would soon take the place of radio and turn men
into female-dominated dupes. Women, he wrote, "will not rest until every
electronic moment has been bought to sell suds and every bought program
censored to the last decibel and syllable according to her self-adulation—
along with that (to the degree the mom-indoctrinated pops are permitted
access to the dials) of her de-sexed, de-souled, de-cerebrated mate."[51] The
mixture of misogyny and "telephobia" that runs through this passage is
clearly hyperbolic; still, the basic idea is repeated in more sober representations of everyday life during the postwar period.

As popular media often suggested, television threatened to rob men of
their powers, to usurp their authority over the image, and to turn them
into passive spectators. This threat materialized in numerous representations that showed women controlling their husbands through television.
Here, television's blurring of private and public space became a powerful tool in the hands of housewives, who could use the technology to invert the sexist hierarchies at the heart of the separation of spheres. In this
topsy-turvy world, women policed men's access to the public sphere and
confined them to the home through the clever manipulation of television
technology. An emblematic example is a 1955 advertisement for *TV Guide*
that conspires with women by giving them tips on ways to "keep a husband home." As the ad suggests, "You might try drugging his coffee . . .
or hiding all his clean shirts. But by far the best persuader since the ball
and chain is the TV set . . . and a copy of *TV Guide*."[52]

This inversion of the gendered separation of spheres was repeated in
other representations that suggested ways for women to control their husbands' sexual desires through television. A typical example is a 1952 advertisement for Motorola television that shows a man staring at a bathing
beauty on television while neglecting his real-life mate. The dilemma of
"the other woman," however, was countered by the enunciative control
that the housewife had in the representation. While the man is shown to
be a passive spectator sprawled in his easy chair, his wife (who is holding a shovel) dominates the foreground of the image, and the caption,
which speaks from her point of view, reads, "Let's Go Mr. Dreamer,
that television set won't help you shovel the walk." Similarly, a 1953 RCA

advertisement for a set with "rotomatic tuning" shows a male spectator seated in an easy chair while watching a glamorous woman on the
screen. But the housewife literally controls and sanctions her husband's
gaze at the televised woman because she operates the tuning dials.[53] Then,
too, numerous advertisements and illustrations depicted women who censored male desire by standing in front of the set, blocking the man's view
of the screen.[54] Similarly, a cartoon in a 1949 issue of the *New York Times*
magazine showed how a housewife could dim her husband's view of televised bathing beauties by making him wear sunglasses, while a cartoon
in a 1953 issue of *TV Guide* suggested that the same form of censorship
could be accomplished by putting window curtains on the screen in order
to hide the more erotic parts of the female body.[55] Television, in this regard, was shown to contain men's pleasure by circumscribing it within the
confines of domestic space and placing it under the auspices of women.
Representations of television thus presented a position for male spectators
that can best be described as passive aggression. Structures of sadistic and
fetishistic pleasure common to the Hollywood cinema were still opera-
tive, but they were sanitized and neutralized through their incorporation
into the home.

In contemporary culture, the dream of social interconnection through
antiseptic electrical space is still a potent fantasy. In 1989, in an issue
titled "The Future and You," *Life* magazine considered the new electronic
space that the home laser holographic movie might offer in the twenty-
first century. Not coincidentally, this holographic space was defined by
male desire. As Marilyn Monroe emerged from the screen in her costume
from *The Seven Year Itch*, a male spectator watched her materialize in the
room. With his remote control aimed at the set, he policed her image from
his futuristic La-Z-Boy lounger. Although the scene was clearly coded as
a science fiction fantasy, this form of home entertainment was just the
latest version of the older wish to control and purify public space. Sexual
desire, transported to the home from the Hollywood cinema, was made
possible by transfiguring the celluloid image into an electrical space where
aggressive and sadistic forms of cinematic pleasure were now sanitized
and made into "passive" home entertainment. The aggression entailed in
watching Monroe was clearly marked as passive aggression, as a form of
desire that could be contained within domestic space. But just in case the
desire for this electronic fantasy woman could not be properly contained,
the article warned readers to "fasten the seatbelt on your La-Z-Boy."[56]

Television is the "other woman" in this 1952 Motorola ad. (Copyright, Motorola Corp.)

"I think it's time you gave a little of your attention to these forty-two-inch screens"

COLLIER'S

GLENN R. BERNHARDT

An angry housewife comes between her husband and another woman in this 1953 *Collier's* cartoon.

As this example shows, the utopian dreams of space-binding and social sanitation that characterized television's introduction in the fifties is still a dominant cultural ideal. Electronic communications offer an extension of those plans as private and public spaces become increasingly intertwined through such media as home computers, fax machines, message units, and car phones. Before considering these social changes as a necessary part of an impending "electronic revolution" or "information age," we need to remember the racist and sexist principles on which these electrical utopias have often depended. The loss of neighborhood networks and the rise of electronic networks is a complex social phenomenon based on a series of contradictions that plague postwar life. Perhaps being nostalgic for an older, more "real" form of community is itself a historical fantasy. But the dreams of a world united by telecommunications seem dangerous enough to warrant close examination. The global village, after all, is the fantasy of the colonizer, not the colonized.

Notes

This essay first appeared in *Sexuality and Space*, ed. Beatriz Colomina (New York: Princeton Architectural Press, 1992), pp. 185–217.

1 See my essay "Installing the Television Set: Popular Discourses on Television and Domestic Space, 1948–55," *Camera Obscura* 16 (March 1988): 11–47; and my book, *Make Room for TV: Television and the Family Ideal in Postwar America* (Chicago: University of Chicago Press, 1992).

2 Katherine Morrow Ford and Thomas H. Creighton, *The American House Today* (New York: Reinhold, 1951), p. 139.

3 Daniel J. Boorstin, *The Americans: The Democratic Experience* (New York: Vintage, 1973), pp. 336–45. Boorstin sees this "leveling of place" as part of a wider "ambiguity" symptomatic of the democratic experience.

4 *Sunset Homes for Western Living* (San Francisco: Lane, 1946), p. 14.

5 Thomas H. Hutchinson, *Here Is Television, Your Window on the World* (1946; New York: Hastings House, 1948), p. ix.

6 For more on this, see my *Make Room for TV*.

7 The data on installation rates vary slightly from one source to another. These estimates are based on Cobbett S. Steinberg, *TV Facts* (New York: Facts on File, 1980), p. 142; "Sales of Home Appliances," and "Dwelling Units," *Statistical Abstract of the United States* (Washington, D.C.: Government Printing Office, 1951–1956); Lawrence W. Lichty and Malachi C. Topping, *American Broadcasting: A Source Book on the History of Radio and Television* (New York: Hastings House, 1975), pp. 521–22. Note, too, that there were significant regional differences in

installation rates. Television was installed most rapidly in the Northeast; next were the central and western states, which had relatively similar installation rates; the South and southwest mountain areas were considerably behind the rest of the country. See "Communications," in *Statistical Abstract of the United States* (Washington, D.C.: Government Printing Office, 1959); *U.S. Bureau of the Census, Housing and Construction Reports*, Series H-121, nos. 1–5 (Washington, D.C.: Government Printing Office, 1955–1958). Average hours of television watched is based on a 1957 estimate from the A. C. Nielsen Company, printed in Leo Bogart, *The Age of Television: A Study of Viewing Habits and the Impact of Television on American Life* (1956; New York: Frederick Unger, 1958), p. 70.

8 James W. Carey and John J. Quirk, "The Mythos of the Electronic Revolution," in *Communication as Culture*, ed. James W. Carey (Boston: Unwin Hyman, 1989), pp. 113–41. For related issues, see Leo Marx, *The Machine in the Garden: Technology and the Pastoral Ideal in America* (New York: Oxford University Press, 1964); John F. Kasson, *Civilizing the Machine: Technology and Republican Values in America, 1776–1900* (New York: Penguin, 1977); Wolfgang Schivelbusch, *Disenchanted Night: The Industrialization of Light in the Nineteenth Century*, trans. Angela Davies (Berkeley: University of California Press, 1988).

9 Carolyn Marvin, *When Old Technologies Were New: Thinking About Electric Communication in the Late Nineteenth Century* (New York: Oxford University Press, 1988), pp. 200–201.

10 For discussions about electricity, see Carey and Quirk, "The Mythos of the Electronic Revolution" and "The History of the Future," in *Communication as Culture*, pp. 113–41 and 173–200; Andrew Feldman, "Selling the 'Electrical Idea' in the 1920s: A Case Study in the Manipulation of Consciousness," master's thesis, University of Wisconsin–Madison, 1989; Susan J. Douglas, *Inventing American Broadcasting, 1899–1922* (Baltimore: Johns Hopkins University Press, 1987), p. 308.

11 For a detailed study of the widespread concern about juvenile delinquency, see James Gilbert, *A Cycle of Outrage: America's Reaction to the Juvenile Delinquent in the 1950s* (New York: Oxford University Press, 1986).

12 Edward C. McDonagh et al., "Television and the Family," *Sociology and Social Research* 40:4 (March–April 1956): 116; and Raymond Stewart, cited in Bogart, *The Age of Television*, p. 100.

13 *House Beautiful*, October 1951, p. 168.

14 Sylvester L. "Pat" Weaver, "The Task Ahead: Making TV the 'Shining Center of the Home' and Helping Create a New Society of Adults," *Variety*, 6 January 1954, p. 91. The hope for a new democratic global village was also expressed by other industry executives. David Sarnoff, chairman of the Board of RCA, claimed, "When Television has fulfilled its destiny, man's sense of physical limitation will be swept away, and his boundaries of sight and hearing will be the limits of the earth itself. With this may come a new horizon, a new philosophy, a new sense of freedom and greatest of all, perhaps, a finer and broader understanding between all the peoples of the world." Cited in William I. Kaufman, *Your Career in Television* (New York: Merlin Press, 1950), p. vii.

15 Stewart's findings are summarized here by Bogart, *The Age of Television*, p. 98.

16 Respondent to Stewart's study is cited in Bogart, *The Age of Television*, p. 98.

17 David Riesman, "Recreation and the Recreationist," *Marriage and Family Living* 16:1 (February 1954): 23.

18 Eugene David Glynn, M.D., "Television and the American Character—A Psychiatrist Looks at Television," in *Television's Impact on American Culture*, ed. William Y. Elliott (East Lansing: Michigan State University Press, 1956), p. 177.

19 Following along the trail of other mass media aimed at youth (e.g., dime novels, comic books, radio, and film), television became a particular concern of parents, educators, clergy, and government officials. The classic tirade against mass culture during the period was Frederic Wertham's *Seduction of the Innocent* (1953; New York: Rinehart, 1954), the eighth chapter of which was entitled "Homicide at Home: Television and the Child."

20 For examples see William Porter, "Is Your Child Glued to TV, Radio, Movies, or Comics?" *Better Homes and Gardens*, October 1951, p. 125; *Ladies' Home Journal*, April 1950, p. 237; "Bang! You're Dead," *Newsweek*, 21 March 1955, p. 35. For more information on this, see my book *Make Room for TV*.

21 *Better Homes and Gardens*, September 1953, p. 154; John L. Springer, "How to Care for Your TV Set," *American Home*, June 1953, p. 44.

22 A similar scene is found in *The Three Stooges* comedy short "Scheming Schemers" (ca. 1946) when the Stooges, posing as plumbers, mistakenly squirt a gush of water through the television set of a wealthy matron who is showing her guests a scene of Niagara Falls on TV.

23 See my book *Make Room for TV*.

24 *House Beautiful*, August 1949, p. 66; "Where Shall We Put the Television Set?" *Good Housekeeping*, August 1951, p. 107.

25 *American Home*, May 1951, p. 40.

26 Lawrence W. Levine, *Highbrow/Lowbrow: The Emergence of Cultural Hierarchy in America* (Cambridge: Harvard University Press, 1988).

27 George Lipsitz, *Time Passages: Collective Memory and American Popular Culture* (Minneapolis: University of Minnesota Press, 1990), p. 8. Also see John F. Kasson, *Amusing the Millions: Coney Island at the Turn of the Century* (New York: Hill and Wang, 1978); and Kathy Peiss, *Cheap Amusements: Working Women and Leisure in Turn-of-the-Century New York* (Philadelphia: Temple University Press, 1986).

28 After reviewing numerous studies from the 1950s, Bogart claims in *The Age of Television*, "In the early days, 'guest viewing' was a common practice" (p. 102); for a summary of the actual studies, see pp. 101–7. For additional studies that show the importance of guest viewing in the early period, see John W. Riley et al., "Some Observations on the Social Effects of Television," *Public Opinion Quarterly* 13:2 (summer 1949): 233 (this article was an early report of the CBS–Rutgers University studies begun in the summer of 1948); McDonagh et al., "Television and the Family," p. 116; "When TV Moves In," *Televiser* 7:8 (October 1950): 17 (a summary of the University of Oklahoma surveys of Oklahoma City and Norman, Oklahoma); Philip F. Frank, "The Facts of the Medium," *Televiser* (April 1951):

14; and "TV Bonus Audience in the New York Area," *Televiser* (November 1950): 24–25.

29   McDonagh et al., "Television and the Family," p. 116.

30   *Esquire,* July 1953, p. 110; Bob Taylor, "Let's Make Those Sets Functional," *TV Guide,* 21–27 August 1953, p. 10.

31   William H. Whyte, *The Organization Man* (Garden City, N.Y.: Doubleday, 1957), p. 314.

32   Harry Henderson, "The Mass-Produced Suburbs," *Harper's,* November 1953, pp. 25–32, and "Rugged American Collectivism," *Harper's,* December 1953, pp. 80–86; John Keats, *The Crack in the Picture Window* (1956; Boston: Houghton Mifflin, 1957); Richard E. Gordon, M.D., Katherine K. Gordon, and Max Gunther, *The Split-Level Trap* (New York: Dell, 1960).

33   "NBC Promo for *Ethel and Albert* for use on the *The Golden Windows*," Clyde Clem's Office, 31 August 1954, NBC Records, box 136, folder 15, Wisconsin Center Historical Archives, State Historical Society, Madison; Gilbert Seldes, "Domestic Life in the Forty-Ninth State," *Saturday Review,* 22 August 1953, p. 28. For a fascinating discussion of nostalgia in early ethnic situation comedies, see Lipsitz, "The Meaning of Memory: Family, Class, and Ethnicity in Early Network Television," in *Time Passages,* pp. 39–76.

34   *I Married Joan*'s Aunt Vera, *My Favorite Husband*'s Gillmore and Myra Cobb, *Burns and Allen*'s Harry and Blanche Morton, and *Ozzie and Harriet*'s Thorny Thornberry were faithful companions to the central characters of the series.

35   "The Great Competitor," *Time,* 14 December 1953, p. 62; Seldes, "Domestic Life in the Forty-Ninth State," p. 28; "Normality and $300,000," *Newsweek,* 17 November 1952, p. 66; "Two-Family Man," *Newsweek,* 5 April 1954, p. 86.

36   *Better Homes and Gardens,* November 1951, p. 162.

37   Sylvester L. Weaver, "Thoughts on the Revolution; or, TV Is a Fad, Like Breathing," *Variety,* 11 July 1951, p. 42.

38   "NBC to Project 'American Family' in 3-Hour Saturday Night Showcase," *Variety,* 3 August 1949, p. 31.

39   *Variety,* 6 August 1952, p. 26.

40   For a review of the show, see *Variety,* 30 January 1952, p. 31. Note that the particular episode I have seen clearly is aimed at a female audience, given its pitch for women's stockings and its promise of a date with Cesana; however, Cesana addresses the home viewer as if she were a man, specifically his pal who has been stood up for a double date. Also note that there was a radio version of this program in which a female host courted male viewers in the late-night hours. Titled *Two at Midnight,* the program was aired locally on WPTR in Albany and is reviewed in *Variety,* 22 October 1952, p. 28.

41   "DuMont Daytime," *Telecasting,* 12 December 1949, p. 5.

42   "CBS-TV's 'Studio Without Walls' New Gitlin Entry," *Variety,* 24 September 1952, p. 43.

43   Joshua Meyrowitz, *No Sense of Place: The Impact of Electronic Media on Social Behavior* (New York: Oxford University Press, 1985), pp. 223–24.

44 *Better Homes and Gardens,* November 1951, p. 218.

45 *Ladies' Home Journal,* January 1952, p. 64.

46 *The Honeymooners* was first seen in 1951 as a skit in the live variety show *Caval-cade of Stars* on the DuMont network. The filmed half-hour series to which I refer aired during the 1955–1956 season.

47 McDonagh et al., "Television and the Family," pp. 117, 119.

48 Cited in Betty Betz, "Teens and TV," *Variety,* 7 January 1953, p. 97.

49 Andreas Huyssen, *After the Great Divide: Modernism, Mass Culture, Postmodernism* (Bloomington: Indiana University Press, 1986), p. 47.

50 Philip Wylie, *Generation of Vipers* (1941; New York: Holt, Rinehart and Winston, 1955), pp. 214–15.

51 Ibid., pp. 213–14.

52 *TV Guide,* 29 January 1955, back cover.

53 *Better Homes and Gardens,* February 1952, p. 154; *Better Homes and Gardens,* September 1953, p. 177.

54 See, for example, an advertisement for Durall window screens that shows a housewife blocking her husband's view of a bathing beauty on the television set in *Good Housekeeping,* May 1954, p. 187. A similar illustration appears in *Popular Science,* March 1953, p. 179. And an advertisement for Kotex sanitary napkins shows how a woman, by wearing the feminine hygiene product, can distract her husband's gaze at the screen (*Ladies' Home Journal,* May 1949, p. 30).

55 *New York Times,* 11 December 1949: magazine section, p. 20; *TV Guide,* 6 November 1953, p. 14.

56 *Life,* February 1989, p. 67.

Portable TV: Studies in Domestic Space Travel

✱ In 1967, the Sony Corporation tuned consumers into a new innovation in product design, a 5-inch mini-portable TV that it called "drive-in
television." The ad for the set shows a man and woman parked at a drive-
in theater, watching their new mini-portable receiver while tenderly embracing under the blanket of night. The advertising copy explains, "For
smooching 'n watchin' this tiny Sony operates off your car lighter . . . you
get a picture that's perfectly brilliant. Even with a policeman's flashlight
shining in."[1]

Sony thus used the popular conception of the drive-in movie as a semi-
private and even illicit space for dating to promote television watching
as an erotic experience to be had outside the home. However, the adver-
tiser staged this scenario of unmarried sex with full awareness of the fact
that most consumers were buying the mini-portables for more traditional
household uses. Assuring the reader that the portable set could also be
watched by "non-driving smoochers," Sony was more interested in selling
a particular fantasy about television spectatorship in domestic space than
it was in making people actually watch TV in their cars. In other words,
the slogan "drive-in television" was directed less at a concrete practice
for watching television than it was at a mode of imaginative experience.
The slogan encouraged consumers to experience TV—and domestic space
itself—as a vehicle for transport through which they could imaginatively

travel to an illicit place of passion while remaining in the safe space of the family home.

Although it is a quirky example, this ad is symptomatic of the more general cultural sensibility surrounding television and family life in the late 1950s through the 1960s. In this "second wave" of television installation, when most American households already had one receiver, marketers were looking for ways to convince the public to replace old living-room consoles or install additional sets throughout their homes. While early design and marketing presented television as living-room furniture, by the end of the fifties manufacturers broadened their design schemes to include (and even emphasize) nondecorative uses for TV. As *House Beautiful* announced in 1958, "For ten years the TV set has pretended to be furniture, which it is not. . . ." In place of the furniture model, *House Beautiful* recommended the purchase of a Philco Predicta, which, it claimed, "may be placed anywhere in the room."[2] While this was offered as pragmatic advice, the idea of moving television sets around the house gave way to much more fantastic visions. Instead of the sedentary viewing protocols that the console implied, portable receivers were marketed as marvelous new "space age" toys that promised audiences a more masterful, even active, relation to everyday life at home. As opposed to their 1950s predecessors, which were promoted as "home theaters" that promised family togetherness and shelter from the evils of urban life, ads for portable sets pictured TV as a vehicle that would drive people away from their mundane domestic lives and into a world of active adventure and romantic (if not sexual) quests.

This essay explores the cultural significance of portability and the related technologies of miniaturization and remote control. In an effort to revise some of the more abstract theories on technological change (and especially Baudrillardian-based arguments that claim that television and new satellite technologies have obliterated conventional boundaries between public and private space and have changed human subjectivity completely) this essay addresses the rise of mobile culture in historical and material terms. By examining the way portable sets were promoted in advertisements and popular magazines aimed primarily at the white middle class, I focus on how marketing and design strategies relate to the changing ideals of middle-class family life in the 1960s.[3] Although advertisements, magazine articles, and other vehicles of popular culture obviously do not directly reflect how people experience television or how they use it in their daily lives, such sources do provide an intertextual context—a set of interrelated texts—through which people learn about new technologies. These sources help to establish a horizon of expectations, and at moments of technological transition they also help to establish a set of possibilities for how we use communication technologies and how we think about them in our everyday lives. The promotional rhetoric on portable television in the 1960s demonstrates the way in which this new technology was designed for and predicated on broader technological transitions in American family life. These changes revolve around a shift from the Eisenhower era's emphasis on nuclear-family consumer lifestyles to the Kennedy-era ideal of "New Frontierism," which stressed active citizenship, physical fitness, adventurousness, and "movements" of all kinds.

In fact, the concept of movement permeated all levels of television culture in the 1960s—not just the set itself. Movement and portability were written into television's aesthetic form, especially with the advent of mobile cameras. Remote news gathering and location shooting allowed television to shed itself of its overwhelmingly theatrical and static sensibility. Attesting to this, one NBC staff designer claimed in 1963, "One of the most important characteristics in the art of television is movement— mobility of cameras in and around, even through, objects. . . . It is this quality of movement that makes designing for TV so very different from designing for the theatre."[4] By the early 1970s, movement seemed so basic to television's cultural form that cultural theorist Raymond Williams devised the word "flow" to characterize not only the programs themselves but their scheduling by networks (he spoke of the way programs led into one another) and their reception by audiences.[5]

Movement was also a major narrative motif of program content and news images. From the famous footage of the Kennedy motorcade in Dallas to the news reports of Civil Rights marches to the trip to the moon in 1969, television was replete with travel narratives of every sort, from the political to the sublime. Meanwhile, series programming such as *Route 66* (1960–1964) and *The Fugitive* (1963–1967) showed men on the run who had moved away from their homes in search of their identity or freedom. Even genres as unlikely as the family sitcom began to stress notions of mobility and related ideas of sexual liberation from housework and suburban domesticity. As the classic family sitcoms such as *Leave It to Beaver*

(1957–1963) increasingly vanished from the airwaves, the domestic comedy began to feature fantastic households populated by witches, genies, and robots who were able to perform the technological feats of portability and remote control with their supernatural powers. In programs like *Bewitched* (1964–1972), the mundane tasks of housekeeping became opportunities for displays of women's liberation, as housewife/witch Samantha Stephens twitched her nose to wash the dishes and then flew off to lunch in Paris.[6] In ways such as these, television's technological and cultural form took on a keen fascination with movement that was intimately connected to notions of social progress and mobile family lifestyles.

Thus, more than simply an object form, the portable TV was the material manifestation of broader conceptual frameworks for television and family life in the 1960s. As a cultural sensibility rooted in the continual relocation of household objects and human subjects in and out of the home, portability came to represent larger social anxieties about postwar transformations in the relationship between public and private spheres. Like the ad for "drive-in television" with its allusion to promiscuous sexuality, these anxieties were mostly rooted in sexual difference and in the reigning ideals of femininity and masculinity that have worked to sanction (and even legalize) the division of spheres since the Victorian period.

I begin this essay, then, with the material object, portable TV, in order to unravel the cultural significance of portability and its relationship to the gendered divisions of private and public space. In particular, I am concerned with the way ads and magazines represented domestic space and how these media encouraged people to experience their daily lives through new transistorized forms of portable and remote-control technologies. I also want to show how sexual difference and the ideological divisions between private/feminine and public/masculine spheres continue to inform the way we think about new electronic technologies as well as the most recent metaphor of portable culture—the "information superhighway." With this in mind, I end the essay by considering the way portable culture has recently manifested itself in a new domestic ideal—the home office—which, despite its apparent "liberating" notions of working mothers and domestic dads, is still a highly gendered and racialized paradigm for everyday space.

From Home Theater to Mobile Home

In the 1950s, when television was hailed as a new "entertainment" and "information" medium, two central and often connected conceptual frameworks were written into its cultural logics and narrative forms. These frameworks, which I will refer to as "theatricality" and "mobility," were constitutive of virtually all statements about TV, statements generated by the industry, advertisers, policy makers, artists, critics, and social scientists and engineers. Theatricality and mobility have not only permeated, but in fact are generative of, television's object and cultural form.

During the period of television's early installation after World War II, popular literature, intellectuals, and corporate executives spoke of it both as a "home theater" that brought spectator amusements into the living room and as a "window on the world" that would imaginatively transport viewers across the globe. Over the course of the last fifty years, theatricality and mobility have continued to generate the ways we speak about television and the related technologies of cable, satellites, and most recently, the Internet. Consumer magazines such as *Home Theater* still package television through notions of theatricality, while terms like "surfing" or "information superhighway" serve as the contemporary version of a much older fantasy about travel to distant locales that telecommunication has historically offered its publics. Theatricality and mobility have also generated the "statements" that television makes, at the level both of its programming and its material design and object form. Live "golden age" anthology dramas are famous for their adaptations of legitimate theater, and even 1990s dramatic formats still aspire to theatricality (think, for example, of *ROC*'s live performances, or of the 1997 season premier of *ER*, which was shot live as it unfolded on stage). Meanwhile, since the radio age, broadcast programs have also promised audiences a sense of mobile transport to distant locales. In the case of television, media events premised on this transportation model range from *See It Now*'s demonstration of the 1951 coaxial cable hook-up of East and West coasts to Pathfinder's recent satellite transmissions from Mars.

Given that broadcasting was developed in the United States for household uses, it is perhaps no coincidence that theatricality and mobility have also been central metaphors for the middle-class home and bourgeois family.[7] Since Victorian times, the theater was a central organizing theme for domestic architecture and family relations. Architects, planbook writers, religious leaders, domestic engineers, women's magazines, and books on interior decor variously imagined the bourgeois home as a stage on which a set of highly conventionalized social roles were played by family members and guests alike. This theatrical conception of the home and human subjectivity within it carried through from the Victorian era to modern housing design. In her work on modernist architect Adolf Loos, Beatriz Colomina has shown that exclusive client-built modernist homes were organized around notions of residence based on the performative nature of everyday life and related notions of visual pleasure.[8] Although presented through mass-production economies and plans that appealed to middle-class tastes, the housing designs of the postwar suburb echoed these earlier modernist homes, emphasizing theatricality and visuality as central structural principles. In this respect, as I have argued previously, television was the popular activity par excellence through which the home theater was envisioned.[9] The arrangement of television in domestic space was guided by theatrical principles of set decoration and optimal audience pleasure, and television itself was often promoted as a substitute for theater-going in the public sphere.

Although the home theater continues even today to define modes of domestic architecture and electronic culture, by the end of the 1950s this metaphor for domesticity and domestic communications began to make way for a new set of metaphors that pictured the house as a vehicle for transport, or what I am calling a "mobile home." At a time when Americans were obsessed with the possibility of satellite technologies and outer-space travel, the mobile model of domesticity was especially realized in images that depicted the home as a rocket.[10] Drawing from previous streamline styles, but tailoring them to the penchant for space flight, ads for all sorts of remodeling products—from Armstrong flooring to Scotchguard fabrics—showed consumers how to sweep away the tacky remnants of 1950s domesticity and make way for decor that gestured toward the planets. Everything from kitchen dinettes to family cars to toothpaste containers mimicked outer-space fashions. Although obviously a marketing gimmick devised to make people buy new domestic trappings, the gimmick was probably effective because it tied what is typically devalorized as "feminine," decorative, trivial pursuits to the so-called "higher" "masculine" goals of national supremacy and citizenship. In other words, this new and improved family home validated itself through appeals to progress; no longer a place of insular stasis, the home was now a motor for change. Mimicking the ideals of Kennedy's New Frontier, and especially his emphasis on space travel as a sign of ultimate national progress, this space-age home gave private life a public purpose.

It was in this context of a new ideal of mobile domesticity and progressive family lifestyles that portable television—as a whole new way of watching TV—was introduced to the public.[11] To understand the specific dynamics at hand, I turn now to the promotional rhetoric that welcomed in the portable sets.

Breaking Up the Family Circle

In its first incarnation, television was primarily marketed as a family activity. Programming was typically developed and scheduled with family audiences in mind. By the end of the decade, however, this family-circle notion of television changed in several ways. First, as new forms of sponsor-network relations evolved, and as Nielsen rating measurements changed, networks began to move away from the singular focus on family audiences and aggregate ratings toward the idea of "demographics" and audience "shares." Networks increasingly developed prime-time programs with individual "demographics" in mind, attempting to draw in, for example, women age eighteen to forty-nine by targeting them with programs that suited their (as opposed to their family's) tastes. While this focus on demographics did not happen overnight (indeed many shows in the 1960s were still marketed with family groups in mind), the general trend in the industry favored identifying the audience as an individual-consumer type rather than a family unit. So, too, this trend favored socially mobile consumers over the stable family group, and in this sense mobility was not simply a metaphor but integral to the economic logic of the industry.

In this industrial context, the family console planted in a central living space gave way to portable receivers that could be watched by individuals and moved throughout the home. In 1963, *Good Housekeeping* estimated that "portables are the most popular models today, comprising about 60 percent of all sets sold."[12] The U.S. Census bears this out: from 1955 to 1969, the sale of black-and-white portable and table-top receivers rose dramatically, peaking at mid-decade as color sets (of all models) began to rise in popularity. Meanwhile, the sale of black-and-white consoles sharply declined; by mid-decade consoles were sold primarily in color models. Overall, this meant that by 1969 over twice as many portable and table-top models were sold than were consoles (7,606,000 versus 3,442,000).[13]

Although advertisers still marketed television—especially color models—as a family medium, they also sought to convince people to watch television alone (and thus to buy more than one TV).[14] One novel marketing twist was the increasing emphasis on what numerous manufacturers called "personal" viewing. As opposed to the family theater of the early 1950s, by the end of the decade manufacturers began to promote solitary room-to-room viewing with advertisements showing mom, dad, and the kids separately enjoying TV programs on their very own portable receivers. Even ads for large living-room consoles displayed television as an individual activity. A 1967 ad for General Electric receivers, for example, shows a couple with their three children sharing five television sets—one of which is a portable receiver piled on top of a console cabinet. The ad equates this personalized viewing experience with the obvious display of consumer capital that it required by offering the five TV sets as a grand prize in a sweepstakes contest.[15]

Despite the rhetoric of festive good fortune and affordable prices, advertisers did recognize the potential psychological risks entailed in their new campaigns to make television watching a solitary as opposed to a family experience. Anticipating consumer resistance, a 1965 ad for Panasonic portables asked, "Can a personal TV get too personal?"[16] While Panasonic reassured potential customers that portable TV could never be too private, the ad nevertheless expressed the anxieties inherent in the transition from a model of television viewing based on the family theater to the portable model of TV spectatorship based on individualized reception. As this ad suggests, the sentimental family iconography that depicted television in the 1950s could not easily be displaced by the spectacle of self-centered, even narcissistic, viewing. Instead, manufacturers for portable television had to respect the residual cultural sensibilities surrounding television. They had to introduce the new "personal TV" as something compatible with, rather than antithetical to, 1950s cultural ideals of family entertainment.

In this regard, advertisers promoted portable TV as a remedy for family fights over program choices on the living-room console. An ad for Admiral TV, for example, presents two portable receivers, one with a man and the other with a woman on screen. With the TV "couple" smiling, and the sets rubbing against each other in such a way as to suggest a physical if not romantic relationship, the ad told consumers to "meet the happy medium" by purchasing two sets.[17] This advertising strategy followed the logic of more eccentric contraptions marketed in the early 1950s—devices such as the DuMont Duoscope (a set with two separate picture tubes that would display two separate channels simultaneously so that people could sit together while watching different programs). But while such contraptions were mainly marketed as ways to maintain the ideals of family harmony while allowing for individual privacy and tastes, the "his and hers" marketing strategy for portable sets was much more concerned with demonstrating the pleasures—even autoerotic pleasures—to be achieved through watching TV alone.

This point is especially demonstrated by a 1964 ad in the Admiral campaign that used the "his and hers" strategy when telling consumers to "make a date with a Playmate," its 11-inch portable model. The ad shows two Playmate portables, one held by a male hand and the other by a female hand. As in the previous example, the sets are positioned side by side, suggesting a sense of intimacy between the TV "couple." Continuing with its romantic innuendoes, Admiral suggested that the Playmate could be taken anywhere, even the bedroom, where the consumer could listen to their favorite program with the Playmate's "private pillow" earphone.[18] A clear instance of product differentiation, such promises of promiscuous "playmate" dates and "private pillow" pleasures made the portable distinct from the family console.

More generally, manufacturers suggested that portable TV was perfect for bedroom viewing, and numerous ads contained hints of the secret desires and solitary (if not masturbatory) pleasures that portable TV would bring to the home. So prevalent was this idea that even mattress and bedding companies made use of the portable TV when advertising their wares. For example, in 1957 Wamsutta Mills advertised its Supercale sheets by showing a woman turning in for the night with a copy of TV Guide in her bed and a portable receiver resting on a nearby dresser.[19] Here as elsewhere, the "bedroom" TV became a sign of personal indulgence, an object that spoke more to narcissistic pleasure than to the 1950s emphasis on companionate marriage.

While the narcissistic identification and autoerotic desire encouraged by such ads were presented as "positive" goals for the consumer, the ads also had more negative, depressing implications. In fact, portable TV was sometimes used metonymically as a kind of shorthand symbol for the perceived crisis of failed passion and dead-end marriage. At a time when divorce rates were climbing,[20] women's magazines and popular weeklies presented articles (typically told from a woman's point of view) in which a husband's loss of sexual interest was represented via the image of a portable receiver. In its January 1970 issue, *Good Housekeeping* capped off this decade-long trend with a story titled "Can Love Live with Indifference?" A large photograph on the first page showed a husband fast asleep in bed, while his wife, sporting a sexy nightgown, stares with furrowed brow at her portable set. The caption reads, "Night after night my husband turned away from me. Hurt, baffled, frustrated—I couldn't believe he was the same man I married."[21]

Whether presented as a luxurious tool for personal indulgence or a depressing comment on romantic estrangement, such images of portable TV should be seen in the context of a more general move away from the suburban family ideals that had been so integral to marketing campaigns for television sets in the early 1950s. While the television industry still targeted the family as its primary consumer unit, it nevertheless revamped its images of ideal families, appealing to domestic consumers in markedly changing terms. Trading in its 1950s emphasis on domestic interiors and sedentary family circles, the industry represented family life in terms that engaged ideals of freedom, sexual liberation, personal achievement, and participation in public affairs—ideals that were integral to Kennedy's New Frontier and to the various social movements of the sixties.

Privatized Mobility

At the most basic level, the move away from domestic enclosures was written onto television technology itself. Names like the General Electric Adventurer, the Zenith Jetliner, and the RCA Globe Trotter spoke to the new emphasis on active leisure and imaginary travel away from home. Television manufacturers especially drew on the public's burgeoning interest in space travel. In 1960, Motorola spoke of its "Astronaut Portable," while a host of manufacturers boasted of "space-age" performance and style.[22] As the case of the "drive-in television" suggests, advertisers also encouraged consumers to imagine portable sets as earthbound vehicles, not only cars but also motorcycles and boats.[23]

Not only did advertisers recommend uses, they also designed the set

This 1962 ad for a GE portable uses the space-age imagery of the
Seattle World's Fair. The small print dubs GE the "TV of
tomorrow." (Copyright, General Electric Corp.)

itself in ways that evoked travel away from home. Numerous manufacturers made portable cabinets look like luggage. In 1959, Philco claimed that its portable was "handsomely encased . . . in leather-like vinyl simulating natural saddle, white or black alligator."[24] Making the visual comparison more emphatic, the Philco ad placed the portable receiver next to an actual suitcase. In 1965, General Electric took this idea to its logical extreme by featuring an ad that displayed four portable sets inside a large coupon that was drawn to look like a piece of luggage. The ad told consumers to "trim along the dotted line and you have your own portable ad. Carry it anywhere, especially to your GE dealer. . . ."[25] Portability thus opened up a whole new set of cultural fantasies about television and the pleasure to be derived from watching TV—fantasies based on the imaginary possibility of leaving, rather than staying, home.

In ways such as this, the stress on mobility made portable television (or at least the fantasies surrounding it) quite different from the console models of the 1950s. While early advertising promised viewers that TV would strengthen family ties by bringing the world into the living room, representations of portable receivers inverted this logic. Rather than incorporating views of the outdoor world into the home, now television promised to bring the interior world outdoors. In this regard, we might say that what Raymond Williams referred to as communication technology's capacity for *mobile privatization*—its promise to link the private family home with the modern industrial city—was now inverted into a related ideal of *privatized mobility*.

Williams, we can recall, developed the concept of mobile privatization in order to explain television's rise as a technological and cultural form. In this context, Williams uses the idea of mobile privatization to describe the inherent paradox entailed in two contradictory yet intimately connected modes of modern social life: geographic mobility (realized through technologies of communication and transportation) and privatization (realized through domestic architecture and community planning). He locates the roots of this paradox in the changes wrought by the industrial revolution. After industrialization, people no longer experience a rooted existence in small agricultural communities. Instead, in a society organized around large urban centers, people live in a highly mobile world where communities are joined together through transportation and communication systems. At the same time, since industrialization there has been an increased emphasis on the ideology of privacy, an ideology that materialized in the private family home. Nevertheless, the private family has always depended on the public sphere for funding, maintenance, and information about the world. Broadcasting, Williams argues, serves as the resolution to this contradiction insofar as it brings a picture of the outside world into the private home. It gives people a sense of traveling to distant places and having access to information and entertainment in the public sphere, even as they receive this in the confines of their own domestic interiors.

In the 1960s, the paradox of mobile privatization that Williams described still structured the statements that people made about television. However, the inversion I refer to as "privatized mobility" characterized a peculiar shift of emphasis. Now, rather than experiencing the domicile as a window on the world that brought public life indoors, the resident experienced the home as a vehicular form, a mode of transport in and of itself that allowed people to take private life outdoors.

In fact, privatized mobility extended beyond the case of television per se; it was written into architectural styles and decorative practices. This period saw the rise of the "mobile home" as a new design for middle-class suburban lifestyles. Differentiating itself from the trailer and its previous associations with Depression era and wartime hardships, the term "mobile home" was coined in the mid-1950s "to refer to a place where respectable people could marry, mature, and die." [26] A popular mode of everyday life, the mobile home perfectly encapsulates the contradictions of portable culture. While most people living in these homes did not use them for travel, the homes nevertheless were promoted in ways that negotiated cultural ideals of travel, adventure, and personal freedom with the values of home ownership, a stable family life, and suburban community.

For the more traditionally homebound consumer, a host of "indoor-outdoor" products boasted of their ability to transform domesticity (and the civilizing customs it implied) into rustic, outdoor lifestyles. In 1966, *Ladies' Home Journal* included an article on a new line of sleeping bags that allowed for an "indoor camp-out." The magazine told readers that the sleeping bags were "an adventure for the whole family. . . . The ideal campsite, of course, the floor." The accompanying photograph to this indoor-outdoor fantasy was a domestic scene in which two children nestled up next to each other in their bandanna-patterned sleeping bags, while Dad, lying in his own bag, watched a miniature portable TV. [27]

In tune with this indoor-outdoor aesthetic, numerous ads for television sets promoted TV's ability to merge domestic space with the world out-doors. In the early 1960s, Motorola's advertising campaign for hi-fi, table, and portable TV models featured brilliantly rendered upper-class homes that incorporated dramatic landscapes into the living room. Sporting the slogan "fresh from Motorola," the ads depicted the home as a nature re-treat. A 1963 ad shows a house made entirely of glass and shaped like a perisphere.[28] The glass home functions as a series of views through which we see hillsides, an ocean, and two large rocks near the shore. The seaside motif continues thematically into the interior space, as a rock formation occupies the center of the living room where it forms a kind of altar for a TV set. Vegetation and steps of flagstone lead up to a hi-fi/TV console.

Other ads in the "fresh from Motorola" series depict the activity of television watching as a kind of outdoor sport. A 1962 ad for a table-top model is especially striking here.[29] Evocative of the Paris home that Adolf Loos built for actress Josephine Baker in 1928, this postwar domestic in-terior contains a glass wall, with a swimming pool behind it. Inside the swimming pool wall a little boy is diving under water. Meanwhile, a TV set, placed against a wall adjacent to the pool, competes for his mother's attention. In fact, she seems unable to decide which view (her boy or the program) to watch. Placed in a position analogous to the mother, the reader for the ad is likewise uncertain as to what constitutes inside and outside in the home, and toward which screen (the pool or the TV set) they should direct their visual attention.

Motorola continued with the swimming pool motif when it advertised its portable model in 1963.[30] In this example, the activity of watching TV takes place in a dome-shaped, all-glass poolhouse, through which the reader sees the adjacent main—and markedly modernist—home in the background. Placed at the edge of the pool, the portable set is tuned to an exercise program that pictures a female figure stretching her body. Mean-while, in the foreground of the ad a woman dressed in a leotard imitates the action on screen. This ad for the portable model thus carries the Moto-rola series to its logical extreme. Portability allows the woman literally to carry her television pleasures outside the home where she becomes an active, rather than a passive, viewer. Her body, just as the receiver itself, is placed in motion.

In ads such as these, portability is more than a technological contrap-tion; it serves to define not only the receiver but the experience of tele-vision spectatorship itself. Portability is thus portrayed as a conceptual

FRESH FROM MOTOROLA.

In this 1963 ad, indoor and outdoor space merge as TV goes back to nature. (Copyright, Motorola Corp.)

Television comes with weather-resistant attachments in this 1967 ad for an Admiral portable. (Copyright, Admiral Corp.)

design for living—a mode of experience that became the dominant ideal for television culture in the 1960s. Distinct from the sedentary domestic culture of the 1950s, and the passive model of spectatorship implied by the "home theater," portable TV assumed an active viewer, a mobile subject. As Zenith proclaimed in 1964, portables were "for people on the go."[31] Moreover, whereas the early cultural expectations for television and its live production practices emphasized TV's ability to simulate the experience of "being at the theater," the 1960s model of portability emphasized television's ability to simulate adventures in the great outdoors.

Some manufacturers even sold their sets with special "weather-resistant" attachments. RCA named its 1967 portable model the Sport, and marketed it with a removable "snap-on sunshield" that would "filter [sun] for better daylight viewing, inside or out."[32] This indoor-outdoor motif was continued in that same year by Admiral, which promoted its "snap-on 'Sun-Shield' TV" that "gives you perfect pictures outdoors!" and "perfect pictures indoors, too."[33] A 1967 ad for the RCA Jaunty used an even more unlikely accessory. The ad shows a pair of flippers and a snorkel and mask laying next to a portable TV, whose screen depicts a woman who looks like she's been diving. Thus, whether through marketing gimmicks or advertising metaphors, advertisers encouraged consumers to think of television as an active outdoor sport.[34]

Despite the promise of exotic outdoor fun, it seems unlikely that actual consumers took these advertisements literally. Nor does it seem likely that people assumed advertisers intended them to do so. In fact, in 1963 *Good Housekeeping* reported that "research has shown that for whatever reasons, portables are seldom moved."[35] From this point of view it seems most probable that advertisers assumed the public wanted the *fantasy* (as opposed to the actual possibility) of being somewhere else while watching TV at home.

In this sense, such sales come-ons evoked what Margaret Morse has called television's capacity to "derealize" space. Morse argues that television is one of several postwar phenomena that encourage people to experience the lived environment in a state of distraction so that they are no longer "present" in the material spaces they occupy (she uses the shopping mall and the freeway as additional examples).[36] Ads for portable television promoted this derealization of space as an ideal state of consciousness and as a highly pleasurable form of experience. Even if most people actually watched their portable receivers at home, the ads supplied a new kind of "psychical reality" for television, giving the public a fantasy of TV watching as an active, and markedly nondomesticated, mode of experience that took place in an imaginary space, outside the material contours of the home.

In addition to its promise of imaginary transport to another spatial realm, advertisers promised that the portable TV would allow spectators to manipulate space, to convert the "here and now" into the "there and then," to make "presence" into "absence," "home" into "not home." Manufacturers boasted of the portable's capacity for multiple hookups, telling consumers they could plug it into cigarette lighters in cars and boats in addition to conventional household sockets. Moreover, the portable television's capacity for electrical conversion allowed advertisers to evoke a range of contradictory meanings and uses for television. With its "indoor-outdoor" convertible sockets, portable TV could appeal to people aspiring to conventional family ideals, or just as easily appeal to consumers who embraced the nonfamilial, "liberated," and even countercultural lifestyles of the 1960s.

Liberated Viewers

Representations of the "mobile home" and the fantasies of portability it contained were predicated on a new set of gender and generational relations that were tied to the movements of the day, especially the sexual "revolution." Advertisers often represented their imaginary television outings as social relations apart from the family unit, and they displayed television in scenes that evoked youth culture or sex out of wedlock.

For example, a 1965 ad for the Zenith Voyager shows a group of young people gathered on a beach at night, barely dressed and watching TV as the tide comes in.[37] In that same year, RCA-Victor claimed its Sportabout portable was just right "for the action crowd." The ad shows a young man and woman on motorscooters, with 19-inch portables rigged onto the back of each bike.[38] Sony's 1967 ad campaign for its 5-inch portable took this "swinging youth" ethos to its provocative extreme. One ad in the campaign promotes the Sony "Sun Set" model by showing people watching it in a nudist colony. Calling it "the Sony for sun-lovers," the ad includes twelve naked men and women watching the mini-portable while resting in tall grass that hides the more private parts of their anatomy. Sony, however, used this visual censorship as a way to provoke—as op-

The Sony for Sun-Lovers

The Sun Set

No longer a family group, the ideal TV spectator is now going "back to nature" in this 1967 ad for a Sony portable. (Copyright, Sony Corp.)

posed to diminish—the reader's sexual interest in the scene by going to great lengths to direct visual attention to what the reader was not allowed to see. For example, the ad draws attention to female genitalia by having women modestly hide their body parts. Meanwhile, a male nude towers over the scene, holding a barbell and flexing his sizable biceps. Sony thus encouraged consumers to imagine the activity of watching TV as an erotic, and emphatically nonfamilial, pastime. Of course, as with these ads more generally, Sony was quick to remind people of the convertible nature of the fantasy, telling readers, "there's nothing to stop you from going indoors and watching the Sun Set after the sun goes down."[39]

In cases such as this, the move away from family life that was built into the symbolic apparatus of portability was accompanied by new images of male and female viewers quite different from the moms and dads of the 1950s home theater. The representation of gender roles in promotional materials for television underwent a marked shift, even if the ads preserved the middle-class family as a dominant design for living.

Representations of female viewers embraced the ethos of liberated lifestyles. While Sony's nudist colony was the most extreme example of the marketing of the sexual revolution, other ads also incorporated new sensibilities about women's social and economic equality. In the context of the widespread popularity of Betty Friedan's *Feminine Mystique* (1963), advertisers addressed women not only as housewives but as people expecting to achieve some degree of economic and professional success.

The association of portability with women's liberation and economic mobility was from the start crucial to the promotion of portable receivers. As early as 1957, *House Beautiful* ran an ad for Magnavox portables that displayed on screen a young woman in graduation cap and gown. At a practical level, Magnavox most likely recognized the market for portable receivers among the growing number of young people living away from home in college dorms. But at a symbolic level, the ad implies that the portable receiver is imbued with the values of women's liberation—particularly its emphasis on the pursuit of professional careers over what Betty Friedan derisively called "occupation housewife." Condensing the set's ability to be carried outdoors with the growing emphasis on girls' achievements before marriage, the caption boasts that the portable "promises performance that surpasses many ordinary 'stay at home' sets." [40]

Ironically, then, while Friedan vehemently attacked advertisers for creating stereotypical images of women, advertisers co-opted burgeoning sentiments of women's liberation and turned them into consumer lifestyles. [41] In this regard, ads for portable TV especially resonated with the new sexual freedoms of career girls promoted in Helen Gurley Brown's *Sex and the Single Girl* (1962). Equating liberation with sex appeal, these ads presented slender, modern-looking women who wore miniskirts and other "mod" garb. As in the "fresh from Motorola" ad for poolside TV, advertisers often presented women in action poses that evoked athletic lifestyles. And unlike the ads from the 1950s that typically presented family groups and domestic milieus, these ads often contained solitary female figures set against abstract backgrounds or negative, empty spaces.

In images such as these, the new woman's increased corporal "mobility" and athleticism typically also served to evoke her economic mobility, discretionary income, and consumer choices. A perfect example is a 1966 issue of *TV Guide* that promoted the new fall lineup of state-of-the-art television sets. [42] On the cover, apparently running toward the reader, is a woman dressed in an orange miniskirt, accessorized with white shoes, white gloves, and a white hat that looks ambiguously like a combination

This 1968 ad for Toshiba shows a "mod" female spectator toting her portable TV in the great outdoors. (Copyright, Toshiba)

of English bobby hat and space helmet. The final and most eccentric touch to this already odd ensemble is a small-screen portable television set that the woman holds in her outstretched arms, as if it were a purse. The visual metaphor used here—portable TV as a woman's purse—is the sixties version of a much longer history of visual culture (movies, fairs, museums) in which women's spectatorship has been linked to shopping. In this particular version, the "new" woman's corporal mobility is conflated with both her economic mobility and her (implied) sexual freedom. Over the course of the sixties, the "TV purse" appeared in numerous ads for televisions sets, to the degree that it became a standard symbol for the new woman. Even the Barbie doll, that ultimate icon of sixties femininity, was given a purse-like portable TV to clutch in her specially designed "Busy Barbie" hands.

To be sure, this advertising imagery resonated with television programming of the time, which increasingly promoted new models of femininity that spoke to the reigning ethos of sexual liberation. Despite censorship concerns at networks, housewives had more athletic bodies and wore revealing clothing like capri pants (*The Dick Van Dyke Show*, 1961–1966) or harem garb (*I Dream of Jeannie*, 1965–1970) in place of aprons. The single-girl sitcom was especially concerned with movement away from the family. Underscoring the centrality of this theme, the credit sequences of some of these shows depicted single women moving away from home. For example, *That Girl* (1966–1971) portrayed single-woman Ann Marie leaving her suburban family home to live by herself in the city. The credit sequence showed Ann frolicking through the streets of Manhattan amid a series of moving vehicles. Following *That Girl*, the breakthrough "new-woman" sitcom *The Mary Tyler Moore Show* (1970–1977) took moving to its logical extreme. The famous credit sequence showed Mary Richards driving from her small-town home to the thriving city of Minneapolis, where she turned in her engagement ring for an exciting career in television. In ways such as these, the technological apparatus and some of the most popular new programs it delivered associated women's liberation with a move away from traditional ideals of family life in the 1950s suburb.

The idea of mobility and travel away from home also was associated with a more active style of masculinity. By the end of the 1950s, and especially in the early 1960s, male spectators shed the family-man status of their early fifties predecessors. In the context of the New Frontier's emphasis on physical fitness and do-gooder countrymen—as well as the more counter-cultural romanticization of beatniks and playboys—male spectators were often represented as sportsmen and adventure seekers. In 1960, RCA-Victor promoted its Sportabout line of portable sets by displaying a procession of male figures (cut off at the waist) carrying the sets across a two-page advertising spread. The first man in line was dressed in a formal black suit, carrying a television set as if it were a briefcase. The second man was dressed in white pants and tennis shoes, and his portable receiver looked like a gym bag. Finally, the third man was dressed more ambiguously in a sporty shirt with formal black pants and shoes, so that the portable TV functioned as both gym bag and briefcase. In this way, the ad encouraged the reader to imagine TV not simply as a sedentary pastime but rather as the perfect marriage of work and leisure. So, too, the image of male bodies dressed for success and proceeding purposefully across the page imbued the ad with a sense of progress and potent masculinity. The ad's copy associates these pictorial allusions to masculinity with the technological capacity of the set itself, calling it a "big-time performer" and claiming it as "high in picture power."[43] Other ads balanced this brand of rugged masculinity with the family-man image that had more traditionally been used to market TV. Addressing men as both husbands and adventurers, GE told the male consumer to "bring your wife and your wanderlust to your GE Dealer's."[44]

As with the case of women, these images of "new" masculinity reso-nated with characters on television itself. Heroes such as Richard Kimble (*The Fugitive*), Tod Stiles and Buz Murdock (*Route 66*), Paladin (*Have Gun Will Travel*, 1957–1963), or Kelly Robinson and Alexander Scott (*I Spy*, 1965–1968) lived apart from women, straying far away from domestic lifestyles. Even if these heroes were often involved in romantic interludes or melodramatic plots about human morality, they nevertheless provided a distinct departure from the family man of fifties television. As critic Joseph Golden argued, "Many of television's most highly rated dramatic series have created an essentially womanless society, and in so doing have defined a provocative breed of male hero . . . [whose] behavioral sterility, so aggressively explored by the European avant-garde in the last decade or so, is a natural for television." Claiming that this hero was a reaction against previous radio and television programs that represented men as lovable boobs ruled by their overly "superior" wives, Golden argued that TV's new womanless hero was an expression of a man's desire for "lib-eration," a "sublimated yearning for one's wife to be dispatched."[45]

The association of television's new virile "avant-garde" hero with the rejection of domesticity was clearly, and at the time unabashedly, misogy-nistic. For our purposes, such associations have particular relevance to the more general dynamics of portable culture, beyond the case of program-ming per se.[46] Portable television technology carried with it a set of highly gendered meanings about private and public life. Indeed, despite the em-phasis on heroic men and emancipated women, the cultural fantasies of 1960s television were by no means revolutionary. Anxieties about sexual difference and the power dynamics between men and women still pro-vided the source material for representations of television and the activity of watching TV.

This is particularly notable with regard to the way domestic labor and leisure were represented. Although female spectators were depicted as up-wardly mobile and less housebound, promotional rhetoric surrounding portable TV still often reproduced stereotypical housewife roles. In fact, even the Sony nudist colony ad, with its explicit allusions to sexual libera-tion, found it necessary to depict one of the female nudes knitting while watching from her place in the sun. More generally, even while women were not typically pictured in family scenes, in the few ads that did show family groups, women spectators tended (like their early fifties predecessors) to perform child-rearing functions (such as helping the child move the TV) or household chores (such as serving snacks).

Portrayals of housewife spectators, however, were never simply about feminine submission to male authority in the home. Instead, such images were complicated by the fact that women spectators actually worked—that is, they took an active and productive role while watching television. Conversely, male spectators typically sat passively and were even rendered as what we now call the couch potato. In this regard, even while male spectators might have been given the luxury of total relaxation, these scenarios belied subtle reversals of gender power in the home. Whereas Western culture typically associates men with activity and women with passivity, these images of housewife spectators and their lazy male husbands often reversed that hierarchy so that women were decidedly in the active role while men were presented as passive subjects, not only "victims" of TV but also at the mercy of their more industrious wives. In this regard, this imagery expanded on similar advertising images of male and female spectators in the 1950s that showed lazy male spectators sprawled out in front of the tube while their wives commented in disapproving ways on their utter neglect of household chores.[47]

By the mid-1960s, when the advertising industry increasingly used ironic humor as a sales strategy, representations of lazy male spectators sometimes took on sinister tones. In these cases, the male spectator was not simply represented as a lazy lounger, instead he was shown to be thoroughly humiliated and degraded.

Sony TV was especially brutal in this regard. A 1965 ad shows an overweight, balding, large-nosed man in polkadot pajamas lying in bed with a 5-inch "lightweight" Sony TV resting on his protruding stomach. The bold-print title caption reads, "tummy television," and the copy continues, "The 5-inch Sony [is] for waist sizes 38 to 46." Just in case anyone imagined that this man might have anything to do in bed except watch his tummy TV, the ad claims, "So that your wife can sleep, we also include a personal ear plug."[48] Several months later, Sony followed up with an ad for its 4-inch model. Visually comparing the smallness of the set to the largeness of a man's pot belly, the ad shows the same male model slumped in a chair, smoking a cigar, while the mini-TV sits perched on its handle

Pee Wee Tee Vee

Comb upon my knee, Sony boy. The 4" Sony pee wee tee vee, otherwise known as pee wee knee tee vee. (It only weighs six pounds so you'll never get water on the knee no matter how long you watch it.) For knee TV the pee wee Sony operates on a built in rechargeable battery pack. Thanks to its flat-faced, non-distorting picture tube and directional master antenna, the picture will stay steady even if you're in a rocking chair. For sitting watching, it has an AC plug that fits in your wall outlet. And the nice thing about it is, when the Late, Late Show finally brings you to your knees, you can always take the Sony off your lap and put it to bed in your nighttable.

The 4 inch SONY television

In this 1965 ad for a Sony mini-portable, masculinity is obviously the butt of the joke. (Copyright, Sony Corp.)

on the man's thighs. Because the TV looks as if it is actually crawling up the man's legs, the ad draws attention not only to his protruding stomach, but even more provocatively to his crotch (in fact, the receiver seems headed for his genitals). The humorous juxtaposition of the miniature TV and the man's anatomy is further emphasized by the boldface caption, which reads "pee wee tee vee"—a slogan that in not-too-subtle ways also suggests the diminutive size of the man's genitals (at least in comparison to his pot belly). In short, it seems unlikely that Sony could have intended this ad to be read in any way other than as a humiliating joke about the male spectator's out-of-shape and decidedly unphallic body.[49] A final ad in this Sony series presents a less humorous but equally degrading image of masculinity. The ad shows an aging male viewer, this time terribly thin, balding, and wrinkled, slumped in a chair on his terrace and drinking a soda. His sense of lonely despair is ironically underscored by the fact that he is watching a young couple kiss passionately on-screen. The caption, which reads simply, "the Sun Set," further suggests that television is a sad substitute for a real-life lover.[50] The enigma this ad poses, of course, is why Sony assumed that such a depressing image of masculinity would make people want to buy television sets. Because images such as these are more associative than they are literal, it seems useful to explore this enigma in relation to a set of cultural fantasies surrounding portability and miniaturization—namely, fantasies of mastery over technology.

Portable Power

While I have argued that portability implied an active relationship to television, it is nevertheless true that this could easily turn onto its opposite—complete human stasis.[51] The transistorized technology of portable TV not only allowed the human subject to move the set in and out the home, it also perfected TV technology to the point where human movement was accomplished by the set itself. Manufacturers promised that as opposed to the old vacuum-tube technology, the new solid-state sets with automatic tuning did not need adjusting. As a 1964 ad for the Westinghouse Instant-On asked, "Why wait 25 seconds or more for your TV set to warm up? . . . Why walk back to tune?" With the Instant-On there is "no wait," "no warm up," "no walk back."[52] These sets were marketed through the ethos of the "time-motion" studies that since the turn of the century had been so much a part of domestic science. In this case, the fully automatic TV set promised to minimize the amount of human movement needed to traverse domestic space.

In addition to the promise of automatic tuning, the portable set was often marketed with a remote control, a device that came wrapped in a set of ambivalences about the relation of "man" to machine. Advertisers promoted the ease and comfort offered by automation, demonstrating how viewers could dominate domestic space and time by commanding the set to perform instantaneously from remote locales. Metaphors of flight were especially applied to the remote accessory, as product names like Admiral's Super Son-R promoted the idea that the viewer was a pilot navigating a ship through the airwaves.[53] Yet, despite these action-adventure fantasies of domestic space travel and mastery over distance, the remote control brought with it the nagging fear that technology would render the human body completely immobile, passive, even redundant. Lazy spectators sat transfixed by the tube as their remote controls performed the human function. At its most extreme, and sometimes in terms quite humorous and self-aware, advertisers staged fantasy scenarios of sadomasochism in which man and machine reversed roles of aggressor and victim, master and slave. Not surprisingly, in these terms, the ads had explicit sexual content.

From this point of view, we might better understand Sony's derisive representations of passive male spectators and their "pee wee tee vees." Sony chose to express the cultural ambivalence about automation by way of a joke that would address anxieties about mastery, a joke that had both a psychological and a social dimension. With its focus on the relative size of male body parts versus TV components, Sony's "pee wee tee vee" humorously rendered social anxieties about technology as "castration anxieties" about male power. In addition, on a more pragmatic level, these ads voiced the paradox of mastery over technology: when people produce sentient machines, human intelligence and productive labor become increasingly less necessary.

This paradox was perhaps most succinctly addressed by the numerous ads for portable sets that focused on the workmanship and "craft" needed to build the miniaturized, automated models. These ads are the postwar version of the nostalgic turn to craft that Susan Stewart has explored in her discussion of the history of miniatures.[54] After the invention of the printing press, miniature books served as promotional vehicles for booksellers. Such miniatures, Stewart argues, contained in them a nostalgic longing for their opposite—artisan labor and craft production. This nostalgic longing for handicrafts restored a sense of human mastery over the production process at the dawn of industrialization. Ads for the miniaturized portable sets recall this strategy, focusing especially on the human skill and mastery required in the manufacturing process. As Zenith claimed in 1966, "Zenith portable TVs are built with the pride and skill of the craftsman. . . . Every connection is carefully hand wired."[55] The accompanying photograph showed two male hands connecting a circuit.

While the Zenith ads used the hand to evoke the idea of human labor, other companies used images of human hands to represent mastery over the consumption of television and TV programs (the hand either holds the portable set by its handle or operates the dials with the remote control). In this regard, the portrayal of the severed hand was more precisely a sign of commodity fetishism, wherein the product stands in for the "loss" (or at the least the perceived loss) of human agency in an automated world. In this case, advertisers rechanneled cultural anxieties about the social effects of television by reconfiguring the power to communicate as the power to consume. Even if the public had little influence on the broadcast institution, they did have the power to turn the dial and move the set from room to room.

This notion of consumerism itself as an act of power was not simply an advertising strategy. Rather, it was part of a much larger set of statements made about television during the 1960s, statements that were especially heard in Federal Communications Commission reform movements of the 1960s and early 1970s. From Newton Minow's 1961 "vast wasteland" speech (which was premised on the idea that the lowly state of the TV arts was in part caused by the public's "bad taste" and widespread largesse) to Nicholas Johnson's consumer activist campaigns (which culminated in his 1970 book *How to Talk Back to Your Television Set*), the decade was bracketed by notions of cultural reform rooted in the rhetoric of American pragmatism and the faith in the consumer's power to police the market.[56]

Given the anticommercial populism behind this brand of consumer activism, it is no small irony that the watchdog rhetoric surrounding television was co-opted by the industry itself. In 1964, Sony launched an ad campaign for mini-portables that used the ethos of consumer activism in ways that both parody and yet simultaneously endorse the reformist urge to resist TV. These ads repeatedly used puns and jokes to express fears about television's negative effects and degraded content. However, they put these fears to rest by suggesting that people could reassert power over their lives by purchasing a mini-portable set. One ad, for example, tells consumers that the miniature TV allows viewers to control their addiction to television:

> Most people can't tear themselves away from their TV sets for a very simple reason. Most television sets are too big to ignore. The Sony Micro-TV . . . demands your attention when you watch it. And it's easy to ignore when you don't. It lets you be the critic instead of a victim because it doesn't dominate the whole house. . . . You can help the kids with their homework. Or read a book. Or study Portuguese. One of the great joys of modern living is to have a Sony portable playing on a raft out on a lake, and to reach over and turn it off.[57]

By assuring potential consumers that they can turn off the set to pursue higher learning or commune with nature, Sony makes the idea of "resistance" to TV one of the micro-portable's most irresistible features. In this way, Sony suggests that the ultimate act of mastery over television is not refusal to buy the product, but rather refusal to use it.

Such master-slave fantasies thus pervaded all aspects of television culture during this period—from the literal technology to the more conceptual issues of control over social life, sexuality, and human subjectivity. Their legacy is still felt today in ads for that ultimate vehicle of portable culture—the computer.

From Mobile Home to Home Office

What interests me about all of these ads for portable TVs is what they say not only about the past but also about the present. I want to turn now to some speculations on the mobile culture of today and the lessons that we might learn from the 1960s.

I began researching the portable television set in response to my frustration with theories of television and new media that make rather grandiose claims about information society and cyberculture—especially the work inspired by Jean Baudrillard. I am particularly thinking of Baudrillard's essay "The Ecstasy of Communication," where he argues that we have experienced a complete break with the Victorian logic of private and public spheres, and with that the end to Freudian-based models of subjectivity and scenarios of sexual difference. This break, he argues, comes with the introduction of television and satellite technologies, which, he claims, makes it impossible to experience home and public life as separate. Rather than experience the home as a private theater in which individuals play roles in scenes, now we are forced into an "obscene" world where private secrets and public information are one and the same.[58] Although his views are sometimes prescient of our worst "information society" nightmares, Baudrillard speaks in fantastic terms that are probably intended more to shock than to explain material circumstances and processes of change. Still, insofar as this brand of fantastic rhetoric has become a kind of cultural cache for cyber enthusiasts and doomsday predictors alike, I think it is important to note that Baudrillard considers this historical shift in wholly ahistorical terms, omitting all of the material details through which these changes were experienced at the time. His work has been interpreted in overly literal and deterministic ways as people envision complete historical annihilations of familiar binaries and ideologies such as public and private, male and female, unconscious and conscious.

By looking at representations of home and technology from the post-war period, we see a very different picture. While the case of portable television does reveal a historical shift in cultural sensibilities regarding domesticity and domestic technologies, this shift was neither simple nor fully achieved. Instead, representations from this period exhibit profound ambivalence about the changes they envisioned. Even while they glorify emerging conceptions of a new space-age mobile family, they harken back to residual ideas about gender roles and the division of spheres that can be traced to Victorian times.

Our present-day world of mobile communications is still structured around these binaries of space and sexual difference, although there are some obvious changes. While the "drive-in television" represented its period's focus on mobile forms of domestic leisure, today's information superhighway is organized around the problem of work. In relation to this changing emphasis, new metaphors of home abound.

Recent ads for Web sites and computers repeat central themes of portable culture but search for new twists. Given that the computer industry has not been as successful as the television industry in selling its products for domestic use, it is perhaps not surprising that advertisers are still experimenting with their sales pitches.

The most typical new configuration is the home office—a hybrid site of work and leisure where it is possible to make tele-deals while sitting at home in one's bathrobe. Promoted in magazines like *Home Office* and *Mac Home,* the home office is a place of high-tech computer workspaces staffed by single moms or stay-at-home dads who keep Pampers next to modems.

Even while it combines traditional forms of male and female labor, and even while men and women are both shown as home workers, the home office most typically appears as a masculine extension of the feminine sphere. Furnishing the home office is presented as a paramount dilemma. Should it recreate the sterile antifeminine spaces of modern industrial design, or should it flirt with feminine flair? The merging of (male) productive labor and (female) reproductive labor poses questions for old modernist ideas about form and function. Frills and hard drives don't mix.

The problem, however, is not simply decorative. The merging of productive and reproductive labor is also riddled with conflicts about male and female roles. These home offices are utopian solutions to tensions felt in everyday life, and their miraculous mergers of private and public, male and female, productive and reproductive work are simply the wish-fulfillment of the advertising industry, which knows that people actually have a much harder time merging these divisions in practice. Indeed, these advertising images are meaningful precisely because people still experience their lives through gendered divisions and are taught to believe that they should be able to overcome these divides through personal achievements. These ads are less a testimony to a sexually liberated world than a symptom of a culture that tells people they should and can do everything at once.

Gender divisions, and especially images of mothers and fathers, are also used by computer companies that manufacture single screens intended to combine traditional forms of TV leisure with office work at home. Again, however, even in images that seemingly merge these traditionally separate kinds of screens, the mergers do not necessarily break down old binaries of femininity and masculinity and their relation to divisions of public and private, work and leisure.

In 1997, for example, Princeton Graphics (a computer hardware company) advertised its Arcadia Home Monitor in clearly gendered terms.[59] Introducing the "birth of Arcadia," the ad uses a two-page layout to show how the computer monitor and TV set have evolved into the Arcadia system. Occupying the center of the layout is a huge-screen Arcadia monitor. The left border of the left-hand page shows a vintage Philco TV set and gives a brief history of TV set design, leading up to the Arcadia digital TV. The right border of the right-hand page shows a vintage computer display and gives a brief history of computer design leading up to full-motion video monitors. The birth metaphor is then carried through as these old technologies figuratively become the mother and father of digital TV. Or as the caption tells us, "Its mother was a TV. Its father was a monitor." The image that dominates the center of the Arcadia screen and the page's layout underscores the point. An old woman appears on the left side of the screen and an old man on the right. Thus, according to the rhetoric of the ad, the new technologies that merge home entertainment with the public world of work are still rigidly divided into gendered categories. Here, as elsewhere, TV is represented as a mode of leisure associated with feminine pursuits while computers are presented as masculine. In fact, as this split-page layout so clearly suggests, even as TV sets and computers increasingly merge into one home screen, this singular screen does not obliterate the distinctions between male and female, work and leisure, or public and private that were associated with the older technologies. Instead, this new home screen incorporates sex-related binaries to such a degree that they reappear in a "birth" narrative which promises consumers that while technologies generate change, the traditional heterosexual family remains the gene pool of all mutations.

Although ads such as these are based in domestic milieus, other images of home promoted by the high-tech industry emphasize the public sphere. The conflation of home and work is also represented through the image of the coffeehouse, or as it is now commonly called, the cyber café. In ads such as these, images of coffee drinking serve as a form of product differentiation, distinguishing the Net from the older mode of network TV. As opposed to the sedentary viewer of the home theater or the outdoorsy sightseer of portable TV, the cyber café signals a different form of engagement for the public: we are no longer spectators, but interlocutors; social actors making the scene and having intense (if noncommitted) encounters with coffee mates.

As personal identity is transformed from social location (the home address) to "home page," people change into noncorporal forms, computer generations rather than genders. For some of the more utopian among us, this new form of social relation offers liberation. Women don't have to be women; men don't have to be men; races don't have to be races. People can make up identities, occupy new dwellings, reinvent themselves.

Despite this utopian rhetoric, the coffeehouse has its own gender bias. Coffee signifies mental stimulation as opposed to TV's image as a plug-in drug that pacifies, feminizes, infantilizes. As a place between home and work, the coffeehouse presents itself as a remasculinized form of communication, a place of productive—as opposed to reproductive—labor. In so doing, it continues with familiar tropes of modernity in which femininity (and the idea of passivity, consumerism, and domesticity associated with it) is the "other" of authentic/male/active culture.

But even in the interactive, male-dominated realm of cyberspace, the "threat" of feminization and domesticity is always somewhere close at hand. The cyber café carries with it the "feminized" culture of gossip, chatter without purpose, passing time without reason, being out of work, and shopping conspicuously for luxury goods like fancy coffee and chocolates. Perhaps to combat these stereotypically "girly" and domestic connections, a string of ads and articles aimed at the cyber café genre show successful, virile guys (and sometimes powerful-looking women) hacking away at computers while drinking cappuccino.[60]

In ways such as these, images of high-tech homes—whether presented as the home office or its public sphere counterpart, the cybercafé—are organized around familiar divisions of public and private space and the gendered divisions that entails. Even if these ads play with these divisions and offer communication technologies as utopian solutions to them, they nevertheless assume that their readers recognize the ideological distinctions between spheres and sexes. Indeed, the prevailing consumer discourses on new technologies aimed at the white middle class continue to present tableaus in which domestic subjectivity is presented through logics of sexual difference and related divisions of public and private space, even if these logics are updated for a computer age.[61]

Mobile Lifestyles and Social Change

While no doubt a new design for living, the mobile home of the 1960s and its more recent manifestation as the home office do not necessarily provide radically new identities for their residents. Even if binaries of private and public, labor and leisure, and masculine and feminine have transformed, it is not the same as complete obliteration. Instead of a total collapse of private and public spheres, we are faced with a much more contradictory environment where different models of domesticity exist in emergent, residual, and dominant forms. Indeed, while I have mapped a series of housing models, it should be clear that the home theater, the mobile home, and the home office do not fall in a straight historical timeline. Instead, they are ideal forms that present distinct possibilities for living that are emphasized in different degrees in specific social contexts.

Given this uneven historical dissemination of domestic ideals, it is probably the case that most of the target consumers for the new communication technologies live in hybrid situations, drawing on models of home that carry with them a host of different historical associations. The living-room TV provides a home theater. Desktop computers and fax machines decorate the home office. Mobile telephones, palm pilots, and laptops continue with themes of portable culture by allowing people to work not only at home, but in cars, on planes, and even, as AT&T tells us, on the beach. In other words, we simultaneously experience different historical styles of domesticity and domestic communications.

Moreover, while I have been dealing with a particular consumer demographic—the white middle class, and a particular cultural ideal—the suburban family lifestyle, it is of course the case that many groups experience home and technology in markedly different ways. In the 1960s, when white middle-class culture was represented through appeals to mobile family lifestyles, mobility meant something very different for people of color and working-class people. Although, for example, the federally funded highways built in the postwar period were designed to bridge suburb and city (thus mostly benefiting whites), they often cut through working-class and ethnic communities, destroying homes and businesses.[62] Meanwhile, as bell hooks has argued, for black Americans travel has been less a romantic metaphor of liberation than it has a constant threat. Black migrations and even everyday transportation have historically been accompanied by acts of white terrorism.[63] Discriminatory seating practices on buses fueled the Civil Rights movement in the mid 1950s, while the movement itself was predicated on a turning away from a social system that had disenfranchised entire communities. Obviously, this politicized notion of movement was worlds apart from the images of mobile family lifestyles meant to counteract white middle-class angst about sedentary family life.

So, too, this different articulation of movement was central not only to transportation technologies such as cars, buses, and freeways but also to communication technologies. Although *Ebony* regularly featured ads for portable television (many of which were exactly the same as those featured in *Life* or *Look*), the newly proposed portable culture and its basis in mobile communication technologies had a different historical resonance for the black community as a whole. Indeed, as I discuss in my essay on the space race, the response to the space age was markedly different in white and black America.[64] In the 1960s, when suburban homes and household appliances mimicked the imagery of outer space and satellite technologies, venues of black culture continually attacked the space race on the grounds of its racist logic. Although popular media aimed at whites imagined outer space as the "final frontier" for family values, the black press saw the space project as a racist waste of tax dollars that might better be spent on housing in inner cities.

Today, as the computer industry makes its way into the American home, similar discrepancies emerge. In July 1999, the Digital Divide Summit held by the Secretary of Commerce demonstrated that numerous Americans were "falling through the net." According to reports presented at the summit, despite signs that upper income blacks are purchasing home computers, "the 'digital divide' between Whites and most minorities continues to grow." In addition, the study indicated that "family structure does play a role in having access to information resources." Among all the race, class, and ethnic groups studied, "family households without two parents have lower levels of phone and computer ownership, as well as Internet access." [65]

In response to the digital divide, state, local, and federal housing agencies have been teaming up with the high-tech industry. In 1995, the Department of Housing and Urban Development (HUD) initiated community computer centers with the goal of helping adults to get jobs and children to do better as school. Known as "Neighborhood Networks" the computer centers now serve low-income residents of HUD-subsidized housing in every state. While HUD's goals might well serve the needs of these residents in positive ways, the Neighborhood Networks plan nevertheless also demonstrates the difference between the way low-income people and higher income groups experience computers in everyday life. As opposed to the promises of private mobilization and domestic leisure that the computer industry offers middle- and high-income families, HUD promotes its Neighborhood Networks through appeals to public welfare and the work ethic. Most important, in the HUD plan, low-income residents are not supposed to question the race and class biases of the education system that has helped generate the digital divide in the first place.

After the passing of the Welfare Reform Act in 1996, public housing agencies and the high-tech industry continue to merge home and work in distinctly class- and race-specific ways. In February 1998, the city of Oakland and IBM announced plans to wire a thirty-year-old housing project for the future. Built in the era of Civil Rights on the flatlands of Oakland's West side, the housing project—known as the Acorn Complex—has since been transformed into a high-tech company town. Individual apartments are now equipped with computers, the complex includes a high-tech learning center, and residents (who began to move in during July 1999) receive IBM computer training courses that they can take in their homes. Those who successfully complete the course are certified by

IBM (which sees this as a "for profit" venture). The last phase of the project, known as "Welfare to Work," will give certified residents jobs with local businesses.[66] Although the idea was originally initiated by the Acorn Complex's tenant association, the ultimate value of this high-tech company town remains open to question. According to the *Los Angeles Times,* the project was at the outset viewed ambivalently. While some residents embrace the project as a way to "level the computer playing field" and give people jobs, the newspaper also reported the more skeptical comments of a professional critic who asked, "Could somebody tell me how some glitzy, multimedia gizmos are going to solve the problem of rats and cockroaches in Oakland's municipal housing?"[67] So, too, some community leaders are skeptical that the project can be duplicated because of the enormous costs involved (HUD reportedly spent 30 million dollars redeveloping the complex).[68] Meanwhile, for its part, IBM speaks as the voice of social justice. A company spokesperson told the *Times,* "This obviously isn't going to be a huge profit generator for us. . . . But we've always been a good corporate citizen."[69]

How are we to make sense of the present conditions of everyday life in the wake of cybermedia? The case of the Acorn Complex poses some radically different possibilities. New media as a cure for poverty and the failures of Civil Rights? New media as a detour through which the ongoing biases of our housing and education systems go unchecked? New media as corporate goodwill, or more cynically put, as a public-relations ploy? Whatever the case, IBM's vision of the home office as company town is radically different from the visions of personal freedom and family bliss offered in middle-class consumer magazines.

For reasons such as this, deterministic treatises on technology and its radical effects on daily life are at best simplistic. Now circulating through a host of both utopian and dystopian speculative fictions, technological determination obscures larger social questions about how we get our ideas of home and family life in the first place. Even if technology is one component contributing to change, social engineering in the form of housing policies, welfare, family planning, transportation, and the like are fundamental in their impact on the structures of everyday life (and communication technologies are intricately involved in the formation of these policies and their implementation).

That said, it is still the case that technology and our ideas about it contribute to the network of forces through which ideologies and practices of everyday life are constituted and achieved. The statements generated about new technologies in popular culture engage the public in dialogues not only on technological change itself, but also on larger issues of home and family life. The portable culture ushered in at the dawn of the 1960s has helped to redefine and also prefigure the various high-tech housing designs of the present. But although this culture was predicated on movements of all kinds, it seems hasty to say that the utopian rhetoric of progressive change at the heart of portability has transformed the world and our perceptions of it in quite the ways that 1960s critics and advertisers predicted. It seems equally hasty to embrace the dystopian nightmares offered today in cyberfiction tales and by numerous theoretical accounts of postmodernity.

Instead, at a time of technological change it might in the end be useful to think about what is not being said about new technologies. We might consider those "structured absences" through which discourses on new technologies evade crucial topics for debate. These topics would certainly include questions of housing as well as media policies that tend to go unaddressed in both consumer advertising and cyberfictions. Promotional rhetoric and speculative fictions about new technologies have typically kept these more fundamental questions at bay. Insofar as the discourse on new technologies has essentially been aimed at the people who can buy them—most typically the propertied class—it has tended to deal mostly with the issues that concern these class interests. As we have seen in the case of portable TV, this technology became a fetish object that stood in for larger social anxieties related to middle-class family life. Even more pervasively, the history of technological innovation demonstrates that a litany of new communication forms, from the telegraph to the computer, were ushered in with similar fears about social life and utopian statements about the future.[70] The fact that this discourse on technological innovation is highly conventionalized and formulaic begs us to consider what is at stake in the compulsion to repeat the same ideas, even as the society itself has noticeably changed.

In this respect, it seems to me that since the nineteenth century and continuing through the present, this utopian (and dystopian) rhetoric about new technologies has served to derail us from asking larger questions about how social change might occur in the first place. Technologies alone will surely not decide the fate of housing and family life, nor will they tell us how to communicate with media and for what social good. Paradoxically, in this sense, while the culture of portability has been based on an obsession with movement, progress, and travel through space, the statements it generates tend to keep people exactly where they are.

Notes

1 *Life*, 6 June 1967, p. 103.

2 *House Beautiful*, October 1958, p. 181.

3 This essay is based on an examination of every issue of *Life, Ladies' Home Journal, Good Housekeeping, House Beautiful*, and *Better Homes and Gardens* from 1956 to 1970. While *Life* addressed a family consumer, and often directly addressed the man of the house, the other magazines were aimed specifically at women. The readership base for these magazines included a range of lower- to upper-middle-class readers, but their representations of the home often spoke to a middle-class dream of luxurious living rather than representing the lived realities of any one social group. All of the magazines also assumed their reader was white, and ads promoted products in specifically racialized terms. *Life* contained the greatest number of full-page ads for portable television during this period, and that fact is reflected in this analysis. As I note later on, however, *Ebony* also often advertised portable sets, frequently with identical ads (sometimes inserting a black viewer in place of the white figure).

4 Jan Scott, in Jan Scott, Charles Lisnaby, and Burr Smidt, "Design in Television," *Television Quarterly* 2:3 (summer 1963): 41.

5 Raymond Williams discusses flow in *Television, Technology, and Cultural Form* (New York: Schocken, 1975), chapter 4.

6 By 1966 all of the classic nuclear family sitcoms were off the air, replaced by broken-family sitcoms (in which a mother or father was missing) or by fantastic sitcoms. For more on these programs, see my "From Domestic Space to Outer Space," this volume.

7 See my "From Theatre to Space Ship: Metaphors of Suburban Domesticity in Postwar America," in *Visions of Suburbia*, ed. Roger Silverstone (London: Routledge, 1997), pp. 217–39.

8 Beatriz Colomina, "Intimacy and Spectacle: The Interiors of Adolf Loos," *AA Files* 20 (1990): 5–15, and "The Split Wall: Domestic Voyeurism," in *Sexuality and Space*, ed. Beatriz Colomina (Princeton, N.J.: Princeton Papers on Architecture, 1992), pp. 73–128.

9 Lynn Spigel, *Make Room for TV: Television and the Family Ideal in Postwar America* (Chicago: University of Chicago Press, 1992).

10 These depictions had very different meanings for white and black America. See my "White Flight," in *The Revolution Wasn't Televised: Sixties Television and Social Conflict*, ed. Lynn Spigel and Michael Curtin (New York: Routledge, 1997), pp. 47–72; and my "Outer Space and Inner Cities," this volume.

11 It should be noted that portable television and the ad pitches for it harkened back

to earlier product designs and ads for portable radio. See Michael Brian Schiffer, *The Portable Radio in American Life* (Tucson: University of Arizona Press, 1991).

12 "A Buying Guide for Television Sets," *Good Housekeeping*, September 1963, p. 154.

13 My calculations are based on the U.S. Bureau of the Census, "Manufacturers' Sales and Retail Value of Home Appliances, 1955–1969," no. 1167, *Statistical Abstract of the United States* (Washington, D.C.: Government Printing Office, 1970), p. 729. Because the *Statistical Abstract* calculates together the sales of portable and table-top models, it is impossible to say from these statistics how many portables alone were sold. Note also that some television sets were designed as phonograph or radio combination models, but these units were negligible in terms of sales rates. These same statistics show that when broken down into color versus black and white, sales of color consoles were dramatically higher than color portables and table tops in 1965, while the difference becomes more negligible by 1969. Meanwhile, by 1969, black-and-white consoles sold dramatically less than black-and-white portables and table tops. Finally, sales of portable radios rose dramatically in the 1950s, so that by 1960 there were more than twice as many portable radios and clock radios than there were furniture models. Most certainly, this increase in portable radios had to do with the fact that television was taking its place as the central family medium. This would mean that radio served as a precursor to the visual culture of portability. For statistics on radio, see U.S. Bureau of the Census, "Manufacturers' Sales and Retail Value of Home Appliances, 1955–1960," no. 1143, *Statistical Abstract of the United States* (Washington, D.C.: Government Printing Office, 1961), p. 821.

14 In 1960, 13 percent of U.S. households had more than one TV. By 1970 that figure rose to 33 percent, and in 1972 to 44 percent. Lawrence W. Lichty and Malachi C. Topping, *American Broadcasting: A Source Book on the History of Radio and Television* (New York: Hastings House, 1975), p. 522.

15 *Life*, 5 May 1967, pp. 54–55.

16 *Life*, 10 December 1965, p. R11.

17 *Life*, 15 April 1966, p. 3. Similar ads for Admiral Playmates ran in *Ladies' Home Journal*, December 1963, p. 44.

18 *Life*, 10 July 1964, p. 42.

19 *House Beautiful*, May 1957, p. 38.

20 While divorce rates were reduced after a postwar peak, they began to rise steadily and steeply again by 1965. See Elaine Tyler May, *Homeward Bound: American Families in the Cold War Era* (New York: Basic Books, 1988), pp. 4–8.

21 *Good Housekeeping*, January 1970, p. 28.

22 *House Beautiful*, September 1960, p. 36.

23 Links between broadcasting and the automobile industry were first forged with the car radio, introduced by Motorolla in the 1930s. There was a significant surge in auto sales after World War II, and again in 1965. See Lichty and Topping, *American Broadcasting*, p. 521. Note, too, that in the 1960s the associative link between television and vehicles was further drawn by automotive companies and dealers, some of which sold television sets during this period. Ford Motor Com-

pany boasted that its product line included Philco portables, while Western Auto, a major automobile supply and household appliance center, regularly advertised portable TVs along with its autocare wares. Thus, at the levels both of advertising semiotics and of hard economics, tie-ins between television and moving vehicles were common.

24   *House Beautiful,* May 1959, p. 62.

25   *Life,* 16 April 1965, p. 95.

26   After 1965, the production of these homes rarely fell below two hundred thousand per year, and by 1979 there were more than ten million mobile-home dwellers nationwide. See Kenneth T. Jackson, *Crabgrass Frontier: The Suburbanization of the United States* (New York: Oxford University Press, 1985), pp. 262–63.

27   Margaret White, "Indoor Camp-Out," *Ladies' Home Journal,* June 1966, pp. 76–77.

28   *Life,* 29 March 1963, pp. 40–41.

29   *Life,* 27 July 1962, pp. 6–7.

30   *Life,* 25 January 1963, pp. 64–65.

31   *Life,* 15 May 1964, pp. 54–55.

32   *Life,* 21 July 1967, p. 14.

33   *Life,* 10 February 1967, p. 18. General Electric also advertised its "play anywhere" TV with a pair of sunglasses resting nearby (*Life,* 11 June 1965, p. 125).

34   *Life,* 7 July 1967, p. 65.

35   "A Buying Guide for Television Sets," *Good Housekeeping,* September 1963, p. 154.

36   Margaret Morse, "An Ontology of Everyday Distraction: The Freeway, the Mall, and Television," in *Logics of Television: Essays in Cultural Criticism,* ed. Patricia Mellencamp (Bloomington: Indiana University Press, 1990), pp. 193–221.

37   *Life,* 17 September 1965, p. 67.

38   *Life,* 30 April 1965, p. 20.

39   *Life,* 14 July 1967, p. 61.

40   *House Beautiful,* June 1957, p. 14.

41   Such images of liberated consumers harken back to the 1920s when manufacturers associated women's newly gained right to vote with consumer choices. As Roland Marchand has argued, such advertisements offered women the ideal of democratic freedom by associating product choices with sociopolitical freedoms. Moreover, he shows that companies often presented these consumer freedoms in highly paradoxical ways by marketing ideals of personal flair and consumer choice through prefabricated and highly conformist "ensemble" sets so that women were told what bedroom sheets matched their complexions or which cars matched their figures and moods. See Roland Marchand, *Advertising the American Dream: Making Way for Modernity, 1920–1940* (Berkeley: University of California Press, 1985), pp. 132–40, 186–87. Portable television followed this paradoxical logic. For example, while the cover of *TV Guide* presented an image of space-age women's liberation, the promotional insert displayed a page of TV "tote alongs" that came in different shapes, sizes, and colors made to match the array of outfits in a woman's ward-

robe. In this way, the "TV purse" became the handmaiden for women's "right" to overconsume.

42 *TV Guide*, September 18–24, 1996, cover.

43 *Life*, 30 May 1960, pp. 78–79.

44 *Life*, 11 June 1965, p. 125.

45 Joseph Golden, "TV's Womanless Hero," *Television Quarterly* 2:1 (winter 1963): 14–15. Golden did acknowledge that these heroes were often lady-killers (in fact, he described how their girlfriends often died). He called these men "womanless heroes" because they did not have wives.

46 In fact, such associations were integral not simply to the television receiver and the fictions it delivered, but also to the innovation of portable cameras, most obviously the Sony Portapak. Introduced in 1965, the Sony Portapak quickly became associated with a new video art movement that constantly distinguished itself from commercial TV. In making such distinctions, critics and artists often associated independent video art with a move away from the domestic forms of commercial television, and they sometimes linked this to a move away from femininity. An early example is Gregory Battcock's "The Sociology of the Set," in *The New Television: A Private/Public Art*, ed. Douglas Davis and Allison Simmons (Cambridge, Mass.: MIT Press, 1978), which was compiled from the now famous 1972 "Open Circuits" conference on the future of television, held at the Museum of Modern Art. In his essay, Battcock argues that a medium becomes "art" when it breaks away from its domestic trappings and stands as an object in itself. By "moving the television set away from the wall" and introducing the "notion of portability," TV became a new "discipline" of "importance equal to that of the era of sculptural communication begun in Ancient Greece" (p. 21). Battcock's historical theory of art is not-too-subtly based on the idea that art is that which sheds itself of domesticity, and he sees portability as exactly that which makes this move away from home possible. Furthermore, he characterizes domesticity as a space of femininity. Professing to have identified "two major developmental steps in the birth of a new, vital medium," he claims the first is "the severance of ties with architecture, the mother form," while the second is "the evolution into the realm of the portable" (p. 18). The "mother"—here associated with both home and commercial TV—literally becomes the abject "other" of independent video. Meanwhile, video is associated with masculine tropes of "vitality" secured through separation from the mother/home.

47 For more on this, see my *Make Room for TV*, chapter 3.

48 *Life*, 5 March 1965, p. R4.

49 *Life*, 8 October 1965, p. 118; *Life*, 14 April 1967, p. 108.

50 *Life*, 14 April 1967, p. 108.

51 In these terms, the ads for portable TV provide a textbook case of the central dynamics at work in the uncanny. In his essay on the subject, Sigmund Freud describes the uncanny as the ambivalent sense of the "heimlich" (that which gives a feeling of being at home or familiar) and the "unheimlich" (that which is not

home, which is hidden from view and provokes fright). He then goes on to analyze the uncanny as an aesthetic sensibility through a reading of E. T. A. Hoffmann's tale "The Sand-Man." In his reading, Freud foregrounds two central plot points that give rise to the uncanny, one which revolves around a disturbance of vision, and the other around automation. As a child, the hero of the tale is haunted by the Sandman, an apparition who throws sand in his eyes before he falls asleep. As a young man, the hero falls in love with Olympia, an inanimate doll that he mistakes for a real-life woman. The disruption of vision and his erotic investment in the automaton are ultimately connected in the tale's denouement, and both eventually drive the hero mad. Freud links both occurrences to what he sees as central causes for the uncanny—castration anxiety and a repetition of that trauma, or else the return to "primitive" animistic beliefs that are otherwise surmounted by "civilized" man (tales of magic or objects come alive are examples here). See Freud, "The 'Uncanny'," in *Psychological Writings and Letters*, ed. Sander L. Gilman (New York: Continuum, 1995), pp. 120–53.

From this point of view, the ads for portable television and remote control seem like postwar versions of the central dynamics staged in tales of the uncanny. Offering consumers the possibility of being at home and not at home at the same time, and presenting the TV set itself as a machine come to life, the ads take the frightening aspects of Hoffman's story and turn them into the stuff that technological utopias are made of. Nevertheless, in line with the general ambivalence at the heart of the uncanny, all the elements in these ads easily transform into opposites, until technological utopia becomes technological dystopia as the human subject is driven mad both by its vision and its love of automation (both of which, of course, are represented in the figure of the television set).

52 *Life,* 24 January 1964, p. 77.

53 *House Beautiful,* June 1961, p. 10.

54 Susan Stewart, *On Longing: Narratives of the Miniature, the Gigantic, the Souvenir, the Collection* (Durham, N.C.: Duke University Press, 1993).

55 *Life,* 18 February 1966, p. 21. This ad also alluded to human hands by showing a television set with a woman onscreen whose hands were clasped as if she were praying.

56 In the 1980s and 1990s, this reconfiguration of consumerism as "power" continues to be central to debates about television. However, contemporary theorists such as John Fiske and Henry Jenkins draw on the rhetoric of French poststructuralist theory, particularly Michel de Certeau, rather than on American pragmatism and reform. While the differences are obviously important, the connections between these two traditions seem worthy of further examination. See, for example, John Fiske, *Understanding Popular Culture* (Boston: Unwin Hyman, 1989); and Henry Jenkins, *Textual Poachers* (New York: Routledge, 1992).

57 *Life,* 29 May 1964, p. R6.

58 Jean Baudrillard, "The Ecstasy of Communication," in *The Anti-Aesthetic: Essays on Postmodern Culture,* ed. Hal Foster (Port Townsend, Wash.: Bay Press, 1983). I think about these issues especially with regard to Baudrillard because his essay

is itself symptomatic of the shift I have been describing in relation to the cultural imagination of the home. In this essay, Baudrillard describes a shift from a model of home as theater to a model of home as spaceship. He argues that this new model of domesticity—or what he calls a home "in orbit"—is the product of an information society in which social relations are thoroughly produced by communication media, initially television but now by satellite technologies. In this world, previous divisions of public and private life have dissolved, and the corresponding metaphors of home as theater no longer apply. The home, he argues, "is no longer a scene where the dramatic interiority of the subject, engaged with its objects as with its image, is played out." Instead, he claims, the resident is placed in the position of an "astronaut in his capsule." We are living "in vivo in a quotidian space . . . with the satellization of the two-room kitchen-and-bath put into orbit in the last lunar module" (p. 128).

Through this figural placement of the home in orbit, Baudrillard attempts to illustrate how the high-tech world of telecommunications has transformed not only the material spaces of private and public spheres but also human subjectivity itself. Within his more general theory of simulation, the home he describes is no longer a fixed place of origin and personal identity; instead, it is a terminal that receives and distributes information. Where Freud described human subjectivity in relation to a series of family "scenes," Baudrillard argues that we now live in the age of the "obscene," where the individual is networked through computer screens (consider, for example, the way people and households are projected in credit reports as so much demographic data). We live in a time where private secrets and public information are one and the same, a time when all kinds of knowledge—from sexuality to product advertising—has become "pornographic," instantly available for public view. For Baudrillard, this instant visibility and physical proximity of information is not—as some would say—a testimony to democracy and freedom of the press. Instead, the dissolution of private and public spheres forces us into "the greatest confusion." In the obscene world that Baudrillard describes, everything is forced to communicate, but nothing makes particular sense.

Again, I believe this thesis too easily ignores the way these transitions in everyday life are experienced at times of technological change. Through a highly ahistorical account of historical change, it ignores all the historical struggles through which change occurs. Moreover, it ignores the highly uneven developments that occasion technological change. That is, not all populations relate to new technologies and modes of domesticity in the same ways—a point with which I end this essay.

Beatriz Colomina's work on modernist architects poses interesting alternatives—and I think correctives—to Baudrillard's theory. In her essay "The Split Wall," Colomina argues that Le Corbusier designed his interiors on principles that were the inverse of Adolf Loos's ideal of insular theatricality. Instead, Le Corbusier thought of modern urban interiors as being externalized, a change he attributes to the city's reliance on media and the diminishing need for the interior space to "defend" itself from the outside world (he argues here against Loos's use of windows to shield the resident from the outside view). Reading Colomina's thoughts on these two modernist architects—one who uses theatricality and the other media as a central points of reference—we see within modernism itself a tension that Baudrillard describes as a postmodern condition. In other words, as I argue in various parts of this essay, Baudrillard makes totalizing claims about differences between modern and postmodern notions of public/private space that are too abstract to describe the complex contradictions and historical struggles through which these two modes of space competed for cultural dominance.

59 *The Web,* May 1997, p. 104 and back inside cover.

60 See *The Web,* May 1997, p. 35; *Wired,* December 1995, p. 165. As the liquid of choice, coffee now is even the major metaphor used by Java, a software brand for the Web, which promotes itself through images of coffee drinking and ideals of revitalization.

61 In this sense, and as opposed to Baudrillard, I think Freud's principles of theatricality and his assumptions about sexuality are still generative of the statements we make about subjectivity in popular discourses on new technologies.

62 For an analysis of the discriminatory practices in transportation, see Robert D. Bullard and Glenn S. Johnson, *Just Transportation: Dismantling Race and Class Barriers to Mobility* (Garbiola Island, B.C.: New Society Publishers, 1997).

63 bell hooks, *Black Looks: Race and Representation* (Boston: South End Press, 1992), pp. 165–78.

64 See my essay "Outer Space and Inner Cities," this volume, and my essay "White Flight."

65 U.S. Department of Congress, National Telecommunications and Information Administration, "Americans in the Information Age: Falling through the Net," Report presented at the Digital Divide Summit, 9 December 1999, and posted at website digitaldivide.gov.

66 For more, see Dan Caterinicchia, "Oakland Housing Wired, Residents Get Training," 9 September 1999, posted at website civic.com.

67 Greg Miller, "Home-Wired Bound," *Los Angeles Times,* 9 February 1998, sec. D, p. 3.

68 K. Oanh Ha, "Oakland tries to bridge digital divide," 29 July 1999, posted at website sjmercury.com.

69 Miller, "Home-Wired Bound," p. 6.

70 See, for example, Carolyn Marvin, *When Old Technologies Were New: Thinking About Electric Communication in the Late Nineteenth Century* (New York: Oxford University Press, 1988); Catherine L. Covert, "We May Hear Too Much: American Sensibility and the Response to Radio, 1919–1924," in *Mass Media Between the Wars: Perceptions of Cultural Tension, 1918–1941,* ed. Catherine L. Covert and John D. Stevens (Syracuse, N.Y.: Syracuse University Press, 1984), pp. 199–220; James W. Carey and John J. Quirk, "The Mythos of the Electronic Revolution," in *Communication as Culture,* ed. James W. Carey (Boston: Unwin Hyman, 1989), pp. 113–41; Daniel J. Czitrom, *Media and the American Mind: From Morse to McLuhan*

(Chapel Hill: University of North Carolina Press, 1982); Susan J. Douglas, *Inventing American Broadcasting, 1899–1922* (Baltimore: Johns Hopkins University Press, 1987); Cecelia Tichi, *Electronic Hearth: Creating an American Television Culture* (New York: Oxford University Press, 1991); Spigel, *Make Room for TV;* and Jeffrey Sconce, *Haunted Media: Electronic Presence from Telegraphy to Television* (Durham, N.C.: Duke University Press, 2000).

Part II: White Flight

From Domestic Space to Outer Space:
The 1960s Fantastic Family Sitcom

✴ It's a warm July in 1969, and millions of Americans sit before their television sets, with hope in their eyes and a beer can in hand, awaiting the
arrival of history. There, on the small screen of the living-room console,
a man steps out of his large, white spaceship and onto a crater-covered
surface. His limbs float in slow-motion gestures, his distant voice breaks
through the static, and then, with a "giant leap for mankind," a small
American flag anchors familiar meanings onto an alien landscape. This
is Apollo 11, the mission to the moon, the realization of a decade-long
American dream, the biggest crowd pleaser in television memory.

Like all technological triumphs, the moon landing was enmeshed in
political, social, cultural, and economic struggles. What I find particularly interesting are the meanings space travel had for television itself —
and for the burgeoning American culture based on watching TV. Above
all, the public's knowledge of space was communicated through the procession of rocket takeoffs and orbits broadcast during the 1960s. But more
than just transmitting a privileged view of the universe, television offered
the American public a particular mode of comprehension. It represented
space, like everything else, as a place that the white middle-class family
could claim as its own. Yet this epistemology of space was not merely an
attempt to colonize the unknown with familiar values. In many ways, the
fascination with space served to defamiliarize the common myths of the

"golden age" of the 1950s and the notions of domesticity that so pervaded television's "message" in that decade.

In the 1960s, television would construct for itself a new generic form founded on the merger between the troubled paradise of 1950s domesticity and the new-found ideals of the American future.[1] We might call this form the "fantastic family sitcom," a hybrid genre that mixed the conventions of the suburban sitcom past with the space-age imagery of President Kennedy's New Frontier. Programs like *I Dream of Jeannie, My Favorite Martian, The Jetsons,* and *Lost in Space* were premised on an uncanny mixture of suburbia and space travel, while shows like *My Mother the Car, Mr. Ed, My Living Doll,* and *Bewitched* played with a seemingly incongruous blend of suburban banality and science fiction fantasy.[2]

These programs have received little critical attention, most certainly because they seem to represent the "lower depths" of television's prime-time past. Typically in this vein, critics tend to view such shows within the logic of cultural hierarchies, seeing their value in negative terms— that is, as the opposite of high art. Rather than leading to knowledge, these programs are said to constitute an escape from reason. Consider David Marc's recent thesis that sees the shows as reflections of the turned-on, tuned-out ethos of 1960s drug culture and locates their popularity in "de-politicization through escapist fantasy."[3] Yet reading these sitcoms as transparent reflections of a desire to escape fails to explain their often satirical and critical aspects. These genre hybrids did not simply reflect a collective desire to flee from the present; rather, the collision of science fiction fantasy with domestic comedy resulted in programs that contested their own form and content. Fantastic sitcoms were a complex organization of contradictory ideas, values, and meanings concerning the organization of social space and everyday life in suburbia. To understand how they emerged, we should read them in relation to historical changes that created the conditions in which they could flourish. In the following pages, I discuss historical shifts that were crucial to the rise of the fantastic sitcom, and then suggest ways to see these shows as popular texts that allowed for diverse, often critical, perspectives on the social world.

Dystopian Visions and a New Space-Age Future

The intricate bond between television and space-age imagery can be understood as a response to a series of disillusionments that began to

The Robinsons, the
quintessential space-age TV
family, are *Lost in Space*.

be most deeply felt in the late 1950s. By the end of that decade, Americans were looking backward at the great white hopes that had somehow led them down a blind alley. The utopian dreams for technological supremacy, consumer prosperity, and domestic bliss were revealing their limits in ways that could no longer be brushed aside. With consumer debt mounting, the stock market felt its first major slide of the decade in 1957. In that same year, Americans witnessed the most stunning technological embarrassment of the times when the Soviet Union beat the United States into space with Sputnik. While these national failures signaled harder times, the promise of easy living and barbecues in every yard was turned into the substance of nightmarish visions as social critics wrote voluminously of the anomie and emptiness experienced in the mass-produced suburbs. And as the walls of Levittown came tumbling down, television, the central household fixture of suburban bliss, also joined the pantheon of fallen idols.

As James Baughman has argued, disappointment in American institutions and lifestyles was typical among liberals and intellectuals who felt disenfranchised in Eisenhower's America.[4] But importantly, I want to stress, such cultural anxieties were also voiced in popular venues. Magazines, newspapers, popular books, and films looked critically at the past and established a set of discursive conventions through which Americans might reflect on their experiences. These critical views anticipated a series of changes in the meanings and practices surrounding television in the next decade.

In this context, critiques of suburbia were especially bitter, particularly when we consider the hopes invested in this new "promised land" at the beginning of the decade. After World War II, suburban towns were a practical alternative to hardships in the city. A severe housing shortage in urban centers was soothed by Federal Housing Administration (FHA) construction loans and low-interest mortgages provided through the GI Bill. These government-financed projects made it possible for builders like Levitt and Sons to offer mass-produced housing at extremely low prices, so low in fact that it cost less to buy a home than to rent an apartment in the city. The suburbs were essentially built for the white middle class, and FHA policies guaranteed the communities' racial makeup. Building loans were predicated on "red-lining" (or zoning) practices that effectively kept all "undesirables" out of the lily-white neighborhoods.

For the white middle class, the suburbs quickly became more than just a practical alternative to the urban housing crisis. They were glorified in popular culture as a new land of plenty—the answer to Depression-era and wartime shortages. Home magazines presented wondrous designs, spacious ranch houses with rolling green yards, shiny pink appliances, and happy white families at play inside. But the practical realities of postwar life necessitated certain alterations of this middle-class ideal. Cramped quarters took the place of the magazines' spacious ranch homes, and rather than gazing out at rolling green yards, residents found themselves sandwiched between the identical houses of their next-door neighbors.

Early in the 1950s, a number of critics expressed doubts about the homogeneous living arrangements and conformist attitudes that characterized middle-class lifestyles, and by the end of the decade the mass-produced suburbs had become the subject of widespread concern.[5] John Keats's *The Crack in the Picture Window* (1956) presented unflattering pictures of the new suburbanites with characters like John and Mary Drone, whose lives were spent deciding how to buy washing machines and avoid their busybody neighbors. William Whyte's *The Organization Man* (1956) was a damning critique of the new company boys, whose willingness to conform to job expectations was mirrored by the peer-pressure policies of their suburban lifestyles. And in *The City in History* (1961), Lewis Mumford criticized the new organization of social space and the homogeneous lifestyles it encouraged.

The postwar cult of domesticity was wearing especially thin for women, and their dissatisfaction began to gain ground in popular thought by the end of the decade. Despite the glorification of the housewife's role, women had joined the labor force at significant rates in the 1950s. In particular, the number of married female workers rose substantially; by 1962 they accounted for about 60 percent of the female labor force.[6] Thus, when Betty Friedan attacked domestic ideology and institutional sexism in *The Feminine Mystique* (1963), she received widespread support.

Popular entertainment forms also expressed dismay with middle-class lifestyles. Film melodramas like Douglas Sirk's *All That Heaven Allows* (1956) and *Imitation of Life* (1959) showed the rigid social codes of middle-class ideals and the devastating consequences that class, race, and gender expectations had for the public. Popular media aimed at youth especially questioned middle-class family values. Rock 'n' roll gave teenagers the chance to participate in a new youth culture, separate from their parents, while youth films like *Rebel without a Cause* (1955) and *King Creole* (1958) made juvenile delinquents into popular heroes, thereby providing teenagers with role models that challenged the suburban family ideal.[7]

If the nation was keen on self-loathing by the end of the decade, one event would provide even more reason for angst. On 4 October 1957, Americans suffered a grave blow to their sense of national esteem when the Soviet Union launched Sputnik and beat the United States into space. Cold-war logic was predicated on America's ability to prevail in all technological endeavors, especially those associated with national security. Thus the advent of a Russian rocket soaring into orbit sharply contrasted with previous conventions for representing American relations with the Soviets. Ironically, just three days after Sputnik's launch, *Life* presented the first of a multipart issue entitled "Man's New World," which claimed that "the present lives and future fortunes of every American man, woman and child are directly and immediately affected by the gigantic technical strides of the past few years."[8]

As Walter McDougall has argued, Sputnik quickly became a major media crisis.[9] Critics expressed anxieties about the nation's technological agenda, claiming that American science had put its faith in consumer durables rather than concentrating on the truly important goals of national security. As Henry Luce, publisher of *Life,* said, "For years no knowledgeable U.S. scientist has had any reason to doubt that his Russian opposite number is at least his equal. It has been doubted only by people —some of them in the Pentagon—who confuse scientific progress with freezer and lipstick output." [10] These criticisms grew out of and reinforced a more general dismay with consumer capitalism that was voiced over the course of the postwar years. Science fiction writers Cyril Kornbluth and Frederik Pohl told of a future dominated by advertisers in their popular book *The Space Merchants* (1953), while nonfiction books like Vance Packard's *The Hidden Persuaders* (1957) and John Kenneth Galbraith's bestseller *The Affluent Society* (1958) attacked various aspects of consumer culture. Such concerns were fueled by the recession of 1957–1958, which created more general doubts about the consumer economy. Private debt increased from $73 billion to $196 billion during the 1950s, so when the Eisenhower administration suggested that the recession could be overcome by increased consumer purchases, not all Americans took solace in the "buy now, pay later" recovery plan. [11] In this economic and discursive context, Sputnik seemed a particularly poignant symbol of America's misconceived goals.

Finally, the United States began a series of attempts to find its own path to glory. Two months after the launching of Sputnik I, on 6 December 1957, America made its first foray into space, with its own rocket, Vanguard I. Vanguard rose four feet off the launch pad and sank in front of swarms of newspaper reporters and television cameras. The popular press called Vanguard such derisive names as "Flopnik," "Kaputnik," and "Stayputnik."

Thus, by the end of the decade, anxieties about private and public goals were being voiced in both intellectual and popular culture. But rather than simply signaling the end of a golden era, this historical conjuncture of disappointments provided the impetus for a new utopian future—one based on the rhetoric of Kennedy's New Frontier and fortified with the discourse of science and technology.

The ideology of the New Frontier promised Americans a way to join the march of history. This was accomplished not through a radical revolution in contemporary lifestyles, but rather through a liberal blend of private ethics with national purpose. The New Frontier was in this sense a popular movement, one that forged an alliance between its own political agenda and the patterns, meanings, and values of the past. In fact, the degree to which the American people were actually fatigued with their existence is not at all certain. In 1960, a nationwide survey in *Look* suggested that "most Americans today are relaxed, unadventurous, comfortably satisfied with their way of life and blandly optimistic about the future." *Look* went on to explain that American plans for the future were "mainly concerned with home and family." As for the larger arena of national purpose and progress in space, *Look* summed up the attitude with the words of one Milwaukee woman who confided, "We are pretty far removed from outer space here on 71st Street." Indeed, as *Look* went on to describe, people were far more concerned with everyday realities. "The chief worry of a lumber dealer in South Dakota," *Look* reported, "was 'having only one channel to watch on TV.'" Importantly, however, the magazine packaged this national complacency within a new and more exciting image. *Look* called the issue "Soaring into the Sixties," and it displayed a rocket on the cover—one that, unlike the flopniks of the past, was clearly taking off.[12] Indeed, just as *Look*'s editors were able to turn a land of happy homebodies into a nation bound for glory, the construction of the New Frontier was largely accomplished through media discourses that envisioned new and potent ways to organize past experiences.

The Kennedy administration eagerly adapted its own political agenda to the new space-age metaphors that were based on the tenets of progress, democracy, and national freedom. The forthright do-gooder citizen to whom Kennedy appealed was given the promise of a new beginning in abstract terms. Ideas like freedom need an image, and the ride into space proved to be the most vivid concretization of such abstractions, promising a newfound national allegiance through which we would not only diffuse the Soviet threat but also shake ourselves out of the doldrums that 1950s life had come to symbolize.

As other historians have argued, the promise of reaching the moon by the end of the decade was a political coup for a president intent on garnering public support. After the embarrassments of the Bay of Pigs and the Soviet launching of Yuri Gagarin into space, Kennedy was able to transform the scrutinizing gaze of defeat into a new look that reached upward to the heavens. Building on the firmly entrenched associations between space weaponry and national security (especially Congress's creation of the civilian-controlled National Aeronautics and Space Administration [NASA] in 1958), the Kennedy administration devised a solid technocratic plan through which to shift public consciousness away from our military expansionism overseas and onto the idea of space travel. In 1961, Kennedy sent Congress a new budget that poured millions into NASA, and a new theatrics of space emerged with astronaut stars appearing on the covers of national magazines.

The goals of the Kennedy administration merged particularly well with those of the television industry, which at this time was facing a public image crisis of its own. By the latter half of the 1950s, the networks had become the target of attacks launched primarily by influential East Coast critics, who began to mourn the passing of television's "golden age." As Baughman has argued, the critics, who were mostly liberals, saw television as an emblem of their disenfranchisement in Eisenhower's America.[13] Dismayed by programming trends that favored popular rather than elite (that is, their) tastes, they were especially upset by the cancellation of "prestige" programs like anthology dramas and *See It Now* (whose ousting in 1958 sparked a particularly heated debate), and they protested the slew of sitcoms, westerns, and quiz shows that had taken the place of what they considered higher television art.

This situation was exacerbated in 1959 when Congress's investigation of the quiz show scandals revealed that the sponsors had fed answers to contestants in the hope of heightening dramatic appeal. The critics seized the moment, blaming the breach of public trust on egghead contestants like Charles Van Doren, shady sponsors like Revlon, the money-grubbing networks, and the negligent regulators at the Federal Communications Commission (FCC). Having been one of the most popular program types, the quiz shows now were proof of the dangers of "low" television. As such, they enabled discourses on aesthetic and moral reform to emerge with a new purpose, creating a basis on which critics, educators, the clergy, and other cultural elites could ridicule popular tastes. After blaming the deceitful advertisers and negligent FCC, the *New Republic* concluded that

> a real investigation would center on a simple question: why is television so bad, so monotonous? The change over the past few years from Elvis Presley to Pat Boone is progress, from the obscene to the insipid. But is that the best TV can do? Must the majority of TV time be given to . . . the weary insouciance of the Bings and Frankies, the smiling but vacuous goings-on of Gale Storm, Donna

Reed, Ernie Ford, Betty Hutton, June Allyson, Mickey Rooney, Ozzie and Harriet?[14]

In April 1959, in the midst of these controversies, the FCC announced a new inquiry into network operations. Ultimately, however, rather than revamping the network system the regulators adopted a reform strategy centered on program quality. In 1961, in his address to the National Association of Broadcasters, FCC Chair Newton Minow called television a "vast wasteland," attacking, in particular, popular entertainment formats. While he was critical about the networks' "concentration of power," his reform program did not attack the structure of commercial television; instead, it ridiculed its products. Popular formats like sitcoms, quiz shows, and westerns were "low TV," while his proposed educational and pay channels would ensure cultural uplift.[15] By focusing on issues of high and low TV, Minow placed himself squarely within the discourses of the culture critics before him, and his position as FCC Chair gave this kind of TV bashing an official stamp of approval.

In the wake of this public-image crisis, the networks found the look-ahead spirit of Kennedy's New Frontier to be a potent metaphor, one that might divert attention away from the scandals of the past and create a new utopian purpose for the medium. In their attempt to restore the cultural validity of television and to ward off the more practical threat of regulatory action, the networks cultivated information programming, lengthening their fifteen-minute news programs to half an hour in 1963 and showcasing hard-hitting documentaries.[16] Perhaps not surprisingly, at a time when the ontological status of the television image was thrown into question by the fraudulent histrionics of the quiz shows, the networks turned with renewed vigor to reality-oriented formats.

In this general programming context, the space race became a privileged focus of attention. Documentary formats found space travel to be a particularly compelling subject of inquiry, and news teams eagerly covered rocket launchings throughout the decade.[17] Here, the political agenda of Kennedy's New Frontier and the networks' search for cultural validity merged harmoniously. Kennedy's promise to land on the moon before the end of the decade became television's promise as well. The space race gave television something to shoot for. It presented a whole new repertoire of images and created a whole new reason for looking at the living-room console.

Information formats, in this and other ways, took up the challenge of national purpose and served, in large part, as an antidote to the attack on television's debased form. But the limits of public discourse foreclosed the possibility that entertainment television could be treated in the same vein. Indeed, as the critics (and Minow) had argued, sitcoms, quiz shows, westerns, and the like were resolutely low. While intended to infuse television with a set of moral guidelines, critical categories of high and low culture enabled the industry to divide its attention. With documentary and news formats to satisfy the reform demands of the wasteland critique, the industry continued to present its "low"—and markedly popular—money-making formats. Still, entertainment programming underwent its own peculiar transition. Although in distorted and circuitous ways, the progressive spirit of the New Frontier and its focus on space-age imagery served as a launching pad for significant revisions in television's fictional forms.

To the Moon, Alice!

In 1966, *Mad* magazine presented a cartoon saga of the perfect American television family, Oozie, Harried, Divot, and Rickety Nilson, who "lived completely and hermetically sealed off from reality." The story's opening panel showed Oozie comfortably reading his newspaper, which Harried had doctored in order to soothe the tensions of the day. Harried stands grinning in the foreground of the panel, where she tells her housewife friend, "I cut out all the articles that might disturb him"; as proof of her deed we see large cut-out areas under headlines that read "Vietnam," "Laos," and "race riots." Nevertheless, Oozie complains to Harried of his action-packed day. "First," he drones, "I pulled the wrong cord on the Venetian blind. . . . Then, Art Linkletter's House Party was preempted by a Space Shot. . . . It's been one thing after another." [18]

As *Mad* so humorously suggested, the middle-class suburban sitcom was vastly out of sync with the problems of the nation. Indeed, its codes of realism (the bumbling but lovable dads, the perfect loving wives, the mundane storylines) were, by this time, codes of satire and parody. If the suburban sitcoms had once explained the ideals and goals of the nation, they no longer seemed to match the real world at all, as is vividly expressed by Oozie's choice of television programs. He prefers the family doldrums of Art Linkletter's *House Party* to the country's national goals in space.

Mad's TV spoof was part of a more general shift in popular representations of family life on television in the 1960s. Programs like *Bewitched, I Dream of Jeannie, Green Acres, The Beverly Hillbillies, The Jetsons, My Living Doll, The Addams Family,* and *The Munsters* poked fun at narrative conventions of the sitcom form and engaged viewers in a popular dialogue through which they might reconsider social ideals. In their own context, they took up the challenge of the New Frontier, but rather than providing a rational-scientific discourse on the public sphere (like that of the 1960s documentary), they presented a highly irrational, supernatural discourse on private life. In other words, they launched a critique of the American family in ways that were antithetical to the norms of television's "high" art forms.

These programs can be understood in the context of other media forms (magazines, rock 'n' roll, youth films, melodramas, and so on) that gave voice to critical perspectives on the social world. Borrowing from the discourses of previous texts and transmuting already established generic conventions, the fantastic sitcom provided a cultural space in which anxieties about everyday life could be addressed, albeit through a series of displacements and distortions. The sitcom format was an apt vehicle for this because it offered ready-made conflicts over gender roles, domesticity, and suburban lifestyles, while its laugh tracks, harmonious resolutions, and other structures of denial functioned as safety valves that diffused the "trouble" in the text. Moreover, its proclivity to deal with "contemporary" subject matter made the genre responsive to larger shifts in the social world.

In the most basic terms, changes in the family sitcom can be charted through a demographic analysis of family structure and living arrangements. In the early half of the 1950s, domestic comedies tended to present a varied demographic group that included families living in urban areas (such as *I Love Lucy, Make Room for Daddy,* and *My Little Margie*), suburban areas (such as *I Married Joan, The Adventures of Ozzie and Harriet,* and *My Favorite Husband*), and notably, ethnic and working-class types like Italian immigrants (*Life with Luigi*), blacks (*Amos 'n' Andy, Beulah*) and working-class families (*The Honeymooners, The Life of Riley*). These programs appealed to television's early audience, which was located primarily in urban centers (especially the Northeast) and which could most strongly relate to these ethnic/urban types. As television became a national medium (by 1955 it was more evenly disseminated throughout the country), producers, networks, and advertisers tried to appeal to a more homogeneous, middle-class audience. In addition, as George Lipsitz has suggested, when the Hollywood majors rigorously entered into television production in the mid-1950s, the ethnic/working-class programs, which tended to be produced by small independents, began to wane.[19]

Concurrent with these shifts, the conventions for representing the family group changed over the course of the decade. Although these developments were somewhat uneven, significant trends can be tracked. Of the seventeen different family sitcoms that aired on network prime time between 1957 and 1960, fourteen were set in the suburbs.[20] Meanwhile, the ethnic variations disappeared, so that by September 1960, they were all off the networks.[21] By the end of the decade, the middle-class suburban sitcom had become the primary form for representing family life. Programs like *Ozzie and Harriet, Leave It to Beaver, The Donna Reed Show, Father Knows Best,* and the more "moderne" *Dick Van Dyke Show* dramatized, with varying degrees of humor, the lives of nuclear families in suburban towns. The families included a contented couple with a modest number of children, and almost always lived near a group of friendly—if quirky—neighbors, who were obviously of the same social class. Donna (Reed) Stone, for example, lived in the perfect suburban town of Hilldale with her physician husband Alex Stone, her two children, and her next-door neighbor, Midge Kelsey (whose husband was also a doctor). Unlike such earlier zany sitcom characters as Lucy Ricardo (*I Love Lucy*) and Joan Stevens (*I Married Joan*), who tried desperately to break out of their domestic spaces, the women in these sitcoms were typically happy housewives who, despite the everyday strains of mothering, had put their faith in the suburban dream.

If these programs were out of sync with the widespread critique of suburbia at the end of the decade, they nevertheless remained on the networks through the early part of the 1960s, and until 1964, several ranked in the top twenty-five on the Nielsen charts. Most strikingly, however, by the fall 1966 season, all had been taken off the air.[22] This trend continued in the coming years; between 1966 and 1969 only three of the thirty-two different domestic comedies aired on network prime time were suburban family sitcoms.[23] Taking their place were two new types that gained ground in the early to mid 1960s: the broken-family sitcom and the fantastic family sitcom.[24]

In the broken-family sitcom, the middle-class family still constituted the focus of the show, but one parent was missing. This corresponded to the rising divorce rates of the 1960s, but in the fictional representation the missing parent was never absent because of divorce (which was a network censorship taboo) but because he or she had died.[25] In this way, the broken-family sitcom signaled changes in family structure, but it also often smoothed over these social changes by including a character who functioned narratively as a surrogate parent. Thus Uncle Charlie in *My Three Sons,* Aunt Bee in *The Andy Griffith Show,* and governess Katy Holstrum in *The Farmer's Daughter* were among a long list of stand-in parents.

In the fantastic sitcoms, families were also often formed in new ways. The genre was populated by unmarried couples such as Jeannie and Tony in *I Dream of Jeannie,* extended families such as *The Addams Family* (with Uncle Fester, Grandmama, and Cousin It), and childless couples such as Wilbur and Carol in *Mr. Ed.* But these sitcoms presented more than just demographic changes; they provided narrative situations and themes that suggested a clear departure from the conventions of the suburban family sitcoms that preceded them. These genre hybrids were parodic in nature because they retained the conventions of the previous form, but they made these conventions strange by mismatching form and content.

Bewitched, for example, employs the narrative conventions of the middle-class suburban sitcom. Its narrative structure revolves around the comedic complications and harmonious resolutions common to the sitcom genre as a whole. Typically, Darrin Stephens has an important advertising account at the office, but his domestic situation leads to problems. Often his mother-in-law Endora finds reason to spark a fight that creates havoc for the rest of the episode. This narrative complication is then neutralized by Samantha, who mediates the dispute, wins Darrin's ad account, and thus restores narrative harmony. The setting—an ideal two-story home located in a middle-class town—also borrows its conventions from the middle-class suburban sitcom. Similarly, the program retains clear gender divisions between public and private space, with Samantha taking the role of housewife and Darrin an executive in a high-rise office building. Gladys and Abner Kravitz function as the neighbor characters of the earlier form. But in all of this something is amiss. Samantha is a witch, and her supernatural powers recast the narrative situation so that the conventional becomes strange. Warlocks, witch doctors, and evil witches populate the traditionally decorated rooms of the Stephens's home, while powerful spells bring Ben Franklin, Mother Goose, and tooth fairies alive. In a similar way, programs like *Mr. Ed, My Mother the Car, I Dream of Jeannie, The Addams Family,* and *My Living Doll* retained the conventional forms of the suburban sitcom past but infused them with talking horses, conversing cars, genies, ghouls, and robots.

This peculiar mixture of domesticity and fantastic situations could be found outside the sitcom form in other popular venues. These series employed discursive strategies that were also used in representations of science and, in particular, space science. During the 1950s and 1960s, the American media communicated ideas about space through tropes of domesticity and family romance. National magazines mixed everyday situations with fantastic scenarios of space travel. In 1958, *Look* quoted lyrics from songs about space written by children of parents at the missile test program at Cape Canaveral. Another article showed how a vacationing family, dressed for summer fun, found Cocoa Beach a perfect place to watch for "imminent missile launchings" while "tak[ing] in the sun and the sights at the same time."[26]

The discursive conjuncture between domestic space and outer space found its standard form in *Life*'s biographical essays, which presented technical information alongside multipage spreads depicting family scenes and life histories of the astronauts. For example, in the 18 May 1962 issue, Scott Carpenter was pictured with his wife Rene on the cover, while the inside story showed family photos of Scott as a child with his grandfather, his pony, his friends, and finally his modern-day wife and children. The snapshots showed them as the ideal American family: playing at home, enjoying a family vacation, and finally in the last pages of the essay, saying their farewells just before the space flight.[27] In this way, the photographic narrative sequence suggested that Scott Carpenter's flight to the moon was one more in a series of "everyday" family activities. This became the conventional narration of *Life*'s astronaut profiles in the years to come.

In a practical sense, this essay format allowed the magazines to appeal to diverse audiences because it conveyed technical, scientific information in the popular format of family drama. Discussions of domesticity made space familiar by offering a down-to-earth context for the often-abstract reasoning behind space flights. When astronaut John Young went to space in 1965, this merger of science and domesticity was taken to its logical extreme. *Life* reported his flight by telling the story of his wife and children, who witnessed the event on television:

> The Youngs watch. In John Young's home outside Houston, the astronaut's family sits at the TV set as the seconds crawl toward launch time. Barbara Young fidgets, Sandy fiddles with a bit of string and Johnny, still getting over chicken pox, stares unsmiling at the screen. At lift off Mrs. Young hugs Sandy. "Fantastic," she crows . . . as [the] ship soars skyward.

The accompanying photographs showed the Young family sitting before the television set, much like other Americans would have done that day.[28] Here as elsewhere, the "fantastic" is communicated through the domestic, and space technology is itself mediated through the more familial technology of television.

Even the space scientists seemed to recognize the popular appeal of domestic explanations for space travel. In 1958, Wernher von Braun told *Life* that "missile building is much like interior decorating. Once you decide to refurnish the living room you go shopping. But when you put it all together you may see in a flash it's a mistake—the draperies don't go with the slip covers. The same is true of missiles." And in 1969, NASA engineer John C. Houbolt told the same magazine that a "rendezvous around the moon was like being in a living room."[29]

The American public responded in kind, tying space-age imagery to their own domestic lives. In 1962, *Life* reported that parents across the country were naming their children in new ways. Lamar Orbit Hill, John Glenn Davis, John Glenn Donato, and John Glenn Apollo were among the list of space-age babies, and as *Life* pointed out, the trend was so consuming that one couple "yielded to the headlines and named their new boy John Glenn—they'd been planning to call him Robert Kennedy."[30]

Big industry capitalized on and added to this space-age fever. In 1955, when going to the moon was more Technicolor fantasy than technocratic plan, Disneyland made space into family fun in its Tomorrowland section of the park (which was further embellished in 1959). In the early 1960s, with the official space race now underway, the World's Fair in Seattle and in New York opened their gates to families who wandered about futuristic pleasure gardens, peering at Ford's 100-passenger space-ship and pondering the NASA exhibit. Meanwhile, women's home maga-zines included recipes for "blast-off" space cakes, promoted "space-age homes," and suggested building "space platforms" instead of porches.[31] Songwriters fashioned romantic tunes like "Space Ship for Two," "Earth Satellite," and "Sputnik Love."[32] Advertisers, eager to employ popular meanings, used space imagery to glorify family-oriented products. Ford, for example, showed a little boy dressed in a space suit, exploring his brand-new Fairlane family sedan and telling consumers that "Ford interi-ors are . . . out of this world."[33]

This merger of science and domesticity thus became a conventional way of thinking about the fantastic voyage into space, but as the above ex-amples show, it also provided a new mode of expressing family relations. In the fantastic sitcom, science fiction fantasy invaded the discourses of the everyday, so that the norms of domesticity were made unfamiliar.

As Fredric Jameson has argued, science fiction tends less to imagine the future than to "defamiliarize and restructure our experience of our own *present*."[34] Although these sitcoms were not science fiction narratives per se, they engaged elements of science fiction fantasy for similar pur-poses. Rather than portraying the future, the fantastic sitcoms presented critical views of contemporary suburban life by using tropes of science fiction to make the familial strange.

Consider again the case of Samantha Stephens, who swore off her supernatural powers to marry a mere mortal. Episode after episode, we find the good witch in her Sears and Roebuck outfits, masquerading as the perfect suburban housewife, happily scrambling eggs as Darrin delib-erates over his next trite advertising slogan. Consider as well the beautiful Jeannie, who gleefully fulfills the wishes of her astronaut master Tony as he desperately tries to hide her from his NASA bosses. And consider finally the exploits of the Jetsons, an average American cartoon family living in the twenty-first century, which turns out to be a space-odyssey version of Levittown. These sitcoms incorporated elements of science fiction to present a heightened and fantastic version of suburban life.

As Tzvetan Todorov has argued, the fantastic exists less as a genre than as a moment in a text, a moment characterized by hesitation.[35] The fan-tastic often occurs at the point at which the hero or heroine doubts the credibility of the situation (can this be happening, or am I dreaming this?). In the fantastic sitcom, the doubting-Thomas character became a stock vehicle for this kind of hesitation. Gladys Kravitz, the busybody neighbor in *Bewitched,* constantly doubted her own visions (or at least her husband Abner did). Similarly, Dr. Bellows, whose psychiatric discourse sought to explain all human aberrations, hesitated to believe the outlandish stories that Tony conjured up in his attempts to hide his genie from the boys at the space project. In addition to this hesitation within the mind of the character, the fantastic also makes the reader uncertain about the status of the text. The story calls its own conventions of representation into question and makes the reader wonder whether the narrative situation is possible at all. In the fantastic sitcom, the elements called into question are not the fantastic aspects per se (we are never made to question whether Jeannie is a genie, nor does the narrative ask if being a genie is possible in the first place). Rather, the moment of hesitation takes place in the realm of the natural. We are, in other words, made to question the "naturalness" of middle-class existence. We are asked to hesitate in our beliefs about the normative roles of gender, class, and race that so pervade the era's suburban lifestyles. In this sense, the fantastic unmasks the conventionality of the everyday.

The fantastic family sitcoms expressed tensions about the classist, racist, and sexist premises of suburban life by revolving around fantastic situations that referred, in hyperbolic ways, to everyday practices of the middle class. In this sense, they can be seen as the 1960s answer to the ethnic and working-class family programs of the earlier decade. Although Italian immigrants, Jewish mothers, and working-class bus drivers might have disappeared from the screen, they returned in a new incarnation as genies, witches, and robots. In other words, fantastic hyperbolic representations of cultural difference took the place of the more "realistic" portrayals. At a time when the Civil Rights movement had gained ground, these programs dramatized the exclusionary practices of the middle-class suburbs, not in realistic ways but through exaggerated, comedic representations.

In fact, fear of the "Other" became one of the central narrative motifs of the fantastic sitcom. In place of the idyllic neighbor characters of the suburban sitcom past, these genre hybrids presented unflattering images of the middle-class community. Instead of *Donna Reed*'s best friend Midge or *Ozzie and Harriet*'s affable Thorny, we had neighborhood snoops like *Bewitched*'s Gladys Kravitz and *My Favorite Martian*'s Detective Bill Brennan, characters who threatened to expose the alien's identity. In this regard, the programs drew on earlier science fiction forms that dramatized the fear of aliens in our midst. Anthology shows like *Science Fiction Theater, The Twilight Zone,* and *The Outer Limits* included episodes that revolved around aliens moving into suburban communities, while science fiction films like *War of the Worlds* and *Invasion of the Body Snatchers* based their plots on alien invasions.[36] The sitcoms incorporated this earlier strategy, but dramatized it in comedic terms.

These programs presented friendly, lovable aliens: good witches, flying nuns, glamorous genies, favorite Martians, humorous horses, motherly cars, and friendly ghosts were among the strange but kindly heroes and heroines. Rather than the aliens advancing a threat, it was the white middle-class suburbanites who revealed their darker sides. *The Addams Family* and *The Munsters* (which engaged the fantastic by turning to horror rather than science fiction) were particularly keen on this theme. These ghouls were friendly, kind, generous folks who welcomed strangers into their homes. But their difference from the white middle class made them unacceptable to suburbanites who feared deviations. Thus, after a glimpse at the cobwebbed decor, slimy pets, man-eating plants, and cream-of-toad soup, houseguests typically fled in a panic from the haunted mansions.

Space aliens often presented similar commentary on the exclusionary tactics of white middle-class suburbanites. A 1967 episode of *The Beverly Hillbillies* is an emblematic example. This sitcom based its entire situation on the theme of cultural difference in a homogeneous, upper-class community. According to the story of the opening credit sequence, "poor mountaineer" Jed Clampett strikes oil in the Ozarks, after which he rounds up his "kin folk" and takes them to the opulent California suburb. Their southern hospitality provides a sharp contrast to their snobby banker neighbors, Mr. and Mrs. Drysdale, who socialize with the Clampetts only in order to keep their oil money in the bank. In one particular episode, Mr. Drysdale hires a group of Italian-speaking midgets to pose as Martians in an advertising stunt for his bank. When the midgets, dressed in Martian suits, land their spacecraft in the Clampetts' yard, the hillbilly family is at first alarmed. Granny, the most fearful of the bunch, calls the spacemen "little green varmints," but Jed's daughter, Elly May, scolds her for this undue prejudice. "Well, Granny," she says, "they can't help it if they's little and green," and taking this to heart Jed declares, "Elly's right. We shouldn't let on that they's any different than us." After this bit of moralizing, their ideals of neighborliness and hospitality overcome their fears, and Granny invites the aliens in for "vittles." Thus, the kindly but naïve hillbillies are more accepting of cultural differences than are their snobby Beverly Hills neighbors.

But this tolerance comes to a halt when cousin Jethro resparks the fear of strangers. Jethro, who constantly boasts of his sixth-grade education, is more schooled than the others. In the narrative logic, however, his education is his Achilles heel, for it makes him more vulnerable to the hollow ideals of middle-class life. In this episode, Jethro's school-book knowledge of Martians leads him to adopt the "get them before they get us" attitude that is reminiscent of middle-class rationales for social segregation. Having read that Martians can turn people into robots, he suggests a plan for extermination. Chilled by Jethro's warning, Granny reaches for her shotgun and shoots the alien spacecraft.

Often, the fantastic sitcoms represented aliens as being specifically female: Jeannies, witches, and sexy robots. These women had to be carefully guarded so as not to reveal their difference from the group outside. Snooping neighbors like Gladys Kravitz kept a constant vigil over the Stephens's home, hoping to catch the good witch in the act; Jeannie was hidden in her bottle, far away from next-door neighbor Roger (until the later episodes when he discovers her secret) and Dr. Bellows, who constantly pried into Tony's domestic life; the Flying Nun kept her aerodynamic secrets safely among the sisterhood at church; Dave Crabtree's mother clandestinely lived her second life in the form of a 1928 Porter automobile; and Dr. Robert McDonald kept the secret of his robot (played by the vampish Julie Newmar) hidden from his next-door neighbor, who had a powerful crush on the "living doll."

This woman-as-alien motif was indebted to earlier science fiction literature and films. In the 1950s, for example, stories that dealt with alien invasion often centered on relations of sexual difference. Science fiction thrillers like *War of the Worlds* (a librarian falls in love with a scientist who battles the space aliens), *Them!* (a woman scientist falls in love with the cop who kills the giant ants), and *Forbidden Planet* (an astronaut falls in love with the daughter of a psychotic scientist) presented tales that intertwined alien forces with gender dynamics. In such films, romance served to address the enigma in a way that scientific explanation could not. While the scientists try to understand the alien through the conventions of rational discourse, their success is always partial. They can destroy the alien, but the basis for explaining its origins and reproduction is

On the set of "First
Woman on the Moon."

never wholly scientific. Instead, the epistemological basis for diffusing the
threat of difference is transposed onto romantic coupling. It is romantic
love and marriage (the reproduction of the status quo and normal gender
distinctions) that finally solve the crisis of the "Other." That is, sexual difference structures all other differences. The demise of the alien—whether
it be Martian, giant ant, or psychotic parent—goes hand in hand with the
bonding of hero and heroine and their acceptance of traditional marks of
sexual identity. However, rather than serving a wholly conservative function, these films actually problematized the ideology of domesticity by
making it strange.[37]

In fact, representations of the space race—whether offered in scientific
or fantastic modes—often evoked this kind of defamiliarization. A perfect
example is an episode from the syndicated series *Men into Space*, which
was produced from 1959 to 1960 and funded in part by the Department
of Defense. The episode entitled "First Woman on the Moon" tells the
story of Renza Hale and her astronaut husband Joe who, on the orders
of his space department bosses, invites her to travel to the moon. Once
Renza is on the moon, however, problems ensue. Renza is bored because

the men will not let her leave the rocket, and her culinary talents go to waste because she cannot get the hang of antigravity cooking. One night, after her Yorkshire pudding is too tough, Renza breaks down. The next morning, she ventures out onto the lunar landscape without informing the crew. After a panicked search, Joe is furious and in a scolding tone tells his wife, "Your place is on earth at home where I know you're safe." In this episode, tropes of science fiction fantasy allow for an exposition of anxieties that women faced in more everyday circumstances. This program turns out to be a thinly veiled exploration of domesticity and the gendered division of spheres that so pervaded ideas about women's place in the 1950s.

If the space race provided a critique of gender in fictional forms, it also gave voice to feminist views in the culture at large. In 1960, *Look*'s cover story asked, "Should a Girl Be First in Space?" presenting the story of Betty Skelton, an American pilot who underwent a series of tests for space travel. But according to Betty, her fellow spacemen, who nicknamed her No. 7 1/2, were not likely to take her along for the ride. As *Look* reported, "Some 2,000 American women, mostly teenagers, have volunteered for space flight," but "what Miss Skelton and other possibly qualified women fear is not that they will be lofted out of the atmosphere, but that they won't." The article even went on to declare that "women have more brains and stamina per pound than men," and concluded as well that physical and psychological requirements for space travel "are so specialized that specific individual qualifications far outweigh any difference based on sex." In this case, the space race provided a photoessay opportunity for deconstructing notions about biologically determined gender difference. However, this was recuperated within more conventional ideas about domesticity; later in the essay *Look* promised that the first woman in space would be "married," possibly even the "scientist-wife of a pilot engineer." [38]

In 1963, when the Soviet Union sent Valentina Tereshkova into space, *Life* ran an editorial that presented even more damning criticism of America's treatment of women. Written by Clare Boothe Luce (who was married to publisher Henry Luce), the article argued that

> Soviet Russia put a woman into space because Communism preaches and, since the Revolution of 1917, has tried to practice the inherent equality of men and women. The flight of Valentina Tereshkova

is, consequently, symbolic of the emancipation of the Communist woman. It symbolizes to Russian women that they actively share (not passively bask, like American women) in the glory of conquering space.

Boothe Luce went on to tell the story of the thirteen American women pilots who, while having proved their physical capacity for space flight in government tests, were barred from participating in the (aptly titled) manned space program.[39] The article (which most likely was published only because of Luce's family ties) pointedly attacked American sexism. The space race thus provided the grounds on which to question the gender-based decisions behind the New Frontier's march of progress.

Such blatant attacks on institutional sexism were atypical of mass media of the times, and 1960s television, which sought to appeal to broad-based audiences, was by no means a venue for this kind of dialogue. However, the domestic situation comedy was, by its very nature, predicated on the gender conflicts of the American family, and in the 1960s hybrid version, these conflicts were augmented by the fantastic scenarios of space-age situations. In a decade that began with Betty Friedan's criticisms of the mass media's "happy housewife heroine," these fantastic sitcoms offered exaggerated and humorous renditions of the June Cleaver syndrome. Thus, *Jeannie* and *Bewitched* revolved around super-powerful women who tried to efface their potential in return for the "rewards" of family life. Like Donna Reed, who sacrificed her nursing career for life with Dr. Alex Stone, these women traded their credentials for domestic bliss. But Samantha and Jeannie, unlike Donna, had more difficult transitions from career to housewife. Their supernatural powers called for exaggerated forms of self-imposed containment. Thus they became super-feminine. Jeannie called Tony "Master" and scampered around the house in pink harem-girl garb, while Samantha took the more conservative route of miniskirts and aprons. In either case, they were perfect examples of Joan Rivière's classic 1929 study "Womanliness as a Masquerade," which showed how successful female professionals felt compelled to adopt a heightened veneer of femininity as a strategy for coping with their "transgression" of normative gender roles. By posing as super-feminine types, these women were able to minimize anxiety about the negative reactions they anticipated from male associates.[40] In the 1960s television version, powerful female characters were shown to threaten gender expectations

Samantha's supernatural power gets the better of Darrin in ABC's *Bewitched*.

of the patriarchal world; their masquerade as ideal housewives might well have alleviated audience tensions about the changing role of women at the time.

Although this basic situation was less than revolutionary, it did provide a premise for a more subversive kind of comedy that poked fun at social expectations about gender roles. The narratives continually showed how Samantha's and Jeannie's power could not be integrated into patriarchal norms, and they dramatized the impossibility of absolute containment. Notably in this regard, they provided an expressive outlet for women's "bottled-up" rebelliousness through a doppelgänger motif. Samantha's look-alike cousin and Jeannie's look-alike sister were wacky, wild, swinging singles who functioned as hyperbolic depictions of nondomestic roles for women. They had numerous lovers, visited maharajahs, and traveled the universe at their whim. Even if these characters were depicted as irresponsible party girls of the free-love decade, they often directly confronted their feminine counterparts, criticizing the boring lifestyles Samantha and Jeannie had chosen. Similarly, Samantha's bad witch mother, Endora (who was estranged from her warlock husband, Maurice), strongly opposed her daughter's marriage to "Durwood" and continually begged her to skip out to exotic locales like the French Riviera. Significantly here, these female doubles underscored the idea that the nondomestic woman was specifically of a jet-set class whose upper-crust lifestyles had little relationship to the everyday concerns of real working/independent women. Thus, while fantastic sitcoms allowed alternative female roles to be depicted, they bypassed the more threatening elements of women's economic and social power by confining that power to a small group of elites.

These programs also parodied middle-class men who strove to comply with bureaucratic dictates. Darrin Stephens, Tony Nelson, and Dr. Robert McDonald constantly tried to keep their strange and powerful secrets within the private sphere of their homes.[41] Like William Whyte's "organization man," these men had to hide any kind of social deviance behind a strict veneer of allegiance to the corporate ideal. In this way they very much adopted the structural position of the woman in the masquerade, only here the men hid their secret source of power by donning the exaggerated pose of the company boy. By dramatizing these scenarios, the fantastic sitcom often inverted the conventional power dynamics of masculinity and femininity, and in the process they made viewers laugh at their own assumptions about gender.

In *Jeannie* this inversion of sexual identity was directly related to and reinforced by the program's burlesque of technological supremacy, specifically the space race. Not only did the sitcom poke fun at gender roles, it also mocked men's dominion over scientific progress. The program retains traditional divisions between public and private spheres; while the suburban home is the woman's place, NASA headquarters—and by extension space itself—is the male domain. However, Jeannie always manages to blur the gendered divisions of private and public spheres. She typically arrives incognito at NASA headquarters where she undermines its scientific breakthroughs with her greater powers. After all, she need only blink herself onto the moon.[42]

Take, for example, a 1968 episode in which Jeannie grants three wishes to Tony's astronaut pal Roger. Roger wishes to change places with Tony, who has been selected by NASA to travel to the moon. Upon his wish, Tony and Roger find themselves in each other's bodies, a situation resulting in confusion about male identity, a confusion that is typical of the series as a whole. In this case, as elsewhere, NASA psychiatrist Dr. Bellows tries to explain the rational causes behind this male identity crisis, but science fails to locate the "feminine" cause. Dr. Bellows, who assumes that Tony and Roger suffer from a deep personality disorder, becomes increasingly confused by the scenario. Finally, after Roger agrees to retract his wish, Jeannie restores the men to their proper bodies, and Tony takes off for the moon.

However, the final tag sequence defies this resolution, suggesting instead that Jeannie's female (supernatural) powers are more potent than those of the male scientists. Jeannie and Roger sit in the Nelson living room watching Tony on television as he travels to the moon. The camera lingers on a shot of the television set as documentary footage (apparently taken from an actual launching) displays a rocket takeoff that is intercut with fictional shots of Tony in the spacecraft and Jeannie and Roger watching the broadcast. Dramatic music underscores the rocket footage, so that the viewer is led to marvel at the feats of contemporary space science. But this moment of revelry is interrupted when Roger reminds Jeannie that he is still entitled to another wish. After Jeannie's characteristic blink, the camera cuts back to the television set where Roger is pictured alongside Tony in the spacecraft. Thus the patriarchal splendors of the space project are ironically cast aside as a woman is able to accomplish the same task with mere wishful thinking.

In 1969, *Green Acres* presented a similar spoof of NASA's scientific domain when precocious child inventor, Dinky, sells a moon rock to Oliver Douglas's wife, Lisa. Douglas, who has left his New York law practice for the pastoral splendors of a Hooterville farm, is hopelessly caught in the scientific rationalism of his city-slicker past, and the moon rocks prove especially disturbing to him. Despite the claims of Lisa (who is always more in tune with Hooterville's antiscientific, screwball logic), Oliver insists that Dinky's rocks aren't really from the moon. As in other episodes, Lisa adopts the attitude of her bizarre Hooterville neighbors, and through this she is better equipped to deal with the enigmatic laws of her universe. She is, in other words, placed on the side of the aliens—the television-watching pigs, inbred farm hands, and, in this case, whiz-kid inventors—that comprise her community. Her husband, on the other hand, searches for "rational" solutions.

Later in the episode, new "scientific proof" convinces Oliver that the rock is from the moon. The evidence is put forward by Mr. Kimball, the double-talking and clearly irrational agricultural scientist, who informs Oliver that several moon rocks were stolen from a traveling NASA exhibit.

To Oliver, this seems a logical explanation. But when he calls NASA head-quarters, the space officials assume he is just another crackpot and tell him to phone Alcoholics Anonymous. As is typical of the series, the episode reveals the limits of masculine rationalization. The final scene shows con-fused NASA officials listening to a closet full of beeping moon rocks, just as unable to explain the phenomenon as Lisa Douglas was. Gender dy-namics are thus reworked, so that women's "alien" logic is just as rational as the conventions of scientific discourse in the male sphere.

In *Bewitched*, the woman's alien powers serve to invert the gender rela-tions of suburban domesticity, and with this, the consumer lifestyles that characterize the suburbs are also parodied. Darrin's job as a junior execu-tive in an advertising firm provides ample situations for a popular version of critical stances toward the consumption ethic to emerge. In a 1967 epi-sode, for example, Darrin takes a cold tablet concocted by Samantha's witch doctor friend, Dr. Bombay. The magic pill instantly cures Darrin's cold, and on seeing this, Darrin's greedy boss Larry decides to make a fortune overnight by packaging the miracle drug. But as Samantha and Darrin soon discover, there's an unfortunate side effect that leaves Darrin with a new, markedly feminine, high-pitched voice. As in *Jeannie*, magic works to transform Darrin's bodily functions, so that his sexual iden-tity — and at times even his species classification — is thrown into question. Whether he's turned into a screeching soprano, a dog, a mule, or a little boy, Darrin has to be returned to his proper manly state before the episode can end.

So, too, Samantha destabilizes the patriarchal structures of consumer capitalism. Since the 1920s, advertisers have particularly targeted women, whom they calculate are responsible for about 80 percent of the family's purchases. Women thus are institutionalized consumers, and advertisers are eager to promote specifically female uses for products. As Judith Williamson has argued, a central way in which advertisements promote product use is through the promise of magical transformation — cold pills instantly stop symptoms, Mr. Clean materializes in your kitchen, skin creams make wrinkles vanish, and dish soap makes hands look younger.[43] *Bewitched* inverts this dynamic by giving a woman the power of transfor-mation. In the episode described above, not only Darrin but also Larry and a drug manufacturer have been afflicted by Dr. Bombay's magic pills, and thus all are at the mercy of Samantha's witchcraft. Being a good witch, she transforms them with an antidote, and their masculine voices are restored. This closure, however, is only temporary, because in the next episode Samantha will once again wreak havoc on the advertising executives.

More generally, these sitcoms poked fun at the consumer lifestyles of suburban culture, particularly new domestic technologies. Jeannie and Samantha, for example, did the housework the extra-easy way, by operating appliances with their magic touch. The Jetsons's push-button food dispensers, the Flintstones's prehistoric lawnmower, Mr. Ed's love affair with his television set, Gomez's proclivity for train wrecks, Grandpa Munster's mad scientist lab, and Jed Clampett's inability to distinguish a garbage disposal from a meat grinder are but a few in a long list of humorous parodies of the technological utopias Americans had hoped to find in their new suburban homes. Indeed, the consumer culture of the 1960s found a way to defamiliarize its own familiar logic.

Conclusion

In the 1960s, the rhetoric of the New Frontier set an agenda for international militarism and heavenly exploration by calling on the traditional moral fiber of the American family. By the same token, the outworn ideals of family life were reinvigorated with new goals of public life. The space race, in particular, provided a popular spectacle through which Americans could view the future in terms of the past and still feel as if they were going somewhere. No longer a nation of homebodies, we moved from domestic space to outer space while still sitting in our easy chairs.

It was in this land of space-age familialism that the hybrid genre of the fantastic sitcom emerged. Blending science fiction fantasy with domestic situations, these programs foregrounded tensions about middle-class family lifestyles, tensions that were part of the culture at large. Their fantastic space-age imagery made the familial strange; it made people pause, if only to laugh, at what had once seemed natural and everyday. This unlikely collision of genres gave audiences the chance to reflect on their own expectations—not only about the sitcom's narrative conventions, but also about the social conventions by which they lived their lives. The extent to which viewers actually engaged in such thought is another question.[44] But when seen in this light, these programs clearly beg interpretations that go beyond the typical assumptions of their escapist, low-art nature.

Indeed, as I have tried to show, the fact that these programs have not been examined is itself a consequence of history. The "wasteland" critique applied to sitcoms in the 1960s makes it hard for us to break the patterns of the past. These programs were effectively the critics' proof of television's threat to "authentic" culture, and contemporary critics have inherited that binary logic. But television shows like *Bewitched* and *Jeannie* are, of course, part of history, and as such they can play a key role in our understanding of cultural transition. Despite the conventional wisdom of "high-brow" thinking, television's popular formats are not necessarily static; they are not doomed to an endless repetition of the same story. Perhaps their lack of reverence for the "classics" and the strictures of a predetermined aesthetic canon gives them a certain flexibility that permits the development of recombinant genres and other unorthodox twists. Examining these programs in connection with other aspects of their cultural environment allows us to understand them in ways that go beyond the categories of high and low art. By reading these sitcoms alongside the more "culturally validated" texts of 1960s culture—especially popular scientific discourses on the space race—we can begin to see how the fantastic aims of space travel merged, in rather unexpected ways, with the everyday concerns of family life.

What is especially interesting in this regard is that by the end of the 1960s the "high" and mighty goals of going to space had themselves come under attack. Although the moon landing had attracted the most viewers ever in television history, the critics were restless once again. As an editorial in *Life* proclaimed, "The first requirement for a sensible post-Apollo 11 program is that President Nixon decline to sign the sort of blank check for an all-out manned Mars landing that vocal space agency partisans are urging on him." Critics particularly lamented the decidedly unpoetic sentiments that resulted from the exploration of the final frontier. *Saturday Review* complained about an "overly colloquial" reporter, who "when the lunar module successfully fired the engine that lifted it from the moon's surface, cried out 'Oh boy! Hot diggity dog! Yes sir!'" Even the astronauts had to admit their disappointment. Reflecting on their journeys in Apollo 8, astronauts Frank Boorman, Jim Lovell, and Bill Anders clearly were at a loss for the kind of poetic language on which high culture thrived. Boorman admitted that while the moon was beautiful it was also "so desolate, so completely devoid of life. . . . Nothing but this great pock-marked lump of gray pumice." And while he had hoped to find "secrets of creation," Lovell confided, "the moon was void." Anders apologized for making "a few poets angry" with his banal descriptions of the lunar landscape, but admitted nonetheless that "the long ride out to the moon was, frankly, a bit of a drag."[45]

If the space program was conceived by some as an empty venture, it nevertheless served a transformative function over the course of the decade. At least in television's fiction forms, discourses on space and tropes of the fantastic invaded the terrain of the everyday. Filling homes with domesticated witches, neighborly ghouls, and ravishing robots, these programs revolved around anxieties about middle-class social ideals. Even if the sitcom form defused these tensions with safe resolutions, the genre denied absolute closure, coming back each week to remind viewers that they too might be living in a suburban twilight zone.

Notes

This essay first appeared in *Close Encounters: Film, Feminism, and Science Fiction*, ed. Constance Penley, et al. (Minneapolis: University of Minnesota Press, 1991), pp. 205–35.

1   Note that there were several sitcoms of the 1950s that included fantastic elements. *People's Choice*, which, rather than a family situation, focused on the career and love life of a single man, included a talking dog, Cleo. The hound was used as a special effect/sight gag rather than as an integral part of the story. Cleo talked in direct address to the audience, but could not be heard by the characters—a narrational device that functioned much like the self-reflexive direct address of *The George Burns and Gracie Allen Show*. The latter also included a fantastic element in the later episodes, a magical television set through which George replayed portions of the program and commented on plot elements. Again, however, this was included as a running gag rather than as an integral part of the narrative situation. *Topper*, which revolved around ghosts who haunted a suburban home, was more akin to the 1960s fantastic shows in its basic narrative premise, but it lasted for only two seasons. While one might see these programs as forerunners, it is in the 1960s that the hybrid genre cycle proliferates and formulates its particular narrative content and organization.

2   Although it did not use the sitcom form per se, *Lost in Space* mixed family drama with elements of science fiction.

3   David Marc, *Comic Visions: Television Comedy and American Culture* (Boston: Unwin Hyman, 1989), pp. 121–56. Marc does suggest that some of these sitcoms reflected new cultural ideals, but he does not take this path of analysis into serious consideration.

4   James L. Baughman, "The National Purpose and the Newest Medium: Liberal Critics of Television, 1958–60," *Mid-America* 64 (April–July 1983): 41–55. See also

his *Television's Guardians: The FCC and the Politics of Programming, 1958-1967* (Knoxville: University of Tennessee Press, 1985). For more on dissident voices of the 1950s, see Paul A. Carter, *Another Part of the Fifties* (New York: Columbia University Press, 1988); and Todd Gitlin, "Cornucopia and Its Discontents," in *The Sixties: Years of Hope, Days of Rage* (New York: Bantam, 1987), pp. 11–31.

5 Although not exclusively concerned with suburbia, books like David Riesman's *The Lonely Crowd* (1950) and C. Wright Mills's *White Collar* (1951) focused on middle-class consensus ideology.

6 For a discussion of this and other aspects of women's lives in postwar America, see Rochelle Gatlin, *American Women since 1945* (Jackson: University of Mississippi Press, 1987).

7 The cycle of 1950s social-problem films also highlighted domestic strife, often connecting it to a wider social unrest. See, for example, *Come Back Little Sheba* (1952), *The Country Girl* (1954), and *A Hatful of Rain* (1957). For more on these films see Jackie Byars, "Gender Representation in American Family Melodramas of the 1950s," Ph.D. diss., University of Texas–Austin, 1983. For discussions of popular culture and teenagers in the 1950s, see James Gilbert, *A Cycle of Outrage: America's Reaction to the Juvenile Delinquent in the 1950s* (New York: Oxford University Press, 1986) and Thomas Doherty, *Teenagers and Teenpics: The Juvenilization of American Movies in the 1950s* (Boston: Unwin Hyman, 1988).

8 "Man's New World: How He Lives in It," *Life*, 7 October 1957, p. 80.

9 Walter A. McDougall, . . . *The Heavens and the Earth: A Political History of the Space Age* (New York: Basic Books, 1985), pp. 141–56. See also Dale Carter, *The Final Frontier: The Rise and Fall of the American Rocket State* (London: Verso, 1988), pp. 120–25.

10 Henry Luce, "Common Sense and Sputnik," *Life*, 21 October 1957, p. 35. Soviets took the occasion to suggest this as well. For example, McDougall cites Leonid Sedov's condemnation of America's fixation on consumer durables: "It is very obvious that the average American cares only for his car, his home, and his refrigerator. He has no sense at all for his nation" (. . . *The Heavens and the Earth*, p. 137).

11 Figures cited in Dewey W. Grantham, *Recent America: The United States since 1945* (Arlington Heights, Ill.: Harlan Davidson, 1987), p. 143. For an interesting discussion of reactions to Eisenhower's economic recovery plan, see Carter (*The Final Frontier*, pp. 35–40). Another recession occurred in 1960–1961, but between 1962 and 1968 a long stretch of economic prosperity ensued.

12 William Atwood, "How America Feels as We Enter the Soaring Sixties," *Look*, 5 January 1960, pp. 11–15. This survey was commissioned by the Gallup Company and supplemented by *Look*'s staff.

13 Baughman, "The National Purpose and the Newest Medium."

14 "Deception on TV," *New Republic*, 19 October 1959, p. 4. For other examples on this, see Barbara Agee, "The Intruder in Our House," *American Mercury*, June 1959, pp. 129–30; Clare Booth Luce, "Without Portfolio: A Monthly Commen-

tary; TV: An American Scandal," *McCalls,* March 1960, pp. 18–19, 176, 178; "Where Are All the Sparkling Shows of Yesteryear?" *Newsweek,* 3 July 1961, pp. 70–71. For a discussion of related issues, see Baughman, *Television's Guardians,* pp. 20–35, and "The National Purpose and the Newest Medium." Also note that while television critics became particularly dismayed about programming trends in the late 1950s, this attack on television developed out of ongoing debates about television's aesthetic and cultural development. In the late 1940s and early 1950s influential East Coast television critics saw television as a medium that promised to channel the elite through the popular, and they formed aesthetic hierarchies based on this idea. In particular, anthology dramas, with their live origination and theatrical/literary base, as well as prestige programming like *Omnibus* and *See It Now,* were the darlings of the television critics, while filmed half-hour series were seen as the lowest form of television art. For more on this, see William Boddy, "From the 'Golden Age' to the 'Vast Wasteland': The Struggles Over Market Power and Dramatic Formats in 1950s Television," Ph.D. diss., New York University, 1984. For a discussion of the more general debates about television's impact on postwar culture and family life, see my book *Make Room for TV: Television and the Family Ideal in Postwar America* (Chicago: University of Chicago Press, 1992).

15 Newton N. Minow, Address to the Thirty-ninth Annual Convention of the National Association of Broadcasters, Washington, D.C., 9 May 1961. The address can in many ways be read as a reaction to the quiz show scandals, and especially to the critics who attacked the FCC for their negligence in the matter. In a brief sentence, Minow deflected attention away from the scandals and onto the "more important" matters of reform: "I think it would be foolish and wasteful for us to continue any worn-out wrangle over the problems of payola, rigged quiz shows, and other mistakes of the past."

16 Documentary series included such titles as NBC's *White Papers,* ABC's *Close-Up,* and *CBS Reports.* By suggesting that these programs were developed at a time when the status of the television image was thrown into question by the quiz shows, I am not trying to make a direct causal link between the scandals and the networks' turn to documentary. Rather, as James Baughman has shown in his work on *CBS Reports,* the turn to documentary has to be seen in the wider context of problems facing the networks in the late 1950s, and in the case of *CBS Reports,* especially the prospect of an FCC inquiry in 1959. See James L. Baughman, "The Strange Birth of CBS Reports Revisited," *Historical Journal of Film, Radio, and Television* 2:1 (1982): 27–38.

17 On the turn to objective science and the interest in the topic of the space race in the 1960s documentary, see Michael Curtin, "Defining the Free World: Prime-Time Television Documentary and the Politics of the Cold War, 1960–1964," Ph.D. diss., University of Wisconsin–Madison, 1990.

18 Mort Drucker and Stan Hart, "The Nilson Family," *Mad,* January 1966, p. 13.

19 George Lipsitz, "The Meaning of Memory: Family, Class, and Ethnicity in Early Network Television Programs," *Cultural Anthropology* 1:4 (November 1986): 381–

82. Lipsitz argues that these programs used the memory of an ethnic/working-class past to legitimate the increasingly consumer society of the postwar era.

20 In this calculation I have included those sitcoms that revolved around domestic situations. Programs that included families but focused on working life were not included, nor was the popular *The Many Loves of Dobie Gillis*, which was mostly concerned with youth culture and student life. One program, *The Danny Thomas Show*, was set in an urban area, while two, *The Real McCoys* and *The Andy Griffith Show*, were set in rural areas.

21 Some of them did appear in reruns. Note also that *The Danny Thomas Show*, which began under the title *Make Room for Daddy* in 1953 and ended its original run in 1964, included an ethnic character. However, unlike other ethnic comedies and dramas, this program did not usually focus on Danny Williams's Lebanese ethnicity as a major condition of the plot, but rather used it simply as a running gag.

22 By 1965, none of the classic family sitcoms ranked in the top twenty of the Nielsen charts. Only *The Dick Van Dyke Show*, which was a more updated version of the classical type, was still a Nielsen success. According to Tim Brooks and Earle Marsh, *The Dick Van Dyke Show* was canceled in the fall 1966 season due to creative decisions. See Brooks and Marsh, *The Complete Directory to Prime Time Network TV Shows, 1946–Present*, 3rd ed. (New York: Ballentine, 1985), p. 218; for more general rating information, see pp. 1030–41.

23 These three were all substantially different from the classic suburban family sitcoms like *Donna Reed*. They include *Please Don't Eat the Daisies* (which was to some degree aberrant because the mother worked at home), *Blondie* (which also deviated from the norm because it was taken from the popular comic strip), and *The Debbie Reynolds Show* (which, like *I Love Lucy*, was based on a housewife who wanted to work; it was also extremely unpopular, lasting only one season).

24 I have not included certain rather idiosyncratic twists in the cycle in this calculation. These include sitcoms that depict childless couples (*He and She*; *Love on a Rooftop*) and one sitcom that depicted an extended family (*The Mothers In-Law*).

25 For divorce rates, see Gatlin, *American Women since 1945*, p. 144; Winifred D. Wandersee, *On the Move: American Women in the 1970s* (Boston: Twayne, 1988), p. 131; Julie A. Matthaei, *An Economic History of Women in America: Women's Work, the Sexual Division of Labor, and the Development of Capitalism* (New York: Schocken, 1982), p. 311.

26 "A Child Writes a Space Song," *Look*, 23 December 1958, p. 58; "The Strange Boom at Cocoa Beach," *Look*, 24 June 1958, p. 24.

27 Loudon Wainwright, "Comes a Quiet Man to Ride Aurora 7," *Life*, 18 May 1962, pp. 32–41.

28 Miguel Acoca, "He's On His Way . . . And It Couldn't Be Prettier," *Life*, 2 April 1965, pp. 36–37.

29 "The Seer of Space," *Life*, 18 November 1957, pp. 134–35; "How an Idea No One Wanted Grew Up to Be the LEM," *Life*, 14 March 1969, p. 22.

30 "Meet Orbit Hill," *Life*, 9 March 1962, p. 2.

31 *American Home*, September 1964, p. 54; *American Home*, December 1962, p. 121; *House Beautiful*, June 1963, pp. 129–30.

32 By 1958, there were at least three hundred such songs, and one music publisher even called his company "Planetary Music." See Gordon Cotler, "Song-Writers Blast Off," *New York Times Magazine*, 16 February 1958, pp. 19, 21.

33 *Life*, 24 May 1963, pp. 54–55.

34 Fredric Jameson, "Progress versus Utopia; or, Can We Imagine the Future?" *Science-Fiction Studies* 9 : 27 (1982): 151, his emphasis. Later in the article, Jameson more emphatically states that science fiction dramatizes "our incapacity to imagine the future" (p. 153), and he goes on to discuss science fiction dystopias in this vein. My use of Jameson emphasizes his earlier point regarding the way science fiction provides opportunities imaginatively to restructure the present.

35 Tzvetan Todorov, *The Fantastic: A Structural Approach To a Literary Genre*, trans. Richard Howard (Ithaca, N.Y.: Cornell University Press, 1970).

36 These programs often presented moralizing narratives that used the alien motif to dramatize the exclusionary tactics of cold war America. See, for example, *Science Fiction Theater*'s "The People at Pecos" and "Time Is Just Its Life," *The Twilight Zone*'s "The Monsters Are Due on Maple Street," and *The Outer Limits*' "Galaxy Being."

37 In fact, many of these films specifically dramatized a threat to family formations. *Them!*, for example, introduces viewers to the giant ants by showing a little girl who has been traumatized by the creatures; Andre in *The Fly* destroys his happy home by turning himself into an alien being in a teleporting experiment; and relatives in *Invasion of the Body Snatchers* lose faith in the veracity of their family ties when the pod people replicate their kin.

38 "Should a Girl Be First in Space?" *Look*, 2 February 1960, pp. 112–17.

39 Clare Boothe Luce, "But Some People Simply Never Get the Message," *Life*, 28 June 1963, pp. 31–33.

40 Joan Rivière, "Womanliness as a Masquerade," in *Formations of Fantasy*, ed. Victor Burgin, Janes Donald, and Cora Kaplan (1929; London: Methuen, 1986), pp. 35–44.

41 As a variation on this plot, some male characters were forced to hide their secrets from both their private and their public worlds. Thus Wilbur hides Mr. Ed from his wife, neighbor, and clients; Dave Crabtree hides his mother the car from his wife, neighbors, and boss. In both of these cases the male character reveals his secret to the viewer in a separate narrative space (a horse stable and a garage, respectively) that is somewhere inbetween the private and the public world.

42 A similar situation occurred in a 1967 episode of *Bewitched*, when Samantha claims that she has beaten the astronauts to the moon through her magical powers of transportation.

43 Judith Williamson, *Decoding Advertisements: Ideology and Meaning in Advertising* (New York: Marion Boyars, 1979).

44 Along these lines, it is important to keep in mind that the genre attracted many

child viewers who would have had a limited knowledge of the classic family sitcom, as well as different social and historical backgrounds from adults in the audience.

45 "The New Priorities in Exploring Space," *Life,* 22 August 1969, p. 30; Robert Lewis Shayon, "Cosmic Nielsens," *Saturday Review,* 9 August 1969, p. 40; "Our Journey to the Moon," *Life,* 17 January 1969, pp. 26–31.

Outer Space and Inner Cities:
African American Responses to NASA

✳ In 1962, a young girl named Rose Viega wrote to President Kennedy, telling him that she wanted to volunteer to be an astronaut so that her penniless father could have "something to brag about." She connected her wish for space travel to the problems her family suffered back on earth. "You see," she wrote,

> we can't find a place to live because of our complexion. We are hunched up in a two room apartment with an old lady friend of ours. There are six of us, my parents and my brother sleep on the floor, while my sister, the old lady, and myself sleep in the bed. I don't like to sleep comfortable while my parents are suffering on the hard floor. We call the number for the apartment and they say to come look at it. But when we go, and they see us they have an excuse of saying it's all ready [sic] rented, or things like that. I think it's a pity for people to treat other people like this.[1]

Today, Rose Viega's letter is shuffled among documents in the White House files at the Kennedy Library in Boston, Massachusetts. What happened to Rose and her family we can only guess. But the letter itself stands as testimony to the ways in which the space race has historically been linked to the politics of housing discrimination back on earth.

Rose Viega's letter is better understood when considered as part of a counternarrative to the dominant mythology of space travel in the 1960s.

While Rose maintains a utopian hope that space will release her from earthly burdens, her wish is fundamentally different from the dreams of a New Frontier as articulated both by the Kennedy administration and by venues of white popular culture. In this essay, I want to explore this counternarrative by looking at the way people of color represented the space race in the 1960s.

The most publicly vocal on the topic were African Americans who spoke out on the space race in the black press, and especially in the national magazine *Ebony*, which was targeted especially at the black middle class. In the wake of the Soviet launching of Sputnik in 1957, and the establishment of the National Aeronautics and Space Administration (NASA) in 1958, *Ebony* followed space science with interest. But the coverage of the space race changed over the course of the 1960s—from cautious optimism to a more biting critique of NASA's agenda. By mid-decade, *Ebony* typically addressed space travel through the genre of "social problem" criticism rather than the adventure/quest narratives aimed at whites.

Urban newspapers around the country also covered the nation's space agenda, although these accounts offer some local differences that suggest the black dialogue on outer space was by no means monolithic. For example, while the *Chicago Daily Defender* covered NASA's missions with enthusiasm, the *New York Amsterdam News* and the *Los Angeles Sentinel* (which otherwise covered world events) almost never included news of space travel.[2] When these papers did report on the space race, it was almost always in connection to NASA's discriminatory practices. Yet, despite these important differences, the black press collectively engaged perspectives on the space race that were formulated through a unifying concern with Civil Rights issues.

While many whites were critical of the space project, nationwide polls demonstrated significant racial differences. According to David Nye, from 1965 to 1969 the strongest supporters of Apollo tended to be Caucasian, male, young, affluent, and well educated. Meanwhile, "the strongest opposition lay within the Black community, where less than one in four people supported the expenditure of $4 billion a year for the Apollo program."[3] This opposition was not a rejection of science or even space exploration per se. Instead, African American criticism of NASA was articulated within the broader context of racial protest. As in the case of Rose Viega, the African American press connected its criticism to a wider critique of government polices regarding all kinds of space—not just outer space but also the changing nature of community space and property distribution in the postwar period. As I have previously argued, mainstream media targeted at whites typically presented the space race in the context of family life.[4] In *Life* and *Look,* astronaut heroes were depicted as ideal suburban dads and their wives as perfect housewives. And while Hollywood science fiction films and television programs did sometimes present stories that dealt with prejudice and colonialism, these media spoke allegorically about race, typically using the figure of the space alien in considering the issues. In contrast, African American responses to the space race (whether positive or negative) were often explicitly tied to a critique of suburban segregation and the plight of blacks in the inner cities.

Indeed, the black press spoke of the space race in the context of institutionalized practices through which social space was being remapped and rezoned. These practices included the Federal Housing Administration's (FHA) "red-lining" and building start policies that allowed for the creation of white suburban communities that systematically excluded people of color. Fueled by discriminatory bank loan and realtor policies, and by the cultural racism of white property owners, the FHA was largely responsible for the unequal distribution of the races in suburban and urban space. Moreover, the laws and policies that did address housing discrimination were typically not enforced (or else whites interpreted them in ways that further exacerbated segregation). For example, in 1948 the Supreme Court's ruling in *Shelly v. Kramer* overturned "restrictive covenants" that were a common and legal method of prohibiting black occupancy in white neighborhoods. The FHA resisted the Supreme Court's edict for two years, and when it did finally announce it would end restrictive covenants, that announcement ironically "served the purpose of alerting developers and encouraging many to hasten their applications for covenant-bound property before the announced deadline."[5]

Although the 1964 Civil Rights Act and the 1968 Fair Housing Act were both intended to prohibit housing discrimination, even this legislation was very difficult to enforce. As Arnold Hirsch explains, housing is in the hands of numerous private decision makers (real estate agents, lenders, buyers, and sellers) who can't easily be scrutinized by centralized government boards. In addition, "competing, prior, and contradictory government policies" had accelerated segregation to such an extent that Civil Rights laws have had little effect on the separation of the races. And finally, Civil Rights legislation could not reverse behavioral patterns that were encouraged by the prior history of housing segregation. According to Hirsch, long after the passing of the Fair Housing Act, people of all races have tended to "conduct their housing searches within limited areas . . . [and] their existing location is the single most critical factor in determining their new location."[6]

Not only did the FHA encourage suburban segregation, as Kenneth Jackson notes, the suburban bias of the "FHA also helped to turn the building industry against the minority and inner-city housing market. . . . Whole areas of cities were declared ineligible for loan guarantees."[7] Meanwhile, urban redevelopment and renewal projects only intensified racial and class inequalities by allowing for the creation of what Hirsch has called "the second ghetto."[8] Although often promoted through the rhetoric of liberal ideals for better housing, urban renewal was largely motivated by private businessmen with a stake in clearing out "bad neighborhoods" and attracting whites back to the city. Consequently, while the practices and goals of urban renewal differed from city to city (and even within cities), the housing projects that rose up across the nation displaced the poor and people of color from their neighborhoods, enforced race and class segregation, and often resulted in substandard housing conditions. More than 60 percent of those displaced by urban renewal were African Americans.[9]

The spatial segregation supported by these housing policies was coupled with the notorious kinds of racism that blacks faced when attempting to travel, even just across town. Bus boycotts, Freedom Riders, and protest marches challenged the Jim Crow practices of public transportation throughout the period. However, at the same time these challenges took place, the federally subsidized interstate highway systems that began to emerge in 1956 privileged white suburbanites by providing commuter routes to the inner cities that they had fled. In the process, many of the freeways further denigrated urban space by cutting "wide paths through low-income and people-of-color neighborhoods," and thus disrupting once stable inner-city neighborhoods and businesses.[10] When coupled with housing discrimination and urban renewal, the new freeway systems contributed to what George Lipsitz calls a "possessive investment in whiteness" that allowed the race to maintain its power.[11] At least in the African American press, the national agenda for space travel was measured against these and other government-ordained practices that fostered unequal access to the spaces of daily life.

In this essay I want to demonstrate how the racism of space science went hand in hand with the racism of housing, community planning, and transportation back on earth. The various forms of racism should be seen as integral to the ways in which whites maintained and reproduced their cultural hegemony in the decades following World War II. Whether in the mundane streets of suburbia or through the fantastic voyage to the moon, whites secured their power through the colonization and control of space. In other words, it was not just that whites dominated *physical geographies* through racist zoning laws, transportation policies, and other practices of segregation, they also dominated the culture's *imaginary geographies* of the universe at large. Indeed, in order to maintain and reproduce its power a group must not only occupy physical space, but it must also occupy imaginary space (the space of stories, of images, of fantasy).[12] In the modern/postmodern world, this is largely achieved through the control of media institutions. But it is important to stress that the control of representation through media is not the same as the control of people or their individual and collective imaginations. Despite the whiteness of both NASA and mainstream media, people like Rose Viega were still able to imagine space travel as something that might improve their everyday life on earth. In the account that follows, then, I explore how NASA became a subject of critical attack in the black press, but I also show how outer space at times posed utopian possibilities for racial pride and progress. Indeed, the counternarratives forged by African Americans were not just negative critiques of racism but also hopeful "replottings" of the prevailing myths about space travel and the white man's journey to the moon.

Science, Race, and the New Frontier

Even before the space age, speculative fictions about space travel were closely tied to racist geographies on earth. We find this, for example, in the minstrel tunes of nineteenth-century popular culture. In 1896, one sheet music company (which aimed its products at white consumers and specialized in songs about outer space) published a minstrel ditty "I Just Got a Message from Mars." The sheet music featured a man in blackface on the cover and told the story of Parson Brown, who promised his black congregation that he would take them to a utopian community on the moon. But when they got there they found that they had been duped, because the moon was no utopia. Instead, it was a place of toil and hardship.[13] Aimed at white fantasies of "racial cleansing," the lyrics were clearly aimed to invoke laughter at the naïve blacks who were tricked (no less by their own parson!) into a new form of racial genocide. From an African American perspective, the song would have resonated with slavery, and from this point of view it is not hard to see how black Americans of the late 1960s began to associate spaceships with slave ships (a point I'll return to later on).

In its own time, the message in "I Just Got a Message from Mars" was not simply testimony to a degraded popular culture; instead, it was symptomatic of attitudes about race within the supposedly more elevated world of nineteenth-century "enlightenment" science. Since the rise of industrialization, people of color were often assigned the role of "modern primitives." They were, in other words, presented as a backward people who could not understand or were terrified by the onslaught of scientific progress. As Carolyn Marvin demonstrates in her discussion of nineteenth-century electrical engineers, the field's professional journals contained numerous "jokes" about people of color who were terrified and confounded by new electrical gadgets. According to Marvin, these racial slurs were part of the way the electrical engineers secured power over new electrical technologies.[14] By forming a social hierarchy of a technically literate elite, and by using race (as well as gender) as a marker of technical illiteracy, the engineers convinced themselves and their publics that they were the necessary guardians of a new modern science. This form of cultural racism thus served as the ideological justification for the marginalization of people of color in scientific professions.[15] Moreover, it also occluded the important contributions they made to scientific discovery and technological invention.

By the 1960s numerous African Americans had played important roles in the sciences, and the kind of racial slurs promoted by the nineteenth-century electrical engineers would no longer have been speakable (at least publicly) by an organization like NASA. In fact, throughout the period NASA's public relations division worried about the organization's image in the area of race relations. Thus, even while NASA employed only one astronaut of color (and this near the end of the decade and after considerable dispute), it tried to present itself as a democratic organization. To be sure, concerns over race relations resonated with NASA and President Kennedy's more general ideological mission to convince the world that U.S. space travel—as opposed to Soviet efforts—was both peaceful and predicated on values of democratic "freedom." Given that the Soviets had already demonstrated their scientific superiority by beating the United States into space, the Kennedy administration decided to sell its space program through its symbolic rather than technical feats. In this regard, NASA's public relations department studied the perception of the space race in countries around the world, concluding that the U.S. space program was most valuable for its ideological ability to convince other nations that America's "free world" and "peaceful uses of space" ethos was superior to communism.[16] For his part, Kennedy promoted the space race as testimony to America's free press by claiming, for example, that while the Russians might have sent the first man (Yuri Gagarin) into space, his flight was shrouded in "secrecy." Conversely, the United States "did not conceal . . . the possibilities of failure," but instead covered Alan Shepard's flight on live TV. This, he claimed, "was a tribute to the strength of a free society."[17] In subsequent years, President Johnson's "Great Society" further envisioned space flight as part of a general campaign for national excellence, coextensive (not economically competing) with the war on "poverty, disease, ignorance, and intolerance."[18] In a 1969 interview, Johnson said that the Apollo project had inspired the country to do something about its educational systems, medical care for the elderly, conservation, and poverty.[19]

Although NASA, Kennedy, and Johnson thus aligned the space project with democratic, free world, and social welfare rhetoric, at times this rhetoric had the uncalculated effect of opening the door for public criticism regarding NASA's less than democratic racial bias.[20] For example, in 1962 four employees in a Massachusetts bank wrote to Kennedy about their concerns with Civil Rights and tied this to a plea for racial justice at NASA. Telling Kennedy that they sympathized with the Civil Rights struggles of black southerners, they stated, "We have not yet been able to understand why the Negro cannot be considered as equal to the White. We would like to ask if at any time it has been suggested that a Negro be given the opportunity to become an astronaut? We somehow feel that if a Negro was given this honor that it would almost make many of the Whites respect the Negro race."[21] In a typical response that smacked of premeditated and well-rehearsed public relations rhetoric, a White House staff person replied, "There is no discrimination whatever against candidates of any race, color or creed, and many hundreds of Negroes are already employed in the space program in countless capacities. If a qualified Negro candidate volunteers for service as an astronaut you may be sure that he will receive equal consideration with other candidates."[22] Over the years NASA continued to respond to racism charges by pointing to its integrated workforce and eventually by appointing one black man, Maj. Robert Lawrence Jr., to the astronaut program. Nevertheless, the space project still implicitly endorsed a scientific culture based on segregation, a culture that mimicked the racial division of populations back on earth. Over the course of the 1960s, African Americans protested not only the white bias of the astronaut programs, but also they claimed that NASA and its contracted industries tended to employ blacks in menial jobs rather than as high-ranking professionals. As we shall see, the corporate culture around NASA was also segregationist, making it difficult for black aerospace workers (of any rank) to live in the areas where whites lived or to participate fully in benefits bestowed by the space program. In the end, it was not until 30 August 1983 that NASA sent its first black astronaut, Lt. Col. Guion Bluford, into space. Even today, astronauts such as John Glenn or Neil Armstrong are commonly remembered for their historic flights, while most people would be completely unfamiliar with the many African American scientists, engineers, and pilots who made (and continue to make) important contributions to the field.[23]

Articulated against this historical legacy of racism, news in the African American press presented an alternative picture. From 1958 (when NASA was first formed) through the mid-1960s, *Ebony* and the *Chicago Daily Defender* reported with interest on the developments of space science. While the *Defender* kept its readers up to date on Soviet and U.S. advances in space technology, *Ebony* featured proud profiles of African Americans who were able to find positions in the aerospace industry. As early as 1958, *Ebony* ran a cover story titled "Negroes Who Help Conquer Space" that celebrated the inroads blacks had made in the aerospace industry. Based on a survey of 109 "leading industries," the magazine reported that "top-flight Negro scientists . . . are performing brilliantly all over the nation in answer to the world's most exciting challenge — the conquest of space. This challenge of space and military preparedness has prompted a quest for scientific and technical know-how that transcends the traditional barrier of race."[24] The accompanying photospread portrayed pictures of civilian and military scientists, demonstrating their range of achievements from research on rocket fuel to the design of test equipment for guided missiles. Over the course of the decade, *Ebony* featured profiles on all kinds of aerospace workers, from biochemists to space vehicle engineers to space antenna designers to missile lab supervisors to office managers.[25]

Although the majority of black aerospace workers were men, *Ebony* did feature profiles on women scientists and engineers throughout the decade. In 1961, the magazine profiled Myra Willard, a research chemist who was one of the few women to join Hughes Aircraft Company's aerospace engineer division and who was project surveyor on Hughes's program to design and build space vehicles to land on the moon. "Last year," the magazine reported, "she became the first woman to win $100 in the company's Published Papers Award Program."[26] Other women space workers included Elizabeth Reddick (a missile school analyst in the army), Evelyn Boyd (a mathematician with the Space Computing Center in Washington, D.C.), Jewell Rich (an associate airframe design engineer in the Glenn L. Martin ICBM plant in Denver), Carole Ann Johnson (a thermodynamics engineer on the "top secret" Atlas missile and Centaur space vehicle projects at General Dynamics Astronautics in San Diego); Joan Foster (an experimental psychologist in the NASA space laboratory at the University of Maryland); and Melba L. C. Roy (the head of a team of mathematicians at NASA's Goddard Space Flight Center in Greenbelt, Maryland).[27] In 1961, *Ebony* featured a front-page story on "Woman Engineer" Bonnie Bianchi who worked as a scientific writer for Baltimore's Martin Marietta Company, which was developing "peaceful uses of energy" for sea and space nuclear power systems. The front-page photo showed Bianchi next to a missile and the caption read, "Woman engineer: beauty in a man's world." The inside article continued with the brains-plus-beauty theme, also noting that Bianchi was "gregarious as well as intellectual." Meanwhile, the accompanying photospread showed her working diligently at her desk and then "selecting lunch carefully [at the cafeteria] to keep her 116-pound figure trim."[28] While this article obviously went to great lengths to maintain traditional standards of feminine beauty even while valuing female intellect, it nevertheless does suggest some important differences between the depictions of women in media aimed at blacks and whites.

In popular magazines and network news aimed at majority audiences, there was almost no coverage of women workers in the space project. When *Life* and *Look* discussed the role of women in the space race, they were almost always cast as the proud, pretty wives of astronauts.

In 1961, *Ebony* features
woman engineer Bonnie
Bianchi on the cover.

Although the mainstream press did report on the 1962 hearings held by
the House Science and Astronautics Committee that investigated charges
of sexism at NASA, this was an exception to the rule. Reading *Life* or *Look*,
one would think that American women had almost no interest in the technical aspects of space science, and certainly (apart from two critical essays
I found on the sexism of NASA), one would think that no woman (black
or white) ever worked in any capacity in the aerospace industry. While
this discrepancy does not necessarily mean that white culture was more
sexist than black culture in some essential sense, it does suggest that for
the black press the issue of race progress outweighed the male bias of scientific professions. In other words, *Ebony* looked for examples of black
space scientists and workers wherever it could find them, regardless of the
gender of the individual.

Given this dialogue on race pride and progress, it is not surprising
that advertisers and manufacturers used the iconography of space travel
when promoting products to the growing ranks of black middle-class
consumers. In *Ebony*, as in the white magazines, outer space was portrayed as a new cultural style that signified participation in a distinctly

modern, high-tech, and even "hip" world. In 1965, *Ebony* ran a cover story titled "Fashions in Orbit," which displayed glamorous black models in "sculptured space helmets" and "white pants with lacing [that] capture [the] packaged 'astronautical' look." Incorporating the sentiments of women's liberation, the story told women to stop being "doormats" and to start dressing for the future. "Why be chained to the everyday world when astronauts float in space?"[29] Advertisers also connected the space race to family life. For example, in 1969 Aetna life insurance advertised its family-oriented service by showing a close-up of a boy wearing a space helmet, implicitly promising that the insurance would provide a better future not only for the family but also for the race.[30] Perhaps the most explicit link in this regard was a 1963 ad for a land/housing developer that went by the name Canaveral Acres and was located right next to the Cape Canaveral space headquarters in Florida. Offering plots in the Canaveral Grove Estates, the company promised that the Cape Canaveral area "is the fastest growing in all Florida, with population, employment, and building up and going up!" In bold letters, at the top of the page, the ad exclaimed, "NOW, PROFIT FROM PROGRESS!"[31]

So, too, as in the pages of *Life* and *Look*, *Ebony* enthusiastically covered the decade's space-themed world's fairs. Its June 1964 vacation issue pictured the New York World's Fair as a futuristic mecca for black families, who were shown exploring the "landscape of the moon" at the Eastman Kodak Pavilion.[32] Three years later, when *Ebony* reported on Canada's Expo 67, it also presented thrilling images of the fair's space-age exhibits. Speaking of the fair's "man the explorer" theme, *Ebony* included a large picture of the dome-shaped U.S. pavilion (designed by Buckminster Fuller), which contained an Apollo module as its central exhibit. However, in this case we begin to see how the black press in fact departed from the "space-age fever" exhibited in the pages of *Life* and *Look*. Even while *Ebony* described the U.S. Apollo exhibit with excitement, the magazine also discussed the real-life problems that black tourists might expect to face when traveling to Canada. In March of that year the New York Urban League leveled charges against fair officials, claiming that hotels and campgrounds near the fair had established discriminatory housing practices. The Urban League also urged President Johnson to cancel U.S. participation in Expo 67 unless Quebec officials would assure the United States that such discrimination would not take place. In its coverage of Expo, *Ebony* reported the Urban League's concerns and then promised readers that "officials of the Quebec province have given assurances that Negro visitors will not be the victims of housing discrimination. . . . The officials say their province's anti-discrimination laws cover hotels, restaurants and camp grounds and they will be enforced rigorously by Quebec police authorities."[33]

As this case illustrates, even while *Ebony* took a deep interest in space exploration and the culture that celebrated it, the magazine was in no way color blind to the racism this entailed. Indeed, although some black leaders of the period took *Ebony* to task for its assimilationalist politics,[34] I think it would be a mistake to see its embrace of space science as evidence simply of a wish to be part of a white American Dream. Despite its intrigue with space flight and its hopeful attitude toward scientific achievement, *Ebony* (and the black press more generally) was not just mimicking white culture or ingesting its values. Instead, the meaning of space travel in the black press has to be seen within the context of black struggles and racial memories.

Civil Rights in Space

As bell hooks has suggested, travel has always meant something different in the black community than it does in the white, because black migrations and even everyday modes of transportation have typically been accompanied by acts of white terrorism.[35] In the period of the Civil Rights movement, it seems likely that black Americans would have associated travel with the terrorism encountered by Rosa Parks and countless others on the bus system in the South. As Robin Kelly argues in his study of Birmingham, even earlier during World War II the bus had became a public "theater" on which the working-class and poor (both men and women) militantly performed their resistance to white racism in acts that were often met by violence or arrest.[36] So, too, by the early 1960s the bus served as a kind of national stage for the Freedom Riders, who demonstrated for their right to interstate travel—often at the risk of death. Within this context of everyday transport and performative acts of resistance, the more fantastic theater of space travel took on meanings specific to African American quests for social justice. Just as the Expo coverage highlighted the discrimination that blacks experienced when on the road to that spectacular space-age event, other articles associated Civil Rights struggles with the prospects that space travel held for the race.

In fact, when looked at from the perspective of these struggles, even the ads and promotional rhetoric resonate with meanings specific to African American experiences. A good example is a 1962 ad for the Greyhound Bus Company that appeared in *Ebony* just one year after the Freedom Riders (who had rigidly maintained a policy of nonviolence) were attacked on Greyhound buses. (The most extreme case was the burning of a bus by white segregationists in Anniston, Alabama.) No doubt attempting to allay fears by convincing consumers of the progressive nature of the company, Greyhound advertised its buses by using the iconography of space travel. The ad features a large picture of the moon and the caption reads, "Who goes to the moon 5 times a day? Nobody . . . but Greyhound does travel that far right here on earth." A smaller photo at the bottom of the page shows a black man and woman sitting comfortably on the bus, with the company slogan "leave the driving to us" printed next to it.[37] Greyhound thus associated the technological progress of space travel with the good treatment blacks would receive on their busses.

More generally, the press spoke of the space race within the context of Civil Rights struggles over transportation, housing, education, and the like. Most explicit in this regard, the front-page headline of the *Defender*'s 22 March 1965 issue reads:

All Systems GO:
King to Montgomery
Ranger to the Moon [38]

While this headline intentionally links the protest march with the forward thrust of a rocket launching, most of the time the connections forged seem less guided by editorial intentions than by the fact that Civil Rights and space travel were both compelling news events that warranted front-page coverage. In this respect, the graphic layouts in the *Defender* juxtaposed news about the space race with stories about bus boycotts, protest marches, and demonstrations. For example, in June 1965 the *Defender*'s front-page story began with the title "History's Biggest Welcome: Chicago Greets Astronauts Today," while the bottom half of the layout stated, "Dr. King Booed in New York." Whether intentional or not, the graphic layout of the two stories asks readers to think about the two events in connection with each other. As the stories suggest, the white astronauts enjoy unbounded geographical mobility as their trip to Chicago is saluted with fanfare (the city staged a homecoming parade for the astronauts known as Gemini Twins), but in his travels to U.S. cities the black hero of the Civil Rights movement is received with protest and threats of violence.

The juxtaposition between these two stories further resonates with racial connotations because Chicago's astronaut parade was itself the site of a Civil Rights struggle over the uses of city space. While the *Defender* noted that the crowd at the parade was "swollen with suburban children," it also reported that people in the inner city were less eager to watch the Gemini Twins float by. Hearing of the city's plans to stage the astronaut parade, Civil Rights groups (who had previously been demonstrating against unfair practices in housing, employment, and education) planned to hold a counterparade. According to the *Defender*, the counterparade would "possibly cause a conflict with the astronaut parade." In response, Mayor Daley threatened police violence to stop the march. While there was some dispute within the Civil Rights movement about whether or not to proceed with the plan, in the end the counterparade did not take place. Civil Rights leader Dick Gregory made a public statement, claiming: "We do not want to use our national heroes to propagandize our own efforts to rid the city of segregation. . . . We do not, at any time, intend to block the routes of the astronauts. America is bigger than our problem. We have an important mission. But we certainly do not wish to embarrass these national heroes." It seems unlikely that Gregory's statement was a product of his earnest respect for NASA. In fact, he had previously addressed the space project with bitter sarcasm in his comedy act, telling jokes about how NASA excluded blacks from its official ranks. Instead, in making this statement, it seems likely that Gregory felt it would be unwise to associate Civil Rights with unpatriotic sentiments—and he was probably especially worried about connecting black protest with the violence Mayor Daley threatened. In place of the counterparade, Gregory and other leaders planned a series of "weekend nuisance actions" and announced that the protests would resume the day after the parade took place.[39]

Making the situation even more complex was the *Defender*'s own attitude about the space project. While the paper covered the counterparade incident, it nevertheless did so within a story that clearly endorsed the astronauts' homecoming parade. Titled "Chicago's 'A-Day': A Big Success!" the story even included two large pictures of the parade that demonstrated the fanfare and excitement for readers. In fact, the *Defender* remained relatively supportive of NASA throughout the decade. But, as in the case of the Chicago counterparade incident, this support has to be understood within the larger context of racial protest. In other words, while the black press wasn't necessarily against space science or even always anti-NASA, it did address space travel through the particular concerns of the Civil Rights struggle. Whereas the mainstream media aimed at whites continually associated outer space with family-man astronauts and what the *Defender* called their "beaming wives," the black press increasingly conceived of the space race in relation to unfair access to that American Dream. In fact, just at the time that magazines like *Life* and *Look* depicted outer space as the final frontier for suburban family lifestyles, the black press exposed space science and suburbia as interconnected forms of institutionalized racism.

These interconnections were especially pronounced in *Ebony*'s coverage of the rise and fall of astronaut candidate Edward J. Dwight Jr. In 1963, when *Ebony* first reported on the "First Negro Astronaut Candidate," it presented Dwight much in the way that *Life* and *Look* presented the all-white Mercury astronauts. The article used scenes of suburban family life, calling Dwight a "family man" and showing him at home tying his wife's apron strings and reading to his children.[40] But when NASA dropped Dwight from the space program in 1965, *Ebony* reported this by focusing on the fact that Dwight was also in the middle of a divorce. In this way, the African American broken family was ultimately connected to the black man's inability to serve as a symbol of heroic space travel. But unlike the white majority who often dubbed black men "irresponsible" providers and blamed them for the high incidence of broken families, *Ebony* connected Dwight's divorce both to the " 'anti-Negro' attitude and social ostracism the Dwights faced at [the] California base" and to the housing discrimination they experienced in the suburbs:

> In an effort to make a home for his wife and family, he tried to rent a good-sized house near Wright-Patterson AFB, instead of settling on one of the barrack-type housing projects set aside for military personnel. Despite his Air Force uniform and silver captain's bars, he faced the same problems as other Negroes seeking homes in white neighborhoods. Finally, a Catholic layman who had seen Dwight's picture on the cover of a Church publication offered to rent him a house in Huber Heights, a Dayton suburb. Soon after the Dwights moved in, the harassment began. . . . Shouts [of] 'niggers go home!' met the

family almost everyday. . . . Not long thereafter, Dwight's marriage went on the rocks."[41]

This story, then, inverts the myth of the ideal, white, suburban, space-age family so central to the images of the space race in white venues. Instead of the suburban dream house, it depicts a failed black family whose demise is caused by discrimination both in the space program and in the white suburbs. Certainly, this message seemed to have echoed the experience of *Ebony*'s readers. In the August 1965 issue (which bore the title "The White Problem in America"), several readers wrote letters chronicling the "demoralization" and "hardships" they too faced in the military.[42] The article also made news in the urban papers. Although the *New York Amsterdam News* and *Los Angeles Sentinel* almost never covered news of space travel, the Dwight story was front-page headlines in both newspapers. The *Amsterdam News*'s "Negro Astronaut Hit by Race Bias" and the *Sentinel*'s "Bias Ejects First Negro Astronaut" both referred to the *Ebony* exposé, adopting the magazine's scathing critique of Dwight's unfair treatment, and the *Amsterdam News* explicitly spoke of the "social discrimination" Dwight faced in his "home life."[43]

A few months after the Dwight incident, *Ebony* published an article titled "Housing—The Hottest Issue in the North," which provided a cautionary tale for the space age. The lead paragraph told the story of a black military officer who worked on a key missile site in the Midwest. "Because he lived so far from the job, he rose at dawn, driving miles to report on time. . . . When someone suggested he move a little closer to the base, the officer explained he was unable to obtain lodgings in the surrounding white community." *Ebony* further added, when the news of this hit the wires, "Americans across the country discovered that race-prejudice . . . could conceivably sabotage U.S. alertness to a nuclear attack." The article then went on to outline the discriminatory practices in suburbs, especially the way urban renewal had devastated African American neighborhoods. Clearly unimpressed with legislation to date, the article claimed, "John F. Kennedy swept the Negro vote on promises of vast reforms, among them an order outlawing housing discrimination." But, "three years later there has been no avalanche" in black homeownership. In addition, the magazine used the example of the officer at the missile site to suggest that even if blacks could buy homes in suburbia they often did not want to live in the "monotonous" white neighborhoods with "look-a-like" houses and shopping malls. What really was at stake, according to *Ebony,* was the devastation of black community life, particularly encouraged by urban re-newal projects in inner cities. The lead photograph pictured Chicago's Robert R. Taylor Homes, the world's largest housing project with a 99 percent black occupancy rate, which *Ebony* called "a symbol of America's residential segregation."[44]

More generally, by mid-decade *Ebony* increasingly connected the space race to substandard housing in inner cities and rural towns as well as to the various forms of housing discrimination blacks faced. Despite the John-son administration's attempts to promote the space project as coexten-sive with the fight against poverty and intolerance in the Great Society, African American critics often drew a direct relationship between racism at NASA and racist government housing policies. They criticized Con-gress for pouring tax dollars into space while at the same time refusing to finance housing starts in inner cities and rural towns. In March 1965, *Ebony* reported on the test blasts for the manned moon rocket that were taking place in northern Alabama. The same article also told the story of the nearby town of Triana:

> Just five miles from the George C. Marshall Space Flight Center at Huntsville, Triana belongs more to the ante-bellum South than the era of astronauts. It is far from space-age—a collection of ramshackle farmhouses scattered randomly around two churches and a restau-rant. City hall is a renovated shack heated by a coal stove, and about the closest thing to recreation in Triana is the chance of sharing a few catfish from the sluggish Tennessee River. Ten minutes away scientists are plotting ways to conquer the universe. Triana does not even have its own water system. . . . The [Marshall] space center is nearby, but unskilled jobs are scarce. Today Trianans (an estimated 250, mostly Negroes) earn an average of less than $3,000 a year.[45]

The story then went on to discuss the way the town's new mayor (who was a programmer and analyst at the space center) was attempting to turn things around. Although the article proposed that the presence of the space center might indeed help raise the standard of living in Triana, it also reported that the mayor's efforts to bring Triana into the space age were met by a "familiar obstacle in Alabama—racism." Responding to this story in a subsequent issue, Wernher von Braun, Director of the Marshall Space Flight Center (and premiere German rocket scientist) congratulated the editors on the "perceptive article" on which he put a decidedly positive spin. Admitting that the people of Triana "live in the shadow of the test stand for the Saturn V moon rocket," he nevertheless concluded that the presence of NASA in the area was a "great leap forward." "Tiny Triana," he went on, "can hear and feel the impact of the Space Age first hand." Thus completely whitewashing the portrait of poverty that *Ebony* had previously painted, von Braun concluded, "Space exploration is causing us to revise our thinking. . . . All for the better I hope!" [46]

Meanwhile, in that same year the *Defender* described the racism in the nearby town of Huntsville, home to the Marshall Space Flight Center. Even while the *Defender* remained optimistic about space science, it too reported on the discrepancies between the highly funded space project and the state of housing in the town. Entitled "Huntsville: Famed for Space, Shamed for Race," the article began, "Huntsville, the space capital of the U.S., has yet to catch up with the space age in its efforts to solve the housing, educational and employment problems of the Negro." The story was especially timely because it appeared just a few days after Governor George Wallace and the State of Alabama hosted an "image building" bus tour that took some fifty journalists from across the country on a visit through the state. Designed to counteract what Wallace claimed was the national media's distorted view of Alabama, the tour showed journalists the "tree lined" streets of Huntsville, with "old homes covering endless blocks." Exposing Wallace's not-too-subtle whitewashing campaign, the *Defender* story gave readers a quite different tour through the streets of Huntsville. The story followed the struggles of Mrs. John Cashin, wife of the Chairman of the Community Service Committee who (with her four-year-old daughter) had been arrested trying to desegregate the lunch counters at Walgreen drug stores. "Fully able to build or buy property valued up to $50,000 . . . [Mrs. Cashin and her "young dentist" husband] are faced with the prospect of buying close to deteriorated property. 'You know there is only one street for Negroes to live on that is not in a slum location,' she said." The article further reported that "only 1 percent of the town's Negroes were employed by NASA and 50 percent of that number are holding menial jobs." All of this gave way to a more general consideration of the urban situation, as the *Defender* claimed that in Huntsville "urban renewal clears up the slums but lessens the amount of desirable housing available for Negroes. Huntsville, like most other cities, fails to build housing for the evicted tenants." [47]

It is interesting to compare the *Defender* article to a study of Huntsville published in 1962 by the business magazine *Fortune*, which presented a very different picture of the town's central conflict. The study discussed Huntsville's almost overnight transition from a nineteenth-century plantation town to a boom city filled with housing developments, new space-themed architecture, and an influx of workers at NASA and related industries. According to *Fortune*, the rapid transition brought on by the presence of the Marshall Space Flight Center had divided Huntsville in two parts. The town's "old settlers" lived in huge houses and ruled city hall. The newcomer space scientists and their wives thought of themselves as paragons of progressivism and clamored for better schools, more cultural events, and an "atmosphere of quiet worldliness." In thus representing Huntsville as a town divided by "warring camps" of old southerners and newcomer "eggheads," the *Fortune* editors never once mentioned the black population, housing discrimination, or the devastation that the urban renewal had wrought. In fact, the only time *Fortune* mentioned the black population was in its description of the town's nineteenth-century past.[48] In contrast, the *Defender*'s story of Huntsville clearly demystified the discourse on urban renewal promoted by business journals like *Fortune*.

More generally, in linking space travel to housing discrimination the black press brought the technical and seemingly rational discourses of science and city planning down to earth where they could be inspected for their more irrational, and clearly biased, foundational myths. As early as 1962, an editorial in *Ebony* did just that by exploring how the white "supremacy myth" had affected the lives of black men and women of all colors. The article is a strategic call to arms that connects NASA's sexism to the racism experienced by blacks in all walks of life, and especially in the inner city. Titled "In the Same Boat," the editorial was written in the wake of the congressional hearings held by the House Science and Astronautics Committee on the subject of women's participation (or lack thereof) in the space program. According to the editor, at the hearings the "male response to the female protests against 'for men only' trips to the moon sounded like a replay of white response to Negro protests against 'for white only' public services and facilities on the planet here below." The article went on to link NASA's white male bias to more general "male fears" about women and black men taking over their territory. "The twin fears—female invasion into a man's world and Negro domination of large

American cities—reflect the insecurity of the male whose only claim to superiority is based on myths. . . . The Negro's delinquency rate on mortgage loans is usually below the national average, and he improves rather than devaluates property purchased in good neighborhoods." Bridging the sexism of NASA to the racism of housing and inner cities, the magazine ended by calling for a coalition among black men and women in general:

> Today, the PTA is not enough to challenge the modern woman, nor will token integration satisfy the young Negro. Woman, still far from free of sex discrimination, should be the last to deny the four freedoms to another minority—and in many noteworthy instances, she is. She, with her infinite capacity for getting things done, and Negroes with their historic capacity for having things done to them, form a power that "superior" man can no longer ignore. If he is wise, he will lengthen his launching pad and add two more seats to his space ship, for his "inferiors" are in no mood to be left behind.[49]

Thus, while the article first considers actual acts of sexism at NASA and actual acts of racism in all walks of American life, it ends by using the spaceship as a metaphor through which to imagine a new political movement that would combat white male supremacy by convincing (presumably white PTA mothers) that it was in their interest to leave their racism at the door and bond with the Civil Rights movement. As one of the first explicit denouncements of NASA—and as the only essay that explicitly connected sexism and racism in such a way—the essay was certainly enigmatic for its time. Nevertheless, it did set the stage for the more sustained discourse of protest that continued in the years to come. That protest was particularly pronounced during the Apollo missions and especially during Apollo 11's historic flight to the moon.

"One Small Step for 'The Man'"

In the years leading up to Apollo 11, the black press became increasingly hostile to NASA's ventures into space, and it continued to see space travel in direct relation to housing discrimination and inner-city poverty back on earth. In a changing discursive and social context that combined the fight for Civil Rights with a new quest for black power, the press became impatient with the slow pace of change in government institutions and it increasingly embraced black cultural forms and heroes rooted in African rather than European ideals.[50]

To be sure, the black community was aware that NASA had in some respects responded to the charges of racism against the space project—especially in the wake of its firing of Edward Dwight. But in 1967, when NASA assigned Maj. Robert Lawrence Jr. as the first black astronaut, the assignment was viewed by many as too little too late, and in fact it was precluded by Lawrence's tragic death in a plane crash later that year. While extremely respectful of Lawrence's accomplishments, *Ebony*'s obituary was nevertheless quite different from the kind of coverage it gave to black space scientists in the early part of the decade.[51] The article referred to the fact that many in the black community viewed Lawrence as a "token," and it referenced the fact that Lawrence himself had laughed at the humor in Rap Brown's "alleged quip about America making a black astronaut 'just so's they can lose that nigger in space.'" Like others before it, this story was also predicated on the binary opposition between the inner city and suburbia. But now that opposition was depicted less as a black versus white binary than as a divide within the black community itself. According to *Ebony*, although Lawrence grew up in the city of Chicago, he was an "atypical urban ghetto youngster who easily obtained 'suburban' habits." Lawrence attended Englewood high school, which was populated mainly by students from the Woodlawn area "where resided most of the families who had begun claiming portions of the Dream made available by post-war tokenism." As his sister-in-law (who had worked for the Student Nonviolent Coordinating Committee [SNCC]) noted, "He was 'not revolutionary' in the political sense," even if he was not "insensitive to the growing criticism of the black man's role in the . . . space program."[52] In this case, even while *Ebony* honored Lawrence's accomplishments, it was clear that the figure of the black astronaut no longer served as a "hero." Instead, he became a symbol of both class and ideological divides in the black community.

Meanwhile, the white astronaut had become an even more contentious symbol. By 20 July 1969, when Apollo 11 landed on the moon, the African American press overwhelmingly addressed the space project within the context of discriminatory practices back on earth. The moon landing came in the wake of the 1968 Fair Housing Act, but the response to Apollo 11 shows absolutely no sign that the press believed the legislation would actually solve problems that plagued the poor and limited the life choices of people of color more generally. Instead, the press saw the moon landing as the final proof of the nation's fiscal and social agenda. While the space project was busy sending white men to the moon, housing projects were undermining the nature of African American life. An article in the September 1969 issue of *Ebony* reminded readers: "Especially to the nation's black poor, watching on unpaid-for television sets in shacks and slums, the countdowns, the blastoffs, the orbitings and landings had the other-worldly alienness—though not the drama—of a science fiction movie. From Harlem to Watts, the first moon landing in July of last year was viewed cynically as one small step for 'The Man,' and probably a giant step in the wrong direction for mankind." [53]

The editorial in the October issue took the critique one step further by drawing historical connections between the Apollo spaceship, slave ships, and the ships of European settlers. Claiming that "Columbus's discovery of America actually lead to one of the most infamous and long lasting rapes of all history," the editorial went on to describe the violence to indigenous people and to African populations who were shipped to the Americas in a "system of slavery of black people unmatched in the history of man." [54] Letters to the editor corroborated these sentiments. One student from Birmingham wrote that she would "proudly give an arm or a leg to be able to cheer Apollo 11 like the white folks on America's globe," but "as black as I am, I dare not cheer some $92.5 billion up in the sky when my black brothers and sisters [in Africa] . . . starve for food, wishing for the disappearance of ghettos, and for economic stability." [55] Another woman from Harlem, New York, wrote, "How magnificent it must have been to see the entire operation being carried out by someone who could have been you, your brother, your son, or more importantly, your father. . . ." But, she continued, "I saw no one who looked like me, nor my brother, nor my son, nor my father. For I am black, and so are they." [56]

Responses in the city papers continued with these themes, although with their own local inflections. In its lead front-page story, the *Amsterdam News* presented a report on reactions in the New York area. Titled "Mixed Emotions: Different Views," the article mostly featured quotes from citizens who "had praise for the endeavor, while at the same time underscoring man's earthbound problems." People commented:

I believe they should take the money and build homes and create jobs for the poor people here, before going up there to interfere with someone else's world.

I do think that billions of dollars should be spent down here on earth to alleviate suffering and injustices against minority groups.

The Moon flight to me and to all black people proves that the whites are not concerned about the black problem. They could have used ten percent of the money spent on the flight to help the black peoples.

The moon has been of interest to man throughout the centuries. I hope the astronauts themselves will catch some larger vision of life. The next time, hopefully, we spend $25 billions of dollars it will be on people.

I think it was a great achievement that man can leave the earth and sweep earthly problems under the rug. This means man can start colonizing the moon and have better excuse for keeping the bread and homes from national ghettoes which are also one of man's achievements.

I don't give a good god damn with whatever they do. I can't even find good employment because of that damn man's walk. Later for that man's walk. I hope they don't even get back.[57]

This story shared the same front-page location with another story about a middle-class black family in Houston whose father was an aerospace technologist in the Crew Systems Division of the Apollo mission. This story (which was at the bottom of the page) continued with the black press's early interest in contributions that black scientists made to the space project. In many ways it used similar conventions to those I've discussed in relation to the astronaut profiles in mainstream media. It followed the moon mission through the point of view of the middle-class NASA family who "gathered in the living room of their gracious home at 3826 Julius Lane in Houston."[58] But while this story presented the NASA family as happy middle-class suburbanites, its placement on the same page with the inner-city testimonials made for a quite different reading experience from the one that *Life* or *Look* had offered in its astronaut profiles. Instead, as in the case of *Ebony*'s homage to astronaut Robert

Lawrence, this black, suburban, space-age family seemed completely out of touch with their fellow African Americans living in the inner city.

Meanwhile, in Los Angeles the *Sentinel* featured damning editorials in the days leading up to the moon landing. Right after the launching of Apollo 11, the editor asked a series of rhetorical questions: "Will the flight to the moon find adequate housing for those people displaced by Urban Renewal? Will classrooms be added for children in overcrowded schools in the nation? Will these funds be diverted to the already over-burdened welfare departments that allow not nearly enough money for clients with large families?" Then, a few days after the moon walk, the *Sentinel* reminded readers that there were "thousands of hungry people who have no warm and comfortable homes in which to watch the first man on the moon."[59] A cartoon on the right side of the page showed Uncle Sam putting a flag on the moon, while the earth, somewhere in the distance, was inscribed with the caption, "First class citizenship for all Americans."[60]

The most complex example is provided by the *Defender*, which presented a highly contradictory set of responses to the trip to the moon. In the days leading up to Apollo's launch, the *Defender* presented coverage of the Southern Christian Leadership Conference (SCLC), which staged a "poor people's campaign" at Cape Kennedy. The 16 July edition featured a front-page photograph of picketers with a sign reading, "$12 a day to feed an astronaut. We could feed a starving child for $8." The next day, the front page sported a large cartoon that showed a black family watching as Apollo 11 soared to the moon. The caption next to the black family read, "Starving," and another caption placed near the moon read, "Cheese? . . . I hope it's cornbread." On that same day, the paper reported that the NAACP supported the picketing by SCLC.

Despite its coverage of SCLC, however, the *Defender* maintained its optimism about space travel and in fact embraced the moon landing in no uncertain terms. Perhaps one reason for this enthusiasm was the fact that reporter Harry Golden was a friend of a public relations officer at NASA who invited him to witness the launching of Apollo 11 (and Golden reported on this with great enthusiasm). More generally, however, the *Defender*'s support for the moon landing was consistent with its decade-long embrace of space flight, even in the face of NASA's alleged racism. On the day after the moon landing, the paper's front page flashed the bold-type headline, "Moon Shot Unites U.S. for Instant." A photo at the bottom of the page showed Neil Armstrong's famous walk and the caption exclaimed, "First Man on the Moon!" The story began, "The first non-racist moment in American history came at 3:17 P.M., Sunday, when two Americans—nestled snugly in their lunar craft—became the first men to walk on the moon. At this moment, people of every race, nationality, age and condition were united in praise for an achievement symbolic of the American genius." Speaking for the race, the magazine added, "This . . . was the unexpressed sentiments of millions of black Americans."[61]

Apparently, however, the *Defender* was not speaking for the race. In fact, the following day the paper published another editorial that clearly backtracked on its previous position. As in the *Amsterdam News,* this essay included testimonials (letters that the paper received in response to the previous day's lead story) that praised the achievement, but added cautionary advice. Warner Saudners, Director of the Better Boys Foundation, stated, "Now that this has been accomplished the same effort should be expended to overcome the social problems of the ghetto, and of poverty. . . ." Edwin Berry, Executive Director of the Urban League, claimed, "I hope that my statements take nothing away from the men who have worked on this fantastic accomplishment, but . . . it seems to me malnutrition of our young people, the ill-housed poor, and the problems in our major cities should have come well before going to the moon."[62] By the following week, the *Defender*'s editor and publisher John H. Sengstacke had reversed the paper's initial enthusiasm almost completely. In his editorial, "Lily-White NASA," Sengstacke admonished NASA for failing to train any black men as astronauts since the death (in 1967) of Maj. Robert H. Lawrence. He thought this exclusion was not simply an oversight but intentional. "The Pentagon," he wrote, "has seen to it that [no other black man] is selected for that training." Then he concluded with a not-too-veiled threat: "In truth, there are virtually no Negroes involved in the National Aeronautics and Space Administration. . . . This is typical American racism in action. Like all other areas of racial bias in American life which had to be assaulted by picketing and militant demonstrations, NASA awaits its baptism of racial fire before it integrates its space program."[63] These sentiments resonated in the *Defender* for quite some time. From fall 1969 through spring 1970, the *Defender* carried cartoons that spoofed the space program, especially with regard to issues of hunger and poverty.[64] While I have no direct evidence, it seems that the *Defender*'s reversal of opinion was most likely the result of reader protests. In any

Before and after the moon landing, the *Chicago Daily Defender* published cartoons like this one, which appeared on 20 November 1969. (Copyright, Sengstacke Newspapers)

case, the incident does bring to light the degrees of divided opinion within the black community, while it also suggests the more widespread feeling (in both urban papers and the national magazine *Ebony*) that the tax dollars spent on outer space would be better used on the inner cities and the ill-housed, ill-fed poor in all areas of the world.

It is important as well to note that the dialogue in the black press was not conducted in complete isolation from white culture. As is often noted, physician Benjamin Spock and novelists Norman Mailer and Tom Wolfe were among the space project's biggest critics. At the time of the moon landing, the mainstream press took an ambivalent stand, at times spectacularizing and at other times criticizing Apollo 11's mission. While less overwhelmingly negative than the black press, these venues also sometimes argued that tax dollars would be better spent on social welfare. In addition, by the time of the moon landing the mainstream media began to incorporate the outer-space/inner-city opposition that had become the common trope for black journalists. What resulted in these cases was a kind of imaginary dialogue between white and black America, a dialogue that revolved less around outer space itself than around the racialized "politics of dwelling" back on earth.

Nowhere was this better rehearsed than in the CBS news special "A Day in the Life of the United States," which was broadcast on the day of the moon landing. The documentary featured reporter Charles Kuralt who took to the road in a quest to understand what Americans were doing and thinking on the day that the Apollo crew landed on the moon. His cross-country voyage provided a special glimpse into the geography of American everyday life, displaying the way "families" were rooted and uprooted as NASA staked its flag on an alien landscape. Claiming that "family life is the prime concern of most Americans," the documentary begins with the birth of a little boy, and then shows families boating, a mother serving breakfast, a family eating dinner while watching the Apollo coverage, and another family at a barbecue. During his travels, Kuralt visits a family in a small Montana town; he watches a Vietnam pilot and his wife reunite at an airforce base in San Francisco; he follows a family of Yugoslavian immigrants arriving in New York, awestruck by the city; he goes to Hawaii where he chats with "natives"; he visits a commune and points out with irony that no one there can operate technology; and he goes to New York City where he remarks, "A city is a machine and the city machine is breaking down." The proposed reason for the urban breakdown was clarified when he traveled to the inner reaches of a "slum's slum" in Chicago. There, the cameras penetrated a barroom on Langly and 43rd streets, gaping at African Americans dancing and drinking "cheap wine" in a world unimpressed by the white man's exploits in space. Significantly, in the era of the Moynihan Report—which perpetuated the notion that the black man's lack of paternal responsibility was to blame for the welfare state—this Chicago barroom was a decidedly impoverished and nonfamilial space, a space quite unlike those seen in previous segments.

This segment was also the only one in which the white Charles Kuralt was substituted with George Foster, an "insider" black reporter who explained:

> We've been here since Jamestown. But we haven't cleared customs yet. Four hundred years of traveling, and it's been economy class all the way. . . . Some of my brothers live another culture, talk another language, and you gotta subtitle them like you'd translate the astro-

nauts. . . . I can tell you this about July 1969 at 43rd and Langly in Chicago, Illinois. I can tell you that nobody there understood or even listened to the language of the moon shot. That man on the right with the rolled up *Chicago Times,* with the headlines about Apollo 11, he told me he bought that paper to look at the want ads.

Here, the discussion about race, urban poverty, and outer space was self-consciously expressed in terms of a breakdown of communication, a use of different language systems in black and white America (and a switch from white to black narrators to drive home the point). Among these different languages were the separate and racialized metaphors used to describe national geography. In this documentary as elsewhere, the metaphorical links between outer space and white suburban family life were consistently set in opposition to the racialized inner city and its degraded "slum" housing that opened onto an equally degraded public sphere (or what this segment actually referred to as a "nigger bar"). This strange exploration of everyday life on the day of the moon landing presented a nation divided between rich and poor, citizen and castoff, black and white, and these divisions all overdetermined the schisms between cities, suburbs, and rural towns. In this documentary as elsewhere, the metaphor of travel—whether interplanetary, international, or cross-country— served as a vehicle for an investigation of American family life, or the lack thereof, in different communities and among different races.

Space Is the Place

While the African American press often linked housing discrimination and poverty to the nation's misconceived goals in space, for some people of color space travel nevertheless did provide a source of inspiration from which to imagine a better life. Just as Rose Viega thought the astronaut program might take her someplace past the discrimination of her racist town, numerous people imagined outer space as a new unbounded landscape on which social relationships might be improved. Starting in the late 1950s, and increasingly by the 1970s, artists working in different media began to write a counternarrative in which space was, to use Sun Ra's famous phrase, "the place."

This counternarrative was less invested in mapping distinctions between cities, suburbs, or even nations than it was in imagining a black diaspora, an imagined space of collective identity formed through shared experience, struggles, and memories. The otherwordly iconography and aural alterity of science fiction stories had a special connection to the construction of this black diaspora. As Janice Cheddie has argued, the "image of the (space) ship, as a vehicle for redemptive return to a pre-diasporic Africa . . . stands prominent in the development in what has been dubbed Afro Futurism," a movement that includes, among others, Sun Ra's avant-garde jazz, the recordings of Lee Perry's Black Arc studio, George Clinton's *Mothership Connection,* and the novels of Octavia Butler and Samuel Delany. Following Paul Gilroy, Cheddie claims that the image of the ship has been central to the African diasporic critique of modernity.[65] The spaceship in these terms serves as a repository for the construction of racial memories, and it allows for the creation of new imagined communities that don't respect national or even (in the case of Sun Ra and other artists) galactic borders. In this sense, the image of the ship allows for an exploration of black double-consciousness in the Western world.

Within this ethos, Sun Ra and his Arkestra (a band that he renamed hundreds of times) depicted outer space as an imaginary place for a newly emerging African diaspora. Linked to "back to Africa" sentiments, Sun Ra's brand of Afro Futurism replotted the Western myth of technological progress through the spiritual, nonlinear cosmologies of ancient Egypt. By the late 1950s, Sun Ra increasingly combined his interest in Egypt with images and sounds of the space age, recording such albums as *We Travel the Space Ways* and *Rocket Number Nine Take Off for the Planet Venus* (both of which were not released until 1966). For performances, he designed costumes that referenced different national and cultural styles, and by the end of the 1950s he dressed in space suits (he was especially famous for his elaborately stylized headgear pieces that were at once crowns and helmets). Space served as a powerful metaphor for black alienation in the Western world, and in this regard Sun Ra explicitly identified with the figure of the space alien, often stating that he did not come from the planet earth, and denying his birth name altogether. By 1972, the cover art to the *Space Is the Place* album presented Sun Ra (in his literal meaning) as an Egyptian sun god with a kind of space-age orb nestled in his head crown. He and his Astro Intergalactic Infinity Arkestra played (what critics called) "free style" jazz compositions[66] while intermittent vocals from back-up singers "Space Ethnic Voices" provided otherworldly sounds. His barely distributed film of the same title also deployed hybrid styles, mixing genres of documentary, science fiction, blaxploitation, and biblical epic. The plot of *Space Is the Place* revolves around Sun Ra who, traveling on a rocket ship propelled by music, locates a planet he finds suitable for the resuscitation of the black race. He then goes back to Oakland, California, to convince others to follow him to space and seek an "alter destiny," but is thwarted by a supernatural pimp who profits from the degradation of black people. Although Sun Ra wasn't happy with the results, the film continued with a counternarrative about space and race that was central to his art. His performances further pursued this counternarrative, with slide shows and lighting that referenced the space-age theme. As biographer/anthropologist John Szwed argues, for Sun Ra "space was both a metaphor of exclusion and of reterritorialization, of claiming the 'outside' as one's own, of tying a revised and corrected past to a claimed future. Space was a metaphor which transvalues the dominant terms so that they become aberrant, a minority position, while the terms of the outside, the beyond, the margins, become standard." [67]

Important to his conception as well was the idea that technology might be embraced for purposes other than Western notions of "progress" (whether progress was seen in purely aggressive, military terms of the cold war or in Kennedy's "peaceful uses of space" ethos). If blacks were imaginatively "going back to Africa" they weren't simply going back to nature (or to their status as "modern primitives" in Western science). Instead, technology (both the spaceships alluded to in the songs and the recording technology and instruments themselves) could be used as a vehicle through which to circulate redemptive memories and to chart a course for the future. In this regard, Sun Ra thought of his art as a science and referred to his band as "tone scientists." In his view, his music was "not science as we know it, but another kind. I've been looking for a solution which goes back to Egypt, and to the whole universe. I think musicians are on a superior level, but unlike scientists, they haven't been accepted for their abilities." [68] Explaining Sun Ra's thoughts within the larger historical context, Szwed argues, "African Americans have always talked cosmology with a pre-modern ease, a discourse distantly rooted in African conceptions of the cosmos, but yet also shaped by modern science and tempered by a wariness of how science had sometimes been used against them." [69]

George Clinton and his band Parliament continued in this vein, although they did so with reference to the mythos of the Nation of Islam, and in particular the mythical prophesy of the "Mothership," a huge spaceship that would supposedly end white domination by attacking the earth and destroying the enemies of Allah. Released in 1975, Parliament's *Mothership Connection* pointed to an African diaspora through an unlikely collision of folk and mass culture. While he did make reference to the pyramids, Clinton (who produced the album) was more interested in putting space into a "funkadelic" mix. The first cut, "P. FUNK (Wants to Get Funked UP)," begins with an allusion to *The Outer Limits*'s famous introductory credit sequence, "There is nothing wrong with your television set. Do not attempt to adjust the picture. We are controlling transmission." But this time Clinton (posing as a DJ/spaceship captain) tells us "do not attempt to adjust your radio" because he and his "extraterrestrial brothers" are controlling radio station WPFUNK, also known as the "Mothership." Thus reclaiming (both everyday and extraordinary) technology for African American uses, Clinton ironically "abducts" the mass media's image of the space alien for his own funky mission. The cover art of the album shows Clinton drawn (pulp fiction and comic book style) in a disco-era spacesuit, emerging from the door of a flying saucer that is soaring through space. The back cover shows him sitting on the UFO parked in front of a tenement building with garbage strewn on the pavement. With its juxtaposition of the inner city and outer space, the cover offers itself to be read as an ironic (and funny) critique of the relationship between the space project and housing projects. Nevertheless, the *Mothership Connection* is very much a utopian voyage that evokes its place in previous genres of black inspirational music. The title song's refrain, "Swing low, sweet chariot, stop, and let me ride" is sung by the band's Extraterrestrial Voices and Good Time Hand Clappers, a kind of gospel choir for the space age. In spoken verse, a voice (which sounds like it might belong to a robot preacher from Mars) says, "Swing low / Time to move on/ Light years in time / Ahead of our time / Free your mind and come fly with me / It's hip on the mothership."

The legacy of both Sun Ra and Clinton's Parliament resurfaced in the 1980s with, for example, Afrika Bambaataa, and again in the 1990s and early 2000 with science-fiction influenced themes voiced by Method Man, Gangsta Nip, Dr. Octogon, and especially Kool Keith's 1999 release *Black Elvis/Lost in Space*. Kool Keith creates hybrid forms by literally "slashing" Elvis with space-themed electronic raps like "Rockets in the Battlefield" and "Livin' Astro." On the front (all-green) cover of the

CD, Kool Keith appears as kind of space-age gangsta Elvis posed against the solar system; on the (all-red) back of the cover he is in a space suit and helmet. A graph-paper grid is laid on top of the images and evokes a sense of digitization that also pervades the music. Yet, despite its "programmed" sensibility, *Black Elvis/Lost in Space* conjures up memories of Afro Futurists from the past. Noting the historical debt that the album owes to its predecessors, *Rolling Stone* writes, "Kool Keith is to rap as Sun Ra is to jazz and George Clinton is to funk."[70]

The hybrid and diasporic imaginings of musicians like Sun Ra, Clinton, and more recent artists like Kool Keith demonstrate that outer space has served as a metaphor for spiritual travel and the reappropriation of the places and technologies of everyday life. That said, it is still the case that Clinton's "mothership," and other such diasporic metaphors of space travel, may not always be so progressive for black women. With its semantic connotations of "woman as vehicle" for male journeys, the mothership does little to address black women's agency in the construction of an (imagined) future and the memory of a collective past. As Cheddie argues with reference to the image of the ship more generally, "its associations with slavery, indenture and migration as a metaphor for displacement is one that is fraught with problems for the Black woman. For although Black women shared these experiences with their male counterparts, the image of the ship as a 'social space' is associated most significantly with the experience of male power."[71] While Cheddie is on point, there are ways in which the space race and the image of the spaceship did open up dialogues about black women's agency, and especially their role within the science and engineering professions. These dialogues took place not only in the pages of *Ebony* with its profiles on women scientists and engineers but also in the science fiction genre of later decades. While not always about space travel per se, Octavia Butler tells stories about alien presence and telepathic communication that highlight female authority and sexual desire. Samuel Delany uses the mise-en-scène of outer space to defamiliarize heterosexuality and explore the boundaries between masculinity and femininity. (And, perhaps more disputably, we might even say that contemporary artists such as Kool Keith are exploring the links between white and black machismo by presenting a hybrid mix of rock icons, space heroes, and gangsta poses.)

To be sure, most people in the 1960s would not have imagined that

MARCH 9, 1978/75¢ 64060 A JOHNSON PUBLICATION **First Visit With New Astronauts**

JET

MAJ. FREDERICK D. GREGORY

DR. RONALD E. McNAIR

MAJ. GUION S. BLUFORD JR.

In its 9 March 1978 issue, *Jet* magazine celebrated the new astronauts, focusing on Guion S. Bluford Jr. who in 1983 became the first African American to travel into space.

their discussions of the space race would lead to these African diasporas and sexual reconfigurations. But, perhaps the most interesting thing about the space race is precisely its unpredictable trajectories. The linear Western logic of the space race and NASA's obsession with being first on the moon did not, in the end, result in a singular destiny. Instead, the cultural meanings of the space race took multiple routes and arrived in unexpected places. One of the compelling reasons for this was the history of race relations itself. While black Americans often took an interest in NASA and hoped to participate in space science, their interests were ultimately formed against a history of struggle over access to the spaces of everyday life. If white America sought to colonize space with images of happy space-age families living in suburban bliss, in African American culture space travel was articulated against the strife of inner cities, unfair housing, the racism of public transportation, unequal access to the scientific professions, and the fight to end those and other inequities. Space flight was also imagined within the redemptive logic of music, poetry, novels, and performances that reclaimed space science for a new place in time.

Notes

1 Rose Viega, letter to President Kennedy, 28 March 1962, White House Central Staff Files, box 655: folder 054, John Fitzgerald Kennedy Library, Boston, Massachusetts (hereafter referred to as JFK Library). See also the reply from Ralph A. Dungan, Special Assistant to the President, 21 June 1962, White House Central Staff Files, box 655: folder 054, JFK Library, where he tells Rose Viega that her letter is being forwarded to NASA "for whatever information they may be able to send you regarding the qualifications of a female astronaut." He also tells her that the President is "dedicated to take every necessary and proper step to end discrimination."

2 In fact, apart from some brief blurbs, the only articles I found pertained to NASA's hiring and firing of black astronaut candidate Edward Dwight, astronaut Robert Lawrence Jr., and the moon landing itself. These articles are discussed later on. I looked at every issue of all newspapers and *Ebony* from 1958 to 1969. Note also that the *Defender* had a national edition that carried considerable amounts of United Press International copy even while it privileged news stories pertinent to the Chicago location. Although I did not read any southern papers or the more special-interest papers like *Muhammad Speaks,* such research would be an important addition to my own efforts. For a general analysis of the black press during this period, see Roland E. Wolseley, *The Black Press, U.S.A.* (Ames: Iowa State University Press, 1971).

3 David Nye, *Narrative Spaces: Technology and the Construction of American Culture* (New York: Columbia University Press, 1997), p. 151. These calculations are based on his summary of nationwide Harris polls from 1965 to 1969 and his review of black newspapers during the Apollo 11 event.

4 See my essay "White Flight," in *The Revolution Wasn't Televised: Sixties Television and Social Conflict,* ed. Lynn Spigel and Michael Curtin (New York: Routledge, 1997), pp. 47–71; and my essay "From Domestic Space to Outer Space," this volume.

5 Arnold R. Hirsch, "With or Without Jim Crow: Black Residential Segregation in the United States," in *Urban Policy in Twentieth-Century America,* ed. Arnold R. Hirsch and Raymond A. Mohl (New Brunswick, N.J.: Rutgers University Press, 1993), p. 90. Hirsch also details the stubborn rates of integration across U.S. cities and suburbs through the 1980s. For more on the FHA and the difficulties enforcing housing legislation, see Kenneth T. Jackson, *Crabgrass Frontier: The Suburbanization of the United States* (New York: Oxford University Press, 1985); and George Lipsitz, *The Possessive Investment in Whiteness: How White People Profit from Identity Politics* (Philadelphia: Temple University Press, 1998). Lipsitz points out that

"Title VIII of the Fair Housing Act authorized the Department of Housing and Urban Development to investigate complaints made directly to the HUD secretary but forbade the agency to initiate investigations on its own. The act gave the HUD secretary only thirty days to process complaints and to decide if action was warranted, but even if the agency pursued cases, it had no enforcement power and could only encourage the party guilty of discrimination to accept 'conference, conciliation, and persuasion.' " He adds that only in rare cases could HUD refer cases to the Attorney General for legal action (pp. 28–29).

6 Hirsch, "With or Without Jim Crow," p. 92.

7 Jackson, *Crabgrass Frontier*, p. 213.

8 Arnold R. Hirsch, *Making the Second Ghetto: Race and Housing in Chicago, 1940–1960* (Chicago: University of Chicago Press, 1998).

9 Lipsitz, *The Possessive Investment in Whiteness*, p. 6.

10 Robert D. Bullard and Glenn S. Johnson, "Just Transportation," in Robert D. Bullard and Glenn S. Johnson, eds., *Just Transportation: Dismantling Race and Class Barriers to Mobility* (Gabriola Island, B.C.: New Society, 1997) pp. 7–8. The editors also note that by cutting through neighborhoods the freeways "isolated residents from their institutions and businesses," "created traffic gridlock," and "subjected residents to elevated risks from accidents, spills, and explosions from vehicles carrying hazardous chemicals and other dangerous materials" (p. 8). In the same collection, a number of authors discuss the effects of transportation in many areas of the United States, and they also discuss activist groups and policies for change.

11 Lipsitz, *The Possessive Investment in Whiteness*. Lipsitz also speaks of education, labor, and environmental policies that allowed for this possessive investment in whiteness. He provides a tremendously useful analysis of the various social polices (and the lack of enforcement of Civil Rights legislation) through which white hegemony has been maintained in the postwar era.

12 While I have designated "physical" space as something other than "imaginary" (or what some might call symbolic) space, this designation is more a function of semantics than it is my actual point. Rather than seeing physical space as separate from the symbolic practices through which space is mapped (city planning, architecture, etc.) or as separate from the symbolic practices that create the imaginary spaces of stories/images, it seems more useful to understand how these kinds of space work in connection with one another to produce our lived experience of space itself. In other words, it's not possible in the end to separate physical space from the symbols used to demarcate it or the codes used to imaginatively interpret and appropriate it. This is why I think media analysis has a crucial place in the analysis of space and critical geography. For classic analyses of space along these lines, see Henri Lefebvre, *The Production of Space*, trans. Donald Nicholson-Smith (Oxford: Blackwell, 1991); and Edward W. Soja's explication and expansion of Lefebvre in *Third Space: Journey to Los Angeles and Other Real-and-Imagined Places* (Oxford: Blackwell, 1996).

13 Gussie Davis, "I Just Got a Message from Mars," 1896, Devincent Sheet Music

Collection, box 94:300, Smithsonian Institution, Washington, D.C. Most of the other sheet music in this box is nineteenth-century love songs about the moon.

14 Carolyn Marvin, *When Old Technologies Were New: Thinking about Electric Communications in the Late Nineteenth Century* (New York: Oxford University Press, 1988). Marvin also discusses the way professional journals stigmatized women, the working class, rural people, and children.

15 Throughout the years of the space race, *Ebony* noted that the scientific profession was still exclusionary. For example, in the December 1959 issue (p. 6), it claimed that the magazine *Science*, the organ of the leading professional organization, the American Association for the Advancement of Science, had only one black worker on staff—the magazine's proofreader.

16 For example, in his 1962 address "The Future of Manned Space Flight, and the Freedom of Outer Space," John A. Johnson (General Counsel for NASA) spoke of America's mission to ensure that space exploration remain free and open to all states, and that "celestial bodies . . . are not subject to national appropriation." (Of course, he never addressed the fact that most nations would not have the money required for space exploration.) For this and other documents regarding public relations at NASA, see NASA Collection, Wisconsin State Historical Society, Madison, Wisconsin.

17 These phrases are excerpted from the script for a speech that Kennedy delivered before the National Association of Broadcasters. See Office of the White House Press Secretary, "The White House Address of the President to the Opening Session of the Thirty-ninth Annual Convention of the National Association of Broadcasters," draft of speech, 9 January 1961–25 May 1961, President's Office Files/Speech Files, box 34, p. 1, JFK Library. Note that the speech was covered on the television news, the original film for which is housed at the JFK Library under the title "JFK Accompanied by Shepard," NBC, 8 May 1961. In the film clip, which appears to be edited, it is not clear whether or not Kennedy actually read any of the written speech verbatim, but his comments are in general keeping with its overall message. For more on Kennedy's use of television for the promotion of the space program, see my essay "White Flight," in *The Revolution Wasn't Televised: Sixties Television and Social Conflict*, ed. Lynn Spigel and Michael Curtin (New York: Routledge, 1997), pp. 47–71. For the classic account of the political history of the space race, see Walter A. McDougall, . . . *The Heavens and the Earth: A Political History of the Space Age* (New York: Basic Books, 1985). For essays on space policy from the Eisenhower through the Bush administrations, see Roger D. Launius and Howard E. McCurdy, eds., *Spaceflight and the Myth of Presidential Leadership* (Urbana: University of Illinois Press, 1997).

18 I am paraphrasing a 1965 speech that Vice President Hubert Humphrey gave before NASA officials. He said, "Let me assure you that the Great Society envisioned by President Johnson is not one limited to the fight against poverty, ignorance, disease, and intolerance. The Great Society requires, in addition, an urgent quest for excellence, for intellectual attainment, for crossing new frontiers in science and technology. Let me emphasize that an adequately funded, well-directed space pro-

gram is an integral part of our nation's commitment to its future, to its greatness."
Given the audience, this statement seems directed at allaying fears that social welfare would cut into the nation's scientific agenda. The speech is cited in Robert
Dallek, "Johnson, Project Apollo, and the Politics of Space Program Planning,"
in *Spaceflight and the Myth of Presidential Leadership*, p. 78. Dallek also explains
that while Johnson supported the moon landing, the budget did not vigorously
support post-Apollo projects.

19 Dallek, "Johnson, Project Apollo, and the Politics of Space Program Planning,"
p. 78.

20 In an interesting argument, Jodi Dean proposes "that the failure of space exploration to inspire, to symbolize the future, is . . . an effect of the contradictions
arising out of NASA's preoccupation with openness, freedom, and democracy. . . .
By Apollo's end, it was more than clear that the astronaut could not represent
Americans or America. The raced, sexed, gendered, and classed specifications of
the astronauts excluded too many Americans." See Jodi Dean, *Aliens in America:
Conspiracy Cultures from Outerspace to Cyberspace* (Ithaca, N.Y.: Cornell University Press, 1998), p. 96.

21 John J. Gilbride, Mildred L. Pierce, Elizabeth Ann Chauppette, and Robert Reed,
letter to President Kennedy, 4 October 1962, White House Central Staff Files,
box 655: folder 054-1, JFK Library. In that same year, Edward Wynne, Assistant General Counsel of the Textile Workers Union, criticized the space project.
In a letter to the White House he said, "I don't think any proposed astronauts
are Negroes. . . . Can't this be remedied? I suppose its international implications
are even more important than the domestic political one. The Russians don't have
any Negroes to shoot into space." Given the rather strange wording of this last
sentence, it is hard to say exactly what Wynne's race politics were, but the full
text of his letter makes it clear he interpreted NASA's anticommunist, prodemo-
cratic stance in relation to the need for black representation in the space program.
Edward Wynne, letter to Meyer Feldman, Deputy Special Counsel to the President, 4 October 1962, White House Central Staff Files, box 655: folder 054-1, JFK
Library.

22 Lee C. White, Assistant Special Counsel to the President, letter to Misses Pierce
and Chauppette and Messrs. Gilbridge and Reed, 12 October 1962, White House
Central Staff Files, box 655: folder 054-1, JFK Library. The letter further stipulated the qualifications needed to become an astronaut. This "qualifications"
clause was a typical way NASA justified the exclusion of women and people of
color from the space program. However, as I discuss later, women and people of
color protested the clause.

23 For review of African American contributions to the space project—both in the
early years and through the decades—see Curtis M. Graves and Ivan Van Sertima,
"Space Science: The African American Contribution," pp. 228-57, and James G.
Spady, "Blackspace," pp. 258-65, both in *Blacks in Science: Ancient and Modern*,
ed. Ivan Van Sertima (New Brunswick, N.J.: Transaction Books, 1991). Additional
reviews of African American women's contributions to space science and space

flight can be found in Wini Warren, *Black Women Scientists in the United States* (Bloomington: Indiana University Press, 1999).

24 *Ebony*, May 1958, p. 19. Responding to this story in a subsequent issue, a student at Illinois Institute of Technology thanked the editor for the "fine article," and added, "I now know that I am not the only Negro who is deeply interested in science." Paul J. Whiteweir Jr., letter to the editor, *Ebony*, October 1958, p. 10, 12.

25 In the latter part of the decade, IBM ran ads in *Ebony* inviting readers to apply for training courses and positions as space technicians, programmers, and analysts. See, for example, *Ebony*, August 1966, p. 19; and *Ebony*, July 1968, p. 118.

26 "Space Age Research Chemist," *Ebony*, April 1961, p. 6. A second profile on Willard was featured in *Ebony*, August 1962, p. 6.

27 "Missile School Analyst," *Ebony*, February 1961, p. 7; "Space-Computing Mathematician," *Ebony*, August 1960, 7; "Negroes Who Help Conquer Space," *Ebony*, May 1958, p. 24; "Space Vehicle Engineer," *Ebony*, March 1962, p. 6; "NASA Experimental Psychologist," *Ebony*, August 1963, p. 6; "Space Center's Section Head," *Ebony*, May 1965, p. 6. In 1962, Ebony also ran a feature on Los Angeles high school student Alexis Jackson, titled "Top Science Scholar Visits Los Almos." The article detailed Alexis's tour of the "space age defense" plant, showing her looking at the Ranger III rocket. See *Ebony*, April 1962, pp. 89–93.

28 "Woman Engineer," *Ebony*, December 1961, pp. 87–92. An article on the Seattle World's Fair similarly used the trope of "beauty plus brains" when discussing a college student who was the "only Negro girl among 40 coeds employed as science demonstrators at the U.S. Science Exhibit." The article told readers that "the little tan miss" Merlie Ann Burton "combines beauty with brains." See "U.S. Science Demonstrator," *Ebony*, September 1962, pp. 119–25.

29 "Fashions in Orbit," *Ebony*, October 1965, pp. 163–68 and cover. *Ebony* also promised that the "Fashions in Orbit" show would tour numerous U.S. cities so that readers could get a close-up look. The "Fashions in Orbit" show was part of *Ebony*'s "Fashion Fair" tour, which regularly traveled from city to city. Liquor companies such as Hiram Walker, Smirnoff, and Heilemann (makers of Colt 45) also represented the space race as hip cultural fashion. See *Ebony*, May 1969, p. 24; *Ebony*, February 1969, p. 35; and *Ebony*, August 1967, p. 81.

30 *Ebony*, November 1969, p. 73.

31 *Ebony*, May 1963, p. 10.

32 "Annual Vacation Guide: The New York World's Fair," *Ebony*, June 1964, pp. 166–74 and cover.

33 "Annual Vacation Guide," *Ebony*, June 1967, pp. 140–42. In April (just one month after the Urban League leveled its charges), fair officials ran an ad in *Ebony* that presented Expo as a nonbiased organization. The ad told *Ebony* readers "*Your* accommodations in Montreal are guaranteed, at government-controlled prices" (emphasis theirs). The ad displayed a huge American flag as a background with a black teenage boy jumping for joy directly over it. The caption read, "your son the American" and the text promised that at the U.S. Pavilion you could watch

your son "glow with pride at the achievements of his own country. He may even meet an astronaut." *Ebony,* April 1967, p. 83.

34 In 1965, on the occasion of its twentieth anniversary, *Ebony* took on these criticisms. The magazine invited author-poet Langston Hughes to write a historical assessment of the magazine. Hughes argued, "The careless charge some critics have made that *Ebony* presents only successful Negroes, colorful sports and entertainment personalities and pretty fashion models is not true. . . . While the main emphasis has been on the presentation of the positive side of Negro achievement, *Ebony* has not hesitated to face the grim realities of such ugly episodes in American life as the Emmett Till lynching or the Birmingham brutalities and to present them in all their horror." Langston Hughes, "*Ebony*'s Nativity: An Evaluation from Birth," *Ebony,* November 1965, pp. 40–46. Meanwhile, publisher/editor John Johnson implicitly addressed the same criticisms by suggesting that the magazine had become more outspoken on racism over the years. His publisher's statement claimed, "From a magazine that gloried in the accomplishments of successful Negroes in the early years, it has become a spokesman for the full and equal treatment of all Negroes in this day and age." John H. Johnson, "Publisher's Statement," *Ebony,* November 1965, p. 27.

35 bell hooks, *Black Looks: Race and Representation* (Boston: South End Press, 1992), pp. 165–78.

36 Robin D. Kelly, *Race Rebels: Culture, Politics, and the Black Working Class* (New York: Free Press, 1994), chapter 3. Kelly argues that the black working class in Birmingham often adopted more militant strategies than did many leaders of the Civil Rights movement and black middle class. He also argues that black women took an active role in the bus protests and that "unlike the popular image of Rosa Park's quiet resistance, most black women's opposition tended to be militant and profane" (p. 68).

37 *Ebony,* November 1962, p. 71. The ad also ran in *Ebony,* January 1963, p. 8. Note that in July 1961, prompted by the Freedom Riders' experience on Greyhound, the *Los Angeles Sentinel* took the bus company to task in an editorial and a front-page news blurb. The newspaper stated, "No living person can remember seeing a Negro drive a Greyhound bus out of the Sixth and Los Angeles Depot." See "Greyhound Negro Driver Countdown," *Los Angeles Sentinel,* 6 July 1961, p. 1.

38 *Chicago Daily Defender,* 22 March 1965, p. 1.

39 Thelma Hunt Shirley and Skip Bossetee, "Chicago's 'A-Day': A Big Success!," *Chicago Daily Defender,* 15 June 1965, pp. 1, 3. There were cases where it seems clear that Civil Rights leaders understood the value of staging protests near NASA facilities and events. Because NASA received so much media attention, the protests would be more likely to be covered on local or even national news. For example, a few months before the Chicago parade, another demonstration was held in front of the Houston Manned Space Craft Center the day that the Gemini astronauts first returned from space. This time, the demonstrators were protesting the pace of integration in Houston schools. According to the *Defender,* the group of pro-

testers was composed mostly of white high school children who were led by a public relations executive for People for the Upgrading of Schools in Houston (PUSH). The picketers carried placards with slogans such as "space age city—stone age schools." In this case it seems probable that PUSH assumed their protest would get media attention if they connected it to the highly mediated events surrounding space travel. See "Picket Space Center," *Chicago Daily Defender,* 7 June 1965, p. 2. Another such incident came on the eve of the Apollo 11, when the Poor People's Campaign arrived at Cape Kennedy in wagons pulled by mules. Protesting against national spending on the space race, they literally made a spectacle of themselves that challenged the spectacle of the launch itself. (Ironically, as David Nye points out, the protesters also "demanded 40 VIP passes to see [Apollo 11] close-up." See Nye, "Don't Fly Me to the Moon," p. 152.)

40   Louie Robinson, "First Negro Astronaut Candidate," *Ebony,* July 1963, pp. 71–81.

41   Charles L. Saunders, "The Troubles of 'Astronaut' Edward Dwight," *Ebony,* June 1965, pp. 29–36. The article spoke of a report written by Dwight that listed "page after page of 'racial pressure.'" The article also said the Department of Defense had not responded to Dwight's charges. Saunders then detailed his conversation with an anonymous source at the Department of Defense who filled him in on the case.

42   Letters to the editor, *Ebony,* August 1965, pp. 12, 14.

43   "Negro Astronaut Hit by Race Bias; Seeks Aid of LBJ," *New York Amsterdam News,* 5 June 1965, pp. 1–2; "Bias Ejects First Negro Astronaut," *Los Angeles Sentinel,* 3 June 1965, p. 1. Both newspapers had earlier covered NASA's appointment of Dwight in 1963; the story was front-page news in the *Sentinel.* See "Astronaut Trainee Itching to Go into Orbit for U.S.," *Los Angeles Sentinel,* 6 June 1963, p. 1. The *Defender,* which continued to be more supportive of NASA, questioned *Ebony*'s, and Dwight's, conclusions regarding racial bias, but it nevertheless reported the allegations.

44   Hamilton J. Bims, "Housing—The Hottest Issue in the North," *Ebony,* August 1965, pp. 93–100. This article was in the issue entitled "The White Problem in America."

45   Hamilton Bims, "Rocket Age Comes to Tiny Triana," *Ebony,* March 1965, pp. 106–12.

46   Wernher von Braun, letter to the editor, *Ebony,* May 1965, p. 17.

47   Rosemarie Tyler Brooks, "Huntsville: Famed for Space, Shamed for Race," *Chicago Daily Defender,* 10 June 1965, p. 6.

48   Paul O'Neil, "The Anachronistic Town of Huntsville," in *The Space Industry: America's Newest Giant,* ed. the editors of *Fortune* (Englewood Cliffs, N.J.: Prentice-Hall, 1962), pp. 49–64.

49   "In the Same Boat," *Ebony,* October 1962, p. 72.

50   For an analysis of African American heroes during this period, see William L. Van Deburg, *Black Camelot: African American Culture Heroes in Their Times, 1960–1980* (Chicago: University of Chicago Press, 1997).

51 It should be noted that *Ebony* continued to report on other black Americans who held positions in the space program. However, as is obvious in this case, its attitude toward the space program itself became increasingly less optimistic.

52 David Llorens, "A Farewell to an Astronaut," *Ebony,* February 1968, pp. 91–92, 94.

53 Steven Morris, "How Blacks View Mankind's 'Giant Step,'" *Ebony,* September 1969, p. 33. According to the article, there was a new demand for black employees in the space industry because these companies were subject to federal contract clauses that stipulated percentages for black employment. However, *Ebony* also noted that "at most companies the proportion of blacks to whites is nowhere near equitable. Though Graumman, for instance, draws its workers from as far away as New York City, a recent count showed only 1,500 blacks among the company's 30,000 workers. And the overwhelming number of blacks was in low pay, low skill positions. In job areas above the production line level, the percentage of blacks in most companies drops off sharply" (p. 35). The article also noted that "in administrative levels, where policy is set, blacks are even more rare than in engineering," a situation that *Ebony* suggested was in part based on the corporate culture of the space industries. One black engineer told *Ebony,* "You have to play golf at the right places and be at the right parties" to climb the corporate ladder (p. 42).

54 "Giant Leap for Mankind?" *Ebony,* September 1969, p. 58.

55 Doris Rutledge, letter to the editor, *Ebony,* October 1969, p. 25.

56 Nona E. Smith, letter to the editor, *Ebony,* October 1969, p. 25.

57 "Mixed Emotions: Different Views," *New York Amsterdam News,* 26 July 1969, pp. 1–45.

58 Gertrude Wilson, "In Houston, NASA Space Families Sweat It Out," *New York Amsterdam News,* 26 July 1969, p. 1.

59 "Moon Conquest: The Progress of Man," *Los Angeles Sentinel,* 24 July 1969, p. 6B.

60 Ibid.

61 "Moon Shot Unites U.S. for Instant," *Chicago Daily Defender,* 21 July 1969, pp. 1–2.

62 "Chicagoans Hail Historic Moon Walk . . . But," *Chicago Daily Defender,* 22 July 1969, p. 3.

63 John H. Sengstacke, "Lily-White NASA," *Chicago Daily Defender,* 29 July 1969, p. 13.

64 See for example, *Chicago Daily Defender,* 19 November 1969, p. 17; 20 November 1969, p. 21; and 20 April 1970, p. 13.

65 Janice Cheddie, "From Slaveship to Mothership and Beyond: Thoughts on a Digital Diaspora," in *Desire by Design: Body, Territories, and New Technologies,* ed. Cutting Edge, The Women's Research Group (London: I. B. Tauris, 1999), pp. 163–67. Mark Dery further analyses black-authored comic books written in the tradition of Afro Futurism. See his "Black to the Future: Interviews with Samuel R.

Delany, Greg Tate, and Tricia Rose" in "Flame Wars: The Discourse of Cyberculture," ed. Mark Dery, special issue of *The South Atlantic Quarterly* 92, no. 4 (fall 1983): 735–43.

66 Sun Ra rejected the terms "free style" and "avant-garde," preferring instead to call his compositions "space music."

67 John F. Szwed, *Space Is the Place: The Life and Times of Sun Ra* (New York: Da Capo Press, 1998), p. 140. Seeing the spaceship as a continuation of the praise of the blues for technologies of motion and travel (he cites the predominance of trains, cars, and buses), Szwed explains Sun Ra's interest in space travel within a larger history of black inspirational metaphors that allowed for imaginary transport (p. 135).

68 Sun Ra, cited in Szwed, *Space Is the Place*, p. 131.

69 Szwed, *Space Is the Place*, p. 133. Szwed points out that whites have mistaken the mix of African cosmologies and science as a rejection of science per se (p. 139). For more on myth and technology in Sun Ra, Perry, and Clinton, see John Corbett, *Extended Play: Sounding Off from John Cage to Dr. Funkenstein* (Durham, N.C.: Duke University Press, 1994).

70 This appears as a promotional blurb on the CD's front cover.

71 Cheddie, "From Slaveship to Mothership and Beyond," p. 173.

Part III: Baby Boom Kids

Seducing the Innocent: Childhood and
Television in Postwar America

✱ In August 1991, Pee-wee Herman moved out of his kidvid playhouse into the pornhouse of the nightly news when a mug shot of the children's idol revealed him to be a fully grown man, a man arrested for exposing himself at an adult movie theater. In true Pee-wee style, the arrest sparked a series of nervous reactions. Psychologists appeared on local newscasts, advising parents on ways to tell children about their TV play-pal, offering tips on how to make youngsters understand the scandal of Pee-wee's adult desires. All grown up and seemingly all washed up, Pee-wee was axed from the CBS lineup, and Pee-wee dolls and paraphernalia were removed from the shelves of the local Toys 'R' Us.

Pee-wee is a perfect example of what Jacqueline Rose has called the "impossibility" of childhood. As Rose argues in her work on *Peter Pan,* the child is a cultural construct, a pleasing image that adults need in order to sustain their own identities. Childhood is the difference against which adults define themselves. It is a time of innocence, a time that refers back to a fantasy world where the painful realities and social constraints of adult culture no longer exist. Childhood has less to do with what children experience (because they, too, are subject to the evils of our social world) than with what adults want to believe.[1] In this regard, the problem with Pee-wee is not so much his indecent exposure, but the fact that he exposes the fantasy of childhood itself. Pee-wee, as a liminal figure somewhere between boy and man, is always on the verge of revealing the fact that children are not the pleasing projection of an adult imagination. He is always threatening to disrupt adult identities by deconstructing the myth of childhood innocence.

The Pee-wee panic was a recent skirmish in an older battle to define and preserve childhood on television. Since the medium's rise in the late 1940s, educators, citizen groups, the clergy, and other social organizations have attacked television for its unwholesome effects on children. Graphic violence, suggestive sexuality, and bad behavior of the Bart Simpson kind are continually seen as threats to youngsters, threats that need to be researched and controlled. But rather than examine television's effects on children per se, I want to look at the *image* of the child that television, and the debates around it, have constructed. In order to do so, I will return to the years following World War II, when television was first defined as a "family" medium. In particular, I want to explore the efforts in that period to make distinctions between adult and children's entertainment, and the need, among the adult population, to keep those distinctions intact. Critics in the popular press established a set of taste standards and reception practices for children's programs that were predicated on middle-class ideals for child rearing, ideals that stressed the need to maintain power hierarchies between generations and to keep children innocent of adult secrets. But even if the advice literature suggested such controls and regulations, the actual children's television programs that emerged in this period played with the culturally prescribed distinctions between adults and children. Drawing on the fantasy figures of children's literature, puppet shows, the circus, movies, and radio programs, these television shows engaged the hearts of children (and often adults as well) by presenting a topsy-turvy world where the lines between young and old were blurred and literally represented by clowns, fairies, and cowboys who functioned as modern-day Peter Pans. Indeed, as we shall see, the narrative pleasure these programs offered was based in large part on the transgression of generational roles that were idealized in the childrearing advice literature of the period.

Presumed Innocent: Childhood and Cultural Power

After World War II, the American public was deluged with images of nuclear family bliss. The ravages of war, it was suggested, could in part be assuaged through the protection of a stable home, a home far removed from the horrors experienced in previous decades. Films such as *It's a Wonderful Life* (1947) showed how family values could insulate individuals from economic hardships and compensate for wartime sacrifices, encouraging Americans to return to the "basics"—mom, dad, and the kids.[2] Advertisements for luxury goods told women to leave their wartime jobs and return home, where they could rekindle romance and purchase their share of washing machines and electric blenders. Meanwhile, in social reality, people were marrying at record rates, and the baby boom, which began during the war and lasted through 1964, created a nation of children who became a new symbol of hope.[3] Children, after all, were innocent; they did not know what their parents knew, they hadn't lived through the hardships of the Great Depression and the war, nor did they bear the blame.

The concept of childhood innocence—and the investment in youth as a symbolic future—was, of course, not a new invention. Since the early centuries of industrialization, children have been conceptualized as blank slates on whom parents "write" their culture.[4] In the American context, this tabula rasa conception of the child gained new force and meanings with the transition from an agrarian to an industrialized society that took place over the course of the nineteenth century. While the agrarian child had been a worker in the farm economy, in the industrial society children were no longer crucial to the family income. This was particularly true for white middle-class households, where the family income was high enough to sustain a comfortable life without the contribution of a child's wages. Stripped of immediate ties to the family economy, the white middle-class child emerged as a new sociological category in whom the middle-class adult culture invested new hopes and dreams. By the turn of the century, with falling birthrates and advances in medical science that decreased infant mortality, parents placed increased focus on individual children, regarding them as distinct personalities who needed guidance and moral support. At the same time, the exploitation of child laborers (who came largely from black, immigrant, and working-class families) created a common cause for "child-saving" movements that attempted to combat child abuse by proposing wide-reaching reforms for children of all classes and races.

While this focus on children had humanitarian goals, the particular battles fought over childhood were linked to power struggles in the adult culture. At the core of this concentration on children was a battle between women and men for cultural, social, and political authority. Especially in middle-class households, the focus on children was linked to women's role in the new economy. Like the child's, the woman's place in patriarchal industrial culture was in the home, and her confinement to the domestic sphere was legitimated by the idea that women were morally obliged to be the caretakers and nurturers for their children. The sentimentalization of the mother-child bond worked to secure the middle-class woman's exclusion from the public sphere. Importantly, however, many women at the time perceived the mother role as an empowering one, and for this reason numerous women turned to mothering as an avenue for increased dominion and prestige.

The "mothers' movement," which took institutional form as the National Congress of Mothers in 1897, gave a public voice to women's issues. Although for some this movement was a complicit embrace of women's domestic confinement, for others it served as a venue for expressing what we might now call "feminist" values. At a time when "genteel" women were expected to leave matters of civic governance to men, women activists justified their interests in the suffrage struggle and other social reforms by invoking the more acceptable female concerns of motherhood and child welfare. "The Age of Feminism," one spokeswoman claimed, "is also the age of the child."[5] As this woman must have understood, the child had become a key to power in the public world. The child, after all, was a link to the future. In a world where Darwin's theories of evolution were taking hold, the child became a vehicle for changing the course of history, for bettering the world through imparting one's goals on a new generation.

Just as women saw the child as a means to their own social power, men began to turn to children as a way to reinvent their authority in the alienating conditions of the industrial world. According to Margaret Marsh, a sentimental vision of childhood was at the core of the "male domesticity" that gained force at the turn of the century. Faced with white-collar desk jobs and increasing feelings of anonymity in the urban world, men were advised to turn toward their homes—and particularly their children—to regain a sense of authority and prestige. Camping trips, family games, and other child-rearing activities promised to refortify men's diminishing power in public life.[6] Again, at the heart of this endeavor was the notion that children were innocent creatures who needed guidance into a world that they would help transform.

This image of children—as both innocents and arbiters of progress—was not only at the center of power struggles at home, it also served to legitimate the institutional power of scientists, policy makers, and media experts who turned their attention to children's welfare. Policy reform movements of the Progressive Era fashioned an image of the child as the means to modernization: as a new generation, children linked the past with the future, tradition with progress. As such, the child was no longer simply the responsibility of the private family, but also a prime concern of public agencies. In 1912, the federal government gave official credence to this logic by establishing the Children's Bureau as an official administration for overseeing the care of the young. The twentieth century thus emerged as the "century of the child," an era in which children became discrete individuals who, with the proper socialization, would carry the nation into the future.[7]

While social reforms and public institutions were based on humanitarian efforts, they often worked to diminish the regional, class, ethnic, and racial diversity of family life by disseminating an American "norm" based largely on white middle-class values and life experiences. By 1915, the emphasis on creating standards for child rearing changed from reform per se to scientific investigation of what constituted the "normal" child, and such investigations became the basis for further social policy.[8] In both its reform and investigatory modes, the child-saving movement was a bedrock for a new organization of childhood experiences: the rise of public schools and decline of child labor ensured that the "normal" child would be an individual educated according to the standards of the dominant class, race, and sex (that is, according to white, patriarchal, middle-class curricula). In addition, the child-saving movement set out to regulate children's play: the rise of municipal playgrounds and national organizations such as the Boy Scouts (1910) and Girl Scouts (1912) helped institutionalize ideas about what constituted children's appropriate use of leisure time.

This normalization of childhood experience and formation of standards for child development were promoted by a stream of media experts who disseminated professional advice. In their book on the history of expert advice to women, Barbara Ehrenreich and Deirdre English have shown how the original goals of the mothers' movement were co-opted by a stream of professional scientists who spoke through the venues of women's media to teach women how to raise their young.[9] Rather than finding increased authority through child rearing, women were repositioned as consumers of information that only scientists and institutions of higher education could produce.

By the 1920s, then, child rearing was no longer seen as a natural instinct of the mother; rather, it was a professional skill that women had to learn by heeding the wisdom of (mostly male) professionals. Women were confronted with a host of scientific advice from "experts" who spoke to them through such popular venues as women's magazines and radio shows. At the heart of this advice was the idea that children were pliable, innocent creatures who needed to be guided by adults. It was the adult's responsibility to generate moral values in the young by guarding the gates to knowledge. By doling out adult secrets only at the proper stages in child development, parents could ensure that children would carry the torch of progress for future generations. A mistake in this regard, the experts warned, could prove fatal—not only for the individual child, but for the moral character of the entire nation. And it is in the context of this moral discourse on knowledge and cultural power that the debates on television should be viewed.

Television and the Gates to Knowledge

As the brief sketch above suggests, childhood is something that adults attempt to maintain through various systems of governance, surveillance, and prescriptive science. And while the protection of children appears to be a consequence of "natural" instinct, the way in which our social system goes about this task is also a function of particular material conditions, ideological concerns, and struggles over social and political power. Childhood, then, historically has been an unstable category, one that must be regulated and controlled constantly. Childhood—or at least the image of the innocent youth to which this category refers—can exist only through a certain disciplinary power that, as Michel Foucault has shown, operates to regulate knowledge.[10] Adulthood brings with it authority, and even more a civic duty to control the dissemination of information about the world. And childhood—as a moment of purity and innocence—exists only so long as the young are protected from certain types of knowledge.

Given this, it is not surprising that mass media typically have been viewed with trepidation by the adult culture. Be it the 1920s movie matinee or the contemporary video game, mass media have been seen as a threatening force that circulates forbidden secrets to children, and that does so in ways that parents and even the state cannot fully control. Worse still, parents may not even know how and where their children have acquired this information. With the mass, commercial dissemination of ideas, the parent is, so to speak, left out of the mediation loop, and the child becomes the direct addressee of the message. Perhaps for this reason, the history of children's involvement with mass media has been marked by a deep concern on the part of adult groups to monitor their entertainment and survey their pleasure. From Anthony Comstock's crusade against dime novels to the more liberal approach of matinee mothers who chaperoned children at the movies, the adult culture has continually tried to filter the knowledge that mass media transmit to the young.[11]

After World War II, this legacy of child saving, and the skepticism about mass media that it presupposed, was taken to its logical extreme when local, state, and federal governments focused with unparalleled concern on the figure of the "juvenile delinquent." Although it is by no means certain that actual incidents of juvenile crimes multiplied after the war, it is clear that law enforcement agencies began to police criminal youth in more rigorous ways.[12] In the late 1940s, the federal government established the Continuing Committee on the Prevention and Control of Delinquency, and law enforcers began to count instances of youth crimes more thoroughly than ever before. It was also at this time that the Senate took a profound interest in juvenile delinquency, and in 1952, under the auspices of Senator Estes Kefauver, began a series of investigations that continued into the 1960s. Meanwhile, women's magazines, child psychologists, and pediatricians such as Benjamin Spock (whose *Common Sense Book of Baby and Childcare* was first published in 1946) advised mothers how to prevent their children from becoming antisocial and emotionally impaired. Although it is hard to determine how many parents actually followed the experts' advice, the popularity of this literature (for example, by 1952 Spock's book had sold more than four million copies) attests to the fact that people were eager to hear what the experts had to say.[13]

Juvenile delinquency was blamed primarily on two separate but related causes—a bad family life and mass media.[14] According to the popular wisdom, the splintering of families during the war left children vulnerable to outside forces that encouraged the development of immoral habits and criminal behavior. Experts argued that the rise in juvenile crimes during the war was largely caused by working mothers who did not properly devote their energies to their young. Thus, as in the past, the mother-child bond served to justify the idea that women's place was in the home. Indeed, at a time when the female labor force was being told to relinquish their jobs to returning GIs, the mass media (and the scientific experts who spoke through these venues) promoted a romantic ideal of motherhood that must have helped to encourage middle-class women to spend the lion's share of their energies on domestic concerns. Then, too, men were told to invest more concern in family life. Like the male domesticity at the turn of the century, this postwar version of the child-centered family provided men with a conduit to power that promised to compensate for their increasing loss of authority in the bureaucratic corporate world. Magazines such as *Esquire* and *Popular Science* told men to take renewed interest in all facets of family life, particularly those that involved family fun and leisure (as opposed to the actual work women performed as housekeepers and mothers). Whether the advice was aimed at men or women, the child emerged as a terrain on which to assert adult power, and the parent in turn relied on the experts' wisdom. Failure to follow this advice could result in "problem" children or, worse still, criminals.

In the advice literature of the period, mass media became a central focus of concern as the experts told parents how to control and regulate media in ways that promoted family values. As a domestic medium that brought the outside world directly into the home, television was at once ally and enemy. Television was often considered to have beneficial effects because it would bring the family together for recreation. In 1952, when the House of Representatives held hearings on the content of radio and television programs, government officials speculated that television was a necessity for family bliss. Representative Joseph Byrson from South Carolina admitted:

> My two younger children spent much of their time watching the neighbor's television. In a year or two, when my youngest son had graduated from a local junior high school, he wanted to go away to school. I believe, if I had purchased a television set at that time, he would have finished high school here in Washington.[15]

Similar sentiments were expressed in audience research of the day. In *The Age of Television* (1956), Leo Bogart summarized a wide range of audience studies that showed many Americans believed television would revive domestic life. Drawing on these findings, Bogart concluded that social scientific surveys "agree completely that television has had the effect of keeping the family at home more than formerly."[16] The respondents in studies around the country testified to the particular ways that television enhanced their family life. In a 1950 study of families from Evanston, Illinois, one parent claimed that television "has given the children a happier home where they can laugh," while another admitted, "My two 16-year-olds like to stay home now. I'm so glad, as I would not know where they were otherwise."[17]

Popular magazines publicized, and perhaps encouraged, such sentiments by advising parents on ways to use television as a tool for family cohesion. In 1948, *Parents Magazine* (which generally took a favorable attitude toward television) published the advice of April Ella Codel, who claimed that television repaired the damage radio had done in her home:

> Our family is rather closely knit, anyhow, yet with practically every room having a radio, it was not uncommon for all to scatter to enjoy particular programs. With the one television set, our family is brought together as a unit for a while after dinner.

The following year, another author for *Parents Magazine* claimed, "All the mothers I have talked to are enthusiastic about television for their children. Certainly it has brought back the family circle in the living room." And in 1955, *Better Homes and Gardens* published a readership survey in which parents praised television's ability to unify the family.[18]

Even while critics praised television as a source of domestic unity and benevolent socialization, they also worried about its harmful effects, particularly its dissemination of debased knowledge and its related encouragement of passive minds and bodies. In 1951, *Better Homes and Gardens* complained that the medium's "synthetic entertainment" produced a child who was "glued to television."[19] Worse still, this new addiction would reverse good habits of hygiene, nutrition, and decorum, causing physical, mental, and social disorders. A cartoon in a 1950 issue of *Ladies' Home Journal* suggests a typical scenario. The magazine showed a little girl slumped on an ottoman, suffering from a new disease called "telebugeye." According to the caption, the child was a "pale, weak, stupid-looking creature" who grew "bugeyed" from sitting and watching television for too long.[20] Perhaps responding to these concerns, advertisements for television sets depicted children spectators in scenes that associated television with the "higher arts," and some even implied that

"Telebugeye" afflicts the young in a 1950 issue of *Ladies' Home Journal*.

children would cultivate artistic talents by watching television. In 1951, General Electric showed a little girl, dressed in a tutu, imitating an on-screen ballerina, while Truetone showed a little boy learning to play the saxophone by watching a professional horn player on television.[21]

As popular wisdom often suggested, the child's passive addiction to television might itself lead to the opposite effect of increased aggression. According to this logic, television decreased children's intellectual abilities, leaving them vulnerable to its unsavory content. The discussions followed in the wake of critical and social scientific theories of the 1930s and 1940s that suggested that mass media inject ideas and behavior into passive individuals. The popular press circulated stories about a six-year-old who asked his father for real bullets because his sister didn't die when he shot her with his toy gun, a seven-year-old who put ground glass in the family's lamb stew, a nine-year-old who proposed killing his teacher with a box of poison chocolates, an eleven-year-old who shot his television set with his BB gun, a thirteen-year-old who stabbed her mother with a kitchen knife, and a sixteen-year-old babysitter who strangled a sleeping child to death—all, of course, after witnessing similar murders on television.[22]

In reaction to the popular furor, as early as 1950 the Television Broadcasters' Association hired a public relations firm to write protelevision press releases that emphasized the more positive types of programming television had to offer.[23] But, as I have shown elsewhere, the controversies grew more heated as grassroots groups and government officials battled to censor the airwaves.[24] Even after the National Association of Broadcasters adopted its code in 1952 (a code that included a whole section on children), the debates continued.[25] In that same year, Representative Ezekiel Gathings of Arkansas spearheaded a House investigation of radio and television programs that presented studies demonstrating television's negative influence on youth.[26] By 1954, Estes Kefauver's Senate subcommittee hearings on juvenile delinquency were investigating television's relationship to the perceived increase in youth crimes, focusing particularly on the "ideas that spring into the living room for the entertainment of the youth of America, which have to do with crime and with horror, sadism, and sex."[27] In the face of such criticism, parental control over children's use of this new medium and the knowledge it disseminated emerged as a number-one concern.

Mastering the Child

The anxieties about television's effects on youth were connected to more general fears about its disruption of generational roles, particularly with regard to power struggles over what constituted proper children's entertainment. At the 1952 House hearings, for example, government officials expressed their discomfort with programming that they found offensive, but that delighted the hearts of children. When describing *You Asked for It* (a half-hour variety format premised on viewers' requests to see various acts), Ezekiel Gathings claimed that while most of the program was "wholesome . . . something like a vaudeville show," he could not abide one act that featured "a grass-skirted young lady and a thinly clad gentleman dancing the hoochie-coochie. They danced to a very lively tune and shook the shimmy. . . . My children saw that, and I could not get it turned off to save my life."[28] This problem of controlling children's program choices was voiced more generally by popular critics, who warned that television might disrupt family unity by inverting the power dynamics between children and adults. According to this logic, the television image had usurped the authority previously held by parents. As television critic John Crosby claimed, "You tell little Oscar to trot off to bed, and you will probably find yourself embroiled in argument. But if Milton Berle tells him to go to bed, off he goes." [29]

Women's magazines published articles and cartoons showing how parents might lose dominion over TV-addicted children who refused to eat dinner, go to bed, contribute to family conversations, finish their chores, or do their homework.[30] In 1950, *New York Times* critic Jack Gould wrote, "Mealtime is an event out of the ordinary for the television parent; for the child it may just be out." In that same year, a cartoon in *Better Homes and Gardens* showed parents seated at the dining-room table while their children sat in the living room, glued to the television set. Speaking from the point of view of the exasperated mother, the caption read, "All right, that does it! Harry, call up the television store and tell them to send a truck right over!" [31]

Television's potential inversion of power relationships between child and adult gave way to humorous speculations about the ways in which adults themselves were becoming more like children. In numerous popular comedies of the period, parents—especially fathers—were shown to regress to a childlike state after watching too much television. In a 1955 episode of *The Adventures of Ozzie and Harriet* titled "The Pajama Game," Ozzie Nelson and his sons, Ricky and David, are shown seated before the TV set. The boys are able to do complicated algebra formulas while watching television, and they maintain their general capabilities for industrious behavior. Ozzie, on the other hand, becomes mesmerized by television, and after his wife Harriet has already gone to bed, he decides to read a novelization of the movie he had been watching on television most of the night. The next morning, Ozzie is in a stupor, unable to wake up on schedule. The episode thus humorously inverts the popular fear that television would interfere with children's activities. Now it is the father who is unable to use the new medium in a responsible, adult way.

In 1954, *Fireside Theatre*, a filmed anthology drama series, evoked a similar theme in an episode titled "The Grass Is Greener." Based on the simple life of a farm family, the program begins with the purchase of a television set, a purchase that the father, Bruce, adamantly opposes. Going against Bruce's wishes, his wife, Irene, makes use of the local retailer's credit plan and has a television set installed in her home. When Bruce returns home for the evening, he finds himself oddly displaced by the new center of interest as his family sits enthralled by a TV western. When he attempts to get their attention, his son hushes him with a dismissive "shh," after which the family resumes its fascination with the television program. Not only does Bruce lose control over his youngsters, but in the next scene he actually regresses to the behavior of his children when he, too, finds himself enthralled by a TV western, slumped in an easy chair, passively addicted to the new medium.

The most explicit and humorous case of infantilization took place in 1955 in the first episode of *The Honeymooners*, "TV or Not TV," when Alice and Ralph Kramden chip in with neighbor Ed Norton to buy a television set. Ralph and Ed become classic couch potatoes, sprawled before the set and enthralled by mindless entertainment. Midway into the teleplay, Ralph sits before the TV set with a smorgasbord of snacks, ready to tune in to a movie. But Ed has other ideas; he wants to watch the children's serial *Captain Video*. Ed takes out his Captain Video helmet and begins reciting the club member pledge, promising Captain Video to obey his mommy and daddy and drink milk after every meal. In case the sense of male regression is not yet clear enough, at the end of the episode Alice scolds the men, saying, "Stop acting like babies and try to grow up a little." Finally, Ralph and Ed fall asleep before the set and Alice tucks them in for the night, covering them with a blanket and shaking her head with motherly condescension.

While the infantilized fathers that such television programs portrayed might have been hyperbolic, they spoke to a more general set of anxieties about television's inversion of the power dynamics between adults and children. Summarizing parents' attitudes toward television, Leo Bogart claimed, "There is a feeling, never stated in so many words, that the set has a power of its own to control the destinies and viewing habits of the audience, and that what it 'does' to parents and children alike is somehow beyond the bounds of any individual set-owner's power of control." [32] In this context, popular media offered solace by showing parents how they could reclaim power in their own homes—if not over the medium, then at least over their children. Television opened up a whole array of disciplinary measures that parents might exert over their youngsters. [33]

Indeed, the bulk of discussions about children and television were offered in the context of mastery. If the machine could control the child, then so could the parent. Here, the language of common sense provided some reassurance by reminding parents that it was they, after all, who were in command. As Jack Gould wrote in 1949, "It takes a human hand to turn on a television set." [34] But for parents who needed a bit more than just the soothing words of a popular sage, the media ushered in specialists from a wide range of fields; child psychologists, educators, psychiatrists, and broadcasters recommended ways to stave off the evils of the new medium.

At the heart of the advice on children and television was a marked desire to keep childhood as a period distinct from adulthood. Critics of the medium feared that television might abolish such distinctions by making children privy to adult secrets. In 1951, television critic Robert Lewis Shayon claimed, "Television is the shortest cut yet devised, the most accessible backdoor to the grownup world." [35] More generally, the issue of accessibility became the primary cause for alarm. Television's immediate availability in the home threatened to abolish childhood by giving children equal access to the ideas and values circulated in the adult culture. In 1950, Phyllis Cerf, the wife of the publisher of *Parents Magazine,* claimed that "television, like candy, is wonderful, provided you don't have too much of it. You can run out of candy, or carefully place it out of your children's reach, but television, once it has come into your home, can go on and on." [36] If Cerf addressed the problem of accessibility mostly through fears about the quantity of television that children consumed, others also worried about the quality of messages that it distributed to old and young alike. Television, it was often suggested, failed to discriminate among its audiences; it addressed all family members with the same message. As *Parents Magazine* claimed in 1952:

> A large part of what children see and hear is intended mainly for adult eyes and ears. Of the things that are intended for children, many are unsuitable or questionable. Some people see no problems or dangers in this. "TV keeps the children from underfoot," they say. Or "TV keeps Billy off the streets. It's a built-in baby sitter." But other adults are concerned. "It's not healthy. All day long it's machine guns, murder and gangs. You can't tell me children don't get dangerous ideas from TV." [37]

As such statements imply, television increased parental dilemmas because it undermined their dominion over the kinds of knowledge that their children might acquire.

In the wake of such criticism, popular media advised parents how to protect their young by filtering out television's undesirable elements. One method of purification came in the form of disciplining the child's use of television by establishing a schedule. Drawing on cognitive and behavioralist theories of childhood that had been popular since the 1920s, and mixing these with the liberal approach of Dr. Spock, the experts recommended ways for parents to instill healthy viewing habits in their children, advising methods of punishment and reward that would reinforce particular viewing routines that adults deemed appropriate for youngsters.

But even if children adopted "healthy" viewing habits and routines, they still might see programs unsuited for innocent eyes, particularly in the early 1950s, when crime, mystery, and sexually suggestive programs often appeared during early prime-time hours. Thus, experts advised parents on how to establish a canon of wholesome programs. A readership survey in *Better Homes and Gardens* indicated that some parents had, in fact, set standards for appropriate and inappropriate entertainment:

> Forty percent of all the parents answering do not approve of some of the programs their children would like to see—chiefly crime, violent mystery or horror, western, and "emotional" programs. . . .
>
> About one-fourth of the parents insist on their children viewing special events on TV. In this category they mention parades, children shows, educational programs, great artists, and theater productions.[38]

In many ways this canon of good and bad TV recalled Victorian notions of ideal family recreation. Overly exciting stimuli threatened to corrupt the child, while educational and morally uplifting programs were socially sanctioned. In the years to come, magazines such as *Reader's Digest* and *Saturday Review* internalized this canon of wholesome and culturally enriching programs, particularly giving their seal of approval to educational fare such as *Ding Dong School* and *Captain Kangaroo*. In all cases, critical judgments were based on adult standards. Indeed, this hierarchy of television programs is symptomatic of the more general efforts to establish an economy of pleasure for children spectators that suited adult concepts of appropriate children's entertainment.

The idea that fun should promote industrious behavior rather than passive reflection was paramount in critical discussions. According to a 1954 article in *Parents Magazine*, the best shows are "programs designed for children with understanding of their growth and development, and which give, if possible, some opportunity for participation."[39] With this assumption in mind, *Parents Magazine* commended programs with drawing and essay contests, claiming that they promoted active forms of play:

> The idea of the drawing program—what used to be called "Chalk Talks" in the old Chatauqua days—promises to become very popular on television. WJZ-TV and its affiliates show *Cartoon Teletales*, with one artist drawing illustrations for stories told by his companion. On WABD New York's *Small Fry Club*, and WTMJ Milwaukee's *Children's Corner*, drawings sent in by children are shown on the screen. And on WCBS-TV there is a program which shows real television originality and inspires creative activity by the young audience: *Scrapbook, Jr. Edition*; among its features is a cartoon strip beginning a new adventure story, and the children are asked to write in their ideas for an ending; then the winning conclusion is drawn by the artist in another cartoon strip shown the following week.[40]

Such programs acted as a Band-Aid cure for the deeper political and economic demands of commercial broadcasting's one-way communication structure. But, while television critics frequently argued that children's shows should encourage participatory forms of play, they never demanded that adult programming should elicit these active forms of reception. Perhaps in this sense, adults wished to protect their young from the undemocratic aspects of their one-way commercial broadcast system, even while they accepted that system as the dominant forum for communication.

The critical expectations for children's television voiced in magazines like *Parents* tell us more about adult taste standards than they do about what children actually found pleasurable. Indeed, adults seem to have watched the shows supposedly aimed at children. Since children's shows were often scheduled during late afternoon and early evening hours, adults would have ample occasion to view these programs. *Kukla, Fran and Ollie*, for example, had a strong appeal for grownups, so much so that when NBC attempted to split it into two fifteen-minute shows in 1951, the network was, in the words of one executive, "swamped" with audience mail from angry adults. Robert G. Pilkington, an insurance underwriter, wrote to the network, complaining:

I have read with interest your general letter sent to me among others in answer to the protests regarding Kukla, Fran and Ollie. . . .

The biggest reason for the change is obviously the greater revenue that can be derived from two 15-minute shows, combined with the lack of sponsorship on many stations. Which leads me to inquire, what is the matter with your Sales Department? Regardless of the popular conception that radio and television is directed to the 12-year-old mentality, there is a large enough segment of your viewing audience appreciative of the KFO type show and buying its sponsors' products to warrant a sales effort in its direction. After one program, I went out, simply in appreciation, and immediately bought some of the goods advertised.

Who ever got the idea that Kukla, Fran, and Ollie is a juvenile show? It's an adult program, pure and simple, and contains too many subtleties to be successful completely except with that mind. Maybe your salesmen and sponsors overlooked that little detail.[41]

Mr. Pilkington's acknowledgment of his enjoyment of a children's show is vivid testimony to the paradox at the heart of television's attempts to make distinctions between adults' and children's narrative pleasures. While cultural ideals may have dictated that those pleasures be kept apart, in practice the situation was never so clearcut. Adults seemed to enjoy what children should have liked, and children seemed to like the very things that adults deemed inappropriate juvenile entertainment.

Perhaps for this reason, the impartation of adult tastes onto children became the number-one goal in the popular media of the time. As Serafina Bathrick has argued, *Parents Magazine* showed mothers how to be "TV guides" who helped their children develop the right sensibilities.[42] In 1954, for example, the magazine claimed:

We can only hope to cultivate good taste in our children by developing good taste in ourselves and helping our children to be sure to see the programs that are good programs. . . . Parents can accomplish a lot by pointing out sequences of bad taste, by reacting themselves to elements of bad taste, by appreciating aloud or indirectly programs which are in good taste. . . . As one expert put it, "Children cannot be protected, in life, from exposure to unwholesome influences, but they can be taught how to recognize and deal with them when they are exposed."[43]

Thus, according to the popular wisdom, by elevating children's taste standards, parents could better regulate the undesirable elements of mass culture. Even if they could not control entirely their children's access to the kinds of messages circulated by television, they could, at least, ensure that children internalized their parents' sensibilities toward program content. Revealingly in this regard, an audience study conducted in Columbus, Ohio, reported that parents found it particularly important to regulate the program choices of pre- and grade-schoolers, but high school students received less parental supervision because "their program tastes apparently are considerably closer to those of their parents." [44]

This preoccupation with the establishment of taste standards reflected a class bias. Summarizing numerous social scientific studies, Leo Bogart claimed that it was mainly the middle class who feared television's influence on children and that while "people of higher social position, income and education are more critical of existing fare in radio, television and the movies . . . those at the lower end of the social scale are more ready to accept what is available." But even if he believed that discriminating taste was a function of class difference, Bogart internalized the elitist preoccupation with canon formation, lending professional credence to the idea that adults should restrict their children's viewing to what they deemed "respectable" culture. As he suggested:

> If television cannot really be blamed for turning children into criminals or neurotics, this does not imply that it is a wholly healthful influence on the growing child. A much more serious charge is that television, in the worst aspects of its content, helps to perpetuate moral, cultural and social values which are not in accord with the highest ideals of an enlightened democracy. The cowboy film, the detective thriller and the soap opera, so often identified by critics as the epitome of American mass culture, probably do not represent the heritage which Americans at large want to transmit to posterity. [45]

Thus, while Bogart noted that working-class parents did not find a need to discriminate among programs, and that the formation of critical standards was mainly a middle-class pursuit, he nevertheless decided that television programs would not please the value systems of "Americans at large." Here, as elsewhere, the notion of an enlightened democracy served to justify the hegemony of bourgeois tastes and the imparting of those tastes onto children of all classes.

For their part, children often seemed to have different ideas. Like Senator Gathing's youngsters who wanted to watch dancers do the "hoochie-coochie," children respondents in audience studies often claimed to prefer programs their parents found unwholesome, especially science fiction serials and westerns. Surveys also indicated that children often liked to watch programs aimed at adults and that "parents were often reluctant to admit that their children watched adult shows regularly."[46] Milton Berle's *Texaco Star Theater* (which was famous for its inclusion of "off-color" cabaret humor) became so popular with children that Berle adopted the persona of Uncle Miltie, pandering to parents by telling his juvenile audience to obey their elders and go straight to bed when the program ended.[47] But other programs were unable to bridge the generation gap. When, for example, CBS aired the mystery anthology *Suspense*, affiliates across the country received letters from concerned parents who wanted the program taken off the air. Attempting to please its adult constituency, one Oklahoma station was caught in the cross fire between parents and children. When the station announced it would not air "horror story" programs before the bedtime hour of 9:00 P.M., it received a letter with the words "we protest!" signed by twenty-two children.[48]

The Children's Hour

If the adult culture attempted to distinguish children's entertainment from adult shows, the actual children's programming that emerged in this period was based largely on the dissolution of age categories. Children's programs were filled with liminal characters, characters that existed somewhere in between child and adult, as the shows played with the cultural concepts of childhood that circulated at the time. Indeed, the pleasure encouraged by these programs was rooted in the transgression of taboos and regulations found in the advice literature aimed at adults.

In the TV playhouse, adults functioned for the sole purpose of fulfilling the child's wish. If in everyday life adults represented rules, knowledge, and the threat of punishment, on television they represented mayhem, entertainment, and prizes. On *Howdy Doody* (1947–1960) host Buffalo Bob was ambiguously a grownup and a cow*boy,* who, like Peter Pan, had not abandoned the land of make-believe. Indeed, children's programs had their own never-never lands—impossible places like "Doodyville," places that mocked the confines of real domestic space.[49] Then, too, children's shows set aside the mundane nature of real time by presenting children with the marvelous antics of "Howdy Doody time," a time in which youngsters need not do their homework, go to bed, or wash behind their ears. In fact, *Howdy Doody* began with a cartoon depiction of a cuckoo clock—literally going cuckoo—as the hands spun feverishly around the dial, signaling the temporary abandonment of the normal schedule for the next thirty minutes of fantastic clowns and puppets.

Johnny Jupiter (1953–1954) similarly transported children from the confines of their living room into a magical world. Johnny was a puppet who lived on Jupiter with his pals Reject the Robot and Major Domo. At their outer-space television station, Johnny, Reject, and Major Domo were contacted by earthling Ernest Duckweather, a teenage techno-nerd who invented a magic television set on which he spoke with his Jupiterian pals. Ernest was a 1950s Pee-wee, a liminal figure who straddled the categories of child and adult. And like Pee-wee (although without the campy wink), Ernest suffered from a case of arrested sexual development, underscored in numerous episodes by his disinterest in the advances of his boss's daughter. Johnny, like other children's hosts, played with the fantasy of childhood itself, presenting himself as a half-boy/half-man who defended himself against the constraints and cares of the grownup world.

By blurring the boundaries between adult and child identities, such programs presented a ripe environment through which to address children as consumers. As both authority figures and wish fulfillments, the casts of clowns and cowboys promised children a peek at toys and sweets behind their mothers' backs. The children's show was a candy store populated by dream parents who pandered forbidden products. Even more important, these programs taught children the art of persuasion, advising them how to tell their parents about the wondrous items advertised on the show. In a 1958 episode of *Howdy Doody*, for example, Buffalo Bob chats about Hostess Cupcakes with Howdy, who marvels at the delicious creamy centers. Bob then directly addresses the children at home, telling them to "make sure to tell your mom to put a package of Hostess Cupcakes in your lunch box when you go to school, or ask her to buy some as a special reward sometime during the week." In this imaginary transaction between Buffalo Bob and the child audience, the parent becomes a functionary through which the child accomplishes consumer goals. Children are taught how to influence their parents' product choices, and in the process the child's narrative pleasure is inextricably intertwined with the pleasure of consumption.

Winky Dink and You (1953–1957), a cult classic of 1950s TV, took this consumer logic to its extreme by making the program completely dependent on the product it advertised. Winky was a flatly drawn Tinkerbell-like cartoon character who cohosted the show with the real-life Jack Barry. Although by current standards extremely low-tech in nature, the program was premised on an interactive use of television technology. *Winky Dink* offered children the possibility of drawing on the television set through the purchase of a special Winky Dink kit, complete with rub-off crayons, an erasing cloth, and the all-important "magic window," a piece of tinted plastic that, when sufficiently rubbed by the child's hands, stuck to the television screen. With this apparatus in place, the child could draw along to the animation on the screen, perhaps filling in features on cartoon characters' faces or completing story narratives by drawing in the necessary scenery and props. In a 1953 episode, Jack Barry showed children how the whole thing worked by picking up a remote feed from the home of Helen, a little girl in Pittsburgh, Pennsylvania. Helen demonstrated how the kit worked, and Barry reminded children (and no doubt their parents as well) of the prosocial skills that would be learned on the show. After Helen erected her plastic screen, Barry told the children at home to "share your Winky Dink kits" by evenly dividing the crayons. And, at a time when television was considered a major cause of eyestrain, Barry told the audience to "notice how that plastic is lightly tinted. That makes it much easier to watch our television show, even for your parents." The consumer message of the show was thus tempered with the rhetoric of public service. In the middle commercial, this mixture of commercialism and goodwill was drawn out in a long speech delivered by Barry, who looked directly into the camera to address the children at home:

> I tell you what, if you had your Winky Dink kits and played along with us, well, there's no reason for any of us to miss all the fun. It's so easy to get your Winky Dink kits. And, you know something, the fun starts as soon as you get your kit. Of course, you can watch the program without a kit, but you can't really be a part of the program without 'em. And you can't have the fun that the other boys and girls who have their Winky Dink kits do have. Now, I know you're just used to watching television shows and you just sit back and watch all

the other shows, but not this show. This show you really get a chance to be a part of 'cause it's different. You get a chance at home to play right along with us, and what you at home draw actually becomes part of the program. But to be a part of the show, you must have one of our Winky Dink kits [Barry holds up the kit and describes its contents].

Thus, the product pitch worked by drawing on the popular fears that television made children passive. Like the "chalk talks" applauded by *Parents Magazine, Winky Dink* encouraged participation from children, but participation came at a price. Buying the Winky Dink kit, the ad suggested, would ensure that children took an active part in the communication process, and with this prosocial message intact, Barry went on to pander to the child audience in the most crass and unabashed way. Still holding up the kit, he exclaimed:

Now boys and girls you *must* have this kit, and here's how you get it. Mark down the address, will you? To get this Winky Dink kit for yourself or for your friends, you send fifty cents [Barry holds up a sign with fifty cents boldy printed on it]. Boys and girls, send fifty cents, got that? Fifty cents, with your name and address [Barry holds up a sign that says to print your name and address] and send it to Winky Dink, Box 5, New York 19, New York [Barry holds up a sign with the address]. Now, I do hope you'll all get your Winky Dink kit right away because you really can't have as much fun as if you have a kit.

Programs such as *Howdy Doody* and *Winky Dink* were products of a world in which the age limits of consumption were shifting, a world in which parents had less and less control over the kinds of objects children would desire and potentially own. Just as Jack Barry saw little need to worry where children would possibly get the fifty cents needed to purchase his or her kit, other industrialists were increasingly appealing directly to children, assuming that they would either buy products on their own or use their powers of persuasion to coax parents into purchasing them. In the postwar years, teenagers, who often held after-school jobs, became a viable market for low-ticket consumer items such as clothing, makeup, and records.[50] And even in the case of high-ticket items—especially household commodities—advertisers discovered that tapping into the new consumer power of children and teens was also a way to urge

Winky Dink promotes itself as educational, artistic, and interactive, but it also teaches children how to be good consumers.

adults to buy more. An editor of *Home Furnishings* (the furniture retailers' trade journal) claimed, "The younger generation from one to twenty influences the entire home furnishings industry." [51]

Children especially were considered to have "nagging" power in family purchases of television sets. Surveys indicated that families with children tended to buy televisions more than childless couples did. Television manufacturers quickly assimilated the new findings into their sales techniques. As early as 1948, the industry trade journal *Advertising and Selling* reported that the manager of public relations and advertising at the manufacturing company, Stromberg-Carlson, "quoted a survey . . . indicating that children not only exert a tremendous amount of influence in the selection and purchase of television receivers but that they are, in fact, television's most enthusiastic audience." [52] Basing their advertisements on such surveys, manufacturers and retailers formulated strategies by which to convince parents to buy products for the sake of their children. In 1950, the American Television Dealers and Manufacturers ran nationwide newspaper advertisements that played on parental guilt. The first ad in the series had a headline that read, "Your daughter won't ever tell you the humiliation she's felt in begging those precious hours of television from a neighbor." Forlorn children were pictured on top of the layout, and parents were shown how television could raise their youngsters' spirits. This particular case is especially interesting because it shows that there are indeed limits to which advertisers can go before a certain degree of sales resistance takes place. Outraged by the advertisement, parents, educators, and clergymen complained to their newspapers about its manipulative tone. In addition, the Family Service Association of America called it a "cruel pressure to apply against millions of parents" who could not afford television sets.[53]

Not surprisingly, the area of consumerism remains one of the most heatedly debated in the discourse on television and youth. Commercials induct the child into the market, and market values appear to be in direct opposition to conceptions of childhood innocence.[54] Yet, once again, while adults historically have argued against the commercialization of children's television, they, too, have been seduced by its consumer fantasies. Indeed, since the 1950s children's programs have found ways to draw adults into the joys of spending money by offering them a ticket for a nostalgic return to a childhood dreamland of make-believe.

The appearance of *The Mickey Mouse Club* in the 1955 fall season is an emblematic example. This show and its 1954 predecessor, *Disneyland,* were created as one big advertisement for Walt Disney's theme park in Anaheim, California. Despite the blatant commercialism of *Disneyland,* it won a Peabody Award for its educational value and an Emmy for best adventure series, and was among the top ten programs in the ratings. Not surprisingly, the program's success paved the way for a new surge of sponsor interest in other children's fare. In its first season, *The Mickey Mouse Club* was similarly successful, although some television critics were initially wary of its Disney product endorsements and its overabundance of commercials (critic Jack Gould was outraged that the premier episode had about twenty ads, one of which cut off a Pluto cartoon).[55] Still, its syrupy doses of prosocial themes—respect for elders, family values, courage—must have tempered adult fears about the commercial aspects of the show.[56]

Like other children's programs, *The Mickey Mouse Club* contained a set of liminal characters that played with culturally prescribed generational roles. The opening credits began with Mickey Mouse himself, who then introduced the Mouseketeers, an odd blend of children—from toddlers to teens—and grown-ups Roy and Jimmy, who dressed just like the children in mouse ears and T-shirts. And like *Howdy Doody, The Mickey Mouse Club* existed in a kind of never-never land. But it took the concept one step further by promising children that its never-never land could in fact become a virtual reality, a real place where children might venture— that is, if they could persuade their parents to take them to Southern California. Of course, as with other Disney products, the theme park was predicated on the pleasure of playing with the culturally prescribed distinctions between child and adult. Disneyland was a place where adults could rediscover the joys of youth in fantasy replicas of narrative spaces (like Frontierland, Fantasyland, and Tomorrowland), which they once traversed in storybooks and movies. The roller coasters and teacup rides offered adults the chance to shake up their conceptions of normal time and space, to look at the world from the perspective of childhood exhilaration and curiosity. Indeed, the fact that Disneyland was promoted as a place of family amusement reminds us that the liminality of children's entertainment is often just as appealing to adults as it is to children. Moreover, as the biggest tourist attraction of the 1950s, Disneyland was dramatic proof that despite the arguments against it, children's commercial entertainment could be marketed as wholesome fun for the entire family.[57]

The End of the Innocence?

The controversy that surrounded children's television in the 1950s, and the assumption that children's viewing pleasures should be monitored by adults, continued into the next decades with increased force. In 1961, one of the first and most influential book-length studies of the subject, *Television in the Lives of Our Children,* reported that by the sixth grade children spent almost as much time watching television as they did in school. Moreover, authors Wilbur Schramm, Jack Lyle, and Edwin Parker speculated that television might contribute to "premature aging" by encouraging American youth to grow up too fast. The boundaries between children and adults might blur, particularly because, as the authors noted, children often watched programs that were made for an adult audience.[58]

As the 1960s came to a close, critics who grew up in the turmoil of the new youth movement began to blame television for the perceived generation gap between themselves and their parents. In his 1973 book *No*

Peace, No Place: Excavations along the Generational Fault, Jeff Greenfield claimed that television threatened to abolish childhood innocence because it allowed youngsters to "eavesdrop" on adult secrets. Similarly, in *Looking Back: A Chronicle of Growing Up Old in the Sixties,* Joyce Maynard said that television played a major role in her premature sophistication.[59] And more recently, in *No Sense of Place,* Joshua Meyrowitz has claimed that television contributes to a "blurring of childhood and adulthood." According to Meyrowitz, television not only exposes "many adult secrets to children," it also "reveals the 'secret of secrecy.' " For example, Meyrowitz argues that by broadcasting warnings about programs that children are not supposed to see, television lets young viewers know exactly what is being forbidden. Television, in other words, makes children privy to the fact that adults are hiding knowledge from them.[60]

Although debates about children and television continue to base themselves around the ideal of childhood innocence, the industrial producers of children's culture have learned more sophisticated ways to tap into children's enjoyment of entertainment that adults deem inappropriate. The 1950s debates over comics and television did not destroy the popularity of magazines such as *Mad,* nor did they diminish the next generation's penchant for the perverse pleasures of Ugly Stickers and Wacky Packs. The recent merchandising of Toxic High stickers, a set of Topps trading cards based on the perverse, violent, and authority-bucking antics at a typical high school, is a case in point. Cartoonist Mark Newgarden (also the brains behind the popular Garbage Pail Kids) admits gleefully, "We did a focus test where we showed it to kids behind one of those two-way mirrors, and the kids went wild for it. And then we showed it to their mothers, and their mothers were aghast."[61] As this "tasteless test" suggests, the strength of a child's toy is now predictable in part by the degree to which the parent disapproves.

Broadcast television has emerged, perhaps, as a more "protected" arena. At the time of this writing, the reform group Action for Children's Television (ACT) has discontinued its two-decade attempt to raise children's program standards. According to the organization's founder, Peggy Charin, ACT's work has been accomplished with the recent passing of the Children's Television Act, which mandates broadcasters' responsibility to young viewers. Ironically, however, these gains come at a time when more and more children are finding their entertainment outside the auspices of broadcast television. Now, cable television, VCRs, and Nintendo games offer youngsters alternative venues for pleasure, venues about which critics are more and more anxious.[62] And, as in the 1950s, such anxieties revolve around the central problem of keeping childhood separate from adulthood. In an episode of *The Simpsons*, for example, precocious son Bart is shown charging his school pals twenty-five cents to watch the Playboy channel on cable TV, while in another episode he beats his father Homer at a video game, to the degree that Homer is reduced to a child, yelling and screaming because he can't score points.

Like the child-saving movement in the early part of this century, the anxieties about children as victims of television and the urge to reform the commercial nature and degrading content of electronic media often have humanitarian goals. But, as in the past, this humanitarian urge is no more than a Band-Aid cure for the public's larger disempowerment and alienation from the channels of expression in our country. In fact, since the inception of television as a privately controlled commercial medium, the American public has rarely argued against its basic corporate structure. Little has been said about the fact that television technology (with its inherent capability for two-way communication) was being developed as a one-way medium used mostly for the financial gain of major corporations.[63] Instead, the only widespread challenge to commercialization of the airwaves has taken place in the name of the child. The child in this configuration becomes an alibi and a conduit for larger issues regarding the commercialization of communication and the price tags attached to free speech on our country's mass media. The discourse of victimization that surrounds the child viewer might, in this sense, usefully be renamed and reinvestigated as a discourse of power through which adults express their own disenfranchisement from our nation's dominant mode of communication.

Notes

This essay first appeared in *Ruthless Criticism*, ed. Robert W. McChesney and William S. Solomon (Minneapolis: University of Minnesota Press, 1993), pp. 259–90.

1   Jacqueline Rose, *The Case of Peter Pan: Or the Impossibility of Children's Fiction* (London: Macmillan, 1984).

2   It should be noted that many films of this period—particularly film noir and family melodrama—depicted dysfunctional families; showing, for instance, how infidelity, missing parents, overprotective mothers, or henpecked fathers could

cause destruction for child and parent alike. See, for example, *Rebel without a Cause* (1955) or *Mildred Pierce* (1945).

3 In the early 1950s, the median marriage age ranged between twenty and twenty-one; the average family started having children in the beginning of the second year of marriage and had three to four children. For birthrates, see Rochelle Gatlin, *American Women since 1945* (Jackson: University Press of Mississippi, 1987), pp. 51, 55, 61; Susan M. Hartmann, *American Women in the 1940s: The Home Front and Beyond* (Boston: Twayne, 1982), pp. 25, 91, 170, 213; Glenna Matthews, *"Just a Housewife": The Rise and Fall of Domesticity in America* (New York: Oxford University Press, 1987), p. 265; Elaine Tyler May, *Homeward Bound: American Families in the Cold War Era* (New York: Basic Books, 1988), pp. 7, 136–37. On marriage and divorce rates, see Hartmann, *American Women in the 1940s,* pp. 163–65; Gatlin, *American Women since 1945,* p. 51; and Tyler May, *Homeward Bound,* pp. 6–8, 21, 59, 117, 185.

4 For a detailed study of the social construction of childhood, see Philippe Aries, *Centuries of Childhood: A Social History of Family Life,* trans. Robert Baldick (New York: Vintage, 1962).

5 Beatrice Hale, cited in Barbara Ehrenreich and Deirdre English, *For Her Own Good: 150 Years of the Experts' Advice to Women* (Garden City, N.Y.: Anchor, 1978), p. 194. Also see Ehrenreich and English's description of the mothers' movement, pp. 192–96.

6 See Margaret Marsh, *Suburban Lives* (New Brunswick, N.J.: Rutgers University Press, 1990) and her article "Suburban Men and Masculine Domesticity, 1870–1915," *American Quarterly* 40 (June 1988): 70–83.

7 The phrase "century of the child" was used to describe the twentieth century's child-centeredness in Arthur W. Calhoun, *Social History of the American Family,* vol. 3, *Since the Civil War* (Cleveland: Arthur H. Clark, 1919), p. 131.

8 For a good overview of the child-saving movement in the early decades of the twentieth century, see Hamilton Cravens, "Child-Saving in the Age of Professionalism, 1915–1930," in *American Childhood: A Research Guide and Historical Handbook,* ed. Joseph M. Hawes and N. Ray Hiner (Westport, Conn.: Greenwood, 1985), pp. 415–88.

9 Ehrenreich and English, *For Her Own Good,* pp. 183–211.

10 The links between power and the regularization of knowledge through discourse runs throughout Foucault's body of research and methodological works. For a series of interviews with Foucault about these broad interests, see Michel Foucault, *Power/Knowledge: Selected Interviews and Other Writings 1972-1977,* ed. Colin Gordon, trans. Colin Gordon et al. (New York: Pantheon, 1977).

11 For more on this, see Mark West, *Children, Culture, and Controversy* (Hamden, Conn.: Archon, 1988); Richard deCordova, "Ethnography and Exhibition: The Child Audience, the Hays Office, and Saturday Matinees," *Camera Obscura* 23 (May 1990): 91–107.

12 For more on this and other aspects of the public concern over juvenile delinquents, see James Gilbert, *A Cycle of Outrage: America's Reaction to the Juvenile*

Delinquent in the 1950s (New York: Oxford University Press, 1986). Gilbert shows that while public officials, educators, psychologists, and other "experts" increasingly focused on criminal youth, "the incidence of juvenile crime does not appear to have increased enormously during this period." Gilbert goes on to show that crime statistics were imprecise and, because the definition of juvenile crime and the policing of it had changed over the course of the century, it is difficult to prove that the postwar period actually witnessed a substantial rise in teenage crimes. Given this, Gilbert argues that the perception of juvenile delinquency in the 1950s was based less on reality than on the way crime was labeled and reported, as well as the general worries about the future direction of American society (pp. 66–71).

13 For more on Spock's popularity and influence, see Charles E. Strickland and Andrew M. Ambrose, "The Changing Worlds of Children, 1945–1963," in *American Childhood: A Research Guide and Historical Handbook*, ed. Joseph M. Hawes and N. Ray Hiner (Westport, Conn.: Greenwood, 1985), pp. 538–44. Strickland and Ambrose also point out that while it is impossible to say exactly how many parents actually practiced Spock's teachings, anthropological and psychological studies conducted during the period suggest that many parents, particularly those of the middle class, did opt for the more permissive methods of child rearing that Spock advised.

14 For more on how juvenile delinquency was blamed on mass media (especially music and film), see Gilbert, *A Cycle of Outrage*, pp. 143–95.

15 House Interstate and Foreign Commerce Committee, *Hearings before a Subcommittee of the Committee on Interstate and Foreign Commerce: Investigation of Radio and Television Programs*, 82nd Cong., 2d Sess., H. Res. 278 (Washington, D.C.: Government Printing Office, 3 June 1952), p. 23. The hearings reconvened on 4, 5, and 26 June 1952; 16, 17, 23, 24, 25, and 26 September 1952; and 3, 4, and 5 December 1952.

16 Leo Bogart, *The Age of Television: A Study of Viewing Habits and the Impact of Television on American Life* (1956; New York: Frederick Ungar, 1958), p. 101. As a cautionary note, I would suggest that in his attempt to present a global, synthetic picture of the television audience, Bogart often smooths over the contradictions in the studies he presents. This attempt at global synthesis goes hand in hand with Bogart's view that the television audience is a homogeneous mass and that television programming further erases distinctions. He writes, "The levelling of social differences is part of the standardization of tastes and interests to which the mass media give expression, and to which they also contribute. The ubiquitous TV antenna is a symbol of people seeking—and getting—the identical message" (p. 5). Through this logic of mass mentalities, Bogart often comes to conclusions that oversimplify the heterogeneity of audience responses in the studies he presents.

17 Paul Witty, "Children's, Parents', and Teachers' Reactions to Television," *Elementary English* 27 (October 1950): 8, cited in Bogart, *The Age of Television*, p. 264.

18 Ella April Codel, "Television Has Changed Our Lives," *Parents Magazine*, December 1948, p. 64; Henrietta Battle, "Television and Your Child," *Parents Magazine*, November 1949, p. 58; *Better Homes and Gardens*, October 1955, p. 209.

19 William Porter, "Is Your Child *Glued* to TV, Radio, Movies, or Comics?" *Better Homes and Gardens,* October 1951, p. 125.

20 *Ladies' Home Journal,* April 1950, p. 237. For a similar cartoon, see *Ladies' Home Journal,* December 1955, p. 164.

21 *House Beautiful,* June 1951, p. 8; *Life,* 26 November 1951, p. 11.

22 For these examples, see "Bang! You're Dead," *Newsweek,* 21 March 1955, p. 35; Norman Cousins, "The Time Trap," *Saturday Review of Literature,* 24 December 1949, p. 20; Don Wharton, "Let's Get Rid of Tele-Violence," *Parents Magazine,* April 1956, p. 93.

23 Edward M. Brecher, "TV, Your Children, and Your Grandchildren," *Consumer Reports,* May 1950, p. 231.

24 For more on early censorship campaigns, see my *Make Room for TV: Television and the Family Ideal in Postwar America* (Chicago: University of Chicago Press, 1992).

25 The networks also tried to police themselves. As early as 1948, NBC executives considered problems of standards and practices in television. *NBC Standards and Practices Bulletin—No. 7: A Report on Television Program Editing, and Policy Control,* November 1948, NBC Records, box 157, folder 7, Wisconsin Center Historical Archives, State Historical Society, Madison. In 1951, NBC became the first network to establish standards for children's shows, crime shows, mention of sex on programs, proper costuming, and so on. See *NBC Code,* 1951, NBC Records, box 163, folder 1, Wisconsin Center Historical Archives, State Historical Society, Madison.

26 House Interstate and Foreign Commerce Committee, *Hearings.*

27 Chairman Senator Robert C. Hendrickson, cited in Committee on the Judiciary United States Senate, *Hearings before the Subcommittee to Investigate Juvenile Delinquency: Juvenile Delinquency (Television Programs),* 83rd Cong., 2d Sess., S. Res. 89 (Washington, D.C.: Government Printing Office, 5 June 1954), p. 1. The committee reconvened on 19 and 20 October 1954, and also met on 6 and 7 April 1955, to continue the debates.

28 House Interstate and Foreign Commerce Committee, *Hearings,* 10–11.

29 John Crosby, "Parents Arise! You Have Nothing to Lose but Your Sanity," in *Out of the Blue! A Book about Radio and Television* (New York: Simon and Schuster, 1952), p. 115. For more on television's threat to parental power, and particularly its threat to patriarchal dominion, see my *Make Room for TV.*

30 As Ellen Wartella and Sharon Mazzarella have observed, early social scientific studies suggested that children were not simply using television in place of other media; instead, television was colonizing children's leisure time more than any other mass cultural form ever had. Social scientists found this "reorganization hypothesis" to be particularly important because it meant that television was changing the nature of children's lives, taking them away from schoolwork, household duties, family conversations, and creative play. See Ellen Wartella and Sharon Mazzarella, "A Historical Comparison of Children's Use of Leisure Time," in *For Fun and Profit: The Transformation of Leisure into Consumption,* ed. Richard Butsch (Philadelphia: Temple University Press, 1990), pp. 183–85. This reorganization hy-

pothesis was also at the core of early studies conducted by school boards around the country, which showed that television was reducing the amount of time children spent on homework. For early school board activities, see, for example, "TV Also Alarms Cleve. Educators," *Variety,* 22 March 1950, p. 29; "Students Read, Sleep Less," *Variety,* 5 April 1950, p. 38.

31 Jack Gould, "TV Daddy and Video Mama: A Dirge," *New York Times Magazine,* 14 May 1950, p. 56; *Better Homes and Gardens,* September 1950, p. 56. Audience research showed that people claimed television was disrupting mealtimes and other traditional occasions for family interaction. See Eleanor E. MacCoby, "Television: Its Impact on School Children," *Public Opinion Quarterly* 15 (fall 1951): 428–30, 438; Bogart, *The Age of Television,* p. 261.

32 Bogart, *The Age of Television,* p. 268.

33 In the context of Benjamin Spock's popularity, discipline was often a tricky matter. One of the central theses in that book is that parents should avoid conflict to ensure that their home created a democratic environment where children felt they too had a say in family matters. In this regard, much of the disciplinary advice centered on finding ways for different family members to coexist harmoniously with television—even in the face of family squabbles over program choices and viewing duration. As I detail elsewhere, much of the expert advice on television focused on ways to avoid conflict. For example, home magazines showed women how to divide domestic space so that family members of all sexes and generations could watch television separately, without interfering with the activities of others. See chapter 2 in my *Make Room for TV.*

34 Jack Gould, "What Is Television Doing to Us?" *New York Times Magazine,* 12 June 1949, p. 7. *Popular Science,* March 1955, took the logic of human agency to its literal extreme, presenting a "lock-and-key" TV that "won't work until Mama sees fit and turns it on with her key" (p. 110).

35 Robert Lewis Shayon, *Television and Our Children* (New York: Longmans Green, 1951), p. 37.

36 Cited in "What Shall We Do About Television? A Symposium," *Parents Magazine,* December 1950, p. 37.

37 Paul Witty and Harry Bricket, "Your Child and TV," *Parents Magazine,* December 1952, p. 37.

38 *Better Homes and Gardens,* October 1955, p. 202.

39 Robert M. Goldenson, "Television and Our Children—The Experts Speak Up," *Parents Magazine,* December 1954, p. 76.

40 Dorothy L. McFadden, "Television Comes to Our Children," *Parents Magazine,* January 1949, p. 74.

41 Robert G. Pilkington, letter to Sylvester L. Weaver, 17 December 1951, NBC Records, Box 182: folder 5, Wisconsin Center Historical Archives, State Historical Society, Madison.

42 Serafina K. Bathrick, "Mother as TV Guide," in *From Receiver to Remote Control,* ed. Matthew Geller (New York: New Museum of Contemporary Art, 1990), pp. 23–30.

43 Goldenson, "Television and Our Children," p. 78.

44 Freda Postle Koch, *Children's Television Habits in the Columbus, Ohio, Area*, Television Committee, Franklin County, Ohio Section, White House Conference on Children and Youth, 1952, cited and summarized in Bogart, *The Age of Television*, p. 262. Specifically, the study reported that 42 percent of kindergarteners to second graders, 47 percent of fourth through eighth graders, and 26 percent of high school students said that they disagreed with parents on program choices. According to Bogart, however, the bulk of children in this study said that parents primarily established schedules for children, rather than restricting content per se (p. 263).

45 Bogart, *The Age of Television*, p. 289. In the 1954 Kefauver hearings, similar findings about the relationship between social class and parents' attitudes toward television were made part of the official record. See Committee on the Judiciary United States Senate, *Hearings*, 21–23.

46 The Reverend Everett C. Parker, summarizing findings from the Information Service, Central Department of Research and Survey, National Council of the Churches of Christ in the United States of America, in *Parents, Children, and Television: The First Television Generation* (New York: n.p., 1954); reprinted and summarized in Committee on the Judiciary United States Senate, *Hearings*, p. 28. The surveys included in Bogart's account include a 1955 study from the *New York Herald Tribune* that studied 1,200 schoolchildren; a 1952 and 1955 study by the American Research Bureau of children ages six to sixteen; H. H. Remmars, R. E. Horton, and R. E. Mainer, *Attitudes of High School Students toward Certain Aspects of Television* (Indiana: Purdue University Press, 1953). These are all summarized in Bogart, *The Age of Television*, pp. 252–56. Also see the *Better Homes and Gardens* survey cited above and also summarized in Bogart.

47 For example, in 1952, the American Research Bureau observed that by the age of seven, one child in four had stayed up to watch Berle. Bogart, *The Age of Television*, p. 254.

48 "Kids Not Kidding," *Variety*, 29 March 1950, p. 33.

49 In his ethnographic study of children who watch *Pee-wee's Playhouse*, Henry Jenkins shows how similar aspects of contemporary programming might appeal to child viewers. He claims that the ambiguity about Pee-wee's status as boy and man and the program's disruption of rule-governed behavior allow young viewers to work through anxieties about the day-to-day power hierarchies between children and adults, as well as their own anxieties about becoming adults. See Henry Jenkins, " 'Going Bonkers!': Children, Play, and Pee-wee," *Camera Obscura* 17 (May 1988): 169–93.

50 For an overview of the rise of teenage consumer culture in the postwar period, see Thomas Doherty, *Teenagers and Teenpics: The Juvenilization of American Movies in the 1950s* (Boston: Unwin Hyman, 1988), pp. 42–61.

51 Sylvia O'Neill, "Are You Guilty of Juvenile Delinquency?" *Home Furnishings*, August 1954, p. 14.

52 "Video's Juvenile Audience," *Advertising and Selling*, August 1948, p. 99.

53 "Television Tempest," *Newsweek,* 27 November 1950, p. 62.

54 For two scholarly articles on the commercialization of contemporary children's culture, see Stephen Kline, "Limits to the Imagination: Marketing and Children's Culture," in *Cultural Politics in Contemporary America,* ed. Ian Angus and Sut Jhally (New York: Routledge, 1989), pp. 299–316; and Tom Englehart, "The Strawberry Shortcake Strategy," in *Watching Television,* ed. Todd Gitlin (New York: Pantheon, 1987), pp. 74–108.

55 For a discussion of the success of *Disneyland,* see William Melody, *Children's Television: The Economics of Exploitation* (New Haven, Conn.: Yale University Press, 1973), p. 41; for a discussion of critical responses to the premier episode (including Gould's), see Jerry Bowles, *Forever Hold Your Banner High! The Story of the Mickey Mouse Club and What Happened to the Mouseketeers* (Garden City, N.Y.: Doubleday, 1973), pp. 16–17. *The Mickey Mouse Club* went off the air in 1957 and returned in syndication in 1962. Although its ratings did fall in 1956, its cancellation probably had more to do with disputes between Disney and ABC. See Bowles, *Forever Hold Your Banner High,* pp. 23–24.

56 In *Forever Hold Your Banner High!,* Jerry Bowles claims that "part of the show's impact had to do with its really not being a children's show at all but, rather, a show that featured children playing roles of little adults. All the values the show taught—reliability, reverence, bravery, loyalty, good behavior, the ickky-sticky grown-up stuff of romantic love—are things adults think kids like to be taught" (p. 21).

57 Disney's success with targeting a dual audience of children and adults was to become a major marketing strategy by the next decade. Prime-time programs such as *The Flintstones* and *Batman* self-consciously aimed to attract different age levels by building in a range of interpretive possibilities. *Batman,* for example, was targeted to appeal as "camp" for adults and as action-adventure fantasy for children. For more on this, see Lynn Spigel and Henry Jenkins, "Same Bat Channel/Different Bat Times: Mass Culture and Popular Memory," in *The Many Lives of the Batman: Critical Approaches to a Superhero and His Media,* ed. William Uricchio and Roberta Pearson (New York: Routledge, 1991), pp. 117–48.

58 Wilbur Schramm, Jack Lyle, and Edwin B. Parker, *Television in the Lives of Our Children* (Stanford, Calif.: Stanford University Press, 1961), p. 156. The authors based this speculation on numerous social scientific studies that also suggested television was making children grow up too fast.

59 Jeff Greenfield, *No Peace, No Place: Excavations along the Generational Fault* (Garden City, N.Y.: Doubleday, 1973), pp. 114–16; Joyce Maynard, *Looking Back: A Chronicle of Growing Up Old in the Sixties* (Garden City, N.Y.: Doubleday, 1973), pp. 51–52. Both of these books are cited in Strickland and Ambrose, "The Changing Worlds of Children," p. 560.

60 Joshua Meyrowitz, *No Sense of Place: The Impact of Electronic Media on Social Behavior* (New York: Oxford University Press, 1985), p. 247.

61 Mark Newgarden, cited in Bill Forman, "Sticker Shock," *Creem* (May 1992), p. 28.

62 A 1988 Nickelodian press release, "Kids Spend $15.8 Billion Annually," under-
    scores the popularity of new technologies such as cable, VCRs, and personal com-
    puters with the younger generation. Some 72 percent of American children say
    they will subscribe to cable TV as adults, and among those already receiving cable
    in their homes, 85 percent say they will subscribe as adults. Among the 73 percent
    of American children in households that own VCRs, almost half (43 percent) re-
    port watching videotapes "every day or almost every day." And the press release
    reported that 24 percent of the nation's children own personal computers. These
    data were compiled by the Nickelodian/Yankelovich Youth Monitor. See the Chil-
    dren's Television clipping file, Doheny Cinema-Television Library, University of
    Southern California. In his recent book on video games, Eugene Provenzo Jr. re-
    ports that video games took off in the late 1980s. For example, two years after its
    introduction in 1986, Nintendo had sold about 11 million units, and in 1990 alone
    it sold 7.2 million units. More generally, by February 1989 "16 of the 20 top sell-
    ing toys in the country were video games or video-game related." See Eugene F.
    Provenzo Jr., *Video Kids: Making Sense of Nintendo* (Cambridge: Harvard Univer-
    sity Press, 1991), pp. 8, 12. For more recent analysis of video games and children,
    see Marsha Kinder, *Playing with Power: In Movies, Television, and Video Games*
    (Berkeley: University of California Press, 1991). For a general discussion of the
    children's marketplace in contemporary culture, see Kline, "Limits to the Imagi-
    nation."

63 Although television's corporate structure was not heavily contested, there were
    heated debates about the commercial uses of radio broadcasting in the 1920s, and
    there were also alternative visions. See Robert W. McChesney, *Telecommunica-
    tions, Mass Media, and Democracy: The Battle for the Control of U.S. Broadcasting,
    1928-1935* (New York: Oxford University Press, 1993).

Postscript

Since this essay was first published in 1993, a number of useful books on children
and media have been published. See, for example, Heather Hendershot, *Saturday
Morning Censors: Television Regulation before the V-Chip* (Durham, N.C.: Duke
University Press, 1998); Henry Jenkins, ed., *The Children's Culture Reader* (New
York: New York University Press, 1998); Marsha Kinder, ed., *Kids' Media Cul-
ture* (Durham, N.C.: Duke University Press, 1999); Stephen Kline, *Out of the Gar-
den: Toys, TV, and Children's Culture in the Age of Marketing* (London: Verso,
1995); Ellen Seiter, *Sold Separately: Children and Parents in Consumer Culture*
(New Brunswick, N.J.: Rutgers University Press, 1995); Ellen Seiter, *Television and
New Media Audiences* (London: Oxford University Press, 1999).

Innocence Abroad: The Geopolitics of
Childhood in Postwar Kid Strips

And suddenly I knew for sure what it is that for me, at least, makes parenthood so deeply worthwhile. It gives one the magic passport without which one can never re-enter the lost country of one's own youth—that nationless land from which one emigrated, willy-nilly, so many years ago.

Parents, August 1952

America's children are at once our most precious national resource and our most weighty responsibility. They represent our future hopes and aspirations. . . . We must interact in the future with any number of new and emerging nations. In order to do this successfully, we will need the talent, dedication, and best efforts of all our youth. . . . So I ask all Americans to reaffirm this nation's commitment to its children.

President William J. Clinton, National Children's Day proclamation, 1993

✱ In fall 1993, President Clinton proclaimed the third Sunday in November as National Children's Day. Reminiscent of the 1913 act that created Mother's Day and the 1924 inauguration of Father's Day, Children's Day honors American youth as a cornerstone not only of the family's sentimental life, but also of the nation's public purpose.[1] Now an official part of our national culture, the child was immediately addressed with an appropriate display of multinational consumer capital as Disneyland opened its gates to honor underprivileged children across the globe. In a television special covering the event, Disney beamed in children from its theme parks in California, Florida, Tokyo, and Paris. With its multicultural medley of Mickey Mouse, Gloria Estefan, and teen rap group Kris Kross, this New World Disney jamboree was a complex embodiment of America's will to conquer foreign markets with its most "innocent" and "universal" of products—children and cartoons.

Disney's colonial quests have, of course, been the subject of previous studies about cultural imperialism—most notably Ariel Dorfman and Armand Mattelart's 1971 *How to Read Donald Duck*.[2] Here, I want to take a somewhat different tack by looking at the rise of a new type of comic strip "kid" that appeared shortly after World War II. It was during this postwar period that comics (and cartoons more generally) discovered a new "geography" of childhood in which kids (both real and imagined) wandered through the fantasy spaces of consumer culture epitomized by the mass-produced suburb and its fantastic corollary, the theme park. It was here, in these new prefabricated spaces, that two postwar kid strips, *Dennis the Menace* and *Peanuts,* would become part of America's national popular culture. Less studied than their Disney competitors, these kid strips (and their various "spin-off" incarnations) have important links to the postwar multinational culture in which childhood innocence has served as a green card for America's will abroad and at home. Like their Disney cousins, these two strips traveled across the globe to numerous markets, spreading a message of American family values everywhere they went. But, even more significant for my purposes, these strips were fundamentally "conquest narratives" in which children explored the new geographies of postwar life—especially the suburbs—and in the process, like any good explorer, defined who belonged there and who did not. The cast of characters in these strips—the white middle-class family—is perhaps less surprising than their relationship to the way American postwar culture more generally defined the boundaries of the nation (and its ideal citizen) by invoking the figure of the innocent child.

The appearance of Charles M. Schulz's *Peanuts* and Hank Ketcham's *Dennis the Menace* after World War II was less a revolution in comic strip style than a reworking of a century-long fascination with the kid strip in

American culture. These strips were the postwar answer to what histo-
rians typically agree is the first modern comic strip, Richard Outcault's
The Yellow Kid (a naughty boy who first graced the pages of the *Sunday
World* in 1895). In the years to follow, a spate of kid strips from Rudolf
Dirks's *The Katzenjammer Kids* (1897) to Outcault's *Buster Browne* (1902)
to Harold Gray's *Little Orphan Annie* (1924) would become part of
America's visual culture, and they would also serve as mascots for a host
of product and media tie-ins from children's shoes to Broadway plays.[3] By
the time *Dennis the Menace* and *Peanuts* appeared, the nationwide audience for kid strips was a well-established American phenomenon.

Like their predecessors, both Ketcham and Schulz masterfully built
media icons out of their child heroes. Schulz began drawing *Li'l Folks*
(his original title for the strip) in 1947 as a weekly feature for the *St.
Paul Pioneer Press*. By 1950, it was picked up for national distribution by
United Features Syndicate and (despite Schulz's objections) renamed *Peanuts*.[4] One year later, in 1951, Ketcham and the Post-Hall Syndicate unveiled *Dennis the Menace* in sixteen newspapers, and by the end of the
year, it was in a hundred of the country's largest papers. The strip soared
to national fame so quickly that by 1953 *Newsweek* already called Dennis
a "national personage."[5] Over the course of their first two decades, both
strips were also syndicated around the world (by 1961, *Dennis* appeared in
forty-three foreign countries and *Peanuts* in thirty-five).[6] Following on the
merchandising successes of their kid strip cousins, these media magnates
included worldwide tie-in deals for *Dennis* objects and *Peanuts* paraphernalia, the latter becoming a major player on the international toy market
as the strip grew to phenomenal popularity in the 1960s. Moreover, unlike their kid strip predecessors, both *Dennis* and *Peanuts* came of age
in the same years that television established itself as the nation's primary
means of communication, and both strips were apt fodder for a medium
that, at least in the 1950s and 1960s, saw itself as the quintessential back-
bone of family fun. In the late 1950s, Screen Gems bought the television
rights to Ketcham's strip and produced the live-action *Dennis the Menace,* which ran on CBS between October 1959 and September 1963 (and
was subsequently rerun on Saturday mornings).[7] In 1965, Schulz joined
hands with producer Lee Mendelson and animator Bill Melendez to make
his first in a long line of award-winning television specials, *A Charlie
Brown Christmas*.[8] Both *Dennis* and *Peanuts* also diversified across a range
of other media, including books, motion pictures, theme parks, records,

home videos, and most recently, video games. These strips, in short, have become international media empires.

The status of *Dennis* and *Peanuts* as media empires was not lost on the U.S. government, which at different points in history saw these sweet family strips as vehicles for international cold warfare. In 1959, in the midst of President Dwight Eisenhower's "People to People Campaign" (Ike's populist attempt to create goodwill between peoples of different nations through cultural exchanges), Ketcham decided to take a trip to Russia in hopes of establishing a "humor exchange." According to Ketcham, his plan "got a lot of attention in Washington" and the Eisenhower administration was "delighted." He was soon contacted by the CIA, whisked to San Francisco and Washington, D.C., and briefed on espionage techniques. Ketcham claims he was asked to "look out for certain shapes and things that I saw from the air" while in flight to the Soviet Union. Although the government equipped him with an 8mm spy camera, Ketcham decided to use his preferred medium, drawing suspicious objects on his pad. "When the stewardess started coming down to find out what I was drawing," Ketcham recalls, "I'd quickly put an eye and a nose on it and a great big grin and hair, and make a series of cartoons."[9] The humor exchange was thus turned into an international spy mission as the father of Dennis battled the Red Menace in this heroic cold war flight. Six years later, airplane attacks on "Reds" of another kind became a long-standing gag in numerous *Peanuts* panels featuring Snoopy and the Red Baron.

Given their interests in international surveillance and aerial combat, it is no surprise that both Ketcham and Schulz lent their characters to the goals of the space project. In the early 1960s, Dennis became the mascot for the U.S. Junior Astronaut Program, which exploited Dennis's image to encourage children to buy savings bonds in support of the space program. Later in the decade, at the height of the space race, the National Aeronautics and Space Administration (NASA) enlisted Charlie Brown and Snoopy as its company mascots for the Apollo 10 lunar orbit mission. In a *New York Times* article titled "Lenin vs. Snoopy," the moon mission served as the occasion for a thorough examination of the very different spirit in which Moscow and Washington approach the cosmos. "The Kremlin," the article continued, "used its Venus rockets to further the cult of Lenin. . . . Apollo 10's astronauts chose to call their two vehicles 'Charlie Brown' and 'Snoopy,' after two comic strip characters who represent no ideology or political party but do exemplify the human condition in a frustrating world." [10] Obviously, the fact that the *New York Times* saw it appropriate to compare Snoopy to a Russian leader underscores the very thing that the author so completely denies. Comic strip characters do suggest ideologies and political choices; they do represent nations.

In their economic and political roles in international competition, both *Dennis* and *Peanuts* seem hardly as "innocent" as their childish heroes. It is this status of children as national mascots, with the kid strip as a case in point, that I want to explore in the following pages. Looking specifically at the rise of these strips in the 1950s and 1960s, I ask a series of related questions: How did the figure of the "kid" come to represent the postwar nation during the height of the cold war? How did this icon of American innocence come to be the figure par excellence of our nation's will to power abroad? And how was the relationship between children and national supremacy played out in the strips themselves, as well as in their related media spin-offs?

Childhood and Nationalism

Prior to addressing these questions, I want first to consider the nature of nationalism itself and the historical trends that placed children at the center of nationalist discourse. Recent work on nationalism has stressed its symbolic dimensions, in particular the way language and texts work to provide what Benedict Anderson calls an "imagined community." [11] The nation, according to Anderson, is a historical construct formed primarily in symbolic texts through which people, living in disparate places and under different conditions, imagine themselves joined together. The development of a "mother tongue," along with the variety of poetry, prose, and songs that perform this language, forge links between people who have no personal knowledge of one another, and they also work to create imaginary boundaries between these people and those of other nations. For this reason, Anderson prefers to see nationalism less as an ideology than as a social bond like kinship or religion. While Anderson doesn't concentrate on the funny pages per se, he does show that the newspaper has historically been a central means for creating these imaginary bonds between strangers. From this perspective, we might conclude that the comic strip also served to tie Americans together by forging a shared visual culture, a set of images that were commonly recognized by people in distant locations. Although not all Americans interpreted these images in the same way, the funnies did form bonds between readers; they did create a "reception" community in which the nation (and its others) could be imagined. In the case of the kid strip, the national image involved has, of course, been the child. We might, therefore, begin to account for the kid strip's popularity by considering how the "kid" allowed a diverse American public to imagine itself as a community tied together by common struggles and distinct from other nations.

If the kid character functioned as a vehicle for imagining the nation, this is because, as President Clinton put it, children "represent our future hopes and aspirations." This concept of the child as a symbolic future for the nation became central to the Progressive Era discourses on childhood that emerged in the late nineteenth century and flourished in the early decades of the 1900s. Tying Charles Darwin's theories of evolution to a sense of national purpose, the Progressive Era's middle-class "child-saving" movement saw children as the key to future generations. Reformers fought to secure the child's (and nation's) destiny by promoting legislation against child labor as well as by establishing government agencies to oversee the social welfare of the young.[12] While the child-saving movement had humanitarian goals, it belied power struggles in the adult culture—struggles between classes, sexes, races, and ethnic and religious groups that did not all have the same ideals for their children.[13] Moreover, because many working-class families depended on their children's wages for basic needs, child labor laws threatened the family's very survival. Thus, as the federal and state governments became increasingly involved in child welfare, numerous Americans questioned the extent to which the government should intervene in family life. Children, consequently, came to represent the more general crisis of American liberalism: the relationship between the state and private sector.

With the national reinvestment in family life after World War II, the child once again was crucial in public debates. During the baby boom years (roughly 1946 to 1964), conceptions of childhood still very much revolved around the dynamic between the state and private life, although the problem was often framed in different ways. Now, it was typically articulated in terms of psychological discourses of personality development in relation to larger national questions about authoritarianism and freedom. In both intellectual and popular culture, critics worried that the overly disciplined child would grow into a sociopath unsuited for the basic goals of the free world. In scholarly literature—most notably Arnold Gesell and Frances Ilg's *Infant and Childcare in the Culture of Today* (1943) and Theodor Adorno et al.'s *The Authoritarian Personality* (1950)—the analysis was connected to the specter of fascism. For Gesell and Ilg, German Kultur was based on "autocratic parent-child relationships," while findings in the Adorno collection suggested that excessively submissive children in authoritarian (as opposed to nurturing, egalitarian) family structures would develop the kinds of personalities that were susceptible to prejudice and authoritarian regimes. In popular media, the problem of discipline was communicated in a more commonsense way as the media provided advice on how to avoid damaging the individual child's psyche. A prime example here is Benjamin Spock's best-selling *Common Sense Book of Baby and Child Care*, which was first published in 1946 and went through 167 printings in ten years. It warned against the pitfalls of too much discipline, paving the way for the popular embrace of a liberal, permissive, and presumably democratic approach to child rearing.[14] Although this permissive approach had its critics, it prevailed as the central axis around which debates about child rearing revolved.

In the cold war climate of postwar America, this discourse on children and authoritarianism was generally linked to discussions about America's supremacy in world affairs. Nowhere was this better demonstrated than in popular magazines, which continually endorsed the American way of life by comparing U.S. children to their foreign counterparts across the globe. While this cross-cultural perspective on childhood was historically rooted in anthropological studies (especially Margaret Mead's 1928 *Coming of Age in Samoa* and her 1949 *Male and Female: A Study of the Sexes in a Changing World*), in the postwar popular literature, critics were less concerned with questions of nature versus nurture than they were with questions of "us" versus "them." According to the logic of the popular press, children of other countries suffered from an ill-conceived relation between the nation and private life, and this in turn robbed them of their childhood.

Most emphatically here, the Communist nation served as the measure of American superiority. Comparisons between American and Soviet children often stressed the ways in which the Soviets had lost their childhood to the disciplinary will of the state. In 1961, *Saturday Review* asked its readers to consider what happens "when the state brings up the child." A cartoon at the top of the page encapsulated the general theme by including a split-screen rendering of an American versus a Soviet family. The American family and their adoring dog were gathered together in their yard, with a church spire set in the distance. The Russian family, however, was metaphorically divided by the state as the parents posed like spies at a barbed-wire fence, secretly gazing at their youngsters who were huddled in a schoolyard that looked ominously like a prison. To demonstrate its graphic point, the article detailed Chairman Nikita Khrushchev's plan to place all children in boarding schools, which "in essence . . . means complete domination of the home by the state and the breakup of the family as the basic unit of the new society."[15] Other articles suggested that not only family life but childhood itself was being sacrificed to the state. The grueling amount of schoolwork and the austerity of everyday life resulted in a world without childhood pleasures, which accounted for "the precociously adult-like behavior of Soviet children."[16]

This trope of lost childhood also ran through articles about children from other nations. In the war-torn, Communist-occupied countries of Eastern Europe and Korea, in the poverty-stricken regions of Western Europe, and in nonindustrialized countries, the hardships of life created such strict demands on youngsters that, as one article put it, they became "children without childishness."[17] Despite their value in creating obedient youth, it was argued, the Old World disciplinary techniques of Western Europe stifled children and impaired their ability to mature into free-spirited individuals prepared for the modern world. The British, with their overly protective nannies turned their boys into "fops"; the disciplinarian Germans transformed "Hans and Gretel" into "sneaks"; the upper-class Parisians created solemn "elderly gentleman"; or even worse, the lower-class Frenchmen, with their untamed passions, abused their young in the most violent ways.[18] A 1956 article in *Look* titled "Lost Childhood" detailed the "new crisis in France" that put youngsters at peril. It described the miserable fate of one Jean-Pierre "who never knew the shining joy of childhood" due to the fact that his "indulgent" mother and his equally irresponsible father were feeding him a steady diet of wine. In between the swigs, as the photo layout demonstrated, his parents delivered him a "stinging wallop." Moreover, the wine and wallops dulled Jean-Pierre's brain, making him vulnerable to the low pleasures of mass culture—specifically comic books. One photo showed his "heavy-handed" mother who "lashes out suddenly at Jean-Pierre when he persists in looking at [a] comic book instead of finishing lessons."[19] Thus, according to popular wisdom, and in a variety of ways, the social customs and political conditions in foreign nations had robbed children of their right to be children. In the process, childhood became synonymous with America—the only place where it still existed.

In the context of this discourse on childhood, freedom, and national supremacy, the postwar kid strip contributed its own folksy wisdom. The figure of the "kid" became a conduit for larger social concerns, not just about family life, but also about the free world itself. As postwar social critics such as John Keats pondered over the massive conformity of "Mr. and Mrs. Drone" in the new suburban middle class, as sociologists such as William Whyte worried about the effects of bureaucracy on the "organization man," and as critics such as Betty Friedan became increasingly critical about the middle-class housewife's confinement in the doldrums of suburbia, the "kid" served as a perfect vehicle for thinking through the authoritarian structures of the postwar world.[20] It is in these contexts that the first two decades of *Dennis* and *Peanuts* might best be explored.

Menace or Egghead? Defining the American Kid

If foreign children suffered from an overdose of discipline, the reigning ethos in *Dennis the Menace* and *Peanuts* was the child's unbridled freedom. In line with the ideals of permissive child rearing, both strips shared a fascination with childhood as a time of exploration, a time when children played without fear of retaliation from their parents or any other social institution.

In *Dennis,* parents functioned like the "helper" characters of the folktale; they were there simply to aid in the adventures of the central hero. Mr. and Mrs. Mitchell practiced the "spare the rod" approach with a vengeance to the dismay of their more authoritarian neighbor, Mr. Wilson, who for all his bellowing, was completely unable to control the boy. Because the daily *Dennis* strips were single black-and-white panels rather than narrative sequences, Ketcham typically presented his hero in a kind of "caught-in-the-act" family snapshot that encapsulated Dennis's misadventures, drawn to scale from the child's point of view. The humor in the strips was initially directed at adults (although later in the series, when Ketcham realized that the strip had caught on with children, he directed it at both audiences). Ketcham often evoked humor by making adults and children alike laugh at the standards of middle-class adult decorum. In numerous panels, Dennis unveiled the secrets of parlor etiquette by telling guests exactly those things his parents would say only behind their backs. Dennis, for example, unwittingly insults what appears to be his father's business associate when he announces, "Aw, do I have to go to bed? I wanted to see Mr. Reid talk through his hat!"[21] In other panels, Dennis upsets authoritarian structures of adult life, misunderstanding traffic cops or misbehaving in church.

Many of the panels set in Dennis's home poked fun at the gender roles of family life, with Dennis serving as a foil for his father's work-a-day world. In one panel from the 1950s, Dennis's father returns home from a day at work, dressed in suit and hat and looking bedraggled. As opposed to his father, Dennis has been overindulged in the pursuit of leisure, and the remains of his fun-packed day—melting ice cream cones, toys, and baseball bats—lay scattered on the floor. The caption reads, "We had a party this afternoon! You missed all the fun."[22] Like the stereotypical fifties' dad, when Mr. Mitchell is not at the office he is working in the garden, and Dennis consistently finds ways to subvert his work into play. In one panel, Dennis shoots his famous slingshot at a hornet's nest while his exhausted father mows the lawn; in numerous others, Dennis finds ways to wreak havoc as his father toils in the smoke and heat of the barbecue pit. Meanwhile, Mrs. Mitchell, the quintessential fifties' housewife, is similarly sabotaged by Dennis's interruption of her household chores. For instance, in one panel, Mr. and Mrs. Mitchell's complete submission to their child's "natural" need for boyish fun is humorously depicted as a complete inversion of the power dynamics between adult and child. As his parents busily wash the dinner dishes, Dennis runs out the kitchen door and cheerily remarks, "So long, slaves."[23]

Analyzing *Dennis* in the context of permissive child-rearing literature, Henry Jenkins argues that the strip constituted a particular version of permissive discourse that was linked to generic conventions of "bad boy" comedy. Jenkins shows how Dennis straddled the line between two postwar notions of "bad" boys. On the one hand, he claims, Dennis was a demonic child, symptomatic of postwar fears that permissiveness might lead to juvenile delinquency. On the other hand (and especially when the series made its way to television), as the quintessential bad boy, Dennis also embodied American ideals. His misbehavior and disrespect for adult authority were often championed as a sign of unbridled curiosity, a natu-

While *Peanuts* still embraced an escape from authority, it did so by drawing on conventions of "gang" comedy rather than the "bad boy" tradition. (Copyright, Fawcett Publications, 1960)

ral and normal part of growing up in the free world. From this perspective, Jenkins contends that Dennis exemplified what critic Leslie Fiedler calls the "good bad boy," a mischief-maker who nevertheless represents a healthy disregard for established order and, for that reason, is celebrated as a sign of American manhood.[24]

The world of *Peanuts* revealed yet another articulation of American childhood. While *Peanuts* still embraced an escape from authority, it did so by drawing on conventions of "gang" comedy rather than the bad boy tradition.[25] Famous for its elliptical treatment of adult characters, *Peanuts* literally evacuated them from the child's world, providing instead a picture of children free to roam the green hills of suburbia. Although the concerns of adult life lurked in the shadows of this pensive strip, the children in *Peanuts* played with these constraints and found ways to resist them outside their parents' domain.

As opposed to *Dennis*, which placed the reader in the child's point of view, *Peanuts* typically evoked humor by having its childish heroes take up the roles of adults—at least insofar as those roles were seen from a child's perspective. In a world without grownups, the *Peanuts* clan reestablished various authoritarian relationships common to the postwar social world. Lucy acted as a domineering mother to her younger brother Linus, the exact kind of mother that Dr. Spock would advise against. In strip after strip, Lucy dominates Linus's activities, bossing her brother with a barrage of yelling and following him through the neighborhood in the most overprotective of ways. Perhaps not surprisingly, Lucy's misguided child-rearing techniques resulted in a classic "authoritarian personality" disorder—insecurity. And her attempts to cure Linus of his blanket dependency by continuously taking the object from him were also completely ill conceived. Just like the domineering mother in the advice literature of the day, the more Lucy attempted to discipline the child, the more maladjusted Linus became.

This aspect of the strip was not lost on critics, who during the 1960s, often read *Peanuts* as a parable for adult relationships. Analyzing the personality traits of Snoopy,[26] Lucy, Charlie, Linus, and the entire *Peanuts* gang became a genre of pop criticism onto itself. In interviews, Schulz even participated in this game, commenting on the way he put "adult fears and anxieties into the conversation of the children." Furthermore, Schulz said he liked to think about the "off-stage" adult characters and their relationships to the kids. These speculations turned into various interpretations of child rearing and the way discipline (or the lack thereof) led to neuroses. In a 1969 interview, Schulz suggested:

> Linus's mother seems to be the peculiar one. As Charlie Brown once remarked, "I am beginning to understand why you drag that blanket around." She seems to be obsessed with his doing well in school, and tried to spur him on by sneaking notes into his lunch which read, "Study hard today. Your father and I are very proud of you and want you to get a good education."[27]

Schulz's interest in education was symptomatic of post-Sputnik America, where concerns about pedagogy were often linked to the fear that the United States had fallen behind the Soviets. After the successful launching of the Soviet satellite in 1957, the media presented a host of anxieties

about America's scientific agenda and, with that, the agenda for education (both in the sciences and humanities). Arthur S. Trace Jr.'s *What Ivan
Knows that Johnny Doesn't* (1961) further fueled these worries, and critics
of liberal education took this as a moment for a thorough critique of the
school system's privileging of emotional growth over hard facts.

Although, as we have seen, the popular press often criticized the Soviets
for their overly austere educational system, as with most expressions of
national supremacy such comparisons were riddled with ambivalence. In
1961, for example, the *New York Times Magazine* argued that the extreme
amount of discipline in the life of Soviet children could be interpreted
from two angles. Admitting that some would see this disciplinary regime
as the path to a conformist society (the authoritarian personality critique),
the article nevertheless also concluded that

> in the realm of education the Communists are giving systematic at-
> tention and major emphasis to training in values and behavior con-
> sistent with their ideals. We can hardly claim we are doing as much
> or as well for our own value system. . . . Yet we are fond of saying
> that the American school is the bulwark of democracy. If this be, we
> had better look to our defenses.[28]

But the debates about childhood and education were even more complex than the "us" vs. "them" logic that ran through this article. It wasn't
only the Soviets that Americans defended themselves against, but also
Europeans. Magazine articles comparing American to European children
often indicated a "nature versus culture" logic in which too much of the
latter resulted in "unnatural" habits—especially of the sexual kind. A 1953
New York Times article about two British boys who moved to America is
a perfect example of the way European intellectualism was connected to
homophobic fears about "sissies." "By American standards," the article
claimed, British boys are "a little foppish," scrubbed and polished "like
apples (whereas to an American taste a little dirt and disorder would be
signs of a real boy)." The accompanying "before and after" cartoon pictured the "demure little Londoners" complete with knee-length schoolboy suits and reading books by A. A. Milne. After eighteen months in
America, the fops had been turned into "real boys"—here depicted as
cowboys and spacemen, shooting each other in the back and reading
space comics.[29] Thus, even if Americans needed to beef up their educa-

tional system to compete with Russia, there was always the nagging possibility that too much intellect would rob the good old American boy of his manhood and turn him into a European dandy.

In the contours of this debate, *Dennis the Menace* and *Peanuts* can be seen to work through a series of tensions and uncertainties about what it meant to be an American. While both strips presented popular visions of American children at play, they expressed different attitudes toward the child that belied fundamental ambivalences at the heart of the nationalist discourses described above.

Dennis was the more anti-intellectual version of American childhood. With his overalls, slingshot, and ruffled cowlick, he was decidedly not a "fop," a point hammered home in panels where he begrudgingly wore his Sunday best. In one such panel, he asks, "Why do I have to dress up? . . . Who am I tryin' to kid?" [30] In another, after having torn his suit in a fistfight, he tells his parents, "I was just sittin' there, keepin' clean, when this kid says, 'Hi, sissy.' " [31] As opposed to the squeaky-clean sissy, Dennis was always ready to battle the elements. He went on camping trips, dug up flower beds, captured frogs, and soiled the civilized space of the family home with the dirty tracks of nature.

As the ultimate nature boy, Dennis clearly didn't care much for science or any other intellectual concerns. When he visited the library on a rainy day, his approach to scholarship was more outdoorsy than philosophical. At the checkout desk, he opens an oversized book, puts it on his head like a hat, and tells another boy, "Better get a BIG book! It's raining cats and dogs!" [32] His disregard for learning and disdain for adult authority carried over into his attitude toward school. Ketcham portrays school as one of a myriad of authoritarian institutions that restrain the child's liberties. In one strip, for instance, Dennis and a friend stand with noses pressed against the schoolyard gate. Obviously wishing to bust loose, they slip a note to a passerby on the other side. The caption reads, "Please take this message to the outside world." [33] Dennis, in short, views school as a kind of prison, an obstacle to his natural rights to freedom, and Ketcham usually asks the reader to sympathize with this child's point of view. In fact, when considering why Dennis never grew up in the strip, Ketcham said, "I don't want him to enter the educational system. . . . He's too old for the playpen and too young for jail." [34] Ketcham's distrust of the school system was reciprocated by the Parent-Teacher Association (PTA) which criticized the television series on the grounds that the "devilish" Dennis set a bad example for children.[35]

In fact, on television, where the live-action Dennis did grow up, the character was presented as an average, even lazy, student. As one episode made clear, Dennis's averageness was a mark of pride for the family. After Dennis puts a piece of bubble gum on an IQ test at school, the computer mistakenly scores him as a genius. As a result of his new egghead status, Dennis loses his school chums and becomes increasingly despondent. The happy revelation that Dennis is, in fact, not a genius comes as comic relief, and Dennis immediately turns back to his menacing ways. In the context of Sputnik and the education race with Russia, this episode took a firm stand against those critics of American childhood who called for greater intellectual achievements. Intellectualism was the opposite of childhood in Dennis; the egghead was the ultimate threat to the pleasures and freedoms of American youth.

Despite the often anti-intellectual tone of both the strip and television version, *Dennis the Menace* was not simply a rejection of intelligence. While loathing the "egghead" and disciplinary education, the strip did appeal to the more populist (and racist) assumption that American boys (or at least white boys) had a natural curiosity, an innate capacity for supremacy in all endeavors and over all "others." For this reason, *Dennis* was considered by some to be an antidote to America's post-Sputnik fears about the state of Johnny's education in relation to Ivan's. As Jenkins notes, some critics of the day embraced Dennis for his natural curiosity and sense of exploration, seeing this as exemplary of "the very qualities we would prize in him twenty years from now in a laboratory."[36]

Like *Dennis, Peanuts* also glorified childhood play in pastoral settings —especially in its many panels depicting baseball games, football practice, and kite flying. But unlike Dennis, the *Peanuts* kids were more than just naturally curious; instead, they often openly welcomed school and intellectual pursuits. As opposed to Dennis, Charlie Brown and his friends read books. As Sally enthuses, "Happiness is having your own library card!"[37] And while Dennis made intellectuals the butt of a joke, *Peanuts*'s humor frequently arose when intellectualism was put into the "mouths of babes." In 1961, when asked the basis of the strip's appeal, Schulz replied, "Well, it deals in intelligent things . . . the characters do talk like adults. . . . It makes their language hilarious."[38]

Despite the humor, Schulz's style of deliberately drawn lines gave his children an aura of seriousness. Charlie Brown's rotund body is weighted by the world, and his huge oval head begs the question, "What is he thinking and why?" Charlie is a literal egghead. Even Snoopy became (over the course of the fifties) a serious thinker with an active fantasy life. In the television series and motion pictures, the use of Vince Guaraldi's modern jazz piano on the soundtrack further suggested the "egghead" status of the strip. And of course, the *Peanuts* kids themselves took up an interest in adult intellect and high culture. Lucy set up shop as the neighborhood psychiatrist, Schroeder played Beethoven on his toy piano, Linus wanted to be an artist and read the classics, and over the years Snoopy donned a variety of erudite guises, from Sherlock Holmes to chess master. Moreover, while Schulz never showed the inside of Snoopy's doghouse, he did make it clear that Snoopy was an art connoisseur who lined his walls with a collection of modern masterpieces from van Goghs to Andrew Wyeths. Even though these examples could be read as parodies of professionalism and "highbrow" arts, they encouraged readers to think about childhood in relation to (and not simply as a rejection of) intellectual concerns.[39]

The different attitudes that *Dennis* and *Peanuts* took toward intellectualism were written into their cartoon styles. *Dennis* had an aura of commercial art, which Ketcham's early years at Disney might have encouraged. The strip's caricatures of family life fleshed out a detailed picture of the modern home filled with middle-class appointments. Ketcham was so concerned with producing an accurate and up-to-date portrayal of middle-class life that when he lived in Switzerland in the 1960s, he used the Sears catalog to follow trends in American domestic appliances and home furnishings.[40] *Dennis* was, in this sense, a genre piece that could be found in previous family comic strip portraits such as *Blondie* as well as in numerous magazine cartoons of the day. To execute his vision, Ketcham adopted a mass-production attitude to the strip, hiring a team of commercial artists to illustrate his creation.

Meanwhile, his character Dennis often espoused a clear dislike for the intellectual circles of modern art of all kinds. In one panel, Dennis is pictured in a neighbor's home where modernist furniture and abstract paintings line the living-room walls. Dennis exclaims, "Gee, if ya like THAT kind of pitchers, I can get ya whole kiddiegarter wall full!" In another, on a trip to an art museum, Dennis stares at modern paintings and complains, "SOME art place! Not even one picture of Santa Claus!"[41]

Throughout the development of his comic strip oeuvre, Ketcham seems to have retained this disdain for modern art. Even in the 1980s, Dennis could still be found in a museum remarking, "I forgot, was Picasso in the second or the third grade?"[42] As opposed to Snoopy, who revels in the European modernist masters, Dennis delights in knocking them off their museum pedestals.

Although Ketcham never directly makes the link, it should be noted that his view of the modernist aesthetic also had nationalist implications during this period. Numerous critics saw modernism, with its roots in the European avant-garde, as patently subversive. The debate encompassed not only museum art, but also the more popular arts of home decor. In 1953, Elizabeth Gordon, the editor of *House Beautiful,* wrote an editorial titled "The Threat to the Next America" that argued modernism was an international conspiracy originating in Nazi Germany with the machine aesthetics of the Bauhaus school.[43] In his (albeit innocent) disdain for the high modernism of the European—and by now American—intelligentsia, Dennis thus espoused a view consistent with a populist notion of a distinctly American art that was skeptical of modernism's international roots.[44]

Schulz, on the other hand, represented an alternative strain in this nationalist rhetoric on the arts. As Serge Guilbaut demonstrates, while some critics mistrusted modern art, others embraced the burgeoning forms of modern American painting—especially abstract expressionism—as exemplary of the individual's freedom of self-expression in the "new liberalism" of postwar America.[45] From this standpoint, American artists like Jackson Pollock were hailed for their ability to use abstraction to express their own individuality. While Schulz did not travel in these fine-art circles, his relation to his strip—and the responses he received—was very much in line with the idea that American art forms were exemplary of the artist's individual freedom, the right to make meanings that weren't necessarily in line with the goals of governments or corporations.

Indeed, unlike Ketcham, Schulz prided himself on the fact that he drew the strip alone, without the mass-production techniques of a Disneyesque enterprise (a point that critics of the times also noted).[46] In 1961, Schulz (reportedly with some "grinning modesty") referred to his strip as a "work of art." Later, in 1969, he revised this slightly by suggesting that while comics are not "great art," they are among the "popular arts."[47] At the time that Schulz said this, the comic form was already being resurrected as "art" by intellectuals and collectors, and critics thought seriously about the philosophical things that comics had to say.

Certainly, Schulz's drawing style encouraged readers to think about his strip's meaning. Over the course of the 1950s, Schulz increasingly moved away from realistic rendering to more elliptical sketches. Unlike Ketcham's detailed mise-en-scène, Schulz's minimalist style (a line or two to connote emotion on the face, and sometimes as little as a horizon line to indicate a setting) asked the reader to imaginatively fill in the empty spaces. In fact, so minimal were his designs that his editors sometimes had to remind Schulz to draw the horizon line in the background.[48] One strip even presents a parable of the minimalist ethos, when Linus draws a picture of Lucy that lacks her famous mouth. When Lucy demands that Linus draw her mouth, he tells her that it's "wrong to rush a work of art," but finally gives in and sketches an unflattering portrait of Lucy's big mouth. In return for his attempts to portray her in this more realistic fashion, Lucy socks Linus in the head.[49] Abstraction, then, has the advantage of discouraging instant recognition, and like other *Peanuts* stories, this one elicited critical reflection on the nature of the comic strip medium itself.

Still, it seems unlikely that Schulz intended these self-reflexive moments in the context of an avant-garde aesthetic. Instead, self-reflexivity in *Peanuts* appears connected to Schulz's deeply religious background. *Peanuts* reflects back on its own moral function as art, continually asking the reader to question the set of expectations one has when reading the funnies. The stories resolve less in "punch lines" than in fundamental queries about the nature of life.[50] Perhaps for this reason, numerous intellectuals, from psychiatrists to semioticians, found *Peanuts* an ideal metaphor for the human dilemma itself. In 1966, the strip even became fodder for Protestant Minister Robert L. Short, whose popular book, *The Gospel according to Peanuts,* envisioned *Peanuts* not through the terms of postwar permissive childrearing, but rather as a puritanical conception of childhood: he saw *Peanuts* as a parable for original sin.[51]

More generally, we might assume, both *Peanuts* and *Dennis* allowed a diverse reading public to think about the various tensions involved in defining the child and, with that, the nation. Were we a nation of eggheads or menaces? Or were we the last bastion of the free world—the only place on earth where children could escape authoritarian control? Like all artifacts of culture, these comics could certainly be read in a variety of ways, but the prospects that they proposed spoke to the larger social imagination where childhood was the ultimate measure of the nation.

It's a Small World: The Child Explorer

In both *Peanuts* and *Dennis,* the concern with freedom and discipline was often communicated through stories about children's abilities to master space in their suburban environs. If in social reality the mass-produced suburb was a place of insular domesticity where gates, cramped back-yards, playpens, and cranky neighbors all served to constrict children's play, in the strips the burbs were places that children could control and dominate. In *Peanuts,* where adults exist only via elliptical allusion, children easily move from home to home. Without their parents' supervision, they open doors for one another, effectively controlling all entrances and exits in and out of the houses. By extension, these children propel the narrative progress of the strip itself, allowing the reader figuratively to move across the space of the story. Just as they control domestic space, the *Peanuts* kids move freely around the idyllic world of nature that constitutes their fictional neighborhood. The only character that seems to have any notion of property laws is Snoopy, who makes sure to keep his doghouse free of all human presence (including, of course, the reader, who is also denied access to the doghouse interior).

Ketcham's strip even more deliberately makes the child's domination over space the fodder for jokes about adult notions of property and propriety in the suburban town.[52] To the dismay of all grown-ups, Dennis constantly appears in places that he does not belong, turning adult property laws on their side. Despite the wishes of his cranky neighbor, he repeatedly appears in Mr. Wilson's home and garden, running amok through the flower beds and intruding on Mrs. Wilson's private parties. When he's bored with Mr. Wilson, he moves on to other neighbors, popping up in the most unexpected places. In one panel, he appears in the bathroom of his new neighbor, who is in the middle of taking a shower. Dennis pulls open the shower curtain and enthuses, "Hi! Remember me? I'm the little boy the real estate guy told you didn't live in this neighborhood."[53] Dennis also created mayhem in public spaces, losing his frog in a crowded elevator or breaking objects at a store. When his parents attempt to discipline his travels, he immediately finds escape clauses. One panel shows Mr. and Mrs. Mitchell trying to open the bathroom door, which

As the title of a 1961 edition put it, Dennis was the "ambassador of mischief." (Copyright, Fawcett World Library, 1961)

Dennis has apparently locked himself behind. But Dennis outsmarts his parents, and entering the room from another door, boasts, "Hi! I'm not in there anymore. I got out the window."[54] More generally, when Dennis doesn't like the rules laid down by his parents, he grabs his things up in a bandanna, ties them to a stick in a hobo style, and runs away from home.

The child's ability to master space was, by the time of *Dennis* and *Peanuts,* a common convention in children's culture. The *Rollo Series,* appearing in the 1830s as one of the very first U.S. school primers, told adventure tales of boy travelers who explored exciting places. In the second *Rollo Series,* for example, young Rollo and his family members tour an array of European cities.[55] In the twentieth century, book series such as the *Hardy Boys*—as well as comics, movies, and radio and television programs—

further popularized the figure of the child explorer. Sometimes in such tales, children journeyed to those locales (such as China or Africa) that were typically exoticized in the Western imagination. In this regard, their exploits took on the colonialist tropes of more well-established "New World" narratives where white Europeans encroached on the "savage" and "primitive" cultures in other lands.

In the postwar kid strip, these conquest narratives took place in the suburban neighborhood itself. Schulz, in fact, admits that he originally wanted to draw an adventure strip like *Terry and the Pirates, Steve Canyon,* or *Prince Valiant.* While his kid strip was less fantastic, Snoopy opened up an imaginary space of endless conquest and foreign intrigue, a surrealistic space that existed somewhere in the "unconscious" of the suburban family dog. In his expansive imagination, Snoopy went to France, the Sahara, Mexico, Alaska, and a host of other places including, of course, the moon. Despite their humorous bent, Snoopy's journeys were imbricated in the more threatening side of travel—namely, military conquest. Inside Charlie Brown's bedroom community was a virtual war zone, embodied most graphically by Fort Zinderneuf, which as a member of the French foreign legion, Snoopy furtively patrolled. In October 1965, Snoopy donned his famous World War I flying ace helmet and set out in hot pursuit of the Red Baron. Schulz decided in the midst of Vietnam that war was no longer funny, and temporarily dropped the Red Baron theme in 1969.[56] But war scenarios continued in the following decades. In the 1980s, Schulz presented television specials such as *What Have We Learned, Charlie Brown?* (1983), which pays homage to the Allied invasion of Fortress Europe, as the *Peanuts* cast tours the Normandy battlefields.[57]

In *Dennis,* the little boy's freedom to roam was also communicated through foreign intrigue. Hall Syndicate and Fawcett Books published a series of junior travel books in the early 1960s featuring Dennis's adventures in various parts of the world, including Hollywood, Hawaii, and Mexico. In 1961, Holt, Reinhart and Winston released a book that detailed Dennis's trip to the Soviet Union, not-so-subtly titled *I Want to Go Home.* Meanwhile, in the book-length collections of strips that Fawcett produced in the early 1960s, Dennis's "bad boy" persona was linked explicitly to his status as a representation not just of childhood, but of nationhood as well. As the title of a 1961 edition put it, Dennis was the *Ambassador of Mischief.* And as the inside cover further announced, he was "zooming far above the range of guided missiles and diplomatic conferences . . . to a new summit of success. On his round-the-world mission of mischief he has disarmed entire nations via press and airwaves" with his "live frogs and devilry."[58]

More typically, Dennis's expeditions were connected to the western genre as numerous panels depicted him in the role of cowboy. At a time when Disney's television portrayal of Davy Crockett turned the coonskin cap and cowboy suit into a popular fad, Dennis wreaked havoc on the suburban ranch house. Clad in his cowboy best, Dennis wakes his father by shooting arrows at his head. In another panel, Dennis plays the masked bandit, sneaking treats from the cookie jar.[59]

While the figure of the little cowboy out on the lonesome suburban prairie was certainly intended in jest, it wasn't necessarily so funny to all Americans, especially those who had been forced out of this new frontier. If in the old West the colonized groups were Native Americans, in the new suburban towns the subjects of exclusion comprised a wider range of ethnic and racial minorities as well as social outcasts that simply didn't fit into the family ideal. Government loans to builders and prospective buyers favored "red-lining" (or zoning) practices that effectively kept people of color out of the neighborhood. Suburban architecture and community space were designed for nuclear families rather than lesbians, gays, or any other group that did not conform to community "standards." This design for living was, of course, inscribed in the strips themselves as the fictional neighborhoods (at least as they were originally conceived) were entirely homogeneous.

In their unbridled travels across the suburban frontier, kid characters, like all cowboys before them, defined who belonged on their turf and who did not. Dennis, for example, often found "indigents" living in the park and commented wryly on their unfamiliar ways. In one panel, when Dennis comes across a beatnik loafing on a park bench, he says to his pal Joey, "I must be growin'! Did you notice he kept callin' me 'man'?" The strangeness of the beatnik is further suggested by the fact that the park is filled with couples — parents and kids, husbands and wives, and even birds huddled together in family scenes. The beatnik is a loner, whose strange clothes and dark shades clearly don't belong in Dennis's world. Similarly, in another park scene, Dennis comes across a bum. "Boy are you lucky!" Dennis exclaims. "You mean nobody never tells you ya gotta get cleaned up?" In the background, a man in a business suit looks on with some surprise, although it's perhaps intentionally unclear whether this man is more shocked at the bum's presence in the park or Dennis's reverence for the tramp's unseemly lifestyle.[60] In these and other strips, *Dennis* implicitly demonstrates who doesn't fit in the suburbs; significantly, these misfits were dropouts (always single men) who served no purpose in the social maintenance of family life. If in the 1950s and 1960s the strip presented these tales of exclusion as innocent good clean fun, by the summer 1993 release of the film *Dennis the Menace,* more sadistic elements of this joke were hard to miss. Indeed, the 1993 film takes this to a violent extreme, when the homeless man is posed not simply as a "moocher," but as a kidnapper who Dennis finally (and according to the film, justifiably) sets on fire.

Most important for our purposes, however, is the fact that these scenarios never once mention the more typical targets of suburban exclusion—people of color. Further, given the postwar suburb's actual ethnic and religious mix of second-generation European immigrants, it is even more surprising that these strips presented a world of Anglo-Americans with almost no representation of national heritage other than an imaginary idea of "Americanness." In this regard, it is especially worth noting those instances when national difference does become a central story element.

A 1962 television episode of *Dennis the Menace* is a perfect example. Here, the "good neighbor" policy is dramatically rendered as a young Chinese girl comes to visit the Wilson household. Dennis immediately develops a schoolboy crush, and the two set up a "date" in which they share their respective cultural heritage. The exchange comes in the form of a culinary lesson on the supremacy of American tastes—not only in food, but in child rearing. At the Wilson's home, Sen Yuen and Dennis share Chinese cuisine (a theme that also ran through various *Dennis* panels in which Dennis goes to Chinese restaurants and creates chaos because of his failure to understand their "mysterious" eating customs). After lunch, Dennis invites Sen Yuen to the malt shop, only to discover that this poor Chinese girl has never eaten a banana split or, for that matter, any really good dessert. Dennis's shock at this revelation dramatically underscores the idea that foreign children simply have no childhood fun. This lesson is then narratively linked to another revelation—that Sen Yuen, like all Chinese girls of her age, is already promised in marriage. As this suggests, Sen Yuen has no freedom of choice in a culture based on marriage contracts. The episode then turns onto a thinly veiled lesson in miscegenation in which Dennis, through a series of narrative confusions, fears that he is her promised groom and runs for his life.

This innocent tale of national supremacy was, then, linked to a story about courtship and the little boy's fears of female sexuality. More often, the adventures of the child explorer were connected to conquests of another kind—romantic ones, which the girls in these strips most aggressively attempted. Lucy's endless struggles to win the affections of Schroeder, as well as Margaret's fierce efforts to get Dennis to the altar, were running gags over the years.[61] As Ketcham notes, "There is a Margaret Wade in every man's life. James Thurber knew her simply as Woman. Threatening, bossy, superior, always pursuing, the incipient castrator."[62] In the television episode described above, this fear of "woman" is directly related to a nationalist discourse that hinges on the competition between two female types: the American "loudmouth" and the exotic, mysterious "Oriental" girl. Dennis initially opts for the latter, which sets in motion a tale of female jealousy between East and West as Margaret desperately tries to win Dennis's affections.

This episode, and the figure of the loudmouth girl, are interesting in light of Nancy Armstrong's observation in "Occidental Alice."[63] In this reading of *Alice in Wonderland*, Armstrong shows how British imperialism depended on a representation of women as both out of control (possessed of consumer appetites) and self-regulated by taste. Armstrong argues that women with unruly appetites had historically been connected to prostitutes or native others, against which the proper British woman was defined. In a burgeoning consumer society, however, British women also became associated with the lust for things. The Victorian consumer, in this context, was marked as a good woman to the extent that she internalized taste as a means of self-control. Reading *Alice in Wonderland* as a parable of this "double-bodied" woman, she reveals how Alice's appetite for food was deemed improper (and potentially threatening to her figure). Rather than suffering distortions to her body, Alice must learn to regulate this appetite through adopting British tastes. Armstrong further shows how the story centers not simply around food, but around orality itself, and the little girl's mouth especially. In the episode of *Dennis the Menace*, we see a curious manifestation of this narrative logic. Now, the bad or unruly girl is Margaret, the Western loudmouth. Yet unlike Alice, who learns to control her appetite, Margaret is doomed to her brash, loudmouth ways. Taste is instead embodied in the Orient. But, as the episode suggests, the Orient is too rule governed, and it lacks the appropriate display of appetite and consumer pleasure. Faced with these two versions of femininity, Dennis finally rejects both, opting to return to the world of boys. In the process, however, the Occident and Orient are set in competition with each other through the figure of the girl.

Competition between female types from different nations is, in fact, something that Ketcham himself recognizes as an ongoing theme of his strip. When speaking about Gina Gillotti, an Italian American in Dennis's otherwise homogeneous suburb, Ketcham immediately compares her to her all-American counterpart, Margaret. He recalls, "We needed another ethnic group. And . . . I thought a cute little [Italian] gal would be fun to do and something to offset the rather brash feminist Margaret and her attempted conquest."[64]

Ketcham's recognition of the need for ethnic diversity was probably less a personal revelation than a response to wider demands and pressures on the comic strip industry generally. Since the early 1940s, African Americans had protested the racist stereotypes in strips such as *Joe Palooka, Happy Hooligan,* and *Barney Google.* But as *Ebony* noted in 1966, the comic industry responded to such protests mostly through omission, so that "Negroes—caricatures or otherwise—became noticeably absent from the comic pages."[65] By the mid-1960s, numerous black artists began to fill the void with a variety of comic strip genres. In 1965, Morrie Turner inaugurated *Wee Pals,* which *Ebony* dubbed, "the first truly integrated strip"; it included not just Caucasians and African Americans, but a multiracial cast who boasted of their "rainbow power."[66] Turner claims that he based his strip on the highly popular *Peanuts,* but his multiracial cast made it difficult to sell outside large urban areas. "They don't want to take a chance of offending some of their readers by having a feature with integrated children playing together," Turner told *Ebony* in 1966.[67] Still, Turner paved the way for a new representation of the American kid, and although in different ways, both Schulz and Ketcham responded to the demands of integration.

In 1968, Schulz introduced a black character, Franklin, who in an early strip was invited to Charlie Brown's home. According to Schulz's biographer, "a worried syndicate executive didn't really object to Franklin's inclusion so much, but: did Charlie Brown have to invite him directly into his home?"[68] Schulz claims that he initially shied away from presenting a black character because he "didn't want to do it with a patroniz-

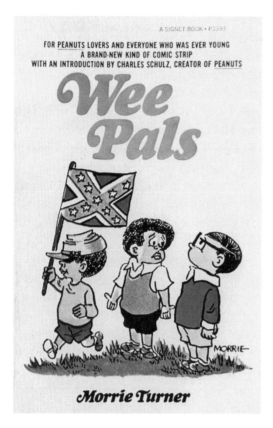

In 1965, Morrie Turner inaugurated *Wee Pals,* which *Ebony* dubbed "the first truly integrated strip." (Copyright, The New American Library, 1969)

ing attitude."[69] It seems likely that Turner's *Wee Pals* provided a model through which Schulz could imagine drawing a black child in less patronizing ways (like Turner, for example, Schulz used diagonal lines rather than the more stereotypical—and controversial—use of solid black to indicate skin color).[70] But Schulz never really developed Franklin's character, nor did he add more racial and ethnic diversity. Instead, race was displaced onto class difference when he included several white children like Marcie and Peppermint Patty who went to a tougher school on the other side of town. Despite these changes, Schulz still centered the strip around his middle-class white suburban town, and as might be expected, some critics were not pleased. In 1970, *Luther* artist Brumsic Brandon Jr. said, "*Peanuts* enjoys a universality among the white community. . . . But to the black community he's a little white boy."[71] One year later, Reverend Cecil Williams of San Francisco's Glide Memorial Church pointed out that "Schulz has stayed away from civil rights and social issues that relate to the Third World and especially black people." [72]

Like Schulz, in the late 1960s, Ketcham also added a black character named Jackson. In his autobiography, Ketcham claims he was "determined to join the parade led by Dr. Martin Luther King Jr., and introduce a black playmate to the Mitchell neighborhood." But unlike Schulz, Ketcham failed to consider the patronizing tone of his character. Ketcham recalls, "I designed him in the tradition of Little Black Sambo with huge lips, big white eyes, and just a suggestion of an Afro hairstyle." In the first panel, Ketcham made race the subject of a gag as Dennis tells his mother, "I have a race problem with Jackson. He can run faster than me!" While Ketcham still contends that this was a "harmless little play on words" and his "Stepin Fetchit" rendering was an "innocent cartoon," Jackson set off protests that began in Detroit and spread to cities across the nation. [73] As Ketcham remembers it, "the odds were against me pleasing everyone, so I just backed away." [74] More generally, Ketcham remains resolute that his characters should not be taken as role models for the real world, whether it be in terms of race, gender roles, or simple behaviors like Henry Mitchell's pipe smoking. Rather, argues Ketcham, "these people behave and look the way they behave and look, and live where they live, because that's the way I want it. . . . This is my space, and I'm going to occupy it in my fashion." [75] Given Dennis's colonialist adventures, perhaps it is no coincidence that Ketcham's description of his comic strip production is itself a colonialist narrative about occupied territories and the rights of the artist literally to own space.

Colonizing the Market: The Meaning of Diversity

To be sure, neither Ketcham nor Schulz did much to diversify their neighborhoods, beyond their token gestures. Instead, they both pursued another kind of diversification that took place outside their fictional strips in the real world of market capitalism. Like their childish heroes, both artists assertively sought to place themselves in as many spaces as possible. Most literally here, in 1956, Ketcham opened the Dennis the Menace Playground in Monterey, California, and Schulz established a separate corporation in 1971 (called Snoopy Co.) to build a theme park on the outskirts of Disneyland. Although Schulz's plans never materialized, he did strike a deal with Knott's Berry Farm, which now includes Camp Snoopy as a separate attraction. Aside from their infiltration of the theme-park tourist trade, both Ketcham and Schulz expanded their narrative spaces outside the strip into a host of related products, from Dennis toy rockets to Snoopy lamps.[76] In fact, as mentioned early on, Schulz was most aggressive in this business; by 1971, *Newsweek* called his strip a "commercial empire" with thirty tie-in companies and a gross national income of $150 million.[77] Over the course of two decades, *Peanuts* had become the most popular strip in history.

Still, at least in the case of *Peanuts,* this forceful colonization of the market was not without its critics, who by the late 1960s began to complain about the proliferation of product spin-offs. Perhaps it is no coincidence that such complaints circulated at a time when comics, and *Peanuts* in particular, were beginning to be conceptualized as "art." One critic for *Look* lambasted the spate of commercial tie-in books by comparing them to Picasso paintings and Nabokov novels. The very fact that this author found it appropriate to compare the *Peanuts* novelty book *Happiness Is a Warm Puppy* to Picasso's *Guernica* suggests that he, like other critics of his time, expected *Peanuts* to be art in the first place. Moreover, this diatribe against *Peanuts* was linked to fears about the commercialization of childhood itself. The critic lamented:

> Schulz first took a part of Charlie Brown away from me when he used his *Peanuts* characters in a series of ads for Falcon cars. I was hurt and puzzled to open a grown-up magazine and see my small friend touting a grown-up automobile. And why shouldn't I be? If there is one quality that particularly binds him to us as a character, it is his own hurt and puzzlement when innocence is betrayed.[78]

Look's adverse reaction to Charlie Brown's adventures on Madison Avenue can be understood in the context of the more widespread ambivalence about consumerism and children that circulated in both intellectual and popular culture. On the one hand, the ability to provide children with wondrous products became a hallmark not only of good parenting, but also of national pride. In the magazine literature that compared U.S. with foreign children, the opportunity to consume came to define the American way of life. In 1958, the vacation magazine *Holiday* reported on the misadventures of one American mother who tried to throw a birthday party for her son while on holiday in Moscow. With the inflated Russian economy, she could purchase only a pencil, some balloons, and a few other "cheap" items, and after searching the streets of Moscow she discovered that Russians didn't have birthday cakes or giftwrap. The birthday party—the quintessential commodity display of affection between parent and child—became in Russia a shopping-spree nightmare.[79]

On the other hand, even as the popular press championed American consumerism, it also presented parents with a stream of contradictory advice against "overindulgence" in the "synthetic pleasures" of consumer culture. Here, mass media aimed at children became key targets of attack. Fredric Wertham's *Seduction of the Innocent* (1953) lashed out at the comic's negative effects on youth, claiming that its violence and perverse sexuality could, among other things, lead to fascist tendencies. Although Wertham coupled his arguments on media effects with a critique of consumerism and American society, at the time his theories became fodder for reactionary antimedia crusades launched both in popular venues (such as women's magazines) and Congress (Senator Estes Kefauver's 1954 hearings on juvenile delinquency featured Wertham as an expert witness).[80] Later in the decade, especially after the recession of 1957 and the Soviet launching of Sputnik, both intellectuals and the popular media became even more critical of the "affluent society," condemning American industry for putting its faith in consumer luxuries rather than in the truly important goals of scientific progress and national security.

Not surprisingly, the postwar kid strip inherited the more general ambivalent attitudes toward children, consumer culture, and national supremacy that circulated during the period. At one level, *Peanuts* and *Dennis* glorified consumerism. These kid strip heroes had expensive toys, went on family vacations, and used their allowances to purchase objects of desire. Moreover, both strips depicted their kids as fervent fans of mass culture who bought baseball cards, watched television, and even read comics. Unlike their Depression-era cousin, Little Orphan Annie, Dennis and the *Peanuts* gang had no hardships to bear. Perhaps most revealingly here, when Little Orphan Annie took a job as a grocery clerk in 1947, venues such as the *Union Times* (a labor newspaper) cried out against the strip's endorsement of child labor: "Any suggestion they [children] be detoured into the bowels of industry or the business world is a menace to the very system and traditional progress that America represents."[81] In *Dennis* and *Peanuts,* the child was unquestionably divorced from the demands of capitalist production and associated with money only by way of consumer desire.

Still, as Jacqueline Rose has argued in her work on *Peter Pan,* in children's literature, money and childhood are always uncomfortably related.[82] From the adult's romantic and nostalgic vision, the child is ideally innocent of worldly woes. But money—even when used for consumption—reminds the reader that children are not immune to the problems that divide the adult world, including the divisions of a class-based society that money so fully organizes. Childhood, then, in popular imagery has often been connected to romantic notions of preindustrial, pastoral values separate from the world of market capitalism. Interestingly, however, in the popular imagination of the day, this return to innocence was not conducted through historical memories of America's own preindustrial, pastoral past, but instead through the geopolitical imagination of the "Third World." Indeed, rather than go back in time, Americans traveled across international space to imagine a world of childhood unsullied by modern life.

Here, popular magazine articles serve as a perfect example. As I mentioned early on, articles about nonindustrialized nations described in painstaking detail the social environments and personal poverty that had robbed children of their natural rights to childhood. Yet at the same time, they often presented romantic tales of the more simple pleasures available to the children of these lands. *Holiday* depicted the poverty-stricken life of a Cuban child named Juana, but in the most romantic way it went on to describe the virtues of her simple island life, which according to the magazine were encapsulated in a rhyme she loved to repeat: "Comer no comemos mucho / Pero rerire si no vemios mucho" (We do not eat very well / but we can laugh, laugh like hell).[83] Similarly, in 1957, *Parents* claimed that Burmese children had more freedom because the "child's life space is not restricted [by] modern inventions to confine the energies of the young." The absence of modern commodities ranging from playpens to television sets helped make the Burmese "informal, spontaneous, optimistic [and] tolerant," as opposed to the "busy, busy, busy" American.[84]

The connections between such images of international childhood and American national policy were especially pronounced in Edward Steichen's *Family of Man* exhibit, which appeared at the Caldren Gallery of Art in Washington, D.C. In a 1955 film made by the U.S. Information Service, Steichen takes the audience on a tour of the exhibit. He starts by admonishing the modern world filled with "hatred and fear," and then uses the image of a Third World child to appeal to us "as human beings." While offered as a humanitarian effort, the exhibit nevertheless was framed within the colonial gaze of the American photographer. Steichen continues, "We begin with a theme . . . a little Peruvian lad blowing the flute, blowing the little song, the song of life. In all his sweetness. The sweetness of a little dark man." [85] Even if Steichen used his image of this Third World child to evoke a kind of universal condition, his conflation of race with childhood innocence worked to infantilize people of color and assert the more sophisticated status of the First World. This becomes especially clear when Steichen contrasts the Peruvian boy to a tuba player in the French symphony or when he compares American children learning about Albert Einstein to a Middle Eastern child learning his "peculiar alphabet." Thus, even when Third World children were presented as "sweet" and untouched by the troubles of modern civilization, these images of childhood nevertheless reasserted the racist idea that in the end the American child was in some way more knowledgeable, sophisticated, and evolved.

While such literal comparisons between American and Third World children did not appear explicitly in *Dennis* and *Peanuts,* the trope of the child native did manifest itself in significant ways. Here, Dennis and the *Peanuts* gang can be seen to be "modern primitives," children who lived in, but were as yet untouched by, the postwar industrial culture. The modern primitive, in this sense, is a figure who negotiates the competing ideals of modernity. On the one hand, as moderns, the kid strip children enjoyed the material goods of consumer capitalism, and in so doing embodied the racist idea that modern capitalism was the product of a more evolved cultural, and even biological, form. On the other hand, as primitives, they also appreciated the simple life of nature and were able to find pleasure in "authentic" folk pastimes. Dennis always likes a good rock collection as much as a new toy rocket, while Charlie and the gang enjoy the "active" pastimes of arts and crafts or piano playing as much as they like to watch television (in fact, in numerous strips they do both at once). In both the strips and television specials, Schulz often criticized the overcommercialization of Christmas and presented moralistic tales in which the *Peanuts* kids learn lessons about the more spiritual meanings of holidays like Thanksgiving or Valentine's Day. Sometimes, as in the case of Linus's furious Halloween search for the Great Pumpkin, Schulz even invented his own ritual traditions, so that in the most paradoxical of ways his highly commercialized kid strip itself took on the status of an "authentic" children's folktale.

The Magic Passport: Childhood, Nation, and Nostalgia

In 1964, at the New York World's Fair, Walt Disney unveiled his popular theme park attraction, It's a Small World. A cruise around the globe, the ride whisks passengers across national cultures, each represented by a group of childlike dolls appropriately attired in native folk costume. Despite their sartorial difference, the children all sing the same "It's a Small World" song and all have the same message to share. And despite the humanist ethos, the small world cruise had the not-so-subtle overtones of Disney's more typical colonialist narrative. Dixieland jazz was the background theme for Africa (which the ride called the "mysterious dark continent"), and at the end of the cruise, the children of the world somehow all sang the English lyrics in a big-finish sing-along.[86]

I want to end this essay with a brief consideration of how these small world politics worked themselves out in the postwar kid strip, which like Disney, also depended on an international market for their phenomenal success. Given the nationalist rhetoric of Dennis and Peanuts, it is particularly interesting that these versions of Americana appealed to readers in distant lands. By 1990, Peanuts could be found in sixty-eight countries.[87] The international success of Dennis and the even more widespread popularity of Peanuts is certainly worthy of an essay of its own, but let me offer a few suggestions.

In the years after World War II, the comic strip industry had numerous problems with its image abroad. Because comics were widely read by American GIs stationed overseas, Europeans often associated them with American military occupation. In this regard, the comic conjured up the image of what one popular book called "the ugly American," the vulgar and uncultured brute who runs roughshod over foreign lands.[88] Insofar as wartime comics were themselves often blatantly racist, militaristic, and xenophobic, they further perpetuated the image of the ugly American in the minds of their readers. In Britain, Western and Eastern Europe, Japan, and the Soviet Union, American comics were variously called "psychological war preparation" and "ideological and moral poison," and several nations banned them.[89]

Despite the fact that American comics were frequently rejected in other nations, Schulz and Ketcham were convinced that their strips spoke a universal language, and U.S. media critics also indicated as much. To be sure, these kid strips were not the first visual media to be considered in terms of universal appeal. As opposed to the language-based texts that Benedict Anderson claims are integral to the "imagined community" of the nation, twentieth-century visual media (even dialogue-based media such as sound films, television, and comics) have often been conceptualized in terms of an *imagined global community* in which people in faraway spaces are joined together by a common lexicon of images. Of course, as is evident from the numerous protests in foreign countries, visual media are not interpreted the same way in all nations. Still, the utopian ideal of universality has been a central mode of understanding—and also legitimating— the spread of U.S. media abroad.[90]

The kid strip took this idea one step further by dealing exclusively with what was seen (at least in America and Western Europe) as a "universal" sign: the child, who according to popular wisdom, communicated the same message wherever it went. Paradoxically here, even while children were often used in discourses of national supremacy, childhood was nevertheless also considered the embodiment of "nature" outside culture. While child-rearing practices endemic to a nation could "ruin" the child, the child itself remained a blank slate. Both Ketcham and Schulz attributed their international popularity, as did many critics, to this "common language" of childhood and its immanent exportability. When asked about the reason for his international success, Ketcham claimed, "Any child, especially a male boy, a male child, preschool, is the same all over the world, regardless of what his culture is."[91] Ketcham's stress on "maleness" is particularly interesting in light of Donna Haraway's analysis of the anthropological sciences, where the "male" specimen is typically considered to be representative of the entire species.[92] Just as in the jungle, in the international image market, the male child seems to function precisely as a form of universal exchange currency—Dennis, Charlie Brown, and even male-coded animal characters like Snoopy are representatives of an essential humanity that exists prior to civilization (which in these strips, is generally associated with the girl characters Margaret and Lucy, who both want to domesticate the boys).

There were, of course, moments when these kid strips did not translate universally across cultures. When Ketcham went to Moscow in 1959, an editor at the humor magazine *Krokodil* asked, "What possible interest would avail readers in the Soviet Union to follow the adventures of a naughty child whose misbehavior is so self-evident due to the defects of a capitalistic society?"[93] And while Charlie Brown was immensely popular overseas, some countries initially failed to see its humor. The strip, for example, took two decades to spark the cultural imagination of France.[94]

By the 1970s, the kid strip became increasingly subject to international controversy. Worried about the amount of *Peanuts* (as well as *Donald Duck* and other American strips) in its nation's press, Brazil's National Executive Comic Strip Commission announced plans to establish a quota system. Despite the fact that U.S. newspapers have historically been entirely devoid of foreign comics, the *Wall Street Journal* found the quota system so offensive that it called for protectionist legislation, and mimicking the "innocent" wisdom of Charlie Brown, cried "Good Grief!" to the whole affair.[95] The *Journal* exclaimed "Good Grief!" a second time when Reverend Cecil Williams suggested that *Peanuts* should deal with Third World concerns.[96]

Despite the defensive logic of big business, the comic came to be a quintessential symbol of American cultural imperialism. In the same year that the *Journal* launched its attack on Brazilian quotas, Chilean scholars Ariel Dorfman and Armand Mattelart wrote their now-classic marxist critique of Disney's imperialist ideology, *How to Read Donald Duck*. An immediate best-seller in Chile, and subsequently in other Latin American editions, this book forcefully demonstrated how companies such as Disney were using "innocence" as a guise for capitalist expansion overseas. Dorfman and Mattelart's harsh criticism of the Duck family made it clear that even the most childish of comics was not a universal language, but instead subject to oppositional interpretations by readers around the world.

Even on American soil, the kid character, as embodied by *Peanuts* and *Dennis,* began to lose ground. Although these two strips remain popular, at the present time they are no longer the reigning symbols of contemporary childhood or, for that matter, the nation. Over the course of the 1960s and 1970s, as collectors, Pop artists, museums, and universities increasingly recognized comics as something more akin to "culture" than to "kitsch," critics increasingly expected funnies to deal with serious problems, from Civil Rights to the Vietnam War to women's liberation.[97] Meanwhile, the growth of underground comics created a new comic book avant-garde in which neither *Dennis* nor *Peanuts* belonged. Dennis is especially resistant to cultural transformation, and aside from some wardrobe and hairdo changes, the strip reads as a monument to its own historical place and time (as one critic said of the 1993 film, it applied "little imagination to an old-fashioned vision of America").[98] Perhaps it is because of their claims to universality (their attempt to speak outside history) that neither *Dennis* nor *Peanuts* did much to remain in step with the times. (And notably here, the new "yellow kid" on the block, Bart Simpson, still exhibits the bad boy charms of his kid strip cousins while the *South Park* kids turn the bad boy comic convention into the ultimate parody, a comic inversion of postwar family ideals.)

Even in their present-day incarnations, *Dennis* and *Peanuts* seem more a part of a "residual" culture that harkens back to a prior time, but is not in sync with dominant contemporary social views. In this case, these comics can be seen as a residue of the cold-war era's conceptions of childhood and national supremacy, conceptions that are no longer the dominant terms of social experience and cultural production. More Americana than American, these two strips of the baby boom generation represent a vision of childhood and suburban life so out of touch with real communities that they no longer provide the "imagined community" that constitutes a nation.

As numerous critics have argued, in a world of global culture and international information flows, nationalism may itself be becoming a residual sentiment, perhaps available primarily through nostalgia rather than any of the social realities that define the current world. The word *nostalgia* was originally intended to describe a soldier's longing for the homeland, but even in its more contemporary meanings of "a return to the past," it still engages nationalist sentiments. It is in this context that we might also understand the recent recycling of *Dennis* and *Peanuts* for the baby boom generation (and their children). The 1993 film release of *Dennis the Menace*, and the spate of Snoopy ties and boxer shorts that are now appearing in men's stores at the local mall, evoke their own romantic longing for a simpler, personal (and national) past where Snoopy fights the Red Baron and Dennis champions the American way. Such recycled objects link together a fragmented demographic group of Americans who imagine themselves as a generation. Still, for this baby boom generation, it seems likely that contemporary kid strip nostalgia is connected to nationalist sentiments, to the desire to return to a cold war past where nations still existed, and the boundaries between "us" and "them" were eminently clear. But, of course, the lines between nations, like the lines of kid strip heroes, are never as clear-cut as they first appear.

Notes

This essay first appeared in *Kids' Media Culture,* ed. Marsha Kinder (Durham, N.C.: Duke University Press, 1999), pp. 31–68.

1   Mother's Day was first celebrated in 1908. Father's Day appeared in 1910; in 1916, President Woodrow Wilson endorsed its celebration, and in 1924, President Calvin Coolidge recommended national observance of the holiday. U.S. Senate Joint Resolution 139 empowered President Clinton to proclaim Children's Day a holiday on November 18, 1993. (President, Proclamation, "National Children's Day, Proclamation 6626," *Weekly Compilation of Presidential Documents* [19 November 1993].)

2   Ariel Dorfman and Armand Mattelart, *How to Read Donald Duck: Imperialist Ideology in the Disney Comic,* trans. David Kunzle (New York: International General, 1971).

3   For a detailed description of the growth of comics and their relation to advertising and consumer product tie-ins, see Ian Gordon, *Comic Strips and Consumer Culture, 1890–1945* (Washington, D.C.: Smithsonian Institution Press, 1998).

4   Initially carried by seven newspapers, the strip took several years to secure its national popularity. In 1952, the first *Peanuts* book was published. See Rheta Grimsley Johnson, *Good Grief: The Story of Charles M. Schulz* (New York: Pharos Books, 1989), p. 28.

5   Hank Ketcham, *The Merchant of Dennis the Menace* (New York: Abbeville Press, 1990), pp. 103, 106. For the national figures in 1953, see "Ketcham's Menace," *Newsweek,* 4 May 1953, p. 57. The same issue of *Newsweek* also reported that Ketcham won the "most coveted prize of comic-strip artists, Billy De Beck award for the outstanding cartoonist of the year." By 1961, *Publisher's Weekly* claimed that *Dennis* was in seven hundred daily and Sunday U.S. papers. See "From Cartoon to Big Business with *Dennis the Menace,*" *Publisher's Weekly,* 9 January 1961, pp. 34–35.

6   For the *Dennis* figure, see "From Cartoon to Big Business," p. 34; the *Peanuts* figure was reported in "Good Grief, Curly Hair," *Newsweek,* 6 March 1961, p. 68. *Peanuts* was reported to be in forty-one countries by 1969. See John Tebbel, "The Not-So Peanuts World of Charles M. Schulz," *Saturday Review,* 12 April 1969, p. 72.

7   For descriptions of Screen Gems's production of *Dennis,* see Screen Gems, Inc., Annual Report, 1 July 1961, *Dennis the Menace* folder, Doheny Cinema Library clipping files, University of Southern California; Jeb H. Perry, *Screen Gems: A History of Columbia Pictures Television from Cohn to Coke, 1948–1983* (Metuchen, N.J.: Scarecrow Press, 1991); and George W. Woolery, *Children's Television: The*

First Thirty-Five Years, 1946–1981, part 2 (Metuchen, N.J.: Scarecrow Press, 1985), pp. 146–48. In later years, *Dennis* returned to television in a two-hour special for first-run syndication produced by DIC Enterprises and distributed by Coca-Cola. See Synopsis/Press Release, Doheny Cinema Library clipping files, University of Southern California. There was an animated *Dennis the Menace* in first-run syndication, which is also packaged for the home video market. In 1993, a theatrical film was released.

8   *A Charlie Brown Christmas* won a Peabody Award that year for "outstanding children and youths' program." For a retrospective of the many specials, see Museum of Broadcasting, *Charlie Brown, A Boy for All Seasons: Twenty Years on Television* (exhibition catalog, Museum of Broadcasting, New York, 15 November 1984).

9   Hank Ketcham, telephone interview by Bill Forman, 4 August 1993, Los Angeles, California. Ketcham further recalls this incident in his autobiography, *The Merchant of Dennis the Menace,* p. 159.

10   "Lenin vs. Snoopy," *New York Times,* 24 May 1969, sec. 2, p. 34.

11   Benedict Anderson, *Imagined Communities: Reflections on the Origin and Spread of Nationalism* (1983; London: Verso, 1992).

12   Viviana A. Zelizer, *Pricing the Priceless Child: The Changing Social Value of Children* (Princeton, N.J.: Princeton University Press, 1994).

13   For more on this point in relation to crusades against mass media, see Lynn Spigel, "Seducing the Innocent: Television and Childhood in Postwar America," in *Ruthless Criticism,* ed. Robert McChesney and William Soloman (Minneapolis: University of Minnesota Press, 1993), pp. 259–90, and in this volume.

14   On the sales of Spock's book, see Dewey W. Grantham, *Recent America: The United States since 1945* (Arlington Heights, Ill.: Harlan Davidson, 1987), p. 201.

15   Abram Kardiner, "When the State Brings Up the Child," *Saturday Review,* 26 August 1961, p. 9. For articles (explicitly or implicitly) comparing American children to those in the Soviet Union and other Communist countries, see "Cuba: And Now the Children?" *Time,* 6 October 1961, p. 41; Hugh Moffett, "The Moffetts Go A-Moseying," *Life,* 13 September 1963, pp. 101–11; J. L., "The Russian Tragedy," *Saturday Review,* 3 March 1962, p. 42; and "Moscow," *Life,* 13 September 1963, pp. 89–91.

16   Urie Bronfenbrenner, "Challenge of the 'New Soviet Man,'" *New York Times Magazine,* 27 August 1961, p. 78.

17   For examples, see George Kent, "Magic Carpet for Europe's Saddest Children," *Reader's Digest,* April 1956, pp. 127–30; Roger Angell, "The Small One," *Holiday,* February 1956, pp. 100–101; "The King's Man," *Holiday,* December 1955, pp. 115–17; and Howard A. Rusk, "Voice from Korea: Won't You Please Help Us off Our Knees?" *Life,* 7 June 1954, pp. 178–82.

18   Alastair Buchan, "Our Small Anglo-American Relations," *New York Times Magazine,* 12 April 1953, pp. 17, 39; Alice Shabecoff, "Bringing up Hans and Gretel," *New York Times Magazine,* 13 November 1966, pp. 180, 182–83; and Ruth McKenney, "Paris! City of Children," *Holiday,* April 1953, pp. 62–66 (for the description of the abusive French parent, see n. 20).

19   Edward M. Korry, "Lost Childhood," *Look*, 20 March 1956, pp. 65–73.

20   John Keats, *The Crack in the Picture Window* (1956; Boston: Houghton Mifflin, 1957); William H. Whyte, *The Organization Man* (Garden City, N.Y.: Doubleday, 1956); and Betty Friedan, *The Feminine Mystique* (New York: Norton, 1963). It should be noted that many of these views were also expressed in a host of popular media.

21   Hank Ketcham, *Dennis the Menace, A.M.: Ambassador of Mischief* (New York: Fawcett World Library, 1961). This is an anthology of panels that appeared in daily newspapers. According to the copyright information, the panels were first published between 1959 and 1961, although they are not individually dated in this book. The book is not paginated, and therefore all subsequent references will not include page numbers.

22   Ketcham, *Merchant of Dennis*, p. 154.

23   Hank Ketcham, *In This Corner . . . Dennis the Menace* (1959; Greenwich, Conn.: Fawcett Publications, 1971). The panels in this collection are copyrighted from 1957 to 1959. The book is not paginated, and therefore all subsequent references will not include page numbers.

24   Henry Jenkins, "Dennis the Menace: 'The All American Handful,'" in *The Revolution Wasn't Televised: Sixties Television and Social Conflict*, ed. Lynn Spigel and Michael Curtin (New York: Routledge, 1997), pp. 119–38.

25   As one of the readers for this essay suggested, *Peanuts* can be seen to inherit some of the characteristics of the Hal Roach series *Our Gang*, as children form the principal cast. Yet unlike *Our Gang*, which expressed class conflicts between rich and poor children, *Peanuts* presented a postwar consumerist ideology about children that placed them in a world where social mobility seemed possible for all.

26   Snoopy, like other animal characters before him, was presented through anthropomorphic logic. Often, he took on the role of an adult, so that the adult-child binary was displaced onto that of animal-human. As Richard deCordova argues in his work on Disney, such displacements might be read in terms of the history of the regulation of childhood. He writes of early cinema: "Reformers were interested in conserving a set of distinctions between adult and child, which the cinema presumably blurred. One way of bringing those distinctions back into focus was to superimpose them on the more culturally stable distinction between animals and humans. That is what the association of animals and children worked to do." See Richard deCordova, "The Mickey in Macy's Window: Childhood, Consumerism, and Disney Animation," in *Disney Discourse: Producing the Magic Kingdom*, ed. Eric Smoodin (New York: Routledge, 1994), p. 211.

27   Charles M. Schulz, cited in Tebbel, "Not-So Peanuts World," p. 74.

28   Bronfenbrenner, "Challenge of the New Soviet Man," p. 79.

29   Buchan, "Our Small Anglo-American Relations," p. 39.

30   Hank Ketcham, *Dennis the Menace: His First 40 Years* (New York: Abbeville Press, 1991). This book is not paginated, and therefore all subsequent references will not include pagination.

31   Ketcham, *In This Corner*. Note that the strip often represented the "sissy" through

Dennis's pal Joey. According to Henry Jenkins ("All American Handful," p. 129), Joey was constantly torn between Dennis's love of boyish games and Margaret's desire to play house. Jenkins offers this example as part of his larger thesis that Dennis portrayed American masculinity as a rejection of all things domestic, suburban, and feminine. Joey, then, illustrates the inability to choose between the man's world of rugged adventure and the domesticated world of women's suburban culture.

32 Ketcham, *His First 40 Years.*

33 Ketcham, *In This Corner.*

34 Hank Ketcham, telephone interview by Bill Forman, 2 August 1992, Los Angeles, California.

35 See the review of the televised version of *Dennis the Menace,* in *National Parent Teacher,* April 1960, p. 25. According to George W. Woolery, "after the first season, the PTA asked the producers to tone down Dennis's shenanigans so he would not set a bad example for young children" (*Children's Television,* p. 147).

36 James L. Hymes cited in Jenkins, "All American Handful," p. 131.

37 Charles M. Schulz, *You Can Do It, Charlie Brown* (New York: Holt, Rinehart and Winston, 1965). The strips in this collection are copyrighted from 1962 to 1963. The book is not paginated, and therefore all subsequent references will not include page numbers.

38 "Good Grief, Curly Hair," p. 68.

39 To be sure, some critics lashed out at Schulz's brainy, adultlike kids, and found his renderings unrealistic to the point of parody. Cartoonist Al Capp made his disapproval the subject of his strip *Li'l Abner,* which featured Schulz in the guise of "Good Old Bedly Damp," creator of "Pee-Wee." See Johnson, *Good Grief,* p. 76.

40 Ketcham, Forman interview, 4 August 1993.

41 Ketcham, *His First 40 Years.*

42 Ibid.

43 Elizabeth Gordon, "The Threat to the Next America," *House Beautiful,* April 1953, editorial. For a discussion of American modern art as it relates to postwar nationalism and cultural imperialism, see Emily S. Rosenberg's exploration of the State Department's 1946 international exhibit titled "Advancing American Art" in her book *Spreading the American Dream: American Economic and Cultural Expansion, 1890–1945* (New York: Hill and Wang, 1982), p. 216. See also Frank A. Ninkovich, "The Currents of Cultural Diplomacy: Art and the State Department, 1938–1947," *Diplomatic History* 1 (1977): 215–37.

44 Ketcham's various museum panels are the comic strip equivalent of Norman Rockwell's *The Connoisseur* (1962) in which Rockwell juxtaposed his popular commercial art style to the intellectual art of abstract expressionism (the painting presented a Rockwellesque rendering of a museum where a patron gazes at a Jackson Pollock–type canvas).

45 See Serge Guilbaut, *How New York Stole the Idea of Modern Art: Abstract Expressionism, Freedom, and the Cold War,* trans. A. Goldhammer (Chicago: University of Chicago Press, 1983). While Guilbaut acknowledges that this "triumph of the

avant garde was neither a total victory nor a popular one" and that it was "threatened by opposing tendencies in the work of art" (p. 3), he nevertheless argues that the avant-garde—particularly abstract expressionism—coincided with what was becoming the dominant ideology of the new liberalism.

46 Robert R. McElroy, "Good Grief, $150 Million!" *Newsweek,* 27 December 1971, p. 42.

47 "Good Grief, Curly Hair," p. 68; Tebbel, "No-So Peanuts World," p. 74.

48 Johnson, *Good Grief,* p. 29.

49 Charles M. Schulz, *Peanuts Treasury* (New York: Holt, Rinehart and Winston, 1968), n.p.

50 While *Peanuts* often engaged profound questions, and while critics and Schulz himself liked to interpret the strip in this way, in his recent biography, Schulz denies that he is trying to send a "message," arguing that he's only "interested in being funny" (Johnson, *Good Grief,* p. 130).

51 Robert L. Short, *The Gospel According to Peanuts* (Richmond, Va.: John Knox Press, 1964). By 1969, this book had entered its twenty-first printing. Its popularity was met with some resistance by the church, which questioned the introduction of popular culture into Christian doctrine. See Edward B. Fiske, "Liturgies Embracing More Pop Art Forms," *New York Times,* 15 May 1967, sec. 1, pp. 1, 48. Despite this, Short wrote a second volume titled *The Parables of Peanuts* (New York: Harper and Row, 1969), and went on to produce a theological reading of science fiction narratives about space, which also used comics (including *Peanuts*) as examples. See Robert L. Short, *The Gospel from Outer Space* (San Francisco: Harper and Row, 1983).

52 Note that in *Dennis the Menace,* the image of suburbia was more nostalgic than modern. It harkened back to the American small town suburb, even while it was in dialogue with the more contemporary mass-produced suburb of its time.

53 Ketcham, *Dennis the Menace, A.M.* Ketcham was particularly fond of these bathroom jokes, which became a running gag.

54 Ibid.

55 For a description of *Rollo* and other early children's series, see Faye Riter Kensinger, *Children of the Series and How They Grew* (Bowling Green, Ohio: Bowling Green State University Popular Press, 1987).

56 Johnson, *Good Grief,* p. 80.

57 In the television special *Bon Voyage, Charlie Brown* (1980), the *Peanuts* gang become exchange students in France and rescue a sad little French girl who has been tormented by her uncle. The program also deals with war-related themes.

58 Ketcham, *Dennis the Menace, A.M.,* inside cover.

59 Ketcham, *His First 40 Years;* and Ketcham, *In This Corner.* Henry Jenkins ("All American Handful," p. 131) notes that in the television series, the western frontier was often translated into the new frontier of outer space, as Dennis became a little astronaut ready to explore the universe.

60 Both of these are in Ketcham, *Dennis the Menace, A.M.*

61 While Charlie Brown pined after the Little Red-Headed Girl and Linus after his

teacher Miss Othmar, unlike Lucy, they never badgered their beloved. Instead, they were the victims of their inability to properly pursue the girls of their dreams. For boys, then, romance represented the failure of masculine prowess, while for the girls it became a weapon of the weak.

62 Ketcham, *Merchant of Dennis*, p. 136.

63 Nancy Armstrong, "Occidental Alice," *Differences* 2:2 (1990): 4–41.

64 Ketcham, Forman interview, 4 August 1993. Just as in the television episode with the Chinese girl, Gina's nationality was often represented by her culinary difference. In numerous panels, Dennis becomes a big fan of Gina, rushing off to get a taste of her mother's Italian cuisine.

65 See Ponchitta Pierce, "What's Not So Funny about the Funnies," *Ebony*, November 1966, p. 50.

66 See Louie Robinson, "Cartoonist with a Conscience," *Ebony*, February 1973, pp. 31–42. In 1968, *Luther*, a well-known kid strip that features an African American boy, also appeared. For more on this, see David A. Andelman, "Comics Find Negro Heroes," *New York Times*, 22 September 1970, sec. 1, p. 47.

67 Morrie Turner cited in Pierce, "What's Not So Funny," p. 53. Despite its slow start, *Wee Pals* went on to achieve national success. By 1973, it was picked up by King Syndicate and transformed into the ABC Saturday morning show *Kid Power*.

68 Johnson, *Good Grief*, p. 66.

69 Andelman, "Comics Find Negro Heroes," p. 47.

70 *Ebony* listed the solid black face as one of a litany of racist stereotypes that had been the subject of black protest. See Pierce, "What's Not So Funny," p. 48.

71 Andelman, "Comics Find Negro Heroes," p. 47.

72 "Good Grief!" *Wall Street Journal*, 24 December 1971, p. 1.

73 Ketcham, *Merchant of Dennis*, pp. 210–11.

74 Ketcham, Forman interview, 4 August 1993.

75 Ibid.

76 In 1953, a comic magazine based on *Dennis* was published by Harry Slater of the Hall Syndicate, who was also in charge of merchandising Dennis products. By 1961, Holt, Rinehart and Winston had already published eight hardcover collections of the cartoons, which were reprinted in softcover by Fawcett. See "From Cartoon to Big Business," p. 35. In 1953, Rosemary Clooney and Jimmy Boyd made a *Dennis the Menace* record for Columbia. See "Ketcham's Menace," p. 57. In that same year, a line of *Dennis the Menace* children's clothing was in production. See "The Menace Gets Dressed," *Look*, 6 October 1953, pp. 87–91. By 1961, a host of other products from paper plates to greeting cards were available. See "From Cartoon to Big Business."

   Determined Publications has made novelty books of the *Peanuts* strip since 1962. The first was *Happiness Is a Warm Puppy*, which was a 1962–1963 bestseller for forty-five weeks. Holt, Rinehart and Winston and the John Fox Press (a religious publisher) went on to handle the higher-priced *Peanuts* books. By 1976, sixteen of the fifty-eight best-selling paperbacks were *Peanuts* books. See Paul Showers, "Snoopy in the Sky with Diamonds," *New York Times Book Review*,

12 February 1968, p. 28. In 1970, Schulz formed a company to build a Charlie Brown–theme amusement park. See *Wall Street Journal*, 12 October 1970, p. 5. The Broadway musical "You're a Good Man, Charlie Brown" is one of the most frequently produced in history (see Johnson, *Good Grief*, p. xii), and the *Peanuts* characters have appeared in a host of other related media and products, from ice rink pageants to clothing, posters, and wristwatches.

77 McElroy, "Good Grief, $150 Million!" pp. 40–42.

78 William K. Zinsser, "Enough Is a Warm Too Much," *Look*, 21 February 1967, p. 11.

79 Santha Rama Rau, "For a Russian Child—Everything," *Holiday*, June 1958, pp. 68–69.

80 For a more thorough account of Wertham's intellectual history as well as a discussion of the congressional hearings, see James Gilbert, *A Cycle of Outrage: America's Reaction to the Juvenile Delinquent in the 1950s* (New York: Oxford University Press, 1986), esp. chapter 6. For the hearings themselves, see Committee on the Judiciary, United States Senate, *Hearings before the Subcommittee to Investigate Juvenile Delinquency*, 83rd Cong., 2d Sess., S. Res. 89 (Washington, D.C.: Government Printing Office, 5 June 1954). The committee reconvened on 19 and 20 October 1954, and also met on 6 and 7 April 1954 to continue the debates.

81 Bruce Smith, *The History of Little Orphan Annie* (New York: Ballantine, 1982), pp. 64–65.

82 Jacqueline Rose, *The Case of Peter Pan: Or the Impossibility of Children's Fiction* (London: Macmillan, 1984), esp. chapter 4.

83 "The Girl on the Cay," *Holiday*, January 1956, p. 96.

84 Helen Trager, "The Burmese Way with Children," *Parents*, January 1957, pp. 32, 44–45.

85 Edward Steichen, voice-over in *The Family of Man*, CBS TV and Robert Northshield Productions, 1956. In the Museum of Modern Art Film Archives, New York, New York.

86 My description of this ride is based on an episode of *Walt Disney's Wonderful World of Color*, originally aired on NBC in 1964.

87 Johnson, *Good Grief*, p. xii. *Peanuts* may well be more popular in Italy, where it was translated into Latin, than it is in America. For instance, Italy's official 1993 entry for the Oscars's "Best Foreign Language Film" is called *Grande Cocomero* after Linus's search for the Great Pumpkin.

88 William J. Lederer, *The Ugly American* (New York: Norton, 1958).

89 Italian Communists called Mickey Mouse and Donald Duck "imperialist warmongers" (see "Italian Reds Bar a U.S. Comic," *New York Times*, 4 April 1952, p. 15); Moscow radio said that Americans were "flooding Western Europe with ideological and moral poison" (see "Moscow Calls U.S. Comics Poison," *New York Times*, 25 November 1953, p. 10); the Justice Ministry in West Germany banned comics portraying "primitive" and "barbarous acts" (see "Bonn Curbing 'Comic' Books," *New York Times*, 21 August 1955, p. 5); East Germany called American comics "psychological war preparation," and Education Minister

Fritz Lange said that distributors of American-style comics would be "punished severely and mercilessly" (see "German Reds Propose 'Punishment' for Comics," *New York Times*, 20 May 1955, p. 3); a Tokyo newspaper dropped *Pogo* because of its rendering of a Khrushchev-like pig (see "Tokyo Newspaper Drops *Pogo* because of Khrushchev-Like Pig," *New York Times*, 21 May 1962, p. 16); and in Britain, the Communist Party played a central role in a postwar campaign against U.S. horror comics that culminated in a nationwide ban on comics (see Martin Barker, *A Haunt of Fears: The Strange History of the British Horror Comics Campaign* [London: Pluto Press, 1984]).

90 For a good case study that shows how Nelson Rockefeller, director of the Office of the Coordinator of Inter-American Affairs, joined hands with Walt Disney in the early 1940s to produce films that would enhance the image of the United States in Latin America, see Julianne Burton, "Don (Juanito) Duck and the Imperial-Patriarchal Unconscious: Disney Studios, the Good Neighbor Policy, and the Packaging of Latin America," in *Nationalisms and Sexualities*, ed. Andrew Parker et al. (New York: Routledge, 1992), pp. 21–41.

91 Ketcham, Forman interview, 4 August 1993.

92 Donna Haraway, *Primate Visions: Gender, Race, and Nature in the World of Modern Science* (New York: Routledge, 1989), esp. chapter 3.

93 Ketcham, *Merchant of Dennis*, p. 163.

94 Nan Robertson, " 'Peanuts' Bridges a Language Gap and Captivates the French," *New York Times*, 26 March 1975, p. 2.

95 "What's Next, Charlie Brown?" *Wall Street Journal*, 19 April 1971, p. 14. It should be noted that in Brazil, a congressional bill to ban U.S. comics had been put forward in the early 1950s. See "Brazil Assails U.S. Comic Books," *New York Times*, 11 November 1953, p. 13.

96 "Good Grief!" *Wall Street Journal*, p. 4.

97 The comics' turn to relevancy was the subject of discussion in the popular press, and for this reason, it seems likely that people beyond critics, collectors, artists, and intellectuals were thinking about the new "horizon of expectations" for topics in the funny pages. See Saul Braun, "Shazam! Here Comes Captain Relevant," *New York Times Magazine*, 2 May 1971, p. 1; Laurie Johnston, "Women's Liberation in the Comics: The Jokes Are on Everybody," *New York Times*, 3 February 1973, p. 34; David Kunzle, "Self-Conscious Comics," *New Republic*, 19 July 1975, pp. 26–27; and "Leapin' Lizards! Look What's Happened to the Comics!" *U.S. News and World Report*, 9 June 1975, pp. 44–46.

98 Todd McCarthy, "Dennis the Menace," *Variety*, 28 June 1993, p. 24.

Part IV: Living Room to Gallery

High Culture in Low Places:
Television and Modern Art, 1950–1970

✱ In 1954, on the occasion of its twenty-fifth anniversary, the Museum of Modern Art presented an episode of the New York television program *Dimension*. Hosted by museum director Rene d'Harnoncourt, this public affairs program served as a promotional vehicle for MOMA's collection of modern art. In the opening sequence, d'Harnoncourt presents a Leger painting and is joined by a professor from NYU's art history department.[1] While the two men show a distinguished command of the modernist canon, they seem less certain about how to convey their knowledge over the new medium of live TV. About five minutes into the program, when the professor decides to show Stuart Davis's painting *The Flying Carpet*, he suddenly realizes the canvas is not in the room. Looking embarrassed, he asks the cameraman to move to another gallery space where the painting is located. Unfortunately for the professor, however, more embarrassment is in store because when the camera moves to the next gallery, it reveals a rather disheveled looking TV floor manager hanging out in front of the painting, smoking a cigarette, so close to the canvas in fact that it appears he is going to burn a hole in it. When the floor manager realizes he is on live TV, he runs out of the frame. The befuddled professor then tries to make the best out of a bad situation and calls the floor manager back, asking him whether he likes the painting. The floor manager replies, "Uh, yeah, I like it, it's big," to which the professor remarks,

"You can tell us what you really think. Because if you don't like it, you won't be the first person who didn't respond favorably to modern art."[2]

Today, at a time when Congress turns its back on public TV, it seems especially useful to consider the historical dialogues that have taken place regarding art and education on our national broadcast system. In light of this, I want to explore the first two decades of television broadcasting, the time when television reached its mature form as a commercial and national medium, with one venue, the Public Broadcasting System (PBS), serving as its forum for the arts.

Insofar as recent television scholarship has been largely defined as the study of popular culture, critics have tended to stay away from topics that engage the problem of art. Even while there has been important work on issues of taste and "quality" television, there is very little work on television's artistic practices and discourses about art.[3] Given that television is integral to the foundations of the postmodern blurring of "high" and "low" culture, it is even more curious that recent art historical work and museum exhibitions on the fate of modernism and the avant-garde after World War II have been relatively silent on the role that television played in collapsing this great divide. While debates about the postwar status of a distinctly American modern art and its relation to popular culture have circulated within art historical circles, art historians have primarily investigated the art world as a privileged term, giving little perspective on how popular media—especially television—served as a vehicle for the wide-scale dissemination of ideas about modern art and its relation to national identity after World War II. Similarly, the recent high and low exhibits at museums such as MOMA and the Whitney Museum of American Art consider how artists used popular culture as a "subject" in their painting, yet there is virtually no understanding of how television used art as a subject.

As Pierre Bourdieu has demonstrated, the value of art in a culture is not neutral, but rather is a product of the way people in a social formation make distinctions among themselves based on notions of "taste."[4] These taste distinctions generally are determined by social class and economic privilege, but also by access to "cultural capital" gained through arenas such as education. Constructed through such social differences, art—or what counts as authentic art versus kitsch—is never universal across time and space; rather it is deeply historical and subject to change as other kinds of social identities and formations of everyday life shift among populations. Television's various representations of art and its own artistic practices have accordingly changed with larger social and cultural reformations. In this essay, I want to consider how television positioned itself in relation to the meanings of the visual arts—primarily painting—in the first two decades after World War II, during the height of the cold war.

Television's discourses on art were rooted in the history of European colonialism (especially the art world's ties to Paris), and the perception both here and abroad that the United States—while an economic and political superpower after the war—was still a *cultural* colony of Europe. It was the urge to distinguish a new (and typically called "modern") American art from European modernism that haunted the screens of American living rooms during the 1950s and 1960s. In the process, television contributed to a redefinition of the American vernacular that was ultimately based on the idea that American modern art was commercial art, with no apologies and no excuses. It is here, in the redefinition of the American vernacular, where the connections to postmodernism seem most clear, especially as they pervade the pop art scene in the 1960s. Also in the process, there was a curious inversion of the ideological relationships between mass culture and modernism, especially as those terms have historically been associated with feminine consumers and masculine producers, respectively. Indeed, as I will show, the history of art on television is also a history of cultural politics imbedded in battles over taste, which were in turn ultimately based on larger social struggles.

Before the Great Divide

To understand television's role in the redefinition of art in postwar America, it seems important to question, as Andreas Huyssen has, the "great divide" thesis that pits a postwar and increasingly postmodern consumer culture against a prewar, supposedly more political, modernism.[5] Moreover, it seems crucial to reject at the outset the facile labeling of television as "postmodern," a label that is all too often used as if it were an MTV promotional slogan (which it is), a label that is thus utterly tautological because it is so characteristically postmodern in and of itself to have a critical term that doubles for an advertising jingle. While there is something different in the air (and on the airwaves) that might amount to a cultural sensibility called "postmodernism," it is important to explore the ways in which television is, a priori, rooted in the logic of modernism and, in particular, to the marriage between the visual arts and industrial technology so crucial to the modern world of twentieth-century Western culture. In the postwar period, television responded to and expanded the definition of modern art—both in the sense of the modern "art for art's sake" movements and in the more avant-garde notion of modern art as a revolutionary tool (the "art for life's sake" position). To disclose television's role in this process, it seems necessary to understand something of the cultural moment that preceded it, particularly that moment, the 1920s to the 1930s, when modern art (in Europe) and commercial art (in the United States) shared their first encounters.

Cultural historians have detailed some of the links between American consumer culture and the influx of European modern art and design.[6] As such research makes clear, the advertising and fashion industries were among the first cultural sites where the public—especially bourgeois women targeted by corporations—encountered modern art.

A fascinating memoir written in 1939 by advertising executive Estelle Hamburger, *It's a Woman's Business,* suggests women were not only the target consumers of this early merger between high and low, but also the producers of it.[7] I want to give some thought to this memoir, not only because it suggests the central importance of women in the imagination of the American "modern" (a point to which I shall often return in this essay), but also because it exemplifies in a most explicit way the nationalist impulse that runs through the discourses found on television three decades later.

In her memoir, Hamburger recalls how during the 1920s she made her way from a copy girl at Macy's to the head of the advertising department in the more upscale and uptown Bonwit Teller. Once there, Hamburger tried to change Bonwit's image from its eighteenth-century French decorative style and its promise of "classic" fashions to one that spoke the language of the here and now. In the process of this transition, Hamburger found herself at the intersection of consumer culture and modern art.

In her chapter "What Is Modern?" she discusses her 1925 trip to the Paris Exposition of Decorative Arts that she said "became the cradle of modern design." She writes: "If America did not take 'Modern' to France in 1925, Americans brought it home. Only a few understood the objectives in the minds of artists who gave it birth. To American designers of furniture, rugs, fabrics, lamps, china, to creators of American advertising, Modern became a new commercial god."[8]

While Hamburger emphasized America's debt to European modern art, it was clear that the American design industry's interpretation of "modern" was also based on its global scavenging of what the business and art world alike deemed "savage" or "ancient" cultures. Hamburger spoke at length of her use of savage and ancient art for modern textile design. She also detailed her debt to the Brooklyn Museum of Art, which she ransacked for nativist and primitivist inspirations. Explaining one such campaign she wrote, "In the window with the Bonwit Teller dresses, hats and jewelry inspired by the African Congo were the treasures from the Brooklyn Museum authoritatively documented with explanatory cards." She goes on to note that when the director of the Brooklyn Museum "saw this marriage of Congo art with current fashion his pleasure was unbounded. It had been his life's labor to build a museum that would not be a mausoleum of dead art, but an inspiration to vital modern industrial design. . . . [He] had the entire exhibit transferred to the Brooklyn Museum, to illustrate, in connection with his permanent display of the Belgian Congo, how the resources of a museum might be employed to inspire the creative impulses of the commercial world."[9]

Clearly, the art world of the 1920s had just as much to gain from its relationship with consumerism as did the consumer culture from its links to the art scene (and both, obviously, benefited from their use of what they deemed "savage" cultures as sources for modern design). At a time when museums were already being criticized as "mausoleums of the dead" (that is, spaces that ripped art from its everyday context), and when movements like DADA were promoting "living art," museum directors could, in one simple stroke, answer to the demands of the art world and also shamelessly pander to the (mostly female) bourgeois public through cross-promotional ties with the world of fashion.

Hamburger's memoir demonstrates that the union of art and industry—high and low—was crucial to the culture of the early twentieth century. Her text maps out a series of relationships between and among art and industry, nationalism and internationalism, modern and primitive, consumer and museum culture, and intellectualism and populism. In addition, given Hamburger's status as a female "adman," her memoir also suggests a struggle between women and men for control over art, culture, and commerce. These relationships would reemerge on television—the new shop window on the world—at a time when the meaning of modern art and consumer culture were being renegotiated in important ways.

In the postwar period, the relationship between art and industry was embroiled in a new set of circumstances that revolved around America's efforts to define itself as a cultural center for the world at the same time that it emerged as a global superpower. During the war, according to Serge Guilbaut, "Companies made use of art and advertising as a way of keeping their trademarks alive before the public," thus creating a merger that contributed to a popular embrace of art after the war.[10] This growing public interest in art was spurred in the early 1940s by increased discussion of the arts in popular media by such government-sponsored campaigns as "buy American art week," and by the sale (through credit financing) of famous paintings at Macy's and Gimbles, two of New York's largest middle-class department stores. During the war, art appreciation was positioned as a form of patriotism linked to the defense of American civilization against Nazi barbarism. The Metropolitan Museum of Art and MOMA both gained respect by linking their institutions to the war effort. In this context, museum patronage increased significantly. The number of art galleries in New York grew from 40 at the beginning of the war to 150 by 1946, and both public and private gallery sales skyrocketed during the war.[11] These trends apparently continued after the war: in 1962, the Stanford Research Institute estimated that "120 million people attend art-oriented events"; that tourism at MOMA was "only outnumbered by the Empire State Building"; and that "attendance at art galleries and museums almost doubled during the 1950s."[12] According to the Stanford report, the new "cultured American" was in part the result of technology that made possible "first class reproductions" at a "cost many can afford."[13] To be sure, people in the art world manipulated the new medium of television to this end, appealing to middle-class publics in the mass-produced suburbs with "free" shows of modern painting.[14]

As my opening example suggests, MOMA, a museum renowned for introducing European modernism to the public, was heavily invested in the subject of television. In 1939, the year MOMA opened its West 53rd Street building (a starkly modern structure that Alan Wallach calls a "utopian" engagement with the technical future[15]), MOMA officials also began to consider television as a technological marvel that might extend the museum's reach past its newly built doors. Consequently, in this same year MOMA became the first museum in the United States to appear on television.[16] In the early 1950s, aided by a three-year grant from the Rockefeller Brothers fund, MOMA established its TV Project in order to experiment with in-house commercial television production and to consider

how TV might become an art medium in itself. By 1955, TV Project director Sidney Peterson characterized the audience for art programs as decidedly suburban and overwhelmingly female. Borrowing sociologist David
Riesman's famous characterization of suburbanites as "the lonely crowd,"
Peterson called the audience for TV art programs "the lonelier crowd,"
and on that basis wrote a detailed report that considered the best ways
to address suburban housewives.[17] Other museums around the country
similarly embraced the new medium. In 1954, the Museum of Fine Art in
Boston wired its building to televise programs (on station WGBH) from
all exhibition floors. For their part, the networks encouraged these ties.
The archives for NBC are full of correspondences from museums, artists,
and other groups in the visual arts. Meanwhile, CBS Chairman William
Paley sat on the board of MOMA and was instrumental in forging numerous links between the museum and his network. In short, the worlds of
museum art and television collided in mutual relations of support, each
publicizing and legitimizing the other. As a curator for the San Francisco
Museum of Modern Art claimed in 1952, "Television programs presented
during an eight month period reached approximately 1,500,000 people,
or ten times the annual attendance at the Museum." [18]

Indeed, as the older, urban (and small town) conception of public culture now stretched across the freeway-linked boundaries of city and suburb, and as shopping practices moved consumers (and would-be museum
patrons) from urban "districts" to corporately engineered malls, the museum and the art world in general became increasingly dependent on the
new electrical space of television for public relations and for the maintenance of their middle-class patrons. It is with regard to all of these issues
that television engaged a particular set of discourses on modern art, one
grounded in prewar mergers of culture and commerce but now articulated
in terms of the historical moment at hand.

Communists, Ugly Americans, and the Modern Vernacular

The nationalist urge to create a uniquely American form of modern
art—different both from European modernism and from the art of the
American past—resulted in a series of disputes regarding questions of
style and taste that ultimately had to do with cultural imperialism. As
Serge Guilbaut has discussed in great detail, debates about the relationship between European modernism (especially its roots in Paris) and a

uniquely American form of modern art engaged intellectuals during the Depression, and increasingly during and after World War II "every section of the political world in the United States agreed that art would have an important role to play in the new America." [19]

For the U.S. government, the construction of this art scene had an important role to play both economically and culturally. With the establishment of the Department of Cultural Affairs in the late 1930s, the U.S. government had officially recognized the importance of culture in securing international good will. Despite many humanist intentions, the major strategic focus of these cultural exchanges was the government's desire to counteract the prevailing image of Americans as militaristic, vulgar brutes (or what one writer later called "the ugly American"), an image that dominated the European and Latin American imaginations. [20] A major mission of the Department of Cultural Affairs—and later, during World War II, the Office of War Information—was to counteract this notion of the ugly American and spread a more genteel, peace-loving image of Americans abroad.

After the war, these forays into cultural imperialism were enacted under the Marshall Plan, as American media industries and government offices applied policies of "containment" and searched for new markets for the "Free World" around the globe. Guilbaut shows how the attempts to construct an American art scene, distinct from Paris and situated instead in New York, coincided ideologically with the new "liberalism" that saw communism as a threat and sought to contain it globally. Modern art and the American avant-garde were nourished by a climate of thought that divorced art from the politics of the thirties and favored the freedom of individual expression that abstract expressionism, with its sense of eccentric psychology, especially provided. At the same time, however, the popular press and government officials often scorned modern artists such as Jackson Pollack for their failure to represent subjects that might be commonly understood, and numerous people suspected that such art was itself "un-American."

In both the domestic and global contexts, these contradictions resulted in a series of struggles over what exactly was meant by the terms American "culture" and American "art." While various attempts were made to export America's fine arts—painting, opera, dance, and so forth—they were often fraught with problems. In 1946, when the State Department put together an international exhibit called "Advancing American Art," the contemporary paintings chosen for exhibition became the site of public and Congressional controversy, as Senator George Dondero of Michigan attacked the work of painters who had once been connected to the Communist Party. More generally, some critics objected to the "ham and eggs" art chosen for the exhibit on the grounds that the paintings were subversive of American values. At its paranoid extreme, rumors circulated that American abstract artists were working as foreign agents by inserting military maps into their paintings. Then, too, in previous decades American art was not often received well on foreign soil, especially in Paris, the capital of modernism. The European art public typically saw American "high" art as a cheap imitation of the real thing, and, moreover, these high art imports had little value for winning the hearts of the more general world population. Ironically, then, despite their status as vulgar and despite the fact that Europeans sometimes deemed them as such, American popular arts often appealed to European audiences (as well as critics) and were thus seen as more viable vehicles than American fine art for the solicitation of international goodwill. The distinctions between high and low were thus enmeshed in cold war sentiments during the period of postwar decolonization, as Americans searched for a way to rid themselves of their status as a cultural colony of Europe.

In this matrix, television played a key role in distinguishing American from European modern art.[21] As one TV critic writing for the *Saturday Review* asked, "How many of us would like to know how American is American Art? Simple questions like these are effective grist for television. . . ."[22] This issue of national identity was crucial, as television sought ways to negotiate the "high" (and typically assumed, communist) world of European modernism with the more all-American popular arts in the United States. In the 1950s, when the television medium grew to become the country's central communications medium, these concerns were continually posed on 1950s "prestige" programs including TV specials and such series as *Camera 3, Omnibus, Wisdom, See It Now,* and *Person to Person.*

In a 1959 episode of *Person to Person,* for example, Edward R. Murrow interviews the premier poster boy of World War II, Norman Rockwell, showing his perfect American family and little dog Lolita at home. Addressing Mrs. Rockwell, Murrow says, "You must have quite a decorating problem. Do you keep many of Norman's original paintings on your wall?" Painting thus becomes a domesticated and familial form, much in line with the Office of War Information's use of Rockwell during World War II to symbolize Roosevelt's "Four Freedoms," which all revolved around the right to private life apart from government intervention. Not surprisingly, then, when Murrow tours Rockwell's studio (also in his home), he points to two of the paintings most notable for this logic—*Freedom of Speech* and *Freedom of Worship*. Making the patriotic message even clearer is the fact that in a previous segment Murrow interviews Fidel Castro. Although Castro presents himself as a family man (he is with his son and dog, and he even shows Murrow his baby pictures), the unkempt beard, the fact that he appears to be wearing pajamas, his missing wife, and the fact that he is in a hotel room rather than his home marks him as decidedly outside the American iconography of family life that Rockwell made famous during the war. Thus, the juxtaposition of Rockwell with the Cuban communist leader speaks, not too implicitly, to the debates about American art and communism that circulated at the time.[23]

Still, Rockwell's association with the patriotic art of the wartime past, as well as his own antimodern stance, made him less than a viable leader in the quest for the American modern. Television thus explored other possibilities, and in the process modern art was often ambivalently presented. In one respect, as with the Rockwell-Castro program, modern art was often disassociated from its communist and elitist connotations. But on television, modern art was also often distanced from Depression-era social realism, regionalism, and WPA-funded art, as well as the Rockwellesque imagery of the wartime past. Modern art, then, meant progress, but of a distinctly American and popular sort.

A 1955 episode of *See It Now* even more explicitly illustrates this point. Significantly titled "Two American Originals," the program was divided into two segments, one that featured artist Grandma Moses and the other jazz great Louis Armstrong. Grandma Moses, who had come to national prominence in the early 1940s, was famous for her so-called "primitive" art that rendered, in a craft tradition, realistic subjects such as houses, pets, and other domestic scenes. For some, she represented the quintessential American vernacular where the term "primitive" assumes a positive connotation, as the art world placed "high" value not only on Moses but on other untraditional artists and art forms (for example, children's art, art therapy, and the art of psychotics).

Murrow's interview took place in Moses' humble home studio where her practical arts and crafts aesthetic was made notable by her folksy decor. In the interview, Murrow asks Moses "Have you decided what picture you're going to paint next, Grandma Moses?" Grandma replies, "I'm going to try to get into something different . . . well, more . . . more modern. I've been inclined to paint old scenes, I suppose, since I'm old." To which Murrow retorts, "Or old enough to go modern."

This curious exchange between the grandmother of American art and television's premier newsman suggests the ambivalent attitudes toward the old and the new, tradition and modernization, that surrounded the definition of the American vernacular for the postwar world. The figure of Grandma Moses offers a resolution for this ambivalence, as she is literally rendered a "modern primitive." As such, she negotiates the contradictory values of the more traditional American representational art (by which I mean the rendering of recognizable subject matter) and the newer forms of abstraction that often worked to negate subject matter (as, for example, with Jackson Pollack's "drippings" or with Larry Rivers's *Washington Crossing the Delaware,* which abstracted portions of the historical scene).

Moreover, as opposed to what President Truman called the "lazy, nutty moderns," Grandma Moses was distinctly American, a point that was "officially" recognized during the period. Truman said that comparing Moses to the moderns was like "comparing Christ with Lenin," and President Eisenhower's cabinet presented him with a specially commissioned Grandma Moses painting depicting the Eisenhower family.[24] In the *See It Now* episode, her nationalism is underscored when Murrow asks her, "Do you ever look at the paintings of a foreign artist?" and she replies, "Some. I never have seen so much. You know I've never been away from home much. Most that I've seen is in pictures." The exchange clarifies that Grandma Moses is truly an American original, untouched by foreign influence. The meaning of modern is thus construed simply as something contemporary, but it remains quintessentially American.

However, as *See It Now* makes clear, being "American" meant nothing if American did not translate as such abroad. In other words, American art for the modern world was art recognized as such in Europe. One of the reasons Grandma Moses was famous enough to be on *See It Now* in the first place was because she was one of the American painters that Europeans embraced after World War II. The segment with Louis Armstrong further suggests the "exportability" of American art, as jazz musicians had historically played to adoring audiences in Europe and had migrated there, especially to Paris, since World War I. So, too, rather than being associated with white militaristic "ugly American" masculinity, the black jazz musician had traditionally been treated by Parisians as an artist compatriot.[25] In Armstrong's segment, Murrow follows the musician as he plays to adoring audiences in Paris, and he concludes by announcing, "Satchmo is one of our most valuable items for export." Thus associating Grandma Moses with the kind of popular cross-over appeal of jazz, *See It Now*'s "Two American Originals" is able to suggest that modern American art is popular art with great potential to capture the hearts of the world population.

Although these issues deserve much more consideration than I can give here, it seems worth pointing out that the perception of American culture in foreign countries increasingly posed a dilemma for television during the late 1950s and through the 1960s, when foreign syndication became a lucrative market. By 1962, the sale of syndicated off-network programs abroad was higher than domestic sales, and in that same year the first private communications satellite, Telstar, was launched. Despite the economic gains, however, in the early 1960s the export of television became a subject of concern during Senator Thomas Dodd's hearings on television violence, as various parties worried about television's cultural/ideological effects overseas, particularly with regard to the image of the "ugly American" that violent programs might perpetuate.[26] In this context, the more "art and education" that U.S. television could export, the better it would reflect on the nation as a whole, and the more conducive it would be to convince people of other nations to join what President Kennedy called the Free World.

Kennedy, of course, imbued his presidency with a sense of the higher arts from the start, using television as a key instrument for communicating his sense of taste.[27] On the occasion of his inaugural address in November 1960, he invited Robert Frost to recite a poem. Poetry manifested itself in yet another famous poem that came to provide the reigning discourse on television during the period: I am speaking, of course, of T. S. Eliot's *The Waste Land*, a poem that perhaps not coincidentally was modernist in nature and written by an American poet who lived in Paris in the twenties. Taking this avant-garde legacy into Kennedy's New Frontier, Newton Minow called television a "vast wasteland" in his 1961 speech delivered before the 9 May meeting of the National Association of Broadcasters. Minow argued that television had broken the public trust by offering "a procession of game shows, violence, audience participation shows, formula comedies about totally unbelievable families," and he recommended more arts and educational television as a remedy.[28]

For Minow and many others, the vast wasteland came to symbolize the cultural demise of America through TV, and Minow's speech reoriented the discourse on television from its obsessive interest in family life during the 1950s to a focus on public interest and national purpose. In the context of the new satellite technologies and Kennedy's cold war zeal for cultural and economic imperialism, television's national purpose was international in scope.

But despite the attempt to make the world safe for democracy, when it came to art network television still represented America as a cultural colony of Europe. The "Camelot presidency" drew shamelessly on British and European art history to prove its appreciation of the legitimate arts. Again, the figure of the woman was integral to this endeavor. One of Kennedy's greatest triumphs was to secure the first American traveling exhibition of yet another famous woman, the *Mona Lisa,* which he got on loan from the Louvre. In a television press conference on the subject, the connections between art and international diplomacy are made explicit as Kennedy positions the loan of the Mona Lisa as "a reminder of the friendship that exists between France and the United States."[29]

And, of course, the first lady herself became the camera's favorite modern woman. The 1962 CBS documentary *A Tour of the White House with Mrs. John F. Kennedy* was an attempt to redecorate the nation with a sense of American history, as Jackie discussed the need to fill the home with antiques that would speak to American heritage.[30] Ironically, however, while Jackie kept pointing out that everything about the house was American, she nevertheless spoke mostly of British and European design, comparing the east room to the palace at Versailles, talking of Shakespeare and ancient Greece, and even boasting that the wallpaper, with its scenes of America, was made in France. Moreover, while Jackie went to great lengths to prove that the redecoration was done on behalf of her fellow Americans, her Europhilia emerged in irrepressible ways. When asked whether she thinks "that there is a relationship between the government and art," or if it is "because you and your husband just feel this way?" she replies, "That's so complicated. I don't know. I just think that everything in the White House should be the best. The entertainment that's given here. And if it's an American company that you can help, I like to do that. If it's not, just as long as it's the best." Although President Kennedy soon told the audience that the purpose of redecorating was to teach young people to "become better Americans," Jackie's penchant for European art made her modernization scheme seem altogether foreign. In this regard, Jackie served as an ambivalent figure who skirted the boundaries of a popular celebration of American modern style and the popular mistrust of European art.

From Momism to Popism

As with its presentation of the first lady, television often represented the idea of modernization through the figure of women art connoisseurs and artists. Sometimes this representation served a familiarizing function by schooling the public on ways to appreciate the much mistrusted European modernists through representing art as feminine, domesticated, and polite. But, as in *A Tour of the White House,* the attempts to contain modernism within the tropes of an aristocratic "refined" femininity never quite worked, because it also posed the threatening presence of Europhile, snooty, eccentric, excessive, and overeducated elites, even when spoken in the whisperingly demure tones of the charm-schooled Mrs. Kennedy.

More generally, in popular culture "modern" women (aristocrats and otherwise) were decidedly suspect. In fact, the "threat" of the modern woman even achieved the status of a popular theory encapsulated by the term "momism." First coined by Philip Wylie in his 1941 book *Generation of Vipers,* the term was widely popular throughout the 1950s. Wylie argued that women were in a conspiracy with industry to rob men of their power and create a culture of sissies. As I have previously suggested, Wylie connected his fears of women to an equally paranoid vision of the broadcast media.[31] In the 1941 edition, and the sixteen more that followed, Wylie claimed that women had somehow teamed up with the broadcast industry by using radio, and later television, as tools for dominating men. The constant "goo and sentimentality" emitted through the wires would turn men into "desexed, de-cerebated, de-souled" homebodies. Not only did such emasculization threaten individual men, it foreshadowed "national death."[32] To this end, Wylie even compared what he called the "matriarchal" use of broadcasting in the United States with Goebbels's "mass-stamping" of the public psyche in Nazi Germany. Wylie's hyperbolic ravings testify to Andreas Huyssen's claim that femininity has historically been aligned with mass culture (and its threatening, degraded status), while high art is seen as the prerogative of male elites.[33] But importantly, when women were represented on mass cultural forms such as television programs, the threat of femininity could just as easily be associated with the foreign (which typically meant communist) threat of both European and American modern art.

Television fiction especially took up these interests, crafting plots around dubious paintings and women out of control. A 1957 episode of CBS's *Telephone Time* titled "One Coat of White" illustrates the point. In this drama, actress Claudette Colbert plays an American tourist in France who falls in love with Lautisse, the greatest living French artist (a name that a critic for the *Saturday Review* called "a provocative amalgam of the names Lautrec and Matisse"). Lautisse, who hasn't painted in years and refuses to let anyone know his true identity, falls in love with Colbert and follows her back to her home in Seattle, where her grown-up children are "horrified by what they consider to be their widowed mother's middle-aged escapade." Colbert is torn between her love for her children and her unsuitable European modernist suitor. The conflict is resolved when the children in Seattle undergo a financial crisis and decide to put the home up for sale. As the *Saturday Review* critic explains:

> The children propose to help its salability by giving its fence a coat of white paint. But Lautisse gets there first and begins to cover the fence's surface with abstract forms which he quite rightly describes as "rather like Miro." His skill gives the game away naturally, his identity becomes known to the children and the public, and within hours curators of some of the leading American art museums have arrived on the scene and are bidding against each other for sections of the fence at fabulous prices per running foot.[34]

While "One Coat of White" has a happy ending, the odd coupling of the American housewife and the French modern artist provides the terms of dramatic conflict, asking viewers to decide whether an American woman ought to be engaged with modern art. Moreover, Colbert plays an older woman, and according to the terms of the narrative, her age, even more than her nationality or sexuality, precipitates the crisis.[35] In this sense, we might say, the older woman represents not just femininity but the American past, especially the recent wartime "patriotic" past that was rendered through images of family life, most notably by Norman Rockwell. "One

Coat of White" thus presents its female heroine and her out-of-control desires for French men as a threat to the isolationist and family values of the previous two decades. However, it resolves the dilemma of the American family's place in an increasingly international postwar world by having the French modern artist literally save the American family home.

Other television genres similarly presented housewives as arbiters of modern art, suggesting links between the suspect nature of European modernism and a potentially out-of-control American femininity. A perfect example here is an episode of the situation comedy *The George Burns and Gracie Allen Show*. Known for her illogical relation to language by way of her famous shaggy dog jokes, Gracie becomes the representative par excellence of the populist scorn for modern art. After going on a gallery tour for a lesson in art appreciation, Gracie decides to try her hand at painting. Misunderstanding the difference between industrial arts and fine arts, Gracie buys supplies from a house painter and decides to make a portrait of George. The painting turns out to be "abstract" despite Gracie's efforts to render her husband in the representational tradition of portraiture.

Predictably, at the end of the episode when Gracie shows the portrait, no one can figure out what the painting is about. One character thinks "it's a yellow cab with the doors open"; another says "no, it can't be . . . who ever saw a yellow cab with bloodshot headlights and a radish hanging inside"; and a third suggests, "someone threw a lighted cigar on a dying water lily in a stagnant pond." Although rendered humorously, the point here is that abstraction poses a threat to consensual meaning as no two people in the scene arrive at the same interpretation. In a television genre notable for its attempts to elicit consensual (mass audience) interpretations by staging and then resolving all eccentricities (even Gracie's) within the "norms" of suburban domesticity, modernism clearly has no place apart from its position of comedic excess—the exact position that Gracie Allen herself always occupies in the program. And in that regard, modernism is literally a woman.

In fact, the episode explicitly makes modern art an issue of sexual difference, as Gracie's "screwball" persona and her proclivity for abstraction are countered by George who takes the opposite position of the "ham and eggs" anti-intellectual, antimodernist, American populist. In one of his weekly monologue segments, George literally walks out of the plot, comes onto the stage to address the home audience, and recalls the time he visited his "highbrow" friend:

> Last time I was at Getz's house he showed me a modern painting he just bought, and he asked me if I liked it. Well, all I could see was some blue triangles on top of a yellow square so I had to be honest. I said, "Bill, maybe I'm old fashioned. I like simple pictures like a little boy and his dog." He looked at me sort of pityingly. He says, "But George, that's what it is." Then he told me it was surrealism and that artists that do that kind of work have to paint the way they feel. Well, if you really feel that bad you should stop painting and go to bed.

In all cases the implication is that no one can understand modern art, and this is not because the art is complex but rather because it is bad. Typically associated with psychosis (and note that George compares it to feeling bad) and also often compared to children's paintings, modernism becomes "outsider" art, which for populists has no value. In *Burns and Allen,* this wry dismissal is linked to an implicit association of modern art with women and madness—or at least madcap comedy.

If *Burns and Allen* treated the eccentric nature of femininity and modern art in comic terms with the woman artist as the butt of the joke, other programs presented more troubling visions, linking issues of nationalism and modernism to unruly women artists. A perfect example here is an episode of *I Led Three Lives,* a syndicated program that revolved around the life of Herbert A. Philbrick, a counterspy for the FBI who posed as a pipe-smoking advertising executive. This episode told the tale of Margaret, a young female art student engaged to Paul, her art school teacher, who supplements his meager earnings as a painter and teacher through his day job as an ad man. At the beginning of the story, when Paul visits Herbert to discuss an advertising campaign, he tells Herbert he suspects Margaret is a communist. Margaret, it turns out, is not only a communist spy, she is a modern artist who plants microfilm in her collages. In one scene, when Herbert visits the art school, Margaret asks, "Did you ever see a collage painting before, Herb? Collage is old fashioned but we moderns go in for it when we want to puzzle people." Then, in more sinister tones, she says, "We take little pieces like these . . . well they should be pieces of your heart. . . . Who are you Herb? . . . Oh, the man who corrupts commercial artists with money. Do you know what you've done to Paul?

You've made him unable to understand my genius." As opposed to Margaret's interest in modernist collage, Paul and Herbert both express their preference for representational art that has recognizable subject matter (and Herb specifically calls modern art "strange"). In the end, in the true terms of momism, it turns out that Margaret has turned communist because she hates her mother.[36] When mother and daughter finally reconcile, Margaret is purged of her communist sins, turns in her modernist collage for a wedding ring, and she and Paul live happily ever after.

This program is interesting not only because of the hyperbolic way it conflates the threat of modernism with the threat of women, but also because it makes the commercial artist into an American hero, a counterspy for the FBI who staves off the communist threat. We might note here that the presentation of the commercial artist as patriot was continuous in many ways with the figure of Norman Rockwell, himself a commercial artist, working for the good of the country. Only for Herbert Philbrick, and for the more general notion of American art after the war, the work itself did not deal with themes of patriotism but rather was simply about products. In fact, the idea that advertising art was not only art but the true American modern vernacular, became increasingly central over the course of the decade.[37] This could be seen not only in fantastic tales of communist infiltration, but also in documentaries on art education.

It is, for example, well demonstrated in two advertising segments that aired during the *See It Now* episode featuring Grandma Moses and Louis Armstrong. In the first segment, the narrator tells us, "Out of the modern Shulton plant come these two brand-new men's products. Old Spice electric shave lotion and Old Spice body talcum." Like Grandma Moses, Old Spice mediates the old with the modern. Meanwhile, the commercial, which is rendered in abstract animation, is itself testimony to the fact that television advertising art in the 1950s was one of the central places where American modern design was developed. (In fact, the design journal *ID* is full of this kind of abstract TV animation as it was constantly used for network promotional ads and logos such as the CBS surrealist-inspired eye.[38]) The second commercial underscores the "art" value attached to industry, as the narrator tells us that Old Spice is a "real American original" and shows us the "magnificent murals that decorate the lobby" of the Old Spice factory. The camera pans across the mural and displays Old Spice bottles in a kind of gallery setting—as if these products are art objects.

An even more striking example is a 1953 episode of *Omnibus* that centers on a visit to the home of the premier Depression-era social realist and regionalist painter, Thomas Hart Benton. Benton is an interesting figure here insofar as his career was itself born of a curious mix of modernism (which he experimented with in art school in Paris) and mass culture (he painted movie sets for Fox and Pathe in the 1910s). His art was marked by an admixture of aspects of modern style into realistic subject matter that emerged as regionalist murals depicting slice-of-life scenes—scenes that were intended to be critical of social inequities, such as labor exploitation. Despite its ethos of social criticism, regionalism was itself co-opted by big business such as Standard Oil, which saw this art as useful for advertisements. At first Benton eagerly accepted commissions, hopeful about the "possibilities of a fruitful relation between big business and art." In 1937, *Life* magazine sponsored *Hollywood*, his painting of union workers at Twentieth Century Fox (which *Life* ultimately rejected because of its controversial subject matter). In 1941, he made *Outside the Curing Barn* as an ad for Lucky Strike cigarettes. But by the postwar period, Benton realized that big business was not interested in art that contained social criticism, and he felt that his liaisons with big business had been a failure.[39] By the time of the *Omnibus* episode, Benton had likewise rejected his connections both to the WPA-funded art inspired by the New Deal and to the modernist artists that emerged from the Depression (especially his former student Jackson Pollack). Holding onto his regionalist aesthetic, he moved to the Midwest, a place that he thought spoke to the folksy values of the real America in way that the New York City art world never could.

Given his rejection of both the "art for business" ethos and big-city modernism, and given his status as a regionalist painter of slice-of-life scenes, Benton would seem to be the perfect representative of the American vernacular. However, the *Omnibus* episode suggests that the vernacular was itself less easily defined because it presents Benton as a confusing hybrid of folk, high, and mass culture sutured together in a family scene. Moreover, if this were supposed to be American, it still depended on two British stage actors, Alistair Cooke (the host of *Omnibus*) and Claude Rains (a family friend), who by way of their Britishness give the program a highbrow feel. At the beginning of the episode, Cooke invites viewers into the Bentons's home for a "typical" night of family life among the art set. Rains exhibits some of Benton's work and reads the poetry of Carl Sandburg. Then, after Rains shows Benton's famous Huck Finn lithograph,

Benton reads from a Twain novel. Folksinger Susan Reed plays the harp and croons a ballad, and Benton's thirteen-year-old daughter reads from the French novella *The Little Prince*. Finally, as the whole family gathers in a sing-along, the camera moves to a painting on the wall, and then an off-screen narrator asks, "Have you ever wondered how the pretzel gets so twisted?"

If you are wondering what this question possibly has to do with the likes of Mark Twain, Carl Sandburg, and Thomas Hart Benton, you should be, because the answer is not to be found within the logic of enlightenment that the Benton family scene strives to portray. Instead, we are now in the twisted pretzel logic of the advertising community where language can be used for convenience, in this case as a transition from program to ad, rather than as something that—as in Twain, Sandburg, or Benton—strives toward reason. Specifically, the pretzel problem serves as a transition to a commercial for AMF industrial machines that are used in pretzel factories. This juxtaposition of Benton's populist interpretation of the American vernacular with the advertisement's image of pretzels and assembly-line technology suggests that even while television presented the great artists of the Depression era and World War II, its commercial nature was fundamentally incompatible with the interpretation of American art proliferated by the Bentons and the Rockwells of the past. Who in the audience would really be able to seriously contemplate the possibility of the folk and high cultural values that Benton here represented when they were simultaneously asked to ponder the hermeneutics of twisted pretzels?

From Pretzel Logic to Henny Picasso

By the 1960s, the issue of art and its links to commercial television had taken on national importance, with television squarely in the center of the debates. Now, the search for the modern American vernacular was no longer posed as a painter's dilemma that television might help to solve; instead it was posed increasingly as a televisual dilemma worthy of grave national attention.

Although critics in the 1950s had considered how television might become the "eighth lively art," and although many people at the networks thought about the adaptation of "high" cultural forms such as opera and ballet and some even pondered the use of television for experimental purposes, by the end of the 1950s the terms of the debate had shifted.[40] Now people began to wonder what the difference was between commercial television and the visual arts, and that sense of relativism began to make itself felt both in paintings and in television programs.

Widely seen as the onslaught of postmodern sensibilities, such relativism is typically discussed from the point of view of the art world's scavenging of "low" forms, and the art critics' various debates on pop, op, camp, minimalism, and the like. What needs to be addressed, however, is the blurring of high and low through the lens of the television camera; that is, how television's representations of the modern visual arts gradually shifted focus to the complex mergers among commerce, the "high" arts, and also, in terms of the technological sublime of Kennedy's New Frontier, the "high" sciences.

It is curious in many ways that television's embrace of the postmodern blurring of high and low should take place in the 1960s, because this decade was ushered in by a spate of modernist-inspired "vast wasteland" rhetoric that in fact tried very earnestly to make distinctions between what was authentic and what wasn't. In the land of the New Frontier, this meant not only the arts but also the sciences, which were equally important in Minow's reform agenda.

This goal of making distinctions between real art and science as opposed to commercial pap was, however, quite difficult to achieve in relation to a medium that was all three things at once—a potential forum for the fine arts, a technology produced through and used as a tool for science, and a form of commerce and commercial culture. Moreover, because art, science, and commerce have all, at different points in American history, been viewed skeptically as "artifice" and even sorcery, it was always hard to decide which of these were "authentic" forms of experience and which were "frauds."[41]

The advent of the quiz show scandals in the late 1950s exacerbated these confusions. What the public had believed to be the hard facts about the arts and sciences that these shows featured were revealed to be the products of fraudulent sponsors who gave contestants answers before the programs. The quiz show scandals and the hearings that ensued made the problem of authentic versus fraud a national dilemma. While the prosecution claimed commercial fraud, the producers (in their own defense) argued they should not have been expected to tell the truth because television quiz shows never purported to be true to life, but rather were a dramatic art form that needed to present heightened conflict. The scandals thus had the effect of relativizing the difference between television's status as art, science, and commerce, as the legal proceedings generated testimony that proved all three possibilities equally viable.

As is clear from this highly publicized example, television's shifting status between the categories of art, science, and commerce caused considerable confusion and resulted in an array of disparate responses among different groups. For some media critics, such as Marshall McLuhan, these contradictions were resolved by privileging the scientific/technical explanation in essentialist prophesies such as "the medium is the massage." According to this logic of technological determinism, television, like all media, is what McLuhan called an "extension of man," or a kind of technical prosthesis that evolved out of the evolutionary thought structures of the human mind.[42] In the scheme of "the medium is the massage," technology determined aesthetics, and commerce simply didn't matter much. For others, like Newton Minow, these contradictions were resolved by making distinctions between good and bad taste, between what was authentic art and what was hard (or real) science, as opposed to what was low art, pseudo science, and thus blatantly commercial trash. For others, however, creating a distinction between the high and the low was not the point. This third group resolved the contradiction between art, science, and commerce by turning to a more postmodern attitude that played with uncertain boundaries among the three. This attitude was taken up by two apparently disparate camps whose opposing views were represented by a coastal divide: Hollywood producers versus the New York art scene. Although the divide between Hollywood and New York was not always geographically coherent (the networks had business offices in New York, and there were, of course, artists and critics on the West Coast), the two coasts did come to represent two different attitudes toward the blurring of high and low.

After 1955, when television had moved its base from New York to Hollywood, the production system fostered a kind of "regulated innovation." Networks and Hollywood studios such as Screen Gems often contracted with independents and sought to produce a variety of different kinds of programming, hoping for a hit. Although the Hollywood industry was not usually interested in avant-garde experimentation, production companies and networks were searching for new looks, especially those that removed prime-time television from its roots in New York "legitimate" and vaudeville theater, which had been the mainstay of the 1950s live anthology dramas and variety shows (both typically shot in New York). These new looks were produced by turning to the nontheatrical arts, including (1) the literary movements of Beat poetry and intellectual science fiction fantasy (which surfaced respectively in programs like *Route 66* and *The Twilight Zone*); (2) developments in popular music (including jazz, but particularly the youth music of folk, rock, and pop); and (3) movements in the visual arts, especially painting, which I am most concerned with here.

The world of the painterly arts embraced television at the beginning of the decade in a ceremonious gesture. In 1962, one year after Minow's famous speech, MOMA held the first TV-art exhibit. Titled "Television USA: 13 Seasons," the show was a retrospective featuring critics who selected the "golden age" programs of the bygone era of fifties TV. The program book for "Television USA" noted that television was divided in "two camps": the industry that is concerned with money and "artists and journalists whose standard of 'success' is the degree to which television realized its potentialities as an art form."[43] Predictably, given Minow's attack on Hollywood genres and its own geographical setting, MOMA selected the news documentaries, variety shows, and anthology dramas that had been produced in New York studios during the 1950s; *Gunsmoke* was the only Hollywood dramatic series that made the list. Clearly, for MOMA the "vast wasteland" referred to anything west of the Empire State—especially anything that emanated from Southern California.[44]

Over the course of the decade, MOMA's canon of New York-produced golden-age plays, documentaries, and variety shows gave way to new developments in the visual arts (especially pop), which seemed to have more in common with Hollywood commercialism than with the fine and performance arts featured in golden-age formats. In the 1960s, Hollywood commercial television seemed increasingly "arty," as premier pop artists like Robert Rauschenberg, Andy Warhol, and Roy Lichtenstein turned popular artifacts, stars, and politicians into a painter's (or sometimes silk screener's) medium, thereby flattening out the differences among them. Meanwhile, commercial television took an interest in pop and the new camp sensibility.[45] In 1966, ABC adapted *Batman* for television, playing on popism's visual iconography and pulp fiction themes with a camp awareness of its own "badness."[46] Moreover, insofar as pop was notable for its use of bright primary colors, the new style (along with psychedelic art) was particularly conducive during this period to the industry's big push for the conversion to color TV (not surprisingly, *Batman* was shot in color). Indeed, programs that worked in the pop tradition (including, for example, NBC's "in living color" *Laugh-In*) also had the advantage of making people want to buy color television sets.[47]

The fact that television was both pop and popular was not lost on the network promotional department at ABC, which "dual" marketed *Batman* both as a camp parody for adult audiences and as an action series for kids, thereby maximizing ratings. For the adult crowd, ABC even held a posh "cocktail and frug" party for the premier episode, which took place at Harlows, the fashionable New York discotheque. Andy Warhol, Harold Prince (director of the League of New York Theaters), and other celebrities attended the event. (Pop icon Jackie Kennedy declined ABC's invitation.) After cocktails, the network staged a special screening of *Batman* at the York Theater, whose lobby was adorned with Batman drawings and stickers that sported slogans proclaiming their status as "authentic pop art." Guests at the York were reportedly unexcited about the show, but in true pop style they cheered when a commercial for corn flakes came on the screen.[48]

As these promotional gimmicks suggest, while pop artists like Warhol and Lichtenstein borrowed popular iconography to make "art," the "low" medium of television borrowed pop's aesthetics of borrowing—in this case essentially using the artist's tradition of the *in-crowd* opening reception as a publicity stunt staged for a *mass audience*.[49] While this scavenging act between the "high" and the "low" is now often seen in postmodern criticism to mark the demise of the myth of "authentic" expression, in the 1960s it was typically championed as proof of what many commercial artists had long argued—that ads and commercial culture were themselves a legitimate "art" form, that advertising could be just as authentically expressive as painting.[50] Even MOMA's "Television USA" 1962 retrospective, which otherwise championed New York produced golden age formats, embraced the TV commercial as a form of art. Its catalogue for the "Television USA" retrospective stated, "Almost everything has been tried to create original commercials. As a result, radical avant-garde experiments which would be frowned upon in other areas of television are encouraged in this field."[51] Consequently, "Television USA" exhibited everything from Bewer's beer to Rival dog food ads as proof of television's avant-garde status.

Several years later, *Television Quarterly*, the journal of the Television Academy of Arts and Sciences, agreed. In 1967, it included an article entitled "Be Quiet, The Commercial's On," which endorsed advertisers' "willingness to experiment" and reminded readers that in critical circles commercials were in the same league as cutting-edge films and filmmakers:

> Almost every article about Richard Lester dwells on his experience as a director of commercials, and suggests that *A Hard Day's Night* and *Help!* are, technically at least, extended commercials. David Karp in the *New York Times Magazine,* insisted that television shows are supposed to be bad, and praised commercials and their use of *cinema verité.* Stanley Kubrick is quoted in the *New York Times* as finding "the most imaginative film-making, stylistically," in TV commercials. Even Herbert Blau, in *The Impossible Theater*, stops to ponder the skill that goes into TV ads.[52]

More generally, *Television Quarterly* promoted this equivocation between art and industry by publishing articles on "taste" and the meaning "culture." Appearing on a regular basis during the decade, these speculative essays were written by such unlikely bedfellows as Andre Malraux, France's Minister of State in Charge of Culture, and the President of the CBS Broadcast group, Richard Jencks.[53] Once again, in the true pop aesthetic of the time, television seemed to be the great equalizer between artists and bureaucrats.

Still, for some veteran golden age critics who had lived through the sponsor boycotts of McCarthyism and the histrionics of the quiz show scandals, the celebration of commercialism as art was a hard pill to swallow. Many continued to express their preference for the older golden age formats. However, because these critics also traveled in New York art circles (and had originally been theater critics), they had trouble ignoring the fact that popism was the latest thing in museums, fashion magazines, and even in the New York theater, where *Superman* and *Mad* were both adapted for theatrical presentation. In this context, many of the East Coast TV critics expressed ambivalence toward TV's pop attitudes. For example, while veteran *New York Times* critic Jack Gould admitted that *Batman* was a "belated extension of the phenomenon of Pop art to the television medium," and as such might "be an unforeseen blessing in major proportions," he also cautioned, with some irony, that pop art had its own inverted standards and that *Batman* "might not be adequately bad" when compared to *Green Acres* and *Camp Runamuck*." [54] Similarly confused about the role of the critic in a television universe where aesthetic hierarchies were turned upside down, a reviewer for the *Saturday Evening Post* claimed: "*Batman* is a success because it is television doing what television does best: doing things badly. Batman, in other words, is so bad, it's good. . . . Batman translated from one junk medium into another is junk squared. But it is thoroughly successful and—this troubles critics for whom good and bad are art's only poles—it can be surprisingly likable." [55] As such ambivalent commentary suggests, the transition from the theatrical conception of television (both legitimate theater and vaudeville) to a painterly one (which increasingly meant pop and psychedelic art) was never smooth or fully achieved. Instead, television seemed caught in a style war that manifested itself in the most curious ways.

The television variety show is a good demonstration of the problem, if only because it included such a schizophrenic mix of the 1950s "vaudeo" aesthetic of variety theater with the newer stylistics. A case in point is the 1967 TV special *Color Me Barbra,* which as the title suggests was CBS's rather obvious attempt to promote its color TV system. This TV special took the popular genre of the variety show and turned it into an occasion for the unlikely combination of European modern art and American vaudeville. "act 1" is set in the Philadelphia Museum of Art, where Barbra Streisand, in the role of a French chambermaid, cleans the museum at night. As she stops to contemplate the artwork, the paintings come to life, and Barbra (seemingly a victim of Stendahl syndrome) projects herself into the canvas. For example, when she arrives in a gallery full of abstract art, Barbra sheds her black-and-white French maid outfit and reappears in a colorful halter-style gown that mimics the abstract patterns in the paintings. Dressed as a canvas, she then performs a modern dance routine. In another sequence, Barbra takes a more somber tone. After looking a little too long at a Modigliani painting, she becomes the girl in the picture, enters a set made to look like a Parisian café, drinks a glass of wine, and belts out the French lyrics to "Non, C'est Rien." Obviously recalling the famous "painting come to life" sequence in *An American in Paris* (1951), the "art into life" conceit not only provided a stage for colorful performance, but also a reason for constant costume changes. In effect, the program doubled as a fashion show in which paintings and haute couture shared the stage.

Barbra Streisand in the museum in act I of *Color Me Barbra*.

Barbra Streisand speaks French in act II of *Color Me Barbra*.

Barbra Streisand at the circus in act II of *Color Me Barbra*.

If "act 1" provided a mix of the painterly arts with the "live" popular arts of TV song, dance, and women's genres, then "act II," which is set in a circus, takes this hybrid form of art and popular culture to its logical extreme. In other words, just in case the museum's largely European collection was a "turn-off" for the nonart crowd, the producers provided a true form of Americana. In fact, the program is quite self-reflexive about this. In the opening part of the circus segment, Barbra greets the audience in French, while English subtitles appear on the screen. However, her "Frenchness" turns out to be a vaudeville gag as she breaks out of the French language to return to her Jewish American persona. Then, as she switches back to English, the subtitles turn to French. The circus act thus neatly undoes all the pretensions of her previous visit with European art. As a whole, *Color Me Barbra* is a perfect example of the networks' aim to present art through vernacular genres and a sense of live performance that would turn modern art into a truly "American" popular form.

While a spectacular example, *Color Me Barbra* was not alone. By the end of the 1960s, the weekly variety show updated its golden age format to make way for the new painterly arts of pop and psychedelia. A dramatic case in point is *Rowan and Martin's Laugh-In*. Broadcast from 1968 to 1973 on NBC (and at the top of the Nielsen ratings for its first two seasons), it featured a pop-influenced, psychedelic, Peter Max–like set design, complete with a brightly colored "graffiti wall." But, the program eclectically mixed the new visual arts with the sensibilities of vaudeville clowns. *Laugh-In* showcased a classic vaudeville couple, straight man (Dan) and buffoonish clown (Dick), and many of its jokes were taken straight from vaudeville. For example, a script for a 1969 episode begins with stage instructions for a "vaudeville crossover" in which Dan remarks, "If Raquel Welch married Cassius Clay, that would be like bringing the Mountains to Mohammed." The stage instructions, in true vaudeville fashion, call for "Music: 4 Bars and Into Vamp." [56]

In fact, *Laugh-In* was itself often very self-reflexive about the ways in which pop and psychedelic art were being incongruously mixed with vaudeville. The graffiti wall, for example, served as backdrop for cast members who literally "pop-ed" out of it to tell vaudevillian one-liner jokes. News segments (which were introduced with a vaudeville-type ditty that went "Ladies and Gents, *Laugh-In* Looks at the News") sometimes included news of pop art. For example:

With crooner Bing Crosby as guest star, *Rowan and Martin's Laugh-In* stages variety show/vaudeville performance against an op art wall.

> Dick: Greenwich Village, New York: Work on Andy Warhol's new underground movie was halted today when the romantic lead, a 300 pound wart hog, died of a heart attack.
> (golf swing)
> Music: drum roll[57]

While the content of the joke was about pop, the form was clearly vaudeville. One year later, the same basic culture clash was evidenced in a "cocktail party" sequence that included a bizarre crossover joke that features Dick imitating vaudevillian Henny Youngman's "one like this" shtick, as he tells Dan, "I got two pictures in the museum, one like this, one like this." To which Dan replies, "Oh that Henny Picasso." The skit closes with an off-screen voice yelling, "Andy Warhol . . . Soup's On!"[58]

As such instances make clear, television was in fact quite self-conscious of its own schizophrenic styles, moving as it was from the 1950s conventions that were developed in New York (and drew on Yiddish vaudeville humor) and toward the 1960s visual art scene based in New York.

Laugh-In also suggests the move from the association of modern art with femininity per se to an increasing representation of modern art as "queer"—both in terms of the "queering" of generic styles (such as the unlikely merger of vaudeville and pop art) and in terms of eccentric (if not explicitly queer) masculinity. As Alex Doty suggests, 1950s variety shows hosts, famous for their use of drag and their "straight" man/oddball couples, always encouraged the possibility of being read queerly.[59] But in the 1960s, the "sexual liberation" found its way to television, not only through overt "swinging singles" content (seen, for example, on programs like *Love, American Style*), but also through the ambiguous sexuality of the pop style with its campy heterosexuality (rendered through subjects such as love comics, superheroes, and Elvis) as well as the unreadable sexuality of its most talked about artist, Andy Warhol. *Laugh-In,* famous for its "love-in" sexual liberation ethos, included regular jokes about gay couples. One skit, for example, features Tony Curtis (well known for his drag performance in *Some Like It Hot*) playing the role of the quintessential Warholian artist, a "flamboyantly dressed" fashion designer/interior decorator who was hired by the military to redo the bunks and military uniforms, which of course he does in pink (he says things like, "a pink Marine is a happy Marine" and "I see the administration building in a psychedelic chartreuse"). By the end of the skit he and the marine officer fall in love.[60] In another episode, a cocktail party skit has the decidedly queer Tiny Tim talking about fop art on the famous gay beach resort, Fire Island. Following this, cast member Judy Carne comments, "TV's really getting arty—last year we saw the Louvre on Channel 4, and next year you're going to be able to see the Artists and Models Ball on Channel 28."[61]

While *Laugh-in* linked the figure of the artist to jokes about gay men, more generally television was filled with representations of male artists who were in some way "eccentric," at least by television's normative Ward Cleaver standards. This figure of the eccentric male "artiste" served at times to critique the boundaries between art and commercial television itself. In the anthology format, such figures as film auteur Alfred Hitchcock in *Alfred Hitchcock Presents* subverted his own genre and his own means of production. Whereas the 1950s live anthology drama presented itself as family programming brought to you by the "goodwill" of sponsors such as Goodyear and were introduced by erudite hosts such as Robert Montgomery, Alfred Hitchcock was an off-beat film auteur known for his penchant for the macabre. What's more, Hitchcock always made fun of the sponsor and the system of commercial TV in general. In this sense, Hitchcock "queered" his own genre, presenting an eccentric masculine "artiste" in place of the paternalistic goodwill and "polite" theatrical enunciative system of the live anthology drama. This eccentric masculinity was similarly evident in *The Twilight Zone*, which introduced its story every week with a highly stylized sequence featuring TV auteur Rod Serling smoking a cigarette (with attitude) and telling us we were "traveling into another dimension."

These new modes of masculinity—and their relationship to the art world—did not go unnoticed at the time. Critic Joseph Golden, writing for *Television Quarterly*, noted that a host of genres, from the medical drama to the western to the single-dad sitcom, featured widowers as their main protagonists. Analyzing why women had been relegated to the "video graveyard," Golden compared television's new "provocative" and "sterile hero" to the "behavioral sterility, so aggressively explored by the European avant-garde in the last decade or so."[62] Interestingly, Golden accounted for the new arty hero via Philip Wylie's treatise on momism; he claimed that "the womanless society of television" was in fact women's fault because they had ruled the airwaves for too long with soap operas that portrayed women as "sexually aloof, emotionally eclectic, and morally rock-like," and turned men into "helpless ciphers" or "in the primeval days of television, lovable boobs."[63] With this, the avant-garde, alienated male hero took revenge against women for their previous broadcast crimes. Thus, at a time when the critical distance between TV and the avant-garde was being blurred, male pop culture heroes in male identified genres (doctor shows, police shows, single-dad sitcoms) were being reclaimed as high art, largely because they had rejected the "normal" heterosexual coupling seen in 1950s television.

Perhaps the most literal incarnation of the "queer" artist was a 1967 episode of *Batman* titled "POP Goes the Joker," in which the Joker decides to steel Gotham City's famous paintings and replace them with his own pop art. The Joker enters an art contest staged at the Gotham City Museum, which has him squared-off against equally bizarre artists whose paintings are all spoofs of European or American modern art. After winning, he sets up an art school for rich women who become partners in his art crimes. The Joker's perverse control of the women of Gotham City and their mutual irreverence toward the art of the city fathers is predictably countered by the equally queer Batman and Robin who retrieve the paintings and return them to their proper place.

In hindsight, "POP Goes the Joker" reads as a bizarre inversion of the more "serious" programs that represented museums on American television during the late 1960s. Intended in part as promotional vehicles for its parent company's new RCA color TV sets, NBC news presented a series of "in living color" documentaries that perpetuated the notion of the museum as a space of nationalism. These programs included documentaries on the Kremlin, the Whitney, and the Louvre. In the 1967 Whitney special, significantly titled *The American Image,* the nationalist pedagogy inherent in this show was explicitly stated by host E. G. Marshall, who introduced the program saying, "Our story is the story of the artists' search, the search for the American dream." The search turned out to be a colonialist narrative in which a title card stating "the land" was followed by close-ups of wilderness paintings, after which the camera focused on frontier paintings showing settlers conquering Indians. The program went on to show twentieth-century cityscapes and ended with postwar abstraction and pop. Despite this colonialist search for an American vernacular, the NBC news division still conceived of America as a cultural colony of Europe, a point that is similarly apparent in the 1964 documentary about the Louvre. Titled *The Golden Prison,* and narrated by French actor Charles Boyer, this program also presents the national archive through a metaphor of landscape. At the outset, Boyer gives the audience a history lesson in Parisian geography, demonstrating through maps that the Louvre has been the center of Paris for centuries. He then advises his American audience, "The way to see the Louvre is with a French man."

Although at the time this kind of nationalist pedagogy was still the dominant discursive mode for representing the museum, it was being challenged by an emergent set of revisionist and revolutionary positions toward art and its collection that was encapsulated by critical terms like "antiart," terms which suggested that the avant-garde was dead, that all art was fundamentally elitist, and that the only position left was to reject art altogether. To be sure, such critics were in historical dialogue with a well-entrenched intellectual critique of museums that people such as Theodor Adorno and Walter Benjamin had participated in during the 1930s and 1940s, and which the DADA movement had challenged even earlier, with its idea of living art and the Cabaret Voltaire.[64] In the 1960s, art critics went one step further by suggesting that art itself could no longer function as a response to social and political crisis.

The art world's rejection of art dovetailed in complicated ways with the more populist "George Burns" dismissal of modern art on the basis of its inferiority and illegibility. Although both camps argued against "elitism," the first group imagined art should *ideally* have a revolutionary function (but no longer could), while the second was conservative in nature, hoping to hold onto the kind of representational art that encouraged consensual viewpoints. But precisely because the two opposing camps shared some common ground (their antielitism), it was easy for television to conflate these radically opposing views and popularize pop and other art movements that implicitly challenged representational art. From the point of view of antiart critics, the Joker, for example, could certainly be championed as a revolutionary dandy who integrated art into his everyday criminal life and sabotaged the city fathers and their elitist canon. Or, from the populist point of view, the Joker could be read as a big joke on the illegible, untalented, and eccentric pop artists of the times. But, even as these alternative positions on pop art and popular culture prevailed, the emerging universe of global television was dreaming up its own possibilities in which the aesthetic hierarchies of "high" and "low" art would merge with the new scientific hierarchies of "high" and "low" tech.

Art into Science

When E. G. Marshall presented the modern art collection at the Whitney museum, he announced that "modernism is born of Einstein" and the theory of relativity. While he was certainly not the first person to put forth this view, the fact that modern art was conceptualized through a scientific revolution was symptomatic of a larger trend in television's relationship to modern art, a trend that was best encapsulated in 1967 when NBC news offered another, very different kind of museum documentary, titled *Bravo Picasso*.

The first global satellite television program to be produced by the networks, *Bravo Picasso* linked together European modernism, telecommunications science, and American commercialism in what the narrator called "an imaginary museum, a museum without walls. Using man's electronic genius to bring you his creative genius." Quite different from the previous "pedagogical" representations of museums, *Bravo Picasso* is instead a simple performance of the point of sale. It is an international auction of Picasso paintings that took place in five separate cities: Paris, London, Dallas–Fortworth, Burbank, and Los Angeles. Bidders from the different cities competed via satellite for bits of the master's oeuvre.

While the program continued with many of the conventions of art education on TV, its focus on the performance of the global sales pitch rendered the national pedagogy seen in programs like *The Golden Prison* an afterthought. For example, while *Bravo Picasso* told viewers that "the way to see them [Picasso paintings] is with a French man," in the same passage it also pointed out that the paintings were from eleven different countries, and in any case the spectacle of metropolises interconnected via satellite made the "Frenchness" issue dull in comparison. In addition, while the figure of femininity still served to organize the representation of modern painting (stationed in Paris, Yves Montand quotes Picasso, saying, "When I love a woman, I don't start measuring my limbs, I love with my heart and my desire"), modernism's objectification of femininity is now undercut by another object relationship—the commodity form—as the program makes a kind of "pretzel logic" transition to an ad for the Avnet company. Standing before one of the many women Picasso "loved" (that is, his famous *Girl Before a Mirror*), the narrator says, "Art has many faces. The dictionary says art is the production of more than ordinary significance. At Avnet business is an art." Avnet (and its cosponsor RCA) went on to show the new uses for satellite communications, computers, and space science for which these two companies were famous. This transition from a romantic conception of modern art to the art of big business continues with the trajectory of the 1950s, but now this merging of high and low is removed from the quest for the national vernacular and taken into the global space of high-tech satellite communication.

Meanwhile, making the situation even more uncanny, the celebrity bidder at this global auction was the premier modern woman (and one-time representative of the nation), Jackie Onassis, who, famous for her utter rejection of fame, bought the painting in absentia on behalf of the Italian Rescue Fund. Lost to the national iconography, the former first lady was transformed into the first home shopper, floating somewhere in the cash flow of a global satellite mall.

Indeed, if any one instance can ever be said to precipitate a movement, *Bravo Picasso* signals, I think, the first truly postmodern media event on television. Its technologically constructed global marketplace, its "no excuses" attitude toward the mercenary nature of art, its utterly irreverent conception of modernism, its first-lady-turned-superstar consumer, its complete disregard for the "meaning" of the art work, and its dramatization of the work's arbitrary market value all encapsulate the central elements of a television culture that moved away from the wasteland's modernist rhetoric of nationalism and public culture toward a postmodern sensibility, where the nation became a thrift shop for modern art. In *Bravo Picasso,* the modern ideal of the national museum that houses artists who express their "nationness" gave way to the postmodern concept of an art mart in global space where the real spectacle is not the work of art, but the staging of the sale of art in the age of satellite transmission.[65]

Newton or Newt?

Given the amount of fervor around the collapse of high and low, it is especially ironic that the technological "hardware" that was finally put in place after all these debates was the formation in 1967 of PBS, funded by the now "old" modern captains of industry, such as the Ford Foundation (which previously funded National Educational Television). By and large, public broadcasting was committed to the Progressive Era ethos of pedagogy and "uplift" for the masses that had been so central to modernity's museum culture, that had merged by the 1920s with advertising and store design, and that still dominates our commerce-oriented museum culture now.

Within this trajectory, the old ambivalences regarding the nationalist roots of American art resurfaced in programs that still express America's debt to Britishness (for example, *Masterpiece Theater*), and that are sandwiched between more indigenous productions of American documentaries, video art, and the theatrical arts. Rooted in Minow's attempts to restore hierarchies of taste to the wasteland, yet appearing at a moment when commercial television and the art world were collapsing these hierarchies (and even declaring them commercially unpopular and artistically retrograde), PBS has been forever lost in its struggle to preserve the distinction between high and low, winding up finally in the imaginary and ever narrowing "middlebrow" in its appeals to its private-donor public.

Clearly, this has been exacerbated by the fact that in making such distinctions, PBS, which is after all the creation of private funding organizations and private donors, and is even governed by a federally appointed private corporation (the Corporation for Public Broadcasting), has had to pretend to speak disinterestedly for what technocrats at the Federal Communications Commission always call the "public" interest. The Corporation for Public Broadcasting has historically been troubled by its failures to define what the public is, what they might be interested in, and what the meaning of public art might be. Is PBS a place for experimental artists or simply a second-rate transmission of the European and British classics? Would it address a nation of philistines with a deeply condescending form of art education, or would it be a venue for the last wave of a critical avant-garde? Would it give in to corporate censorship, or would its leaders fight for some degree of autonomy from sponsors? Undecided about its own public image, and structurally dependent on large funding corporations, private donors, and Congressional dollars, PBS—and the funding cuts it suffered—needs to be understood within a genealogy of discourses about the meaning of modern art on television. As my research on the topic begins to suggest, those discourses have everything to do with implicit and related battles over nationalism, sexuality, race, and class.

By looking at television's historical representation of the arts, this generation of popular-culture critics might usefully reinvestigate our own implicit and explicit embrace of popular culture over "high" culture. The scholarly investment in popular television and popular audiences, which itself grew out of the well-intentioned "antielitist" critical environment of the 1960s, can nevertheless lead to a troubling complicity with Speaker of the House Newt Gingrich, who saw Rush Limbaugh as the preferred substitute for public television and the public sphere more generally. While I am certainly not advocating a return to Newton Minow's paternalistic attempts to restore a certain form of privileged middle-class "taste" to the wasteland, and while I am often unhappy with the way public television has turned out, I think it is time to imagine a form of critical engagement that allows us to understand the connections between popular television and the broader visual cultures of modernism and postmodernism.

It seems particularly important for popular television (and television studies) to engage more with the work being done in video and to think more about why video and television (both the producers and the critics) have remained so detached from one another. Despite all the talk of the mergers between high art and low TV that has been going on since the 1960s, the truth is that art and commercialism did not actually merge quite as fully as people seem to believe. Instead, in the late 1960s art was simply reassigned a new word — video — that made it distinct from television. Video and its Portapak technology grew in the art world context of New York and posed a challenge to Hollywood through a resurrection of personal authorship, nonstudio work, and a penchant for spontaneity over formula. In critical circles, the logic of the high and low distinction became wedded to medium-specificity arguments as numerous critics began a frenzied debate over the essential properties of video versus television.

Still, in some ways, by posing themselves as countertelevision or medium specific, video artists and critics got weighed down by the discursive baggage surrounding modern art on television in the previous two decades. At MOMA's famous 1972 "Open Circuits" conference, which considered the future of television, these medium-specificity arguments turned onto the older gendered modernist logic that associated mass culture with women and high culture with men. In his essay for the book that came out of the conference, Gregory Battcock spoke of early television as part of the "mother form" of architecture. Noting new developments in both portable television sets and video aesthetics, he continued, "By moving the television set away from the wall one moved it away from its mother," and with this move we have a new "era of visual video communication of importance equal to that of the sculptural communication begun in ancient Greece. . . ."[66] Through this logic, television was dressed in the cloak of femininity and thus devalued, while video was remasculinized as a form of "high art" and public culture. In other discussions, however, video art did not fare so well. Like other forms of modern art, video art has been seen as somehow "foreign" to American tastes. Video's connections to the European avant-garde (especially through the French new wave and the work of Jean-Luc Godard) made it susceptible to the populist distrust for modernism exhibited throughout American culture, and certainly, as we have seen, on American television. Moreover, during the "hot war" years of Vietnam, the more immediate foreign threat was Asia: Sony was the company behind the Portapak and its premier artist was the New York–based Nam June Paik. (And, of course, video artists even took on the military language of the war in Vietnam insofar as they were known as "guerrilla" artists.) Ensconced in these gendered and nationalist tropes, the video art world often self-identified by distancing itself from what it perceived to be TV's degraded status, while the public reception of video art increasingly disparaged its artistic aspirations, once more associating modern art with elitism, inscrutability, and even the threat of subversion.[67]

It should be obvious at this point that the contemporary issues surrounding art on television are deeply historical and political in nature, and these historical struggles are neither resolved through nor derailed by a new postmodern sensibility. Rather, the legacy of relationships between modern art and television continues to inform the way we make distinctions among "public" television, commercial television, video art, and even new technologies such as the Internet (with its collectors and fan lines) and CD ROMs (which now include interactive museums). Despite my desire to conclude with an appropriately modernist utopian statement about the way these technologies might integrate art into the practices of everybody's everyday lives, it seems disingenuous at best to make such a statement, especially given the complicated politics involved in the prior criticism that has done so. But it does seem important, at the very least, that popular-culture critics start thinking seriously about their own relative silence on the state of the arts in television, because if we don't speak, you can be sure the people in Washington will.

Notes

This essay is a somewhat revised version of an essay by the same title that appeared in *Disciplinarity and Dissent in Cultural Studies,* ed. Cary Nelson and Dilip Parameshwar Gaonkar (New York: Routledge, 1996), pp. 313–46. Thank you to the editors for their permission to use this piece in this volume.

All transcriptions are author's, unless otherwise noted.

1 Note that the gallery "mistake" and the smoking technician were actually written into the script by MOMA. See *Dimension,* script, air date: 16 October 1954, series 3, box 18, folder 3, Museum of Modern Art Library, Museum of Modern Art, New York (hereafter referred to as MOMA Library). The museum's intent was to include an untutored "doubting Thomas" character who might be more like the TV audience. See Untitled notes, ca. 1954, p. 2, series 3, box 18, folder 3, MOMA Library. See also Sidney Peterson, *The Medium,* 1955, p. 103, series 3, box 14, MOMA Library. Other film and TV documentaries made use of the convention of the "doubting Thomas" character that was dubious of modern art. The professional art critic would then educate this skeptical character, and in the process also educate the home audience. This allowed the museum to avoid direct didacticism, in this case making the viewer believe that he or she was more sophisti-

cated than the disheveled technician and thus more open to modern art. Note as well that the skeptic was usually a woman or a working-class man. See my "Live From New York: Television at the Museum of Modern Art, 1948–1955," *Aura* 6, no. 1 (Spring 2000): 1–24. See also my *High and Low TV: Modern Art and Commercial Television in Postwar America* (Chicago: University of Chicago Press, forthcoming).

2 MOMA continued to advertise its collection on television. For example, in a joint venture with the television program *Camera 3*, it publicized its show for the seventy-fifth anniversary of Picasso, and in another *Camera 3* museum director Alfred Baar presented a detailed study of Picasso's *Guernica*.

3 In the United States, scholars have devoted some attention to performance arts such as ballet, the symphony, and theater. See, for example, Brian G. Rose, *Television and the Performing Arts: A Handbook and Reference Guide to American Cultural Programming* (New York: Greenwood Press, 1986). For the British view of the translation of fine art to television, see John Walker, *Arts TV: A History of Arts Television in Britain* (London: Arts Council of Great Britain, 1993).

4 Pierre Bourdieu, *Distinction: A Social Critique of the Judgement of Taste*, trans. Richard Nice (Cambridge: Harvard University Press, 1984).

5 Andreas Huyssen, *After the Great Divide: Modernism, Mass Culture, and Postmodernism* (Bloomington: Indiana University Press, 1986).

6 See Neil Harris, *Cultural Excursions: Marketing Appetites and Cultural Tastes in Modern America* (Chicago: University of Chicago Press, 1990); T. J. Jackson Lears, *Fables of Abundance: A Cultural History of Advertising in America* (New York: Basic Books, 1994); Terry Smith, *Making the Modern: Industry, Art, and Design in America* (Chicago: University of Chicago Press, 1993); Sarah Burns, *Inventing the American Artist: Art and Culture in Guilded Age America* (New Haven: Yale University Press, 1996); Cecile Whiting, *The Taste for Pop: Art, Gender, and Consumer Culture* (Cambridge, Eng.: Cambridge University Press, 1997); Dickran Tashjian, *A Boatload of Madmen: Surrealism and the American Avant-Garde, 1920–1950* (New York: Thames and Hudson, 1995); and Michelle Bogart, *Artists, Advertising, and the Borders of Art* (Chicago: University of Chicago Press, 1995).

7 Estelle Hamburger, *It's a Woman's Business* (New York: Vanguard, 1939).

8 Ibid., p. 178.

9 Ibid., pp. 141–42.

10 Serge Guilbaut, *How New York Stole the Idea of Modern Art: Abstract Expressionism, Freedom, and the Cold War*, trans. A. Goldhammer (Chicago: University of Chicago Press, 1983), p. 89.

11 Ibid., p. 91.

12 Stanford Research Institute, "Long Range Planning Service," 1962, p. 2, Papers of August Heckscher, White House Staff Files, 1962–63, John Fitzgerald Kennedy Library, Boston, Massachusetts (hereafter referred to as JFK Library).

13 Ibid.

14 Although the Stanford report did not make this correlation, it is interesting to

note that as art became cheaper and more available to see through technological reproductions in mass media, according to the same report, "the price of original paintings rose over 600% in the U.S." ("Long Range Planning Service," p. 4).

15   Alan Wallach, "The Museum of Modern Art: The Past's Future," in *Art in Modern Culture: An Anthology of Critical Texts,* ed. Francis Frascina and Jonathan Harris (New York: Harper Collins, 1992), pp. 282–91. Note also this was the same year RCA debuted its commercial television system at the New York World's Fair.

16   This is reported in Betty Chamberlain, draft of letter to Federal Communications Commission, ca. 1951, series III, box 19, folder 12.d., MOMA Library.

17   Sidney Peterson, *The Medium.* For more on MOMA's TV Project and Peterson, see my essay "Live from New York" and my forthcoming book *High and Low TV.*

18   Allon Schoenor, "Television, An Important New Instrument of Mass Education for Museums," speech presented at The Role of Museums in Education, Seminar at the United Nations Educational Scientific and Cultural Organization, 27 September 1952, Brooklyn, New York, p. 1. The transcribed talk is in Papers of Davidson Taylor, NBC Records, box 278, folder 10, Wisconsin Center Historical Archives, State Historical Society, Madison (hereafter referred to as Wisconsin Center Historical Archives). It should be noted that despite these statistics, not everyone in the museum world felt that television had achieved its goal in disseminating art education. In a report for MOMA, Douglas Macagy predicted that "the museum will do for painting what radio did for the symphony," but at the same time he also remarked, "When compared with radio's achievement in music, television has accomplished next to nothing on behalf of the visual arts, and many wonder why" (*The Museum Looks in on TV,* 1955, p. ii, series 3, box 14, MOMA Library).

19   Guilbaut, *How New York Stole the Idea of Modern Art,* p. 55.

20   The term "ugly American" was coined by William J. Lederer in his book by the same title (New York: Norton, 1958). I am using it to cover the concept that prevailed at the time, but it should be noted the term itself was not in popular circulation during much of the period.

21   As Guilbaut suggests, mass media such as radio and magazines had in the 1940s popularized ideas about modern art in America (see his *How New York Stole the Idea of Modern Art,* chapter 2).

22   Katherine Kuh, "The Unhappy Marriage of Art and TV," *Saturday Review,* 21 January 1961, p. 61.

23   Note that while Castro would have been conceived as "foreign" and communist at this point, he was not yet widely seen as a "subversive" threat.

24   Karal Ann Marling, *As Seen on TV: The Visual Culture of Everyday Life in the 1950s* (Cambridge: Harvard University Press, 1994), pp. 76–77.

25   For a discussion of African American jazz in Paris since the 1920s, see Tyler Stovall, *Paris Noir: African Americans in the City of Light* (Boston: Houghton Mifflin, 1996).

26   William Boddy discusses these issues on foreign syndication in his work on the Thomas Dodd television violence hearings. See his "Investigating Video Violence

in the Early 1960s," in *The Revolution Wasn't Televised: Sixties Television and Social Conflict*, ed. Lynn Spigel and Michael Curtin (New York: Routledge, 1997), pp. 161–83.

27   One of the Kennedy administration's greatest exploits was a closed-circuit TV program titled *An American Pageant of the Arts* that was aired to promote Kennedy's plans for the construction of the National Cultural Center. Produced by Robert Saudek at Omnibus, the program was broadcast on 29 November 1962 to paying audiences in one hundred cities across the country (ticket prices ranged from $100 to $200 according to venue). The program included an eclectic mix of musical and comedy acts from the "serious" conductor (and host) Leonard Bernstein, the poet Robert Frost, and "legitimate" actors like Colleen Dewhurst to the likes of popular entertainers like Danny Kaye, Gene Kelly, Tammy Grimes, Benny Goodman, and Harry Belefonte. For a description see *An American Pageant of the Arts*, 1962, p. 3, Papers of August Heckscher, White House Staff Files, 1962–63, JFK Library.

28   Newton N. Minow, "The Vast Wasteland," speech delivered before the Thirty-ninth Annual Convention of the National Association of Broadcasters, Washington, D.C., 9 May 1961.

29   A tape of this is available at the JFK Library.

30   The program was simulcast on NBC, but ABC did not run the *Tour*, opting instead to feature its police show *Naked City*. See Jack Gould, "Mrs. Kennedy, TV Hostess to the Nation," *New York Times*, 15 February 1962, p. 18.

31   See the passage with direct quotes in my "The Suburban Home Companion," this volume, pp. 51–52.

32   Philip Wylie, *Generation of Vipers* (1941; New York: Holt, Rinehart and Winston, 1955), p. 215.

33   Huyssen, *After the Great Divide*, chapter 3.

34   James Thrall Soby, "Art on TV," *Saturday Review*, 13 April 1957, p. 29.

35   This theme of the older woman and her liaison with a modern painter was repeated in a 1953 episode of *Armstrong Circle Theater* titled "The Secret of Emily Duvane," which is located in the UCLA Film and Television Archive. This episode, which is set in Singapore and deals with a woman and her extremely colonialist-minded husband, is an incredibly rich example of the way older American women are presented as modern primitives.

36   Michael Rogin discusses the links between communism and momism in American film of this period. See his *Ronald Reagan, The Movie: And Other Episodes in Political Demonology* (Berkeley: University of California Press, 1987), pp. 236–71.

37   As early as 1945, premier art critic Clement Greenberg, most famous for his work on the opposition between the "avant-garde" and "kitsch," noted the trend of industry's co-optation of modernism, and warned, "We are in danger of having a new kind of official art foisted on us—official 'modern' art. It is being done by well-intentioned people like the Pepsi-Cola Company. . . . Official 'modern' art of this type will confuse, discourage and dissuade the true creator" (*Nation*, 1 December 1945, p. 604).

38 It is also worth noting that cartoon art used for television reviews in major peri-
odicals often employed abstract styles to depict television and television programming. In this regard, through the institution of TV criticism and its links to commercial art, the reading public would have occasion to acquaint themselves with
elements of modern design. An article in *Television Quarterly* even compared the
editorial cartoon (in both print media and on television) to the French new wave
film *Last Year at Marienbad*. See John Chase, "The TV Editorial Cartoon," *Television Quarterly* 6:2 (1967): 4–19.

39 Erika Doss, *Benton, Pollack, and the Politics of Modernism: From Regionalism to
Abstract Expressionism* (Chicago: University of Chicago Press, 1989), pp. 205–19.

40 For a detailed study of the arts on television, see Rose, *Television and the Performing Arts*.

41 Along these lines it is interesting to note that numerous fiction programs thema-
tized the fraudulent nature of art in stories about forgery. One critic pointed out:
"The most drastic proof of art's descendent popularity is that it so often supplied
the dramatic plot for ambitious TV programs. I don't how many times during the
past two years I've watched mystery stories in which the theft or forgery of a painting has been the subject of complicated exercises in skullduggery and sleuthing."
See Soby, "Art on TV," p. 29.

42 Marshall McLuhan, *Understanding Media: The Extensions of Man* (New York:
McGraw Hill, 1964).

43 Jac Venza, ed., *Television USA: 13 Seasons* (New York: The Museum of Modern
Art Film Library; and Doubleday, 1962), p. 15.

44 The artistic aspirations of Camelot were also exhibited back in Hollywood where
industry people got the city of Los Angeles to front seed money for the Hollywood
Museum, which was, according to its founders, intended to raise film, television,
radio, and recorded music to the status of art. The Museum Commission was
formed by the Los Angeles Board of Supervisors in 1959. The advisory council included Desi Arnaz, Jack Benny, Frank Capra, Walt Disney, William Dozier, Jack
Warner, Arthur Miller, Ronald Reagan, and Harold Lloyd. The founding document is worded as follows: "The goal is to portray these four communicative arts
as having a justification not only as entertainment media but also as important
contributions to humanity . . . the Museum will be of aid in a positive way in
overcoming the damaging effect of the constant and growing criticisms of the industries by numerous private and public groups." See Sol Lesser, Untitled document, 1962, n.p., White House Staff Files, JFK Library. In line with Kennedy's use
of art as a strategic force in "free world" rhetoric, the museum promoters sent
a telegram to Secretary of Defense Robert S. MacNamara, saying that the mass
media represented in the museum would help create better understanding among
nations. See Schumach telegram to Robert S. MacNamara, 1963, n.p., Papers of
August Heckscher, White House Staff Files, JFK Library. Although there were
ground-breaking ceremonies in 1963, the museum did not materialize.

45 One year before *Batman*, ABC aired the short-lived and still black-and-white series

Honey West, a female spy show that was inspired by the popularity of James Bond, but also used pop pulp fiction themes and sometimes pop iconography. The program played with the "threat" of the modern women and her eccentric visual style, presenting Honey as a high-tech femme fatale dressed in leopard print, who kicked, whipped, and even wrestled male enemies. For an analysis of the program, see Julie D'Acci, "Nobody's Woman: *Honey West* and the New Sexuality," in *The Revolution Wasn't Televised*, pp. 73–93.

46 For more on *Batman* in relation to pop and camp, see Lynn Spigel and Henry Jenkins, "Same Bat Channel/Different Bat Times: Mass Culture and Popular Memory," in *The Many Lives of the Batman: Critical Approaches to a Superhero and His Media*, ed. Roberta Pearson and William Uricchio (London: British Film Institute, 1991), pp. 117–46.

47 The networks had considered exploiting art for the marketing of color TV even before the FCC set color standards in 1952. Networks CBS and NBC had affiliated with MOMA and the Metropolitan Museum of Art in these early years. The mix of vaudeville/variety show and fine art was present from the start. In 1951, CBS aired its inaugural color broadcast featuring Ed Sullivan, Arthur Godfrey, and "femcee" Faye Emerson along with a Renoir on loan from the Met and a Picasso on loan from MOMA. As I detail elsewhere, MOMA's Alfred Barr was nervous about loaning the Picasso to CBS, largely because he feared the network might place the painting next to commercial advertising for Pepsi. See Alfred H. Barr Jr. letter to Mr. Rickey, 20 June 1951, Series 3, box 19, folder 12.d., MOMA Library. By 1954, NBC had joined forces with the Met to present its first nationally broadcast color program. The museum used the color broadcast to promote its newly "modernized" building and to court a national audience. See *A Visit to the Metropolitan Museum of Art: NBC*, script, air date: 8 May 1954, The Papers of Davidson Taylor, NBC Records, box 279, folder 69, Wisconsin Center Historical Archives. For more on this, see my essay "Live from New York" and my book *High and Low TV*.

48 "Discotheque Frug Party Heralds Batman's Film and TV Premier," *New York Times*, 13 January 1966, p. 79.

49 It could, of course, be argued that pop borrowed mass culture's borrowing strategies before this, insofar as both film and broadcasting had relied heavily on the fine arts for subject matter, and they both borrowed forms of exhibition from the world of theater and the arts. However, in this case it seems to me that television borrowed a particular kind of borrowing strategy from pop, one that was playfully ironic and self-reflexive. The *Batman* reception was filled with this kind of playful irony and self-reflexivity, as was the program itself.

50 In *Fables of Abundance*, T. J. Jackson Lears shows that this debate regarding the status of advertising as art took place as early as the 1890s (pp. 282–98).

51 Abe Liss in Venza, *Television USA: 13 Seasons*, p. 38.

52 Gerald Weales, "Be Quiet, The Commercial's On," *Television Quarterly* 6:3 (1967): 24.

53 Andre Malraux, "The Meaning of Culture," address before the French National

Assembly, 9 November 1963, excerpted and reprinted in *Television Quarterly* 3:1 (1963): 44–55; and Richard W. Jencks, "Is Taste Obsolete?" *Television Quarterly* 8:3 (1969): 5–21.

54 Jack Gould, "Too Good to Be Camp," *The New York Times*, 23 January 1966, sec. 1, p. 17.

55 John Skow, "Has TV, Gasp, Gone Batty?" *Saturday Evening Post*, 7 May 1966, p. 95.

56 *Rowan and Martin's Laugh-In*, script no. 0283–21, air date: 24 February 1969, p. 4A, Doheny Cinema Library, University of Southern California, Los Angeles (hereafter referred to as Doheny Cinema Library).

57 *Rowan and Martin's Laugh-In*, script no. 0283–14, air date: 6 January 1969, p. 27, Doheny Cinema Library.

58 *Rowan and Martin's Laugh-In*, script no. 0283–20, air date: 17 February 1969, p. 93, Doheny Cinema Library.

59 Alexander Doty, *Making Things Perfectly Queer* (Minneapolis: University of Minnesota Press, 1994).

60 *Rowan and Martin's Laugh-In*, script no. 0283–25, air date: 24 March 1969, pp. 194A–E, Doheny Cinema Library.

61 *Rowan and Martin's Laugh-In*, script no. 0283–20, air date: 17 February 1969, p. 92, Doheny Cinema Library.

62 Joseph Golden, "TV's Womanless Hero," *Television Quarterly* 2:1 (1963): 14.

63 Ibid., p. 17.

64 For a discussion about the history of debates about museums, see Daniel J. Sherman and Irit Rogoff, eds. *Museum Culture: Histories, Discourses, Spectacles* (Minneapolis: University of Minnesota Press, 1994).

65 This new form of postmodern media event, constructed through the merger of science, art, and commerce, was embraced not only by the television broadcasters but also by the New York art world—at least in the pages of one of its premier journals, *Art News*. Writing for the journal in 1971, Alan Kaprow (who was known for his staging of "happenings") embraced the television medium as a welcome alternative to the traditions of modern art. He wrote, "That the LM Mooncraft is patently superior to all contemporary sculptural efforts; that the broadcast verbal exchange between Houston's Manned Spacecraft Center and the Apollo astronauts was better than contemporary poetry; that, with its sound distortions, beeps, static and communication breaks, such exchanges also surpassed the electronic music of the concert halls." Alan Kaprow, "The Education of the Un-Artist, Part 1," *Art News* 69:10 (1971): p. 28. Kaprow was part of the decade's general interest in breaking down high and low aesthetic hierarchies, and taking this to its terminal extreme, he was critical even of the "anti-art" crowd (that is, those who were against art), and instead championed what he called "non-art," or media like television that were integrated into everyday life. Later in the essay he predicts that the new "inter-media" environments of computers, video, etcetera (what we would call the information superhighway) will be the spaces where this type of non-art takes place.

66 Gregory Battcock, "The Sociology of the Set," in *The New Television: A Public/Private Art,* ed. Douglas Davis and Allison Simmons (Cambridge: MIT Press, 1978), pp. 21.

67 It should be noted that in the early years there was some popular interest in video art, especially as the work was publicized on NET, PBS, and also some commercial stations. In 1972, *TV Guide* even ran a rather sympathetic article on the video art movement. See Neil Hickey, "Notes from the Video Underground," *TV Guide,* 9–15 December 1972, pp. 6–10.

Barbies without Ken: Femininity, Feminism, and the Art-Culture System

> It must be remembered that the toy moved late to the nursery, that
> from the beginning it was adults who made toys, and not only with
> regard to their other invention, the child. The fashion doll, for
> example, was the plaything of adult women before it was the
> plaything of the child.
>
> Susan Stewart, *On Longing*[1]

> *Mattel executive* (addressing a group of Barbie doll collectors): How
> old do you think the average girl is who plays with Barbie?
> *Barbie collector:* Forty.
>
> "Barbie behind the Scenes"[2]

✱ Although Barbie recently turned forty, she is still a popular girl. In the
early 1990s, Mattel estimated that two Barbie dolls are sold every second
somewhere in the world, and when placed head to toe there are enough
Barbies to circle the earth more than three-and-a-half times.[3] In the course
of her orbit around the planet, she has evolved from a child's plaything
into a subject of intense cultural interest. While one woman has paid huge
sums for plastic surgery to turn herself into this living doll, another group
calling itself the Barbie Liberation Organization (BLO) has created mass-
cultural subterfuge by performing "corrective surgery" on the voice boxes

of Talking GI Joe and Teen Talk Barbie, so that Joe now says, "Wanna go shopping?" and Barbie grunts, "Vengeance is mine." Meanwhile, a growing number of scholars, journalists, fiction writers, and poets have become riveted on this 11½ inch fashion queen, so that now there is a subculture of intellectuals engaged in "Barbie studies."

In Barbie's miniature dream house there is room enough for almost anyone's fantasy. Since Barbie's introduction in 1959, this has been Mattel's credo and the reason for Barbie's success. Her plastic form is doubled by her equally plastic ability to be molded to almost anyone's desire. Clearly, part of Barbie's longevity is her plasticity—her ability to be reappropriated and interpreted by different groups in a variety of ways. While Mattel does worry about its trademark reputation and Barbie-bashing groups like the BLO (the company even sued one female occultist who channeled Barbie on a 900 number), Barbie's plastic quality has generally worked well for the toy company, which simply wants lots of people to buy the doll, but cares less about what they do with Barbie once they have her. For example, although Mattel denies that its Earring Ken doll is gay, it is clear that the company knows a lot of its consumers are, and it is also clear that Earring Ken has delighted that particular market. In fact, today Mattel markets across two distinct groups—children (its largest consumer base) and an increasingly expanding community of adult Barbie collectors, some 250,000 worldwide.

For more than ten years, I have been involved in the huge collectors' culture organized around Barbie dolls. The collectors' group is global, and although the largest group is from the United States there is a sizable Japanese following and there are numerous collectors around the world. As might be expected, collectors in the United States are predominantly white, and their venues of representation and collective experience are for the most part populated by white lower- to upper-middle-class publics. Despite the whiteness of the group, people of color do collect Barbies and they do express interest in making her fit their life experiences. In 1997, for example, the "International Black Barbie Doll Club" established itself in Van Nuys California. This small group of six primarily comprises African American members, although it welcomes anyone interested in black Barbies.

Beyond these demographics, the racial politics of collectors are not easy to capture. On the whole, collectors represent themselves through ideals of racial tolerance and friendship. The collectors' premier magazine, *Barbie Bazaar,* often promotes and encourages collectors to embrace Mattel's multiracial product lines that include "Black," "Hispanic," and "Native American" dolls, as well as Mattel's "Dolls of the World" series. Still, as Ann Ducille argues, Mattel's racial and national diversity tends to work on the logic of commodity fetishism.[4] As fetish objects these multi-cultural dolls stand in for the lack of race relations—and the disavowal of racial struggles—within the collectors' group itself. Like Barbie, the collectors' culture puts on a pretty face that masks the more difficult problems entailed in gender and racial identity. Yet despite the image of multi-cultural harmony that floats on the surface of most collectors' venues, the practice of collecting Barbie is always bound up with her cultural legacy as the quintessential white girl of cold war America.

Just a glance at collector price guides shows that even in her new multi-cultural incarnations, Barbie's "whiteness" is still taken for granted and naturalized as the norm. White Barbies are listed as just "Barbie," while the other dolls are listed by their race. As Richard Dyer argues, this as-sumption that white is the norm has historically been a mark of white privilege in a world where white operates as the dominant term.[5] White people get to be just "people"—and thus stand for all of humanity—while everyone else is a specific racial or ethnic type. In this regard, even while many Barbie collectors often have very good intentions regarding racial harmony, the culture of Barbie collecting—like most forms of white cul-ture—is based on this taken-for-granted form of white privilege.

The collectors' group is more diverse with regard to gender and sexual orientation. While the majority of collectors are women, there is a large constituency of men, some of whom are openly gay. As we shall see, the mixed composition of the group often leads to complex power dynamics. Yet, despite underlying conflicts, male and female collectors participate together in annual conventions and seasonal shows; they have their own museums, such as the Barbie Doll Hall of Fame; and they regularly meet in each other's homes where they exchange information and display col-lections to one another.

What interests me about the world of Barbie collectors is the way artifacts of popular culture are assigned values by the collectors and the way various groups ascribe meanings to objects that they reappropriate for purposes not originally intended by corporate giants such as Mat-tel. In this essay I am particularly concerned with what I see as three intertwined topics: the relationships among intellectual feminism, popular feminism, and femininity; the relationships among high, craft, and mass culture (especially concerning the gendering/queering of pop art, "women's" crafts, and mass production); and the theorization of subcultural communities that form around mass-produced goods such as Barbie. What also interests me is the fact that I am somewhat of a collector, and so I want to know about my own implications in this activity—both as participant and as academic observer.

Feminists, Fashion Dolls, and Femininity

The dual activity of playing with toys and toying with theories is by now a well-known practice in cultural studies, as so many of us try to understand the logics of those popular cultures that appeal to us but also terrorize us with their insistent commodity forms. Since the mid-1980s, feminist critics have tried to understand the dynamics of audience participation with and pleasure in mass-culture texts.[6] Feminist work in this area has particularly concentrated on "women's genres," such as soap operas and romances. But there is also a large body of work that explores women's participation in cultures that have historically revolved around genres aimed at male audiences—including science fiction, sports, and rock and rap music.[7]

The early feminist work on audience cultures was a reaction against the patriarchal dismissal of mass forms as "feminine" and, therefore, degraded texts. It was an attempt to authenticate, or at least take seriously, genres such as the soap opera and romance novel—genres that the canons of male-centered literary and art criticism deemed unworthy of study. It was an attempt to see these forms as cultural spheres in which women could extract not only individual narrative pleasure, but also could enter into an interpretive community that operates both in terms of, but also at times against the grain of, everyday female experience in Western patriarchies. Originally, then, the studies of fan cultures and audiences were motivated in terms of a dialogue with male-centered literary and art criticism, inheriting much of their critical power from text-based feminist studies, such as Tania Modleski's work on soap operas.[8] The polemic revolved around the sexism of institutional canons and the resulting degradation of female forms and female pleasure.

Soon, however, the internal dialogue in such studies shifted its focus to the dynamics between the intellectual studying women's fan culture and the fan culture itself. In other words, the feminist polemic of institutional sexism turned to anthropological questions of self and other—questions about the role of the intellectual and her or his place in studying popular cultures. How, for example, could a feminist study women's fan cultures without somehow adopting an "I know better" condescending attitude toward them? How could feminists account for the potential race and class bias at the core of ethnographic audience studies generally? How could they deal with the problems of surveillance and voyeuristic pleasure that ethnographers produce for themselves and their readers at the expense of their ethnographic subjects? And how could feminists guard against becoming unwitting "informers," who provide insider information that culture industries can use for their own audience and market research? Perhaps as a way to cope with these very real problems, many scholars—including the ones described here—have turned to self-critique. That is, in the by-now classic ethnographic move, numerous mass-culture critics explore their own power relations to the cultures they study.

Barbie is herself a quintessential example of these critical trajectories. In one respect, as an object of considerable dispute, she continues to be attacked as the embodiment of American culture's willful socialization of rigid gender, racial, and nationalist hierarchies. Yet her critics have also uncovered ample evidence that Barbie has generated a more playful attitude among her many publics. In her ethnographic study *Barbie's Queer Accessories,* Erica Rand considers the way lesbians and lesbian publications like *On Our Backs* have appropriated Barbie's image in ways that acknowledge the queer pleasure she evokes. By talking to women about their childhood memories and current fantasies of Barbie, Rand shows that even while Mattel promotes Barbie as the ultimate heterosexual virgin, Barbie is never just that. Like many recent ethnographies of mass culture, Rand often questions her own position vis-à-vis the women she studies, and she is particularly concerned about the ethics of being an academic insider who translates women's experience into feminist theory. Remaining critical of Mattel, while nevertheless attempting to explore women's experiences with popular culture in nondismissive terms, Rand represents current strains within feminist approaches to mass culture that preserve a negative critique of culture industries even while they attempt to understand the possible utopian (and, for some, "resistant") pleasures that women and girls find in these products.[9]

As feminist scholars continue to explore industrial culture and the female subcultures that form around it, corporate giants are also taking note of the fans and fanzines invested in their products. Companies like Paramount and Mattel see fan productions as a lucrative market for memorabilia, collectibles, and related products. But they also see various fan activities as a threat to their trademarks, and they are attempting to censor fanzines and Web sites through litigation. In 1997, Mattel filed a federal lawsuit against Miller Publications, which produces *Miller's* price guides and fanzine. Jill E. Barad, Chief Executive at Mattel (and the most powerful woman in the toy industry), claimed that *Miller's* tampered with Barbie's image by, for example, showing "Barbie with alcohol [and] pills." [10] In addition to suing for copyright and trademark infringement, Mattel has made numerous efforts to institute itself as the "official" voice of the collector group. Not only has it produced Barbie lines for the collectibles market, it endorses one fanzine, *Barbie Bazaar*, as its official publication (the licensing deal gives Mattel the right to review *Barbie Bazaar* before publication).[11] Mattel is now even trying to persuade local collector clubs that grew up on a grassroots basis over the last fifteen years to obtain official fan club licenses from the toy company. Rage at these and other corporate practices became so intense in summer 1997 that one collector formed the "pink anger" Web site, which called for a boycott and a letter-writing campaign. The pink anger Web site was instantly translated into Japanese and German, and was joined by a "pink tidal wave" movement that further protested Mattel's anticollector practices.[12]

Yet, despite all their "pink anger," collectors don't necessarily agree with feminist intellectuals who critique Mattel's racism and sexism and generally worry about the effects Barbie has on little girls. In fact, although collectors often consider themselves feminists, and although they often agitate against Mattel, most collectors view Barbie as a positive role model for women. In this regard, Barbie has been a primary vehicle through which the strained relations between different views of feminism surface in our culture.

Take, for example, the cultural struggle that took place a few years ago when Mattel marketed a doll known as Teen Talk Barbie. The doll dabbled in a variety of girl talk, including the phrase "math class is tough." The American Association of University Women (AAUW) found this phrase to be beyond the limits of acceptable doll discourse, arguing that the doll sent the wrong message to young girls. The AAUW's efforts to get Teen Talk Barbie off the market were widely reported in newspapers, magazines, and on television. To mediate the battle between the educators and the toy company, the mass media ushered in a third party— adults who collect Barbie dolls. Realizing that they had a natural ally in these groups, journalists and talk show hosts began to interview collectors about their take on the Teen Talk controversy.

For example, Ev Burkhalter, curator of the Barbie Doll Hall of Fame in Palo Alto, California, appeared on CBS's morning show. When the host asked her about the AAUW's attack on Barbie, Ev responded with what is a typical attitude among collectors: Barbie is, in fact, a wonderful role model for women. She has been a veterinarian, an astronaut, and a soldier—and even before real women had a chance to enter such occupations. More generally, collectors rewrite women's history from the perspective of Barbie's progress from her incarnation in 1959 through her series of brilliant careers. From this point of view, Burkhalter suggested that the claims of the AAUW were utterly misguided.

In ways such as this, the mass media's coverage of the Teen Talk controversy set up a series of narrative oppositions that pit the intellectual against the popular. The AAUW became the "Miss Crabapples" of the 1990s—dour schoolteachers who scorn the popular, but ultimately misunderstand its logic because they fail to see how ordinary people actually engage with mass culture. Meanwhile, the media positioned the collectors as heroines (albeit somewhat childlike heroines) of the popular, who resist the negative aspects of Mattel's doll and use it for their own purposes.

More generally, in a survey of print media from 1985 to the present, I found that the media continually pitted the "lowbrow" populist pleasures of Barbie enthusiasts against the elitist stance of intellectual feminists, who, reportedly, revile the pleasures of girl culture that Barbie stands for. A 1986 article on Barbie collectors in the *Wall Street Journal*, for example, starts off by quoting Ev Burkhalter, who says, "A lot of women see in Barbie what they would like to be." A few paragraphs later, the article compares this populist embrace of Barbie as a model of femininity with the academic feminist response. Quoting Robin Lakoff, a member of the Women's Studies Program at UC Berkeley, the *Wall Street Journal* tells of the dark side of Barbie collecting: " 'You have to look at the reasons why people consider Barbie a desirable feminine image,' Prof. Lakoff says, 'and that's a rather dangerous thing. . . . The role of an ideal woman is to look pretty; she encourages the superficial idea that clothing is all. The

Barbie image,' says the professor, is 'the airhead who consumes.'" The article goes on: "Professor Lakoff, who never had a Barbie, suggests a reason for adult women's attraction to the doll. 'People like to hang on to the security of childhood.'"[13] By pitting the collector against the intellectual, the *Journal* succeeds in making feminism seem totally antithetical to femininity. The anti-Barbie stance is coded as a feminist rejection of beauty, fashion, and those activities such as shopping that are deemed to be feminine weaknesses in our culture. Feminism is hereby rendered as an elitist point of view that denigrates other women by claiming that their pleasures are immature and immaterial. Like so many others, the *Journal*'s piece of popular journalism makes it appear that feminism is at battle with that amorphous category "ordinary women," and it does so by portraying feminism as a narrowly conceived cultural style that is the direct opposite of the pleasures of both femininity and mass culture. As a more recent issue of *Spy* magazine succinctly put it, critical commentary on Barbie is reserved for the domain of the "oversensitive feminist," not "for most people."[14]

But at least in the case of Barbie culture, this opposition between ordinary people/mass culture and intellectual/high culture is ultimately misleading because these categories are precisely what is at stake in the process of collection. It is the movement between these zones that reveals some of the central dynamics involved in the collection of commodities like Barbie. That is, it is exactly the practice of playing with categories of high/intellectual culture and those consumer pleasures that get categorized as lowbrow, frivolous, and feminine fun that seems so essential to collectors.

James Clifford's essay "Collecting Art and Culture" can serve here as a useful point of departure. In what he calls the "art-culture system," Clifford shows that the meanings and values assigned to objects are socially constructed and thus open to historical redefinition. His system suggests how, for example, commodities such as souvenirs move from the realm of "inauthentic" kitsch to the sphere of authentic folk art, or how an artifact of folk art can move from the flea market to the art gallery. Such movements, Clifford argues, require semiotic revaluations that are deeply informed by a society's larger ideologies and social practices.[15]

While Clifford's work refers mostly to museums, I want to use the collectors' magazine *Barbie Bazaar,* as well as the various display activities that go on at collector shows and conventions, as my primary objects of analysis. By looking at the semiotics of display within the magazine and other "shopping" and social arenas, it is my intention to analyze the way this culture self-represents, more than it is to describe the "deep structures" of need, intent, and desire that motivate individuals to participate in the culture. My choice to bypass psychological and functionalist explanations is based on my wish to avoid the cultural stereotypes about collectors—that is, the idea that collectors are obsessive-compulsive neurotics and that toy collectors in particular are merely acting out regressive personality traits. This explanation, it seems to me, leads critics away from the more interesting problems regarding the relationship between object relationships and social relationships in postmodern culture. One collector recently complained of the litany of questions posed to collectors by their critics: "WHY do you collect? WHAT trauma in your life brought you to this point? WHAT is your angle? Are you a woman jealous of Barbie's looks, and acting out a fantasy? Maybe you are a bitter man because your family didn't let you have the toy you wanted. Why are you collecting TODAY? We're treated as if the hobby were so insipid that we needed to justify it by psychosis or at least neurosis."[16] To be sure, one of the things that joins collectors together as a subculture is a rejection of the "perversions" ascribed to them by mainstream culture. For that reason, any understanding of collectors' cultures should by definition avoid the "regressive hypothesis" in favor of other forms of inquiry.

What follows, then, is not a "psychological" profile of the collectors but rather a more art historical set of questions about how collectors define and display objects. In the sense of Clifford's formulation, I ask how Barbie has been alternatively categorized as a form of art or culture. In addition, I aim to show how the art-culture system is also a system of gender and sexuality.

Barbie as Craft

Barbie Bazaar was founded in 1988 by a group of women in Kenosha, Wisconsin. Although it began as an independently published " 'zine," it had obvious promotional benefits for Mattel, so much so that now the toy company licenses it as the exclusive Barbie collectors' magazine. With a worldwide circulation of over 110,000 it works as a major international forum for collectors, with articles and graphics culled from the collector group at large. While the magazine does not reflect directly what the

Art is the cover story of this September/October 1994 issue of *Barbie Bazaar*. Note that "sewing" is featured too. (Copyright, Murat Caviale Inc.)

collectors themselves think, it does provide a sense of how this culture organizes and displays itself. It shows us how the culture represents itself and how it wants to be regarded by others inside and outside the group.

In *Barbie Bazaar,* popular collecting always stands in relation to the more dominant art collection discourses and practices that organize objects into high, craft, and mass culture. I use the term "craft" here (as distinct from the more wide-ranging term "folk") because I have in mind a specific range of contemporary artisan/vernacular productions typically associated with (but not limited to) women's "local" community formations. These practices—such as sewing, curio display, baking, and diorama and knickknack making—are fostered in community centers, in national girls clubs such as the Girl Scouts or 4-H, and through mass media "how-to" discourses. It is the movement between the categories of mass, craft, and art that is at stake in the way collectors display and write about Barbie.

Barbie collecting started in the mid-1970s, when the mothers of the first generation of children who had owned Barbies began expressing their own interest in the toy. In 1979, a Barbie encyclopedia appeared;

the book was followed the next year by the first annual Barbie convention, which was organized by collector Ruth Kronk in New York. In 1981, the publication of a price guide upped the stakes of this heretofore informal collector's culture and drove the prices to new heights. Local and then national annual conventions followed, giving the collectors a shared sense of community and purpose. The growth of Barbie Web sites and chat rooms in the 1990s connected people around the globe on a daily basis.

The adult recognition of Barbie created both a new use-value and a new exchange-value for the doll—ones that weren't initially planned by Mattel. This value was predominantly located in what can be seen as an emerging craft culture based on women collectors who designed homemade costumes for the dolls, collected and restored vintage outfits, and built elaborate curio displays. While Mattel has since embraced this collectors' culture by selling high-priced lines of dolls (such as the Stars'n' Stripes collection or the Designer Classique collection), the collectors' culture began in a relatively autonomous way, largely through craft productions.[17]

In *Barbie Bazaar* the artisan practices of craft give way to an expression of local identities that seem to counteract the very status of Barbie as a national mass-market icon. Collectors adorn Barbie with their own local "accents," representing her in ways that speak to their particular regional identities. Issues typically feature stories on local collectors' clubs that are usually named for their geographical location. And against the idea of commodified, ready-made fashions that Mattel's Barbie so fully epitomizes, *Barbie Bazaar* displays a thriving craft culture based on homemade, one-of-a-kind dresses that serves as a representation of one's own identity politics. A particularly striking example is several women across the country who sew nun habits for Barbie.[18] Women also make replica Barbie costumes for themselves and model them in club meetings, using their bodies as media on which to display their sewing talents. In ways such as this, collectors represent themselves not simply as consumers of mass culture but as cultural producers who collectively make their own artifacts and create their own stories.

The craft displays in *Barbie Bazaar* are clearly gendered—that is, they are associated with a women's culture that takes place in domestic spaces and occasionally in community centers where collectors are presented as folksy family types. Pets, cakes, and other signs of domesticity are typically pictured along with collectors in photographs they send into the magazine. When men do appear in these photos they, too, are represented in tropes of femininity; they are shown as participants in a girl culture.

This movement from mass to craft culture might be seen in relation to Michael Thompson's study of the social construction of value in his book *Rubbish Theory: The Creation and Destruction of Value*.[19] Thompson theorizes how objects change their status from, for example, "transient" or declining value (such as the used car) to "rubbish" (or an object with no value) to "durable" (such as an antique piece of furniture). Such transitions, he argues, are governed by larger systems of social power. People at the top of the social system are most able to control the value of objects and attempt, of course, to make their objects into durables. However, rather than seeing this system as completely bound to preexisting class relations, Thompson's theory is dynamic because he wants to explain how the status of objects changes over time in relation to the groups who imagine new meanings for them. For example, in his chapter on Stevengraph collectors, Thompson shows how the value of the object changes along with the gender of the people who control it. "In the early days," he claims, "Stevengraph-collecting, like knitting, was largely a feminine occupation. The great names are Mary Dunham, Mrs. Wilma Sinclair Le Van Baker, Mrs. Therle Hughs, and Alice Lynes, but the transition proceeds so Stevengraphs are transferred to male control."[20]

Although I intend to return to Thompson's last point regarding male control, for now I want to concentrate on the "feminine" side of his equation. Perhaps it is no coincidence that Thompson likens Stevengraph collecting to knitting, a traditional female craft. Indeed, while Thompson doesn't theorize its importance, at least in the case of Barbie collecting I would argue that "craft" serves a central and gendered role in the transition from rubbish to durable. Craft accounts for that flexibility in the system in which women's groups, traditionally disempowered in the sphere of production, exert their influence on the market economies and cultural practices of late capitalism through innovation and creative pursuits. It is through the largely antiquated and anachronistic practice of artisan labor that women turn rubbish into durables and thereby affect the flows and values of objects in our postmodern global markets and cultures.

This situation recalls Susan Stewart's more general comments about the production of miniatures and the collection of them, which coincided with the invention of printing and was first witnessed in the manufacture of miniature books. According to Stewart, while the miniature is a celebration of new technologies and industrial modes of production, it contains within it a "longing" for its opposite:

> We cannot separate the function of the miniature from a nostalgia for preindustrial labor, a nostalgia for craft. We see a rise in the production of miniature furniture at the same time that the plans of Adam, Chipendale, and Sheraton are becoming reproduced in mass and readily available form. Contemporary dollhouses are distinctly not contemporary. . . . Whereas industrial labor is marked by the prevalence of repetition over skill and part over whole, the miniature object represents an antithetical mode of production: production by hand, a production that is unique and authentic. Today we find the miniature located at a place of origin (the childhood of the self, or even the advertising scheme whereby a miniature of a company's first product is put on display in a window or lobby) and at a place of ending (the productions of the hobbyist: knickknacks of the domestic collected by elderly women, or the model trains built by the retired engineer).[21]

The miniature, then, is premised on a desire for craft production and artisan labor. And, as Stewart's comments suggest, its "place of ending," which I am concerned with here, is connected to portions of the population traditionally outside of the public sphere of labor and in some sense "feminized" and domesticated.

These "feminine" and domestic aspects of collecting often escape the marketing plans of companies such as Mattel by inserting a kind of "unpredictability" into the more "rational" (read, masculine) practices of capitalist production. In fact, this notion of feminine unpredictability and its relationship to both women's craft and mass production serves as the central organizing principle in the story of Barbie's creation, which tells the tale of Mattel's cofounder Ruth Handler.[22] As both Handler and the collectors often recall, when she first pitched her idea for Barbie, her male colleagues at Mattel were adamantly opposed to the doll because they thought she was impractical for factory production. But Handler (spurred by her daughter Barbara, who liked to play with paper dolls) challenged the boys at the top, and the rest is history. Central to this success story is (1) the domestic aspect of Barbie's creation—the fact that she was conjured up by a woman and her daughter; (2) the practice of playing with paper dolls, a children's toy that initiates little girls in the craft of sewing by teaching them how to cut out patterns for dressmaking; and (3) the triumph of women's intuition. In this regard, Barbie's creation myth is itself founded on the notion of the domestic economies of craft, which in turn positions Handler as a "crafty" woman, able to compete, through intuitive logic, in the man's world.

To be sure, since Handler's enormous success Mattel has recognized the importance of craft and has incorporated it into techniques of mass production. Back in the late 1950s, Mattel did this by setting up operations in Japan and drawing on its cheap female labor pool of skilled sewers. Through this colonialist practice, the toy company achieved some of the detail of handmade craft while also maintaining the volume necessary for competition on the American market. Meanwhile, Mattel modeled Barbie's wardrobe on the premise of haute couture, thereby using Japanese women's sewing skills to achieve a sense of European high style. Thus, from the outset Barbie was premised on the contradictions between mass production and handicraft production. Her outfits refer ambiguously to the factory mode of ready-made dresses, the homemade mode of domestic labor, and the more high-end/haute couture mode of handmade design. (And, obviously, the name Barbie Bazaar refers to this contradiction in terms.) On the current collector's market, Mattel exploits the contradictions between these production modes, encouraging nostalgia for craft while cutting corners on the labor-intensive frills.

In the late 1980s and 1990s, Mattel began to mark out two specific, if sometimes overlapping, collectible markets—one based on geographical space (the "Dolls of the World" line) and one based on historical time (the vintage reproduction dolls). Both of these markets operate on nostalgia for craft production, although in different ways. When manufacturing the international dolls, Mattel adopts the craft aesthetic, dressing the prototypes in mass versions of "native" artistry and primitive/historical styles. Native American Barbie, for example, wears traditional beaded garb and a mock handmade leather skirt. Hawaiian Barbie wears a grass skirt and a lei. Swedish Barbie wears a calico dress and apron. These designs are exotic precisely because they refer back to craft-based cultures where modern factory production hasn't taken hold. However, because these outfits bear the signs of mass production—cheap fabric, Velcro fasteners, and plastic accessories—they contain within them the contradictions between mass and craft production.

In fact, with its vintage line, Mattel capitalizes on these contradictions.

The clothing for the vintage dolls recalls a time when mass production was still more like handicrafts. Although these dolls are fashioned after the originals, they are clearly *not* produced with the labor-intensive care and the eye for detail of their 1960s counterparts. Paradoxically, however, it is because these reproductions are a pale imitation of the "real" thing that they evoke nostalgia for craft production among collectors. Collectors often compare the shoddy 1990s dolls to the fancy fabrics, the tiny buttonholes, the precise hems, the intricate accessories, and the superior materials used for the original Barbie. Knowing this is part of the game, Mattel sometimes produces high-end versions of the reproductions (for example, when collectors complained that the reproduction of the 1959 ponytail doll did not have curly bangs, Mattel put out a limited edition of curly-bang dolls that were priced at about $350 each). In all of these ways, the collectors' craft aesthetic has helped to turn the vintage dolls into a durable good at the same time that it has been incorporated by Mattel itself and sold back to collectors in mass-produced form.

From this point of view, it would be impossible to say that craft exists in isolation from mass production. So, too, it would be impossible to say that collectors' crafts give expression to a pure form of female self-hood and social relations that exist outside of industrial culture. Instead of seeing craft as a direct expression of female subjectivity, it seems more useful to see craft as a "medium" for self-disclosure, a medium that is highly conventionalized and related to other conventional forms of women's autobiographical self-disclosure (for example, letter writing, diary writing, photo albums, and scrapbooks).

Indeed, in *Barbie Bazaar* craft production is typically related to biographical and autobiographical narratives, not only about Ruth Handler and other female Mattel executives but also about the collectors themselves. At the level of the image, the magazine often portrays collectors by printing snapshots of club meetings that readers send to the editors. Here, women appear to be representing themselves for themselves. In other words, much as in the family photograph, the snapshots are coded as being interesting primarily to the group depicted. Such snapshots are typically paired with confessional narratives in which people (usually women) discuss how they became collectors. Often the women confess to their "obsessive" relation to the doll, writing about how they can't seem to stop buying Barbies and voicing their anxieties that their husbands will seek retribution for their overconsumption.

Although the content of these narratives is often based on being "out of control," the act of biographical and autobiographical storytelling moves in the opposite direction—that is, toward "self-control." In their transition from overconsumer to auto/biographer, the women use the miniature world of Barbie to make authoritative statements about the self. In this sense, it seems likely that these confessional narratives about their obsessive relation to Barbie paradoxically work to assert a sense of personal mastery over the cultural stereotypes that picture collectors as obsessive, hysterical, undisciplined shoppers. In addition to placing the author in a position of subjective control over the object and the cultural objections to it, these stories might be seen to provide a sense of mastery for the reader. As Stewart argues, narratives featuring miniature worlds such as *Tom Thumb* are generally "linked to nostalgic versions of childhood and history" and present "a diminutive, and thereby manipulatable, version of experience."[23] In *Barbie Bazaar*, these autobiographical confessions provide a story world in which readers are able to imaginatively manipulate their relation to Barbie (and all the social relations Barbie comes to stand for) through their relative sense of size.

Yet, despite the mastery at hand in these confessional narratives, mastery is not the same thing as absolute freedom from or resistance to the more troubling ideologies and practices through which Barbie achieves her popularity. As Michel Foucault has demonstrated, the confession has historically worked to constitute people as "subjects" of disciplinary control through a number of social institutions—from religion to psychoanalysis to the law.[24] By extracting confessions, modern social institutions create people as "normal" or deviant types and, through various disciplinary techniques, they make people internalize these discursively produced identities. Following Foucault, Eve Kosofsky Sedgwick has considered the contemporary popular appeal of self-help discourses (especially those that revolve around addictions to things and codependencies to loved ones) as a most recent manifestation of this discursive/disciplinary regime. In her essay "Epidemics of the Will," Sedgwick asks why addiction has now been generalized to the point where it is attributed to all sorts of social habits—from working to eating to shopping. She asks why one's attachment to objects is pathologized as an "addiction" at exactly the moment in late capitalism where social relations have become completely dependent on commodities. Why is it abnormal to have affection for objects in a world where our experience of ourselves and others is mediated through material forms? Addressing this, Sedgwick argues that the self-help/addiction narrative proposes an impossible fantasy of self-control. She makes us wonder why we so easily accept the idea that the healthy subject is one that needs no objects. Sedgwick additionally claims that pathologies of addiction are particularly attributed to people who are otherwise labeled out of control and are demonized as such in our culture (and she especially shows how addiction to objects is attributed to gay men). For this reason, Sedgwick argues that this epidemic of the will and the therapeutics of self-help are not simply misguided but are in fact tools of a disciplinary society that consistently pathologizes and attempts to purge those behaviors that don't fit reigning social norms.[25]

From this point of view, the autobiographical confessions in *Barbie Bazaar* and the collectors' fantasy of mastery and "will power" are less liberating than they are symptomatic of a disciplinary social system. These confessional tales both propose and naturalize a "normal" and "deviant" relation to consumerism: the normal female consumer makes purchases that promote the gender and generational hierarchies of heterosexual family life (for example, dolls are for kids not for grown-ups). The abnormal, "out-of-control" woman (here depicted as both childlike and compulsive) defies the roles and routines of family life (and the techniques of market research that represent them) by shopping for objects that are not aimed at her demographic. In this regard, even while the autobiographical/confessional stories in *Barbie Bazaar* often stage scenarios of mastery over miniatures, it is difficult to celebrate them as proof of some authentic, autonomous womanhood that triumphs over mass production.

In fact, it seems to me that in *Barbie Bazaar* these stories of self-disclosure are less about female autonomy than they are about the difficulties women have achieving femininity in the first place. These stories and their accompanying craft displays provide a way for women to voice some of the contradictions entailed in actualizing the kind of ideal womanhood that the classic white Barbie so vividly embodies. In particular, they provide a vehicle through which collectors investigate the problems of growing up female in our culture.

In numerous confessional tales, Barbie becomes a token of exchange between two female selves—the girl and the woman. Barbie is a narrative figure through which the authors and readers can manipulate the problems entailed in female maturation as well as its links to mother-daughter relationships. One of the tried-and-true conventions of this genre is the story about how a girl's mother threw away her Barbie dolls when she hit puberty (as the publisher told me, "I don't know how many times I've heard that sad story").[26] But there are also stories of reconciliation between mother and daughter who have overcome their differences and collectively share the joys of Barbie as adults. In this regard, the adult rediscovery of Barbie works to repair the divide between girl and woman, daughter and mother. Perhaps in this respect it is no coincidence that the largest collector group comprises female baby boomers, and the second largest is formed by the generation of women who were the mothers of baby boomers. And Barbie collecting is very much a mother-daughter experience.

Barbie also serves to spark autobiographical memories of 1960s girl culture. Stars such as Patty Duke, Twiggy, and the Beatles are typically evoked in autobiographical memories and craft displays of the doll. One photoessay, for example, portrays renderings of the cover art for the Sergeant Pepper, Yellow Submarine, and Abbey Road albums, with Barbies doubling for the Beatles.[27] Female bonding is also a common theme. Collector Susan Miller recalls, "I soon found out at school that every girl in my class wanted a Barbie doll," and she recounts how she and her sister played with the dolls together.[28] Rather than seeing such memories as a form of regression back to childhood, I would argue that these autobiographical stories create a way for adult women to hold the stages of girlhood and womanhood at a distance. As Philippe Lejeune claims, autobiography allows the speaker to simultaneously occupy the place of the child and the place of the adult remembering the child. Because autobiographical writing narrates from this double (or what Lejeune calls ironic) point of view, it allows for shifting modes of identification, with the adult writer narrating the tale about her younger self remembered in the story.[29] In the case of Barbie culture, the reader of these autobiographical stories is encouraged to see herself as a child playing in the fantasy world of Barbie's teenage romance, and at the same time she is asked to imagine herself from the perspective of the married adult woman who remembers herself as a romantic teen. In this regard, the stories implicitly ask women to think about the difference between these adult and girlish selves. In the process, they stage a rather ambivalent transition from the homosocial communities of girlhood to the heterosexual world of adult life.

Similarly, the dress-up activities that take place at conventions and club meetings are designed to investigate the difference between girlhood and womanliness, only here this takes place at the level of the body and the female craft of sewing. The women who sew and model replica Barbie costumes for themselves play a game of childhood dress-up in which they implicitly compare the difference between their adult bodies and their girlish ones. The most striking thing about this practice is how much fun the women have looking "wrong" in classic Barbie garb such as Solo in the Spotlight or Dinner at Eight.[30] Thus, rather than thinking about this as an instance of "camp" or "drag," we might view it as analogous to the autobiographical doubling between feminine selves that takes place in collectors' culture more generally. In fact, the only time when dress-up seems to fall in line with camp sensibilities is when women appear along with their husbands dressed as Ken. These instances, which are always marked by an implicit humiliation of the husband, typically spark nervous laughter that seems directed at the dynamics of gender inversion. That is, the laughter seems to derive from the feminization of the husband, who appears as a male model in the goofiest of Ken's outfits (including, for example, Ken's Bavarian leiderhosen from the 1960s travel series or his Romeo tights from the theater series of the same decade).

Thus, even while Barbie collectors' culture is complicit with the general hegemony of heterosexual marriage and coupling, collecting also provides a way for women to play with those gendered structures of everyday life. If, as I have argued, this happens implicitly through craft production and narrative constructions, it certainly also happens more explicitly through the topics addressed in *Barbie Bazaar*.

Just as Ev Burkhalter represents Barbie as a career woman and female role model, so, too, does the collectors' magazine typically present stories that focus on Barbie's ability to break into traditionally male professions. During the Gulf War, *Barbie Bazaar* put Mattel's new Gulf War Barbie on the front cover, and it recommended that this doll serve as a reminder of Mattel's marketing slogan, "we girls can do anything."[31] The May/June 1991 editorial stated, "Yes indeed, women in the United States have come a long way," and praised "Barbie and all the women in uniform . . . [who] serve[d] their country along with our brave men."[32] The following year, the editor embraced Mattel's "Barbie for President" gift set claiming, "It is time for a woman president, and Barbie had the credentials for the job." While obviously acknowledging the humor involved, *Barbie Bazaar* did not see any conflict between Barbie's feminine and feminist traits.[33]

Drawing on the discourses of the liberal women's movement, such

In its February 1999 photospread recounting the greatest women of the century, *Barbie Bazaar* honors Civil Rights heroine Rosa Parks by dressing an African American Barbie in her image. The text describes Parks as "demure." (Copyright, Murat Caviale Inc.)

stories typically see progress in terms of women's equal participation in the male world. In fact, the publisher told me that one of the reasons she loves Barbie is because Mattel probably has the largest number of women executives of any major corporation (and the magazine often publishes feature stories on these women). The magazine celebrates Barbie as an arbiter of female equality and social mobility for women of all colors and nations. Still, as is obvious from my examples, *Barbie Bazaar* doesn't question the constituent philosophies of patriarchy—such as military aggression overseas or the failures of representational politics at home—nor does the magazine provide any critical perspective on Mattel's hegemonic moves to incorporate ethnic and national difference by fashioning a "Barbified" world culture whose beauty standard still revolves around the all-American white-skinned Barbie.

Instead, the magazine seems more interested in demonstrating to its readers that race doesn't matter in Barbie's world. Despite the fact that Barbie is often seen as an emblem of white domination, *Barbie Bazaar* ignores this critique in favor of printing success stories about women of color who have become Mattel executives or started their own ethnic fashion doll businesses. For example, in the same issue that embraces presidential Barbie, the magazine ran a feature story on Helena Lisandrello, the African American president of Hamilton Toys Inc. who produced a line of "realistically ethnically mixed high fashion" dolls. Quoting her, the magazine writes, "This isn't about competing with Mattel. I am a big Barbie doll fan, but I feel that everyone ought to be able to express themselves in a different category." [34] In this way, the feature suggests that Lisandrello's ethnically correct dolls were inspired by her positive feelings for Barbie, rather than any racial anger. In short, *Barbie Bazaar* deals with race, but never racism. By disavowing Barbie's historical status as an icon of white, blonde, Aryan culture, and by ignoring the fact that many people have attacked her as a racist symbol, the magazine instead promotes the idea that Barbie's world is equally available to all, and that her message of social mobility has the same meaning for everyone, regardless of race, class, creed, or nation.

This philosophy of equality through the inclusion of all women in white society and culture emerges in craft practices promoted in the magazine. The most stunning example is a feature on how to turn a white Barbie into a black Barbie by dying the doll's plastic skin. Applauding *Barbie Bazaar* for running this feature, one woman wrote: "I am an African American collector and sometimes it is hard to find the dolls I want in the black version. Thanks to Julie Neises' article, I learned to make black versions of the dolls. Thanks again to *Barbie Bazzar* for yet another informative article." [35] The writer mailed in photos of vintage dolls she had dyed black. Whether we take this as proof of the woman's ironic reading of Barbie, or whether we assume her response is virtuous, within the context of *Barbie Bazaar* the craft of "blackface" is used to suggest that the only thing that separates whites from African Americans is skin color. The magazine assures us that Barbie, and her "we girls can do anything!" motto, stands as a symbol for all women.

In line with its interpretation of feminism as a road to social mobility for all women, *Barbie Bazaar* delights in role reversals where men are on bottom and women are on top. A cartoon from the September/October 1992 issue displays Barbie's airplane, and the caption reads, "In a strike for women's liberation Barbie pilots the airplane while Ken serves meals."[36] More generally, the magazine features stories that ridicule Ken. Collectors constantly write of how inadequate Ken is and how they remember pairing Barbie with GI Joe dolls or even slimy monster toys. Evacuating Ken from Barbie's life is thus a major narrative pleasure in the women's autobiographical stories. Discussing this, publisher Marlene Mura told me with a playful laugh, "Hardcore Barbie collectors think that Ken's really just an accessory."[37] A letter to the editor seconds this opinion, adding, "In Barbie's world, Barbie rules, Ken drools."[38] And while the magazine obsessively displays Barbie in bridal gowns and wedding scenes, it also continually reminds readers that despite all the veils, Barbie has never really been married to Ken. Always a bride, never a wife, seems to be the logic here.

Such jokes about the inadequacy of Ken spill over into the "real" world of marriage when collectors laugh about how their overvaluation of Barbie leads to an undervaluation of their husbands. An article titled "Thoughts of a Barbie Husband" recounts how one man literally suffered "a loss of living space" because of his wife's collecting hobby: "Slowly the collection grew until the smiling blonde [Barbie] needed her own room. So away went my research room and I was compelled to do what all husbands of Barbie wives must do—build shelving—lots of shelving. . . . I think my wife and Barbie now have their eyes on the den for expansion. While I wouldn't have it any other way, as the collection continues to grow I can only hope they will leave me my own room somewhere in the house."[39] Written in the voice of the displaced but obviously resigned husband, this tale (which is somewhat of a conventional story among collectors) plays on the female pleasure of controlling domestic space and the male movements within it. More generally, female collectors often speak of the way they control domestic space via their collections and occupy territories previously inhabited by their husbands. Whether this displacement of the husband is the intention of the collector or just a side effect of a growing collection, the fact that this tale of male evacuation is repeated so often by collectors suggests that, at least at the level of representation and fantasy, the idea of valuing Barbie over one's husband holds a certain attraction for collectors.

In all of these ways, the movement of Barbie from the realm of mass culture to the realm of craft culture is marked by ambivalence. It re-

Barbie is rendered as if painted by Picasso in this 1990 *Barbie Bazaar* photospread by Julie Neises. (Copyright, Murat Caviale Inc.)

inforces gender stereotypes about art and women's culture while it nevertheless also provides a basis on which to critique aspects of heterosexual romance and marriage. Making this situation even more contradictory is the fact that the craft/feminine uses of Barbie are accompanied by a completely different value system that operates in distinct separation from it. *Barbie Bazaar* not only displays Barbie as a craft object but also pictures her as an object of high art.

Barbie as Art

Barbie moved into the zone of authentic art via the related aesthetics of pop, camp, and haute couture. This movement took place sometime in the mid-eighties and was particularly sparked when Barbie enthusiast Billy Boy published his 1987 book *Barbie: Her Life and Times*. Billy Boy was part of Warhol's entourage and was also a Parisian fashion designer, making him the perfect figure to bring Barbie out of the world of kitsch collection and into the world of art. This logic was not lost on Billy

Boy, who began his book with a photographic still of Warhol's *Barbie*. In his introduction, Billy Boy transfers the Warhol aesthetic onto the doll by equating his childhood love for Barbie with his grown-up passion for the French fashion model Bettina. He writes, "Bettina, the legendary and extremely groovy French fashion model . . . was the archetypal fashion model, and not surprisingly she and Barbie had a lot in common."[40]

Throughout the book, Billy Boy assigns value to Barbie by reading her through a "pop" aesthetic in which artifacts of high culture (particularly high fashion) are made equivalent to artifacts of mass culture. For example, he compares a 1960s Barbie comic book to a Lichtenstein canvas. More generally, Billy Boy draws comparisons between Barbie's outfits and the fashions created by European fashion designers. The last chapter displays modern-day Barbie outfits designed by the likes of fashion leaders Yves Saint Laurent and Emilio Pucci, as well as artist Keith Haring.

Billy Boy's book solidified an ongoing transformation in the gendered collection of Barbie dolls. Recall here Thompson's comments on the history of Stevengraph collecting and its gendered logics. In that case, Thompson argues that the transformation from women "knitters" to male control over the object took place over time, as men began to buy up the women's collections, set up their own shops, and write the authoritative books. He concludes, "Items controlled by women were transferred [from rubbish] to the durable category by transferring control to men. . . . Women have been excluded from durability just as they have been excluded from the Stock Exchange and from Great Art!"[41] Although women collectors continue to run Barbie cottage industries (such as *Barbie Bazaar* itself), it is true that as Barbie's value increased she moved from a craft object (the domain of women knitters) and became more associated with the culturally defined "masculine" prerogatives of high finance and high art. In 1985, the voice of the nation's stock exchange, the *Wall Street Journal,* reported that "money seems to have attracted some of the men (collectors) who have begun showing up at Barbie club meetings and conventions. . . ."[42] As opposed to the obsessive, out-of-control female over-consumers, now collecting was being redefined as a sound investment associated with male business know-how. And as in the case of the Stevengraph, numerous men did start to corner the market by buying up women's collections (Joe Blitman of Joe's Barbies, who claims he was influenced by Billy Boy, is the most successful dealer in the country). So, too, men such as Billy Boy wrote the authoritative books, and more recently dealer Joe Blitman produced the authoritative "how to" collect Barbie video.

More generally, the assignment of art value to Barbie has become one of the central aspects of the collector's fascination. *Barbie Bazaar* depicts the doll through conventions of fashion photography. The magazine often includes a page of artfully posed dolls that it calls the "gallery" portrait. Moreover, following Billy Boy's Warholian example, the magazine features paintings of Barbie that play on the relation between mass culture and the painterly traditions of high art. For example, one photoessay, titled "Barbie Meets the Masters," shows how Barbie would look if she were rendered by Picasso, Gauguin, Botticelli, and Matisse.[43] *Barbie Bazaar* also presents displays of Barbie standing near, for example, the *Mona Lisa*.[44] And artists working in the Warhol tradition regularly exhibit their artistic interpretations of the doll. A feature on artist Mel Odom presents his Barbie portrait and statue series, including such works as his Warhol-influenced canvas *Sissy Summer* and his surreal sculpture of Barbie with tree branches for arms.[45]

As in the case of Mel Odom, most of the artists in *Barbie Bazaar* are men (and about a third of the writers are men).[46] But it is also clear that their status as "men" is complicated by their "queer" relationship to masculinity because, after all, like Odom they are "sissies" who play with dolls.[47] In a 1993 story on Barbie collectors published in the gay-oriented newspaper, the *Advocate, Barbie Bazaar* editor/publisher Karen Caviale states, "I don't know too many men into Barbie who are not gay."[48] But even if she is willing to say as much to the *Advocate,* her magazine never explicitly uses the word gay or talks about gay sexuality and politics.

Instead, in *Barbie Bazaar* gay culture is expressed through aesthetic sensibilities. The art values that the magazine assigns to Barbie are largely implicated in pop and camp reading codes that have historically been associated with gay men. In this case, however, pop and camp aesthetics are themselves often achieved through the more domestic/feminine craft forms of homemade clothing and diorama display. For example, collectors refashion Barbie into classic camp stars, such as Marilyn Monroe, by sewing new costumes for the doll or redesigning her hair and facial features. Or they make dioramas of camp film classics such as one that features a Joan Crawford Barbie and a Bette Davis Barbie in the classic scene from *What Ever Happened to Baby Jane?* where Jane feeds her invalid sister her sister's dead bird for dinner. In this regard, while pop and camp serve to provide a queer relation to the doll, it should be understood that we are talking about a hybrid aesthetic practice in which pop and camp are here mediated through craft production.

More generally, in Barbie culture gay collectors do not speak publicly of their sexuality, but rather represent it through their queer interpretations of the doll. For example, Billy Boy, who appeals to many gay collectors, advertises his limited edition Sexy Men dolls, who take on the body dimensions of gay stereotypes—complete with beef-cake muscles and tattoos. There are also sadomasochist Barbies, genitally correct Kens who appear in pornographic poses, films and videos with drag queen Barbies and lesbian Barbies, and a book titled *Mondo Barbie* that presents pornographic poetry and short stories featuring the doll. In *Barbie Bazaar*'s less explicit imagery, numerous cartoons depict campy send-ups of the dolls, mocking Barbie and Ken's relationship. One strip called "Sister, Sister" even presents Barbie's best friend Midge in a nun habit. In the strip, Midge is a private-eye dressed in nun gear, equipped, for some mysterious reason, with a golf club, to spy on Barbie who takes the role of a glamorous bank robber dressed in babydoll pajamas. Midge is not quite the equivalent of the women's homemade craft nuns; instead, she looks like the campy "twisted sisters" of gay culture.[49]

Coming-out narratives also occupy a large amount of space in the magazine. Male authors reflect on their desires to play with Barbie and Ken as kids, and they recount the heterosexist social taboos that barred them from exploring these interests. A feature on artist Mel Odom writes of his portrait *Sissy Summer*, which "represents a young boy's longing for the beautiful Barbie doll and the ridicule a young boy may have felt because this desire was not . . . accepted by the social mores of the 1960s." The feature then refers to his "dive into the Barbie underground" where he met Billy Boy.[50] Elsewhere, in articles like "And Then . . . I Met Ken" (a four-part series in 1990), male author A. Glen Mandeville is able to imagine his desire for Ken. In the first article of the series, the title appears above a photograph of Barbie and Ken. An epitaph spoken from Barbie's first-person point of view reads, "I never bothered with romance or gave any boy a second glance and then . . . I met Ken!" However, the title "And Then . . . I met Ken," takes on a kind of slippage when Barbie's first-person voice shifts to the autobiographical voice of Mandeville himself, who speaks about his own first encounter with Ken. Remembering his childhood, Mandeville writes: "I was one such boy who viewed

Ken as everything I wanted to be. I bravely bought the doll and all his outfits. . . . The early Ken dolls represented a gentility that GI Joe would lack . . . many, myself included, were not interested in 'conquering,' yet unless a boy's toy taught aggression, it was not too well received by parents." [51] Thus, as the narrative agency shifts from Barbie to Mandeville, the story transforms the heterosexual meaning of its title, "And Then . . . I Met Ken," to a homosexual one. But, even while such columns follow the logic of coming-out narratives, it should be noted they don't go all the way. Instead, *Barbie Bazaar* is careful to keep any direct mention of gay politics out of the magazine.

So silent is the magazine on these issues that some gay collectors think *Barbie Bazaar* is clueless about the sexual in-joking that takes place in its pages. For example, one gay collector told the *Advocate,* "*Barbie Bazaar* is faggier than *Blueboy,*" but the "editors are just too dense to realize how nelly their stories are." Still, the staff of *Barbie Bazaar* is a lot more savvy than this collector assumes. As Karen Caviale told the *Advocate,* "A lot of Barbie collectors are pretty campy people. . . . I don't think any of our suburban housewife readers are going to be offended by a gay angle to any Barbie story." [52]

While *Barbie Bazaar* represents its suburban housewife reader as being both aware of and not bothered by references to gay male culture, the magazine rarely hints at the possibility of a lesbian relation to the doll. And when it has, lesbian innuendo has resulted in reader complaints. The publisher told me that readers thought the "Sister, Sister" feature was tasteless (although she did not say why, we may assume the homoerotic coupling of Barbie and Midge had something to do with the complaints). Even more explicitly, one letter to the editor protested a cover photo of Barbie dressed as George Washington. (This was *Barbie Bazaar*'s playful response to the first issue of *George* magazine, the cover of which showed Cindy Crawford posed as Washington.) Clearly missing the irony, the reader complained that this unpatriotic act was also sexually perverse: "I was both disgusted and angry when I saw Barbie doll dressed as George Washington," she protested. "Is she a cross-dresser now?" [53]

Barbie Bazaar, then, presents an eclectic mixture of mass, craft, and high art values. It bunches these values together without any reflection on the corresponding politics at stake. The female uses of Barbie are coded as craft, the male uses as high art. Moreover, even while the actual artistic practices sometimes merge into hybrid forms (such as the craft diorama of *What Ever Happened to Baby Jane?*), the feminine sphere of craft and the gay male sphere of pop and camp operate in almost complete political separation from one another, in a kind of liberal tolerance that nonetheless almost never crosses boundaries. In Barbie collector's culture, queer sexuality is the classic "open secret," a fact that everyone knows but disavows. And ironically, that disavowal is largely enacted through display.[54]

Arts and Crafts and Mass Culture

In the long run, what do all these Barbie dreams accomplish? Are these collectors' activities a sign of hope—a sign of Barbie's ability to liberate people from sexual stereotypes? Or are they just proof of Mattel's ability to make Barbie everybody's dream date?

While collectors open up the possibility for people to create scenarios that exceed and sometimes oppose Barbie's dominant cultural meanings, they still work to reinforce conventional wisdom about art and culture. The collectors' playful attitude toward the categories of high, mass, and craft culture is circumscribed by the gender distinctions that also pervade our dominant ways of thinking about art and culture. Women's cultural activities are associated with folk crafts that take place in domestic spaces in low- to middle-class suburban locales. The "high" art values ascribed to Barbie are associated with male artists who live in a high-class world of fashion that takes place in exciting metropolitan areas around the globe.[55] Even while the pop and camp aesthetics disrupt these gendered categories, *Barbie Bazaar* repackages pop and camp so as to reproduce essentialist divisions between male arts and female crafts. More generally, in the world of Barbie culture the status of "artist" is typically conferred on men (stars such as Odom and Gary Mandeville are often singled out).[56]

That such gendered distinctions are cultural and not natural is well indicated by the fact that our society works hard to teach women at an early age about their place in our art-culture system. Mattel's *Barbie* magazine, which is aimed at children, reinforces these distinctions by teaching little girls to reappropriate Barbie through the "feminine" crafts of baking, diorama display, and needlework. For example, the July/August 1993 issue teaches girls how to make pink frozen fruit pops and pasta necklaces.[57] Like *Barbie Bazaar*, the children's magazine typically displays snapshots sent in by little girls who appear with their collections and tell a short autobiographical story. In the children's magazine, these activities are always presented as trivial girl play associated with domesticity — not as authentic art. By advising little girls how to reappropriate Barbie through craft, Mattel also teaches them to imagine themselves in the domestic economies of homemaking as opposed to the public economies of the art world.

Meanwhile, for its part the art world has also worked to reinscribe this distinction. In the high and low exhibits staged at museums over the last decade, high is generally defined as male artists working in the pop tradition (such as Warhol), and low is usually defined as mass culture (again produced by male-run corporations). Women's crafts (such as Barbie displays) typically have no place in such fine art museum exhibits and are generally carted off to the craft museum or the museum of science and industry as production with use values (the functional arts) but no authentic exchange value in the art world. I witnessed this exclusion several years ago when I was invited to give a talk on the vernacular arts at the Whitney Museum of American Art's high-low exhibit. The show, which was mostly an homage to Larry Rivers's influence on pop art, included a sanctioned-off space — distinctly separated from the art — where television programming was displayed on monitors (apparently the low/vernacular aspect of the exhibit). When I delivered a lecture on Barbie during the exhibit, the craft dimensions of the collectors' culture were completely unassimilable into the logic of high and low being offered at the show. No one seemed to understand why I was interested in Barbie — at least until I got to the part of the paper that spoke about her pop appropriations. Clearly, at the Whitney the vernacular meant mass culture, high meant pop art (produced almost exclusively by great male painters), and craft meant nothing. Craft, and women's contemporary crafts in particular, did not have a place in this system.

Recently, however, museums have begun to take note of the new subgenre of Barbie "art." [58] Whether done by men or women artists, this work is typically defined in terms of the "high" arts of painting, sculpture, photography, cinema, video, performance art, and literature and not in terms of the "feminine" crafts of sewing, diorama display, snapshots, and baking. [59] Museums such as London's Victoria and Albert and Berlin's Martin-Gropius Bau have held Barbie exhibits. (The latter, titled "Art, Design and Barbie," was held at the Martin-Gropius Bau in 1994, and included 130 artists from Germany, Austria, and Switzerland.) Similarly, marking Barbie's move from kitsch to avant-garde, New York's chic performance space, the Kitchen, held a Barbie Cafe evening that featured electronic hookups with Los Angeles and Paris, where superstars Raquel Welch and Lauren Hutton, and feminist matron Betty Friedan and the postfeminist Camille Paglia, were scheduled to appear. (Welch, Hutton, and Paglia all backed out in the end and appeared only via tape and phone links.) At the Salon de Barbie, on the Kitchen's second floor, numerous examples of Barbie art were on view, including David Levinthal's Kodalith prints *The Barbie Series 1972–73* and Maggie Robbins's sculptures *Barbie Fetish* and *Berlin Barbie*. John Hanhardt, then video curator at the Whitney, was also on hand.

Perhaps not surprisingly, this Barbie art movement has been incorporated by Mattel itself. During Mattel's 1994 Barbie Festival, held at Disney World on the occasion of Barbie's thirty-fifth birthday, the toy company presented a Barbie art gallery space that housed a series of art genres. Included was a mural-size reproduction of Seurat's *Sunday Afternoon on the Island of La Grande Jatte* with Barbies pasted on it, as well as a Monet reproduction with Barbies floating on lily pads. In conjunction with the festival's publicity campaign, Workman Publishing distributed a book titled *The Art of Barbie,* which shows images of Marian Jones's *Nude Barbie Descending a Staircase* (a time-lapse photograph whose title, of course, refers to Duchamp) and William Wegman's *Dream House* (which includes one of Wegman's dogs standing inside a pink plastic dollhouse).[60] These Barbie pieces give a curious twist to Thomas Crow's argument about impressionism's (and Seurat's in particular) debt to mass culture.[61] Where Crow argues that the impressionist/modernist avant-garde often appropriated the low forms of mass leisure to articulate the contradictions of industrial capitalism, the Barbie/Seurat mural ingeniously turns this modernist moment around into a postmodernist vicious cycle. Here, in the Barbie/Seurat, the "low" form of mass production speaks back to its own modernist appropriation by gluing itself onto an oversized reproduction of a modernist "masterpiece." (Even more curiously, the Barbie/Seurat mural is covered by a mock-window frame, so that the spectator is positioned to look at the work of art as if she or he were in a domestic space gazing out at the grounds of an upper-class estate, rather than in the commercialized public sphere to which the painting originally referred.)[62]

In this regard, it seems particularly important to note that Mattel's brand of corporate hegemony does not work simply by incorporating the popular reappropriations of the collectors' subculture. Instead, in post-modern culture hegemony also works by incorporating "high" art move-ments (in this case the Warholian-based and haute-couture use of Bar-bie), which in turn are rearticulated by corporate artists (in this case the commercial artists at Mattel). In this respect, we should remember that avant-garde "art" practice has an important relationship to popu-lar culture and hegemonic incorporation. While influential thinkers such as Dick Hebdige wrote about the significance of the avant-garde in re-lation to youth culture and popular music, the place of the avant-garde has been generally overlooked in more recent literature on fan subcul-tures.[63] This has resulted in a situation where the "popular" is reductively equated with mass culture in ways that work to reinforce, rather than to reinvestigate, the complex relationships among popular/artisan produc-tion, avant-garde practices, and corporate hegemony.

In more general terms, then, the case of Barbie collectors provides some relevant twists and turns for the study of subcultures and analyses of postmodern cultural production and consumption. Collectors have a cen-tral place in the market and cultural economies of postindustrial capital-ism. Barbie collectors are just one group of baby boom adults fascinated with the transformation of mass market "rubbish" into highly valued con-sumer "durables." Items such as comic books, GI Joes, and even cereal boxes are the objects of intense longing for numerous collectors of the baby boom generation. Like Barbie collectors, these groups often use arti-san forms of labor and cottage industry sales practices that harken back to early modes of capitalist production.

In this regard, we might revise Fredric Jameson's famous definition of postmodernism in which he (following Mandel) equates different cul-tural styles (realism, modernism, postmodernism) with different his-torical modes of production (early capitalism, monopoly capitalism, postindustrial capitalism).[64] Jameson theorized postmodernism mainly through male pop artists, such as Warhol, and the retro mode of Holly-wood cinema, arguing that postmodern culture is characterized by the blurring of high and low. In other words, Jameson (as so many others) evacuated "craft" from his theory, looking only at the binaries of "art" versus "mass." The third term of craft, I want to argue, complicates this binary logic, adding the "unpredictable" and "feminine" terms of artisan labor into the mix. Once we recognize the importance of craft and arti-san labor in the general circulation of goods (and their uses) in postmod-

ern society, it becomes difficult to buy into the rigid divisions of historical modes of production and their equation with the cultural styles that
Jameson sets up.

Instead of Jameson's rigid divisions, it might be wiser to say that postindustrial capitalism is characterized by an admixture of production practices from different historical periods. Here, the cottage industry and arti-
san/craft labor associated with the early phase of capitalism are taken
up by relatively disempowered groups (in Barbie culture, mainly women
and gay men) and mixed with the more postindustrial, global flows of
late capitalism characterized by a multinational corporation such as Mattel. The fact that multinational corporations and artisan labor are mutually dependent on one another is nowhere better demonstrated than in
the strange merger of Disney World, Mattel, and the collectors' cottage
industry businesses that all sold goods and reaped profits at the thirty-
fifth anniversary Barbie festival. For such reasons, it might be wiser to use
Jameson's concept of postmodern "pastiche" (or the admixture of historical periods he locates in Hollywood nostalgia films), not only, as he
does, to characterize an *expressive style of postmodern culture*. Instead, I
would argue, pastiche also characterizes a *style of postmodern production*
itself in which different historical modes of capitalism interact with and
reinforce each other.[65] Collecting, it seems to me, is the central practice
that informs this pastiche of production styles in late capitalism.

In addition to raising questions about the production process, collectors' cultures also complicate theories of cultural consumption in cultural
studies, especially those theories based on ethnographies of fans. This
group doesn't easily fall into the narrative oppositions we so often find in
cultural studies, oppositions that pit "resistant" popular appropriations
of mass-culture texts against "dominant" meanings in them. Nor does
this group display the utopian aspects of community that numerous ethnographies of fans locate in these cultures. Instead, Barbie collectors often
reproduce—as oppose to resist—the sexist, classist, and individualist ideologies of Western capitalism, even as they creatively reappropriate the
doll for their own ends. Collectors have competitive businesses based on
selling the dolls, and customers at shows are often worried that the most
successful dealers are eager to rip them off with repainted dolls sold at inflated prices. At the Barbie festival, for example, the "consumer beware"
ethos dominated much of the show, as collectors cautioned one another
against bad deals at various booths. And, mimicking the practices of

art collectors, *Barbie Bazaar* continually warns readers against "frauds." Meanwhile, even the practice of shopping is laced with competition. Collectors eager to get the best dolls hide information from one another, and they aggressively sort through bins of vintage clothing hoping to find the hat for the "career girl" outfit before another collector does. So intense is this competition that *Barbie Bazaar* ran a feature titled "Salesroom Etiquette," describing the "hordes of crazed collectors," some of whom have taken to an "alarming trend" of stealing dolls they can't afford.[66] In this regard, the collectors reproduce cultural stereotypes about feminine and gay male consumers, even while they often also make friends with one another on the basis of their collecting interests.

Moreover, much as Mary Douglas and Baron Isherwood have argued about the tribal potlatch, the exchange of goods is often marked by status relations within a culture.[67] For example, membership in local Barbie clubs is sometimes limited to people with extensive and expensive collections. In practice, then, utopian ideals of community are often compromised by the competitive and status-oriented context of the larger logic of commodity culture that collectors may at times evade, but never ultimately escape. For such reasons, we should not view the "popular" as one collective block that reads against the grain of mass culture to create a better, more authentic public sphere. Instead, the popular is a fragmented group of divided interests and divided politics. In other words, the popular is not an essential category.

By the same token, the "dominant" or "mass" is not easily read as a hegemonic block. Instead, if one were to do a sustained corporate ethnography of Mattel, my guess is that it would soon become clear that many of its employees are avid collectors who sincerely believe in the utopian values of friendship and collectivity among girls and boys that Barbie epitomizes for them. At the 1993 Barbie Round-Up held at the Hacienda Hotel in Las Vegas, Barbie executives spoke enthusiastically about the friendships that Barbie had ignited among them during their many years at Mattel. For them, Barbie's entourage of best friends and ethnic sisters constituted a model of corporate culture that posed a distinct difference from the male-dominated environments at other corporations.

At Disney World's thirty-fifth anniversary festival, this notion of corporate sisterhood was further suggested at the "gala" dinner banquet. There, Barbie's "mother" and one-time Mattel executive Ruth Handler offered a long speech on the history of her rise to power in the then male-

dominated corporation, a speech in which she mostly recalled the relations of family and women's friendship that she built during her tenure
at the toy company. Handler's speech was followed by one from Mattel's
contemporary and markedly postfeminist chief executive, Jill E. Barad
(who was then president of domestic operations). Barad claimed to have
"reposition[ed] Barbie as having substance" through such publicity/good-
will stunts as the Barbie Summit, which brought together forty children
from twenty-eight countries to attend workshops on the world's problems
(the event coincided with the release of the Barbie Summit doll, who came
in a variety of national types). Barad's new brand of corporate multicultural feminism was still rooted in a notion of sisterhood, one that was
most aptly transformed into the 1980s Barbie marketing slogan "we girls
can do anything!" At the end of her dinner speech, in an attempt to rally
excitement among the collectors, Barad repeated the slogan, and with a
campy wink to the gay collectors, she added "and boys" to the phrase.

Barad was followed by closing remarks from yet another female employee who literally wept as she spoke of the close friendships she experienced while working at Mattel. While this outpouring of emotion seemed
genuine in a personal sense, Mattel's more synthetic corporate logic soon
overtook the aura of authenticity as the employee suddenly broke into
song (or rather began to lip-synch). She was joined on stage by an all-
female chorus of Mattel employees (as well as dancers dressed as dolls)
who lipsynched "you got to have friends" to a cover of the seventies hit.
This moment of staged authenticity highlights the paradox involved in the
movement from mass culture to more communal forms of cultural experience. In Barbie collectors' culture it is finally impossible to separate the
decidedly theatrical aspects of such sisterly corporate displays from moments of authentic female bonding because both serve (in Baudrillard's
sense) to mutually produce each other.

Barbie Activism

How then are feminists to deal with objects like Barbie and the female
communities they foster? Given the levels of simulation and dissimula-
tion involved in these communities, how can feminists forge any kind of
social transformation by thinking about objects like Barbie and the cultural practices that surround her? This "what's the political point?" question brings me back to my opening remarks concerning the feminist intel-

lectual's relation to mass culture and aesthetic hierarchies more generally. By accepting the term "popular" or "mass" or "high," we always buy into the idea that a culture can be essentialized as this or that "thing" that can be known and nailed down for further intellectual categorization and analysis. This line of thinking buys into the binary oppositions between the intellectual and the popular, between the high and the low, and between feminism and femininity in a way that doesn't do justice to the complex connections between and among them.

In the case of Barbie, the identity politics of mass culture resist the simple narrative oppositions between the intellectual and the popular that the media set up around the Teen Talk doll controversy. This is well demonstrated by the following two anecdotes that encapsulate some of the complexities involved.

Anecdote 1: In a conversation with *Barbie Bazaar* publisher Marlene Mura, I discovered that the opposition between intellectual and popular culture doesn't really work at all. When I asked her how she felt about Mattel's Teen Talk Barbie and the actions of the American Association of University Women (AAUW), I expected her to defend the doll by telling me that Barbie was a feminist role model who had a string of important careers. She did say that, but she also told me something else: it turns out she is herself a member of the AAUW.

Anecdote 2: This story concerns the ever-changing and increasingly metacritical world of Barbie. While watching television a few years ago, I discovered that my cartoon counterpart Lisa Simpson was also engaged in serious feminist thought about her new Malibu Stacey doll. Like Barbie, Stacey said a litany of offensive phrases, boasting of her love for shopping and inability to succeed at school. Deciding that the doll is sexist, Lisa Simpson goes to her creator (played by Kathleen Turner) and begs her to make a better doll with the "wisdom of Gertrude Stein and the good looks of Eleanor Roosevelt." But ultimately Lisa's feminist doll fails because Stacey's evil toy company markets a new, improved model that quickly makes Lisa's doll obsolete.

As a popular parody of the feminist Barbie critic, *The Simpsons* episode brings me back full circle to the question of the intellectual's role in studying popular culture. It seems, in fact, that popular culture is so full of its own self-reflexive metacritique that the feminist intellectual is no longer needed, or else is at best redundant. Perhaps in this sense, the more we try to assert critical distance, the closer we are to the object itself. Like the logic of capitalism that haunts Lisa Simpson's feminist fashion doll, the work of theory in the age of mass culture has its own planned obsolescence. Indeed, we constantly have to reinvent new ways of distinguishing ourselves from the objects we study. And while I have discussed at length cultural distinctions and the sexist hierarchies inherent in the high/low logics of art collection, I still am not quite comfortable being at one with mass culture. As an intellectual, I still don't want to be Barbie, even if as a collector I want to have her.

In addition to suggesting this intellectual dilemma, Lisa Simpson's crusade in toyland tells us something about feminist and political action. Lisa's problem—and the one that the AAUW encountered—is related to women's place in the art-culture system more generally. Lisa and the AAUW imagine that their voices will be heard if they complain to corporations and ask for reform. The reform desired is to literally have their feminism embodied in Barbie's body—a desire that seems somewhat less than revolutionary at best. Indeed, while Mattel was a bit rattled by the AAUW, in the long run the company's basic foundation wasn't disturbed. Instead, Mattel simply took it on the chin and opened up a new line of career-girl Barbies that were basically simple wardrobe revisions on a much older theme. Mattel doesn't mind equating beauty with intellect. In fact, so long as the 11 1/2 inch Barbie body remains intact, Mattel is quite willing to accessorize her with a number of fashionable perspectives—including feminism itself. Like all successful capitalists, Mattel is very good at accommodating dissent.

So, in the long run, how do feminists—intellectual or otherwise—deal with corporate giants such as Mattel? Perhaps the Barbie Liberation Organization provides a glimmer of hope. This anonymous group of concerned consumers switched the voice boxes of Talking GI Joe and Talking Barbie, and then they planted their tampered toys in toy shops so that unwitting consumers bought these gender bending dolls rather than the ones Mattel originally intended. It seems to me that this maneuver has some radical promise. First, unlike the reform campaigns of Lisa Simpson and the AAUW, the BLO disassociates bodies from voices in a way that gets out of the bind of Barbie's essentialist feminine form. Second, the BLO doesn't accept women's place in the art-culture system. Rather than the homework economy of the female collectors' culture—its baking, sewing, and diorama display—the BLO takes up an interest in the male-defined domain of technology. The BLO distributes literature that teaches con-

The Barbie Liberation Organization (BLO) issued this flyer when it conducted its consumer activist campaign and switched the voice boxes of Teen Talk Barbie and GI Joe.

sumers how to use saws and circuit switchboards in order to transform the dolls. Moreover, it teaches consumers how to subvert consumerism itself by returning the tampered dolls to toy shops.

But I don't want to conclude this piece with simply a call to technological arms and consumer warfare against Barbie. These tactics hold merit, but the BLO should not be seen as a priori more politically pure than other collectors who embellish, sabotage, or otherwise manipulate the doll's meaning and social function. In fact, the founder of the BLO clearly operates within the terms of the collector's market itself. When I asked him if I could get one of his gender-bending Barbies, he quoted me a price of $500 and told me he was currently out of stock. The Smithsonian Institution and John Hanhardt, then video curator at the Whitney museum, were among his clients. In this sense, the BLO has conceptualized consumer sabotage not simply as activism, but as activist art. And like other forms of activist art, this one has a market.

Conclusion

The case of Barbie demonstrates that the mass market and the art market are intimately linked through collection practices that give way to their own production communities. These links are often forged by craft appropriations, many of which are in turn reevaluated and transformed into objects with both financial value and artistic worth.[68]

This reassignation of value to craft, however, is not necessarily a cause for celebration. As Lucy Lippard writes:

> Much has been made of the need to erase false distinctions between art and craft, "fine" art and the "minor" arts, "high" art and "low" art—distinctions that particularly affect women's art. But there are also "high" crafts and "low" ones, and although women wield more power in the crafts world than in the fine art world, the same problems plague both. The crafts need only one more step up the aesthetic and financial respectability ladder and they will be headed for the craft museums rather than people's homes.[69]

The case of Barbie collectors demonstrates that distinctions of high and low do not only separate art from craft, they also operate within craft itself. Moreover, such distinctions are intimately bound up with the gendered terms of power in our culture. In the case of Barbie, art and craft are further distinguished by the relations within the fashion industry—relations between "homemade" dresses that housewives sew for their families and "haute couture" that fashion designers produce for wealthy clients who frequent their urban salons. As we have seen, this "high" end of the fashion crafts initially gave way to Barbie's reinterpretation through pop aesthetics, and by the 1990s Barbie has become a subject for numerous artists working in a number of media and genres.

Even as various groups vie for power over the collectors' market, they nevertheless share a common project of reappropriation, reinterpretation, and redecoration. Their productions have created new markets around the doll. Understanding the value of these collector markets, Mattel now has created niche product lines that incorporate collector tastes and styles into the more standardized techniques of mass production.

This, however, only summaries the art-culture system that has formed around Barbie in the United States, and to a lesser degree in Western Europe. In fact, the art-culture system in which Barbie operates is a global system, with people around the world, some living in diasporaic situations, participating in collectors' culture and making their own versions of the doll. This global traffic in Barbie culture is a subject of its own.[70] But for now, we can at least assume that the activities in the United States and Western Europe should be considered in relation to art, craft, and mass production practices on a worldwide basis. The sources of influence and exchange are most likely to be as complex in this regard as those that obtain for such global goods as world beat music, ethnic curios and souvenirs, and used clothing. In the case of Barbie—the ultimate American girl who has always been produced in Asian factories—the terms of this global exchange are imbedded in postcolonial racism, sexism, and labor exploitation. Any examination of the global collectors' market would have to assume that collecting Barbie cannot possibly mean the same things to people in places where she has been produced as well as consumed.

In the end, Barbie collecting presents a set of problems that call for an investigation of the power dynamics of art and culture within and across historical time and national space. Collectors are so varied in their tastes and distastes for Barbie, and they are so divided in their sexual, national, ethnic, and class relations, that they cannot be understood as a single communal "subculture," in the classic sense of that term. Instead, they are an eclectic group of people who compete for cultural and economic power in a world where consumption and production are increasingly intertwined.

While feminist intellectuals and activists have largely focused on Barbie's sexism, racism, and negative influence on little girls, their condemnations of Barbie have, quite paradoxically, become part of the culture industry around her. Talk show hosts and journalists are eager to incorporate the feminist "side of the story," and as in the case of the BLO, activists understand the market value of their own critical interpretations of the doll. While important in its own right, this kind of intellectual criticism and consumer activism does not exhaust the set of questions we need to pose about mass culture. By investigating the complex relations among mass, high, and craft productions, we might better understand the cultural dynamics of objects like Barbie—objects that, no matter how objectionable, eventually achieve a place on the wall as objects d'art.

Notes

This essay is based on my script for a video titled *Twist Barbie* that I made with the Paper Tiger collective in 1993. Thank you to Dee Dee Halleck and the collective. I am also grateful to the collectors and to the many people who sent me Barbie dolls, Barbie paraphernalia, and news of Barbie over the years.

1 Susan Stewart, *On Longing: Narratives of the Miniature, the Gigantic, the Souvenir, the Collection* (Durham, N.C.: Duke University Press, 1993), p. 57.
2 This discussion took place at the "Language of Objects" exhibit, "Barbie behind

the Scenes," curated by Deidre Evans-Pritchard, California Folk Art Museum, Los Angeles, 18 May 1994.

3   "Barbie Fun Facts," Mattel Toys press release, 1993. Mattel Corporate Communications sent me this press release in 1993. No exact date appears on the document.

4   Ann Ducille discusses Mattel's marketing of black, ethnic, and national dolls since the 1960s, and she considers the problems entailed in the commodification of race in her "Dyes and Dolls: Multicultural Barbie and the Merchandising of Difference," *Differences* 6:1 (1994): 46–68.

5   Richard Dyer, *White* (London: Routledge, 1997).

6   For some of the notable early examples of ethnographic and qualitative audience-based research on women's genres, see Janice Radway, *Reading the Romance: Women, Patriarchy, and Popular Literature* (Chapel Hill: University of North Carolina Press, 1984); Ien Ang, *Watching Dallas: Soap Opera and the Melodramatic Imagination*, trans. Della Douling (London: Methuen, 1985); and Dorothy Hobson, "Housewives and the Mass Media," in *Culture, Media, Language*, ed. Stuart Hall et al. (London: Hutchinson, 1984), pp. 105–14. Since these studies, of course, a large body of work on these issues has been generated.

7   See, for example, Constance Penley, "Brownian Motion: Women, Tactics, and Technology," in *Technoculture*, ed. Constance Penley and Andrew Ross (Minneapolis: University of Minnesota Press, 1991), pp. 135–61; Tricia Rose, *Black Noise* (New York: Routledge, 1996); and Henry Jenkins, *Textual Poachers* (New York: Routledge, 1992).

8   Tania Modleski, *Loving with a Vengeance: Mass-Produced Fantasies for Women* (London: Methuen, 1984).

9   Erica Rand, *Barbie's Queer Accessories* (Durham, N.C.: Duke University Press, 1995).

10 Denise Gellene, "Barbie Protesters Aren't Playing Around," *Los Angeles Times*, 10 May 1997, sec. A, p. 113.

11 In a response to collector protests, *Barbie Bazaar* published editorials meant to dispel what it called "rumors." Although this Mattel-licensed magazine claimed that Mattel doesn't censor its content, these editorials were very much in line with the way Mattel would want collectors to perceive the legal issues on trademark and copyright. See *Barbie Bazaar*, May/June 1997, p. 26, and July/August 1997, p. 26.

12 Collectors also protested the inferior quality of various dolls and the fact that Mattel was flooding the market with collector series (and thus driving resale values down). The toy company has agreed to address consumer complaints about product quality and distribution volume, but it refuses to change its mind about copyright and trademark infringement. Barad claims she "loves the collector," but, "What I do in my job, first and foremost, is protect Barbie." Gellene, "Barbie Protesters Aren't Playing Around," sec. A, p. 113.

13 Carrie Dolan, "Many Adults Are in Barbie's Corner as She Fights Jem," *Wall Street Journal*, 18 December 1986, sec. 1, p. 18.

14 This article was about a man who had his collection stolen by a pornographic

videomaker for whom he worked. The commentary about feminism was a "hook" paragraph that began by suggesting, "For most people, Barbie dolls and pornography wouldn't seem to go together. Oh, if you really wanted, you might find some oversensitive feminist who will point out something salacious about Barbie. . . . Well, those inclined to be critical might find Barbie more suitable to star in a sheltered youth's masturbatory fantasy than to serve as a plaything for pre-adolescent girls." See *Spy*, March 1993, p. 16.

15   James Clifford, "Collecting Art and Culture," in *The Predicament of Culture: Twentieth-Century Ethnography, Literature, and Art* (Cambridge, Mass.: Harvard University Press, 1988).

16   A. Glenn Mandeville, "The Many Faces of Barbie," *Barbie Bazaar*, January/February 1995, p. 28.

17   Mattel regularly advertises its collector series in *Barbie Bazaar* and, as might be expected, is generally supportive of the magazine.

18   In 1991, the Good Habits Collection, created by Gayle Elam and Our Mutual Friends of Oregon, was advertising eight different Barbie habits, complete with matching undergarments and religious jewelry, for sale at $55 a costume. *Barbie Bazaar*, March/April 1991, p. 21. In a ploy for equal representation, some collectors have fashioned rabbinical outfits for Ken dolls.

19   Michael Thompson, *Rubbish Theory: The Creation and Destruction of Value* (New York: Oxford University Press, 1979), p. 7.

20   Ibid., p. 33.

21   Stewart, *On Longing*, p. 68.

22   This is a rather bare-bones account of Barbie's creation myth. As Erica Rand points out, there are competing origin myths for Barbie. See her *Barbie's Queer Accessories*, pp. 29–38. Collectors are especially riveted on producing revisionist histories that take account of Barbie's debt to the German Lilli doll. I would speculate that this fascination with tracing Barbie's origins to the German Lilli doll serves the purpose of transforming Barbie from American kitsch into an object of high art, and thus greater "durable" value, because like all "true" art, Barbie has roots in European culture.

23   Stewart, *On Longing*, p. 69.

24   Michel Foucault, *The History of Sexuality*, volume 1, trans. Robert Hurley (New York: Vintage, 1980).

25   Eve Kosofsky Sedgwick, "Epidemics of the Will," in *Incorporations, Zone 6*, ed. Jonathan Crary and Sanford Kwinter (New York: UrZone, 1992), pp. 582–95.

26   Personal interview with Marlene Mura, 12 September 1992. All subsequent references to my conversation with Mura are taken from this interview and from email correspondence on 30 October 1997.

27   Julie A. Neises and Charles P. Neises, "Barbie Meets the Beatles," *Barbie Bazaar*, January/February 1991, pp. 44–46.

28   Susan Miller, "Life with Barbie," *Barbie Bazaar*, March/April 1993, p. 18.

29   Philippe Lejeune, *On Autobiography*, ed. Paul John Easkin, trans. Katherine Leary (Minneapolis: University of Minnesota Press, 1989).

30 This sense of "looking wrong" bears interesting connections to theories of femininity and gender performance developed out of Joan Rivière's classic 1929 essay "Womanliness as a Masquerade," in *Formations of Fantasy*, ed. Victor Burgin, James Donald, and Cora Kaplan (1929; London: Methuen, 1986), pp. 35–44. In this case, the festive practice of masquerade seems precisely intended (whether consciously or unconsciously) to undo the more metaphorical masquerade that Rivière sees as constitutive of femininity.

31 *Barbie Bazaar*, January/February 1991, cover and p. 6.

32 *Barbie Bazaar*, May/June 1991, p. 4.

33 Karen F. Caviale, "Vote for Barbie!?" *Barbie Bazaar*, November/December 1992, p. 8.

34 Cited in Maria Toth, "Candy Girl!" *Barbie Bazaar*, November/December 1992, p. 36. In success stories such as these, *Barbie Bazaar* never questions the degree to which black dolls that are modeled on the logic of the white Barbie actually present alternatives. For more concerning these issues with respect to Mattel's marketing, see Ducille, "Dyes and Dolls," and Susan Willis, *A Primer for Daily Life* (New York: Routledge, 1991), p. 120.

35 This letter appeared in an editorial column. See "Talkin' Barbie," *Barbie Bazaar*, September/October 1997, p. 87.

36 *Barbie Bazaar*, September/October 1992, p. 6.

37 Interview with Marlene Mura, 12 September 1992.

38 *Barbie Bazaar*, July/August 1997, p. 30.

39 *Barbie Bazaar*, May/June 1994, p. 26.

40 Billy Boy, *Barbie: Her Life and Times* (New York: Crown Trade Paperbacks, 1987), p. 10.

41 Thompson, *Rubbish Theory*, p. 33.

42 Joan Kron, "Who'll Tell Ken? His Little Barbie Is Hanging Out with Other Men?" *Wall Street Journal*, 14 March 1985, sec. 1, p. 33. In my 1992 personal interview with Joe Blitman of Joe's Barbies, he told me that most men weren't really in it for the money, but that this served as a way to explain away the stigma associated with men and women who collect Barbie.

43 Julie A. Neises, "Barbie Meets the Masters," part 2, *Barbie Bazaar*, March/April 1990, pp. 31–32.

44 *Barbie Bazaar*, March/April 1991, p. 32.

45 *Barbie Bazaar*, March/April 1989, p. 6.

46 This figure comes from publisher Karen Caviale, cited in R. L. Pela, "Malibu Whitehouse," *Advocate*, 26 January 1993, p. 48.

47 Symptomatically here, the *Wall Street Journal* article cited in note 42 above alludes to the "queer" nature of male collectors even as it defends against this possibility by positioning men as rational business people in it for the money. The article claims, "A few years ago Mr. Eames, 46 years old and married, came out of the toy closet, so to speak. He joined a doll collectors' club. 'The giggling has pretty much stopped now,' the magazine tells us because Mr. Eames has built a highly lucrative 'world-class' collection" (p. 33).

48 Caviale, cited in Pela, "Malibu Whitehouse."

49 "Midge in Sister, Sister 2," *Barbie Bazaar*, July/August 1992, p. 16.

50 Editorial, *Barbie Bazaar*, March/April 1989, p. 6; and Karen F. Caviale, "Mel Odom," *Barbie Bazaar*, March/April 1989, p. 38.

51 A. Glenn Mandeville, "And Then . . . I Met Ken," *Barbie Bazaar*, January/February 1990, p. 25.

52 Pela, "Malibu Whitehouse."

53 Marcia Elliott, letter to the editor, *Barbie Bazaar*, May/June 1997, p. 26.

54 Lynne Cooke and Peter Wollen introduce their anthology *Visual Display: Culture Beyond Appearances* (Seattle: Bay Press, 1995) by reminding readers of Jacques Lacan's seminar on Edgar Allan Poe's "Purloined Letter," in which Lacan demonstrates that display can provide the best method of concealment. Using this as a paradigm for understanding museums and other exhibition venues, Cooke and Wollen argue that "it is only through display that truth is revealed—not, of course, directly, but obliquely and en travesti. It is through modes of display that regimes of all sorts reveal the truths they mean to conceal" (pp. 9–10).

55 The ideological reviling of the "domestic" is, of course, not specific to Barbie's art-culture system but is generally regarded as a reigning ideology of modernism. Recent art historical work has begun to reexamine the place and function of domesticity in modern art, suggesting that even if domesticity was often seen as the "other" of art, domestic design and everyday life have played an important role in the development of modern styles. See, for example, Christopher Reed, ed., *Not at Home: The Suppression of Domesticity in Modern Art and Architecture* (London: Thames and Hudson, 1996); Griselda Pollack, "Modernity and the Spaces of Femininity," in *Art in Modern Culture: An Anthology of Critical Texts*, ed. Francis Frascina and Jonathan Harris (New York: Harper Collins, 1992), pp. 121–35; Cecile Whiting, *The Taste for Pop: Pop Art, Gender, and Consumer Culture* (Cambridge, Eng.: Cambridge University Press, 1997); Penny Sparke, *As Long as It's Pink: The Sexual Politics of Taste* (London: Pandora, 1995); and Katy Deepwell, ed., *Women Artists and Modernism* (Manchester: Manchester University Press, 1998).

56 When women do take on this artist status they are often ambivalently figured as somewhere between highbrow fashion artist and lowbrow housewife/seamstress. A story on Patte Burgess, for example, depicts her as the designer of "glamorous haute couture for Barbie" but also a retired grandmother who began making Barbie dresses for her granddaughter. See "The Ultimate in Barbie Fashions," *Barbie Bazaar*, May/June 1995, pp. 47–49.

57 "Now You're Cooking," *Barbie*, July/August 1993, p. 14; and "Make Your Own Pasta Necklaces," *Barbie*, July/August 1993, p. 37.

58 This Barbie art movement was noted by a long story in the *New York Times* in 1991. See Alice Kahn, "A Onetime Bimbo Becomes a Muse," the *New York Times*, 29 September 1991, sec. H, pp. 1, 24–25. It has also been the subject of the cover story "Art, Design, and Barbie" in *Barbie Bazaar*, September/October 1994, pp. 18–23. Note that the re-evaluation of Barbie art within fine art circles has coincided with a more general embrace—or some would say appropriation—of craft

aesthetics in the art world. During the 1990s craft was no longer cubbyholed as a "feminist" issue/aesthetic in the arts and came to be seen instead as a more pervasive postmodern aesthetic. Not only craft, but also related artifacts of thrift store venues, were increasingly brought into the purview of the "fine" arts. In September 1993 *New Art Examiner* ran a special issue entitled "Freedom, Function, and Fashion: The Craft Issue" and again in April 1996 its special issue "A Dialogue with Objects" was devoted to the topic of crafts in the fine arts.

59 When functional arts do appear they are rearticulated in the guise of modernism as with a recent ad in *Barbie Bazaar* by the Vitra Design Museum that offers miniature chairs for Barbie modeled on designs by modernist furnituremakers such as Eames and Mies Van Der Rohe. See *Barbie Bazaar*, January/February 1995, p. 11.

60 Craig Yoe, ed., *The Art of Barbie* (New York: Workman, 1994).

61 Thomas Crow, "Modernism and Mass Culture in the Visual Arts," in his *Modern Art in the Common Culture* (New Haven: Yale University Press, 1996), pp. 3–37.

62 Mattel also installed a video art wall of Barbies and a more postpop interpretation that displayed Barbies sailing in Barbie boats on their way to the Statue of Liberty (who had a Barbie, as opposed to a torch, in her outstretched hand). After the festival, Mattel went on to market its own Water Lily Barbie inspired by Claude Monet.

63 Dick Hebdige, *Subculture: The Meaning of Style* (London: Methuen, 1979).

64 Fredric Jameson, "Postmodernism; or, the Cultural Logic of Late Capitalism," *New Left Review* 146 (1984): 53–92.

65 Although he does not speak of craft production in the terms I do here, Edward W. Soja's analysis of Los Angeles's contradictory production economies is instructive. See his *Postmodern Geographies: The Reassertion of Space in Critical Social Theory* (London: Verso, 1989), chapter 8.

66 Ann Walcher, "Salesroom Etiquette," *Barbie Bazaar,* January/February 1994, pp. 10–11.

67 Mary Douglas and Baron Isherwood, *The World of Goods: Towards an Anthropology of Consumption* (New York: W. W. Norton, 1979).

68 In fact, craft has become so highly esteemed in this system that collectors have recently begun to reevaluate "vintage Barbie licensed" craft kits that were originally produced in the 1960s by companies like Standard Toycraft Industries. Kits like the Barbie Weaving Loom Set now go for up to $350 on the collector's market. See Karen F. Caviale, "Barbie Vintage Crafts," *Barbie Bazzar,* September/October 1997, pp. 47–49.

69 Lucy R. Lippard, *The Pink Glass Swan: Selected Feminist Essays on Art* (New York: New Press, 1995), p. 130.

70 For relevant discussions of the anthropology of art and commodity culture in relation to global/local markets, see George E. Marcus and Fred R. Meyers, *The Traffic in Culture: Refiguring Art and Anthropology* (Berkeley: University of California Press, 1995).

Part V: Rewind and Fast Forward

From the Dark Ages to the Golden Age:
Women's Memories and Television Reruns

✳ A few years ago, when my niece was five years old, I told her a story about the time when, as children, my sister and I dressed up in my mother's Jackie Kennedy ensemble, complete with pink jacket and pillbox hat. This story was curiously meaningful to me and fun to tell, but as far as my niece was concerned, I might as well have been talking about the Jurassic period. This five-year-old had obviously already formed a picture of the past that was totally alien to her own present. Clearly, that picture came primarily from reruns of the 1950s sitcom *I Love Lucy* which my sister and I still love and still watch. My niece, who had already seen her fair share of *Lucy,* interrupted my nostalgic tale: "Do you mean," she asked, "the days when everything was in black and white?" At first I thought she was precociously demonstrating her ability to critique early television's simplistic portrayal of good and evil, but then I realized that this child really believed that the world itself was black and white in the 1950s and 1960s because that was how television pictured it for her.

This five-year-old's mistake might seem a cute anecdote for the family diary, but television's representation of the past, and its relation to the historical consciousness of viewers, is more generally regarded as a matter of public importance. I open with this anecdote because I want to explore the intersection between the private histories of viewers and the way public histories (especially histories of women) are constructed through television reruns. And, most important, I open with a family anecdote be-

Jan. 4-10

TV GUIDE

79¢

IS ROSEANNE THE NEW LUCY?

Not since the '50s has one woman so dominated television

Comic genius or exhibitionist?

In our Special Report, we talk with Roseanne, her friends, foes and —for the first time— the family answers her shocking charges of abuse

OUR NEW CRITIC ADMITS: **I LOVE TV** *by Jeff Jarvis*

0 "739178" 1

Roseanne masquerades as Lucy Ricardo on the cover of this 4 January 1992 issue of *TV Guide*. (Copyright, News America Publications Inc.)

cause the problems I want to address hinge on the generational politics between women, especially with respect to the role that television plays in creating images of women's pasts and the idea of women's progress now.

Television Reruns, Official History, and Popular Memory

The question I want to deal with in this essay originated as a pedagogical problem. In the senior-level course I teach on television history, I regularly assign a term paper that asks students to define and research a topic of their choice. The open-ended nature of this assignment leaves plenty of room for the imagination but also makes for some rather "generic" topics. Every year, one of these topics is the changing role of women on television. And every year, my students set out to prove that female characters have changed for the better and that these changes reflect progress in the wider society. Knowing that such papers usually serve to reproduce (rather than to challenge) reigning mythologies about women, history, and progressive social change, I warn students against this topic or ask them to reconsider their aims. But despite my warnings, women (and to a lesser degree, men) in my classes produce a rather predictable teleological historical narrative that derides the 1950s and traces the "progress" of contemporary society and culture.

Why do so many undergraduates want to write this paper? The more jaded among us probably think that the popularity of this topic can be traced to those shady research companies that sell ready-made essays to desperate students. But I prefer a less cynical explanation, and I would instead like to consider some of the reasons why this particular topic speaks to the concerns of so many female undergraduates. To this end, I shall present a set of oral interviews and writing projects I conducted with women college students. This "data," it should be understood, cannot speak for itself, but it can begin to reveal some possibilities when considered with larger questions about the logic of popular memory, especially with the role that television plays in providing young women with a sense of women's history. Indeed, the students' desire to write this paper—even with the clear and present danger of a bad grade—suggests to me the stubbornness of a particular way of thinking about the past that television itself promotes and perpetuates.

Let me leave the question of the undergraduate population aside for a moment in order to show how this historical sensibility works on our television screens. The example comes from an episode of *Kate and Allie* (1984–1989), a "single-mom" sitcom based on the premise of two divorced women sharing a home with their children. This 1987 episode features two dream sequences that parody female characters of vintage sitcoms: Lucy Ricardo and Ethel Mertz (from *I Love Lucy*) and Mary Richards and Rhoda Morgenstern (from *The Mary Tyler Moore Show* [1970–1977]). The sequences respectively poke fun at the stereotypical 1950s housewife and the equally stereotypical "new woman" working girl of the 1970s. In the *Lucy* segment, which is rendered in vintage black and white, Kate (as the frumpy Ethel) and Allie (as the glam housewife Lucy) plot one of Lucy's famous schemes to break into show business behind Ricky's back. In the *Mary* segment, the women (who sport seventies hairdos and polyester clothing) occupy a replica set of Mary Richards's apartment while chatting about the sexual lives of Mary's co-workers (a clearly liberated topic). In both flashbacks the past becomes a cartoonish masquerade—a parody of feminine (and televisual) styles—that renders both versions of femininity outdated and even absurd.

Like other forms of contemporary television, this episode is full of intertextual references to television history, but I use this specific case to demonstrate the way television remembers itself—the type of popular history it depicts. Like my undergraduate students, this program compares the past with the present, suggesting that women have indeed "come a long way" on television and, by extension, in the culture at large. In contrast to Lucy and Ethel and Mary and Rhoda, Kate and Allie appear to be "newer women" who mark the enlightenment of our time by alluding to the "dark ages" of old television.

Beyond the individual text, television more generally promotes this kind of historical consciousness because it constantly juxtaposes present-day programs with reruns from the past. Historians tend to isolate television into periods—the "golden age," the "vast wasteland," "the turn towards relevance," and so forth. Such periodizations are based on programs that are representative of prime-time network production during specific moments of television history. But this ignores television's overall institutional practices, particularly its local scheduling flows and syndication packages.[1] For this reason, these periodizations begin to collapse as conceptual categories once we recognize that audiences are potentially interpreting new shows within the context of the syndicated reruns that surround them on the daily schedule.

The advent of the nostalgia network is perhaps the best case in point. I am referring here to the children's cable network, Nickelodeon, which at prime time transforms itself into Nick at Nite, a cult lineup of "classic" television reruns.[2] Above all, Nick at Nite was a wise business move for Nickelodeon, which is owned by Viacom—one of the largest U.S. syndication companies. Viacom (which merged with Paramount and CBS, and is also the parent company of MTV) owns a ready-made stable of old network programs that it more typically sells to local and independent stations, as well as foreign markets.

The popularity of Nick at Nite's reruns probably has less to do with the universal appeal of television art—its ability to last through generations—than with the network's strategies of recontextualization. Nickelodeon created a new reception context for old reruns by repackaging them through a camp sensibility. In one series of promos, for example, vintage sitcom star Dick Van Dyke informs us of the network's mission to preserve our "television heritage" by airing such indispensable sitcoms as *The Donna Reed Show* (1958–1966). Nickelodeon also runs cult marathons targeted at the youth market. To inaugurate its revival of *The Partridge Family* (a sitcom that originally aired 1970 to 1974 and starred teenage heartthrob David Cassidy), the network ran a week-long marathon of episodes (four a night) followed by a Saturday-night special hosted by Cassidy (which the network dubbed "Very Very David Cassidy"). In a brilliant stroke of youth market saturation, Nickelodeon's sister station MTV aired its own *Partridge Family* marathon that same weekend.

As is obvious from these examples, Nickelodeon specializes in sitcoms, especially ones about women and about family relationships. And because it eclectically places sitcoms from different decades back to back with one another, it implicitly narrates a history of women's roles on television. More explicitly, it promotes a certain way of thinking about this history through satiric promotions that, for example, poke fun at Donna Reed as television's ideal sacrificing mother, or compare Mary Tyler Moore's "new woman" role as Mary Richards to her earlier role as housewife Laurie Petrie on *The Dick Van Dyke Show* (1961–1966). In an even grander gesture of this historical sensibility, Nickelodeon produced (in connection with ABC) its own situation comedy, *Hi Honey, I'm Home* (1991), which details the fantastic exploits of the Nielsens, a 1950s sitcom family who was taken out of rerun on the local TV schedule and relocated to a "real-life" 1990s suburb in New Jersey (a postmodern conceit if there ever was one). The Nielsens, who appear in vintage black and white and are appropriately attired in campy sitcom garb, cannot quite get the hang of modern living, particularly because their neighbor Elaine is a divorced single mother who continually slips into monologues about women's liberation and derides Honey Nielsen for her "housewifey" ways.[3]

Such tongue-in-cheek programs and promotions speak to a young, television-literate generation by constructing a vision of the past that implicitly suggests the "progress" of contemporary culture. And, as Nick at Nite's programs and promotions imply, the female characters on these television reruns are to be viewed by today's generation through the screen of its distance from the past—through its more "hip" attitudes and culture. Granted, the network mixes its message of distanced hipness with a fair-sized dose of romantic nostalgia for the good old days of television when everyone lived in shiny happy suburbs. But despite this nostalgia, the idea that the viewer is somehow more enlightened than the characters (and audiences) of the past is absolutely central to the interpretation the network solicits. Thus, both in its individual texts and in its institutional strategies of syndication, television recontextualizes the past in terms of contemporary uses and perspectives. Indeed, like my students, television engages in a kind of historical consciousness that remembers the past in order to believe in the progress of the present.

Of course, on one level this sense of history is not simply wrong; there have been real changes for women in the last four decades. However, such enlightenment notions are based as much on forgetting the past as on remembering it. As historians have widely noted, progress in history is often uneven; in the case of women, it refers largely to white middle-class women who benefited most from the women's movement, while women of color have seen less gain. Moreover, whether intentionally or unintentionally, the gains that white women have seen have often been at the *expense* of women of color—not only because feminist movements have historically worked to reenact racist power hierarchies and social agendas, but also because feminism has historically conceptualized the category of "woman" as being synonymous with "whiteness." As bell hooks reminds us, while this "in no way invalidates feminism as a political ideology" that works against sexism, it is nevertheless a fact that "every women's movement in the U.S.A. from its earliest origin to the present day has been built on a racist foundation."[4]

In addition, historical narratives that chart women's progress often celebrate women's enlightenment in the present at the expense of undercutting their agency in the past. But, as feminist historians such as Elaine Tyler May have argued, women in the 1950s were not simply passive dupes of patriarchy; instead they made rational choices based on available options at the time, and they often expressed discontent with their roles.[5]

Similarly, despite popular wisdom, 1950s television was not based on a simple consensus ideology, or at least not one as simple as we might first assume. Historians and fans of television will recall the endless plots on situation comedies that revolved around middle-class housewives who chose between privilege and autonomy on a weekly basis. For example, Lucy Ricardo perpetually tried to get out of the house and into the workforce, and even the more idealized dramas such as *Father Knows Best* (1954–1963) questioned their own assumptions about gender roles in plots that worked through tensions about women's place.[6] Moreover, a number of series featured working-class and ethnic women such as the Jewish Molly Goldberg (*The Goldbergs*, 1952–1956), the Norwegian Marta Hansen (*Mama*, 1949–1956), and the black maid Beulah (*Beulah*, 1950–1953). Although many of these programs had highly stereotypical characters (and some were challenged at the time of their initial broadcasts), for better or worse they form part of our "television heritage," a part that Nick at Nite and other syndication outlets often exclude from our view of the cultural past. This process of exclusion, then, creates an image of the past that is highly one-dimensional, an image that has no doubt helped to shape the historical consciousness of my students.

But this is not to say my students are simply "bad girls" who disregard their history professors in favor of the lessons taught on their television screens. Instead, I believe they are caught between two ways of thinking about the past—one properly "academic" and the other conventionally "popular." As opposed to the professional ideals (if not always practices) of exhaustive data gathering, accuracy, and conclusive analysis, the histories told in the texts of popular culture simplify the complexity of historical events. This process of simplification isn't a matter of intellectual deficiencies. It is not that people are incapable of dealing with the more complex situations that professional historians study. Rather, this way of thinking about the past has a logic and purpose of its own.

This historical sensibility can be considered by way of the concept of popular memory. As I use the term, popular memory is history for the present; it is a mode of historical consciousness that speaks to the concerns and needs of contemporary life. Popular memory is a form of storytelling through which people make sense of their own lives and culture. In this regard, it diverges from official, professional history (by which I mean those histories deemed legitimate by schools, museums, textbook publishers, and other arbiters of social knowledge). Whereas official history typically masks its own storytelling mechanisms, popular memory acknowledges its subjective and selective status. Popular memory is playful about the past, and while it certainly elides the complexity of historical events, it never claims to do otherwise. As in the parodic vision of the *Kate and Allie* episode or the campy images of Nick at Nite, this form of storytelling is less concerned with historical "accuracy" than it is with the uses that memory has for the present. Rather than implicitly proposing a divide between fiction and science (the central concern that underlies the texts of professional history), popular memory self-consciously mixes these modes together, and often in a self-reflexive way. For this reason, it would be foolhardy to judge it by the standards of official history. Popular memory does not set out to find "objective," "accurate" pictures of the past. Instead, it aims to discover a past that makes the present more tolerable. Indeed, as I want to show in this essay, the undergraduates in my classes had a particular vision of the 1950s that glossed over historical contradictions in order to present a simplified portrait of the 1950s housewife—a portrait that made contemporary struggles in women's lives seem less difficult.

The opposition I am suggesting between popular and official pasts, however, is not absolute. As Michael Bommes and Patrick Wright have argued, popular memory is intimately connected to the more dominant perceptions of history that circulate in a society, and to think otherwise "is to risk treating 'the popular' as if it were wholly unified, fully achieved and therefore capable of sustaining a memory wholly apart from the dominant constructions of the past."[7] Indeed, the enlightenment models used by my undergraduate students can also be found in the more official textbook versions of women's history. Then, too, popular memories are often constructed and disseminated by dominant social institutions such as television, to the point where such memories become what Britain's popular memory group has called "dominant memories." For this reason, the term "popular memory" should not be understood in terms of transcendental consciousness or even the more poststructuralist notion of "resistance"; instead, popular memory is enmeshed in knowledge circulated by dominant social institutions.

Just as popular memory is dependent on more official pasts, official history is bound up in the larger stories that a society tells about its past. Historians have long debated the divide between science and fiction that professional history strives toward.[8] As contemporary critical historiographers such as Hayden White have argued, the narrative aims of official history make it subject to storytelling mechanisms that simplify the past to make it accessible to people in the present.[9] And, as Dominick La Capra adds, facts and fictions are intimately intertwined in any historical account because the documentary record is not a neutral record of data, but is itself already "textually processed" by the culture in which it is produced.[10] According to this point of view, then, the official record and the means for explicating that record can never exist outside of the stories and discursive logics of the larger social world.

Because popular memory and official history are intimately connected, generic hybrids abound. It is in this in-between place that I would put history films and telehistories. As numerous scholars have demonstrated, history films and telehistories often displace, rewrite, and "reprogram" the past, and they encourage audiences to mistake "belief" for "truth." [11] The various television docudramas of John and Jacqueline Kennedy are good examples of the hybrid status of such texts. On the one hand, these docudramas often announce themselves as authoritative accounts through the use of period costumes, voiceovers, news footage, and famous speeches. On the other hand, they invite audiences to play with these truths by self-consciously acknowledging their deviations from hard fact. Both publicity and the texts themselves delight in conjecture, relating scandalous stories of Kennedy's affairs and Jackie's compulsive shopping sprees. Even while these docudramas stage the "official" single-bullet theory closure with motorcade footage of Kennedy's death, the story (by its very nature) cannot help but conjure up the other possible "endings" that circulate in the rumor mills of popular history. In this regard, I would argue that film and television histories contain within them a popular version of what Michel Foucault called "counter-memory." [12] That is, while they draw on strategies of professional history to authenticate themselves as the "official story," they also narrate another past that often implicitly contradicts the official version. In a quite paradoxical way, they invite alternative readings even as they position themselves as authoritative accounts.

Thus, whether produced in the halls of academia or pictured on our television screens, memory and history are not mutually exclusive domains. Still, as I want to argue, they have different uses and different goals. The question for analysis is not whether popular memory has "ideological effects"—because all history does—but what kinds of effects it aims to have. Why is it popular to remember the past in this way in the first place?

History Lessons

In order to explore the above question, I returned to my undergraduate students in the hope of discovering some clues as to why they construct historical narratives about television and women that affirm the present by glossing over the complexity of the past. I did this research at the University of Wisconsin–Madison where most students are from the Midwest. Almost all of the students were white, and their ages ranged from nineteen to twenty-one (the few older students and students of color had to interact in that context). About half of the students came from the suburbs, about a quarter were rural midwesterners, and about a quarter were from urban areas (especially Milwaukee, Chicago, and New York). Very few of the students had taken a women's studies course at the university. I conducted three oral discussion sessions, with undergraduate women in my large introductory media course. Each discussion session included about twenty women and ran for approximately one hour. In addition to these discussion sections, I conducted three hour-long sessions in which a total of seventy-four undergraduate women wrote five-page essays. The essay assignment read as follows: "(A) What do you think women were like in the 1950s? What did they do on an average day? What did they hope for and dream about? What did they fear and worry about? What were their relationships with men and women like? (B) How do you know these things about women in the 1950s?" Both the students in the discussion group and those who wrote essays also filled out a short survey asking them to list favorite reruns from different decades and also asking them if they thought any women on television serve as good role models.[13]

The point of this study was not to produce generalizable data, but rather to open up a dialogue about the relationship of history to memory, as well as television's place within that complex relationship. My use of the word "dialogue" here does not refer to a utopian democratic situation, because I could see from the start that my students still recognized my position of power in this conversation and that they wanted to please me.[14] Many of the students knew me as their television professor so, understandably, many also knew that I was probably fishing around for information on how television helped form their vision of the past. I think these students might have even overestimated television's influence on their image of the past in order to please me. (However, I do believe from their essays and discussions that the students certainly did use television reruns as a prime source of historical information; it is the extent of television's role in their memories that I question.)

But again, my point was not to erase myself or to fool the students into being open books from whom I could collect objective data. For this reason, I did not set up a "control group" of students who were unaware of my research interests. Instead, I wanted to see how our conversations developed and how I could use this dialogue as a point of intervention between my own status as a professional media historian and the popular texts that I teach. Although I had assumed that the students' narratives (both written and oral) would present highly generic, stereotypical images of 1950s housewives, I was somewhat overwhelmed by the incredible conformity of the images they had. Poodle skirts, ponytails, and pointy eyeglasses were mentioned time and time again. Typical descriptions from the written essays read as follows:

> Women in the 1950s could be described as much more passive than the women of today. . . . The goal of women was to find the "perfect man" and settle down. . . . I think back to the television show *Leave It to Beaver* and imagine life for women as being similar to June Cleaver's.

> In the 1950s, women were very different than they are today. Most women were not expected to go to college and make something of their lives. . . . It is easy to see from shows like *Donna Reed, Father Knows Best*, and *Leave It to Beaver* that the mother was a supermom who got up early in the morning to fix breakfast and make her kids lunches, clean the house, and help solve problems.

> I would say that women in the 1950s wore more plain styles than today. The mental image I get of the fifties is the happy Cunningham family on *Happy Days*. I can just see Joni [*sic*] in her long black poodle skirt and her pink cardigan. . . . I guess then *Laverne and Shirley* would be another vote for the Joni [*sic*] look.

> Women in the fifties were very different than the women of today. . . . When one pictures a typical woman in the fifties, one's thoughts tend to be geared toward a woman like Marion Cunningham from *Happy Days* or Mrs. Cleaver from *Leave It to Beaver*. Women in the fifties wore big puff skirts, tight sweaters, polyester pants.

These comments are typical of other student essays and discussions on a number of levels. First, although I did not ask the women to compare the 1950s to the 1990s, their primary mode for thinking about the past was through comparison with the present—a situation that suggests that the past was relevant to the students insofar as it was pertinent to their own lives. In making the past relevant, they also engaged in a process of familiarization; they made sense of the past by describing it in terms of a repertoire of images with which they were acquainted. As the above examples suggest, the women used television as their key source of familiarization. It was through television that these women claimed to know most about the 1950s.[15]

As the examples above show, many women used actual 1950s reruns and nostalgia sitcoms such as *Happy Days* interchangeably, and in fact many had trouble differentiating between them.[16] By imposing a contemporary logic on historical events, nostalgia sitcoms help to do the work of familiarization for their audiences, allowing viewers to remember only those details of the past that seem useful for the present. Through their ambiguous status as a "contemporary past," these television programs provide a sense of intimacy with, and even mastery over, history because they distill the complexity of historical events into recognizable styles and stories. In a discussion session, one woman even said that she felt the nostalgia shows were better historical sources than the actual 1950s reruns because "they take the epitome of everything from the fifties and put it into one show, whereas programs like *Leave It to Beaver* . . . just seem old. There isn't anything characteristic of . . . the fifties [whereas in] *Happy Days* . . . they don't miss a thing." [17]

At this point in my research, I felt that I had spent a good deal of time to discover a fairly obvious point: television serves as one of our culture's primary sources for historical consciousness. The next logical conclusion, drawn by so many critics of the medium, would be that television caused these women to have a skewed sense of their own past; it was television's "fault," so to speak, that these women had highly stereotyped notions about their heritage. However, I discovered something different. While it is true that the students used television programs as a key source for thinking about the past, they were in fact very self-critical of the fact that so many of their memories came from television. Indeed, even while they wrote and spoke at length about the 1950s, they often reflected on the inadequacy of their sources. Responding to my essay question that asked how they knew about the 1950s (but did not ask them to evaluate their sources of knowledge), many students addressed these problems head on. One woman wrote:

> I am not exactly sure of the things that I have just cited, I could be entirely wrong. What I know about the fifties woman is what I have

taken directly from the television screen. I based a lot, or most, of my knowledge on June Cleaver.

Another stated:

> Most of my ideas, I admit, came from television. Shows like *Leave It to Beaver, My Three Sons,* and *Lucy* are just a few examples. Perhaps it is [because of] TV that all of my opinions or a lot of them are stereotypical. . . . It is amazing how TV has shaped my idea of women throughout time.

And one woman even wrote:

> While I am aware that the Cleavers were not the typical family, it is their image that projects itself into my head upon mention of the 1950s. . . . Okay, okay, I admit it, born and raised in the seventies I am a true product of the TV age. My perceptions of days past are based on reruns!

More generally, the students noted that the images they had from television were more stereotypical than typical, and some students also acknowledged that these television images were more exclusive to the white middle class than representative of all women. Along these lines one woman wrote, "I realize *Leave It to Beaver* is such a white bread show and doesn't depict your normal family." Another claimed, "I'm speaking about the stereotypical middle class. Obviously not everyone was like this." And another student warned, "Please note that I am describing women of the 1950s of the middle class. When thinking of the working woman I imagine her with a 'service' job. A waitress working at the local diner."

Some argued that family pictures and stories help shape their sense of the past and serve as a kind of "reality" test for the images on television. In a discussion session, one woman claimed, "It's hard for me to think those shows are real as far as a real portrayal of the fifties because my grandmother always told me that she had no time for social life. She was busy cleaning and sending my dad to work." Another said, "I saw photo albums and no one was happy. They are real pictures so I tend to side with them." Thus, as John Nerone has argued, the personal past can serve as a critical tool for analyzing a social memory circulated by dominant institutions like television. In addition, Nerone shows how a memory that belongs to a specific social group—such as an ethnic group—can be used by people to challenge a dominant social memory.[18] In this case, students from rural areas typically used their group identity as rural Americans to contest the urban and suburban images of women on 1950s TV. For instance, when talking about 1950s programs, one woman explained, "I thought that's how people in the cities may have lived. I lived very far from any towns . . . so when I grew up I thought that's what women in the cities did." Another woman commented, "I think it depends on rural or urban communities too. I don't think rural women were as able to go to the beauty parlor that often." Thus, while these women believed that television programs might have reflected part of our national past, they used their own regional and personal memories to contest the dominant social memory that television constructs.

In general then, the women were quite self-conscious about their use of television as a primary source of knowledge for the 1950s. They almost all agreed that the past of which they spoke was largely fictional and open to question. But still they continued to believe that the present was better than the past, and their stories almost all suggested that women had come a long way since June Cleaver and Marion Cunningham. In essence, then, they used evidence about the past that they themselves deemed faulty in order to make truth claims about progress in the present. Again, I would suggest that historical accuracy was not finally what mattered in the stories that they told. Instead, these women were engaging in a mode of popular memory that simplified the past in order to affirm the present. In this regard, the storytelling mechanism in which they engaged might be considered to be one of disavowal: these students seemed to disavow their disbelief in television in order to legitimate the idea that women's lives have substantially improved since the 1950s. Almost all of the students agreed that we are now living in an age of enlightenment where women have more choices and more career opportunities. Within this construction of the present, the past served as a comparative index by which people could measure their relative liberation. In this regard, television reruns and nostalgia shows might well have served the purpose of legitimation because they provide us with pictures of women whose lives were markedly less free than our own.[19] In fact, when I asked the students in one session if the stereotypical depiction of women in television reruns made them angry, one woman said, "No, I think it's some-

thing to laugh at now . . . take it for what it was, it's not that way now."
Another claimed, "It kinda makes you glad you are alive today and not
back then." Television thus served as a central form of legitimating the
present.

I use the word legitimation here with some trepidation because it's a
loaded term. It suggests that these women are in some way busy justifying their own oppression, implicitly condoning contemporary sexism
by affirming their culture's progress. In some instances, I do think that
is the case. In fact, for some women, faith in progress seemed to close
off the need for a feminist movement in the present. Numerous women
constructed stories that put the women's movement squarely in the past
tense, implicitly justifying the backlash against feminism that was part
and parcel of Reagan's and Bush's America. In a discussion session one
student said, "Women overcame the feminist movement in the seventies
and eighties. I think women realized they don't have to be like men to be
equals, thus, femininity is coming back into style along with a career and a
family." The word "overcame" seems particularly interesting here because
this woman spoke as if women's gains were won *in spite of* rather than
because of women's political movements. Moreover, as with many students in the sessions, this woman tended to speak as if all women shared
the same common goal of a career coupled with a heterosexual marriage.
This idea of "having it all," as many students put it, was continually put
forward as the solution to what the students perceived as a prior kind
of antifeminine feminism that they associated with the 1970s women's
movement. One student even used the term "ball-buster dyke" to describe
the stereotypical feminist of the past who had not come to terms with
her feminine self. Although this statement was the most extreme, many
students seemed complicit with backlash discourses that have pitted femininity against feminism and, I think for this reason, many were wary of
using the word feminism to describe their views and values.

As the discussion above already suggests, thinking about the past also
sometimes turned to a nostalgic longing for the "good old days" when
girls were girls and boys made money. One woman wrote:

> The fifties is my favorite time, and if I could have lived at any moment
> in time, it would have been then. The young women did not have the
> worries that we have today of being a 'career woman' and 'a good
> mother' at the same time. Housewives in the fifties may have been

upset at their roles in society, but they did not know anything else so I think they were content.

In statements such as these, nostalgia served to legitimate sexism by making it tolerable and even preferable to the confusing events of present-day life. In a less direct way, such statements also justified the racism and class inequities of the present by suggesting that somehow all women had it better back then and that a return to the good old days would be possible for everyone. However, even when students romantically remembered the past as a better place, they typically mixed this nostalgia with a firm belief in future progress. The students often rendered the future as an ideal past where women could enjoy the privileges of stylish clothes, romance, luxury housing, and other personal benefits (all values that they associated with the 1950s) and still have the personal freedom, intelligence, political power, and discretionary income of the ideal postfeminist woman. Nostalgia in this regard is not the opposite of progress, but rather its handmaiden. Like the idea of progress, nostalgia works to simplify history into a timeline of events that leads somewhere better. For these women, the idea of having it all was rendered through this mixture of nostalgic longing and progressive faith in a brighter future.

Thus, the process of thinking historically led these women to some quite ambiguous and contradictory statements. While they legitimated contemporary sexism and racism through the idea of historical progress, their nostalgia for a better past also forced them to consider the constraints of their own present. In this regard, the gaps and inconsistencies in their logic often seemed to lead them beyond their own assertions into what appeared to be hesitations, stumblings, uncertainties. Many of the students recognized that their statements about history were inconsistent. In this way, even while they seemed to embrace the backlash around them, the process of thinking historically also allowed many students to reconsider and to critique the sexism of the present. By comparing their contemporary lives to an imaginary past of poodle skirts and pointy glasses, these women might in some way have been opening up possibilities for thinking about change. Indeed, when considering their lives in terms of the simplified images of 1950s television, numerous students criticized the inequities of their own time. For example, one woman wrote:

I think women were probably happier in the 1950s, although more equal today. I'm not putting down equality, but women still are not fully equal, and in the fifties women's lives were less complicated. Most women who work today have to work and still have the main responsibility for the children.

For these women, the dark ages are over, but the golden age is still to come.

Curiously, as well, while the students generally did not connect sexual inequality to racial inequality, when I asked them if they had female role models on contemporary television, they most often named Clair Huxtable (Phylicia Rashad) of *The Cosby Show*.[20] Having grown up on *Cosby*, many of these women (almost all of whom were white) saw her as the ultimate woman who had combined a successful law career with a loving family life. Clair had it all. And only two students ever mentioned the fact that Clair was an African American woman. Most students seemed just as color blind as *The Cosby Show* does to the problems many black women face. The reasons for this, I am sure, are complex and require much more analysis than my evidence can sustain.

Tentatively speaking, I would say that the students might have felt it inappropriate to bring up the question of race because I had not asked about it in the first place. Then, too, in our oral discussions, they might have felt it "racist" to notice race. At any rate, when I asked them about this issue, they fell silent. We might interpret the students' identification with Clair as a sign of hope: that is, the presence of more black female characters on television helps break down racism by creating lines of identification between races. Or, we may interpret their responses as a measure of success for the much-criticized *Cosby* strategy: that is, *Cosby*'s attempt to elide race and class issues in favor of presenting ideal role models allows these students to comfortably identify with the upper-crust lifestyle of Clair without even thinking about the issues of race and class that affect women's ability to succeed. These two alternatives do not exhaust the possibilities, but they do suggest the difficulties involved in interpreting the silences in discussions such as these.

Generating Knowledge / Knowing Generations

It is difficult, at best, to reconcile the ideas of progress and nostalgia that run through so many of the students' narratives with my own understanding of feminist history and my own relative discomfort with enlightenment models. But again, that would be to judge popular memory by the standards of a more official, professional history. That would be, I think, to misunderstand the storytelling mechanisms at work in popular memory and the reasons why people remember in the first place. Popular memory is bound up with its use-value in the present. It provides people with a way of making sense of an alienating and imperfect world. It operates as an often self-acknowledged fiction, a strategy for *believing* in what people themselves often seem to *know* isn't so. Within this, television seems to have a tenuous position. Its dual status as entertainment and information places the knowledge it distributes somewhere between fiction and science, between memory and history. At least in the case of the students in this study, that ambiguity is not lost. For them, television serves less as a document than as a dialogue. It allows people to tell stories about an ephemeral American past—stories that recast and redress the concerns of contemporary life.

For my part, the question that the study raises doubles back on my original problem: the dialogue between myself and my students. In the opening section of this essay, I displaced my teaching problem onto my students, chiding them for writing bad papers and punishing them with a bad grade for not learning the lessons of feminist cultural history. But finally, the problem really belongs to me and, I suppose, many of us who teach the history of popular culture. It seems likely that my students are participating in a larger tendency to use television reruns and nostalgia programs as a source for popular memory. Indeed, the stories about the past that are heard most loudly and consistently are those that are broadcast on our national media. Although it would be hasty to assume that viewers are simply duped by these television images (indeed my students clearly understood that television is not an accurate picture of the past), alternative histories and countermemories are still typically excluded from the mass media, and for this reason they are often erased from consciousness. Moreover, as I mentioned early on, television even erases its own past; it selects only a few programs for syndication and leaves out countless others.

In distinction to such exclusions, professional history demands the opposite response—inclusion—but this academic impulse to simply know and teach it all is not always that simple. For example, *Amos 'n' Andy* (1951–1953) was taken out of rerun syndication in 1966, only after a long struggle by the National Association for the Advancement of Colored

People to cancel the show for its racist portrayals. Sometimes, then, exclusion and simplification are not merely "ideological" tools forged in favor of producing a consensus view of the past. Sometimes, as in the case of the *Amos 'n' Andy* reruns, exclusion of the past is in dialogue with the continuing hurts of the present. In this light, the desire in professional history to "include" often becomes highly problematic. What do your students do, for example, when you show them *Amos 'n' Andy* in the classroom? Is this an occasion for continued racism among students (as I think it often is) or is it a moment of discovery for them (as I think it can also be)?

These ethical issues are important, but they should in no way turn into an apology for continued exclusions. As Herman Gray has argued, the observation and analysis of racial exclusion, marginalization, and even hegemonic incorporation on U.S. television should not be the end point of television criticism. If it is, Gray warns, the critic simply reproduces the exclusionary logic of television itself. Instead, drawing on the work of George Lipsitz and Stuart Hall, Gray insists that it is necessary to find voices—both in texts and among black audiences—that speak to black experiences and interpretations.[21]

Gray's point is crucial. However, in the context of my study here and television pedagogy more generally, I want to suggest that the act of "giving voice" presents its own difficulties. Students of color are a very small minority in media programs, and that continues to create real problems in terms of their ability to "voice" their perspectives, at least in the classroom. A number of black students have told me that they strategically avoid classes that are centrally about race (especially when these classes are taught by white teachers) because they do not wish to be used as the example of race among a class of white peers (who, of course, have the luxury of believing that they do not signify "race").

For women of color the problem, I suspect, is exacerbated. This was demonstrated to me in one of my television classes when the only black female student in the class purposely stayed home on the day that I showed *Julia* (1968–1971), the first U.S. sitcom to feature an upwardly mobile black woman character in the leading role. Significantly, this female student had an especially interesting way of coping with her discomfort in the classroom while still giving voice to her feelings. That morning, as I waited for class to begin, I received a fax from this woman that contained her analysis and criticisms of *Julia*, which she wanted me to read to the class. The fax described her memories of watching *Julia* as a young girl with her other black female friends, and it recalled how they had laughed at the "whitewashing" of black culture that went on in the show. This woman certainly had memories of television that (as she told me later) formed a very important part of her personal history and her sense of black womanhood. But her only means of recovering that history (at least in the context of this mostly white classroom) was through ventriloquism, through having the teacher stand in as her dummy to recount her memories for her.

Aside from these problems of visibility and invisibility, voice and silence, I would like to conclude with a related pedagogical problem that might be called the persistence of memory over history. Let me clarify this point with an example. On several occasions after I read this paper at conferences, people asked me, in essence, why I am not a better teacher. Why do I not teach away these students' misconceptions about the past? Why do I not show them all the programs on early television, tell them more about women's pasts, and thus give them a better sense of history? This question presupposes that academic history can cure students, that through the exhaustive inclusion of all the facts it can deliver people from the likes of Nick at Nite. But in practice, the problem is much more stubborn than this. For, as I mentioned early on, popular memories of the past have a way of asserting themselves in spite of the history lessons learned in educational institutions. Popular memory is, I believe, popular because it speaks to the concerns of the present in a way that professional histories often do not.[22] It gives people ways to use the past in the context of everyday life, perhaps because the version of the past it offers is simple and open to application as a "moral" lesson.

But my point, once again, is not to blame my students for embracing a reductive picture of historical events. Nor do I want to blame the texts of popular culture that engage their historical imaginations. Instead, I would suggest that we cannot simply "correct" popular memory by teaching it away. Indeed, we need to stop thinking that television or movies or comic books are simply wrong or "ideological" and that professional/official history is in some way a scientific antidote to such trivial misconceptions. Rather than deriding the popular and returning to a more "legitimate" historical/cultural canon (as the cultural literacy advocates would suggest), we need to examine the relationships between popular memory and professional history. We need to understand why popular versions of the past are so persistent and so appealing, even among people who "know" differently. Moreover, we need to consider how our own teaching can explore the relationships between popular memory and professional history. In this regard, we should confront our own imbrication in the popular memories that circulate in the world in which we live. To what extent is our "professional" historical text informed by these popular narratives? How does our desire for progress and our nostalgia for the past help to shape the historical narratives that we write?

In this study, for example, I clearly had a big stake in wanting my students to desire the feminism of my own youth. Indeed, this research was based on what might well be my own nostalgia for a feminist movement that many of today's college women reject. For me, the sticky problem in this study is my blanket assumption that my students *should* desire feminism (which I no doubt associate with the "golden age" of my own university experience) in the face of a student population that considers feminism to be part of the "dark ages" of 1970s television. And in many ways, as so many women have suggested, the feminist movement of the 1970s was laced with its own race and class power structures, structures that certainly do not need to be revisited on our students.

In this sense, the professional historian is always embroiled in her own desires and her own sense of what should constitute the future. The historian is not immune to the nostalgia and enlightenment thinking that motivate our more popular versions of history. In many ways my nostalgia for the good old days of 1970s feminism is precisely the kind of simplification and disavowal that underlie the popular memories I have discussed here. On closer introspection, I can certainly remember a time in college when I (like my students) resisted academic feminism completely, so that my current embrace of the good-old feminist past is nothing if not a historical revision.

For such reasons, we need to consider popular memory and professional history as part of a more intertwined social dynamic. By bringing popular memory into a dialectical tension with professional history, we might find a way to explicate the biases and blind spots of both. We might find a way to begin to address the things that divide women, divisions that leave women vulnerable to the authoritative, patriarchal will of historical discourses that pervade not only our television screens or our academic classrooms, but also the private stories that we tell ourselves each day.

Notes

This essay first appeared in *Screen* 36:1 (spring 1995): 16–33. Thank you to Charlotte Brunsdon, Julie D'Acci, Bill Forman, and George Lipsitz for their thoughtful suggestions and assistance.

1 There is surprisingly little academic interest in reruns, even while they comprise so much of the television experience. The majority of work that deals with reruns concerns cult programs and fan cultures. See, for example, Henry Jenkins, *Textual Poachers: Television Fans and Participatory Cultures* (New York: Routledge, 1992). For a previous study that speaks more directly to my interests here, see Lynn Spigel and Henry Jenkins, "Same Bat Channel/Different Bat Times: Mass Culture and Popular Memory," in *The Many Lives of the Batman: Critical Approaches to a Superhero and His Media,* ed. William Uricchio and Roberta Pearson (New York: Routledge, 1991), pp. 117–48. Most recently, Phil Williams has explored the industrial history of the rerun in his "Feeding Off the Past: The Evolution of the Television Rerun," *Journal of Popular Film and Television* 21: 4 (1994): 162–75.

2 As Karen Lury tells me, British readers will recognize that Nick at Nite is similar to the cable/satellite stations UK Gold and Bravo.

3 This was the first cable-network cooperative venture for a sitcom series. In the summer of 1991, Nickelodeon aired the sitcom first on ABC and then repeated it two nights later on Nick at Nite. It was cancelled after its summer run on ABC, but continued for another season on Nick at Nite.

4 bell hooks, *Ain't I a Woman: Black Women and Feminism* (Boston: South End Press, 1981), p. 124.

5 Elaine Tyler May, *Homeward Bound: American Families in the Cold War Era* (New York: Basic Books, 1988).

6 For a discussion of these issues, see Patricia Mellencamp, "Situation Comedy, Feminism, and Freud: Discourses of Gracie and Lucy," in *Studies in Entertainment: Critical Approaches to Mass Culture,* ed. Tania Modleski (Bloomington: Indiana University Press, 1986), pp. 80–95. In a somewhat different context, Horace Newcomb and Paul M. Hirsch discuss the ways that *Father Knows Best* expresses anxieties about women's roles. See their "Television as a Cultural Forum," in *Television: The Critical View,* fifth ed., ed. Horace Newcomb (New York: Oxford University Press, 1994), pp. 503–15.

7 Michael Bommes and Patrick Wright, " 'Charms of residence': The Public and the Past," in *Making Histories: Studies in History Writing and Politics,* ed. Richard Johnson et al. (London: Hutchinson, 1982), p. 225. In this passage, Bommes and Wright are considering the reasons Michel Foucault abandoned the notion of popular memory in his later work. Although Bommes and Wright expose the problems with the notion of "popular," they attempt to resuscitate its usefulness as an area for critical debate.

8 On this issue especially, see Michel de Certeau, "History: Science and Fiction," *Heterologies: Discourse on the Other,* trans. Brian Massumi (Minneapolis: University of Minnesota Press, 1986), pp. 199–221.

9   See, for example, Hayden White, *Tropics of Discourse: Essays in Cultural Criti-cism* (Baltimore: Johns Hopkins University Press, 1978). More generally, within the academy there is an expanding field of critical historiography (represented by White, Michel de Certeau, and Dominick La Capra, among others) that addresses issues of narrativity, scientism, subjectivity, and objectivity, and the relationships between official and popular history. In addition, there is now a growing interest in the relationship between memory and history.

10 Dominick La Capra, *History and Criticism* (Ithaca: Cornell University Press, 1985), pp. 34–35.

11 See the interview with Michel Foucault in *Cahiers du Cinéma*, no. 251/52 (1974): 5–15. The French text was translated by Martin Jordin for *Radical Philosophy* 11, and reprinted in "Film and Popular Memory: Cahiers du Cinéma/Extracts," *Edin-burgh '77 Magazine*, no. 2 (1977): 22–25.
    Critical theory of the history film became important in France in the first half of the 1970s, and later in the decade these discussions reverberated in Britain and the United States. In the *Cahiers* interview, Foucault used the term "popular mem-ory" to describe popular stories told by groups (orally and in song) who did not have access to official historical writing. He claimed that in the twentieth century the popular memories of the class struggle had increasingly been "reprogrammed" by such apparatuses as cheap novels, school curricula, and the history film. (This position on memory and history seems a rather odd one for Foucault to take, be-cause it sounds more like anthropology than his preferred method of archaeology.)

12 Foucault briefly describes "counter-memory" in relation to a philosophical ques-tion about alterity in history. See Michel Foucault, *Language, Counter-Memory, Practice: Selected Essays and Interviews by Michel Foucault*, ed. Donald F. Bou-chard (Ithaca, N.Y.: Cornell University Press, 1977). George Lipsitz later reused and redefined the term in his innovative book *Time Passages: Collective Mem-ory and American Popular Culture* (Minneapolis: University of Minnesota Press, 1990). I would argue that Lipsitz uses the phrase "counter-memory" in a way more analogous to Foucault's earlier notion of "popular memory" (see the *Cahiers* interview cited in note 11 above). As Foucault did in that interview, Lipsitz dis-cusses how folk traditions, songs, and oral storytelling give voice to the historical memories of people who don't typically have access to historical writing. But un-like Foucault, who spoke of the increasing loss of working-class memory in the face of mass media, Lipsitz argues that these memories have a material and cul-tural base in various ethnic and working-class communities, and he also shows how these memories speak (although in tempered and distorted ways) through popular novels, popular music, television, and film.

13 I had the students fill out these surveys *after* they had written their essays, in order to minimize the problem of "leading" them into writing about television. Because I did not have the same concerns in the discussion groups, these students filled out the surveys at the beginning of the sessions, and we used them as a point of discussion throughout.

14 For an important discussion of how power relations such as this affect the atmo-

sphere of women's media classes, see Charlotte Brunsdon, "Pedagogies of the Feminine: Feminist Teaching and Women's Genres," *Screen* 32:4 (1992): 364–81.

15 While I don't have the space to consider this at length, it is interesting to note that the students almost never used films as references for the past.

16 As will be evidenced in a later quotation, some students also confused programs from different time periods; thinking, for example, as one student did that *The Mary Tyler Moore Show* was an example of 1950s television.

17 Perhaps this statement also lends credence to Fredric Jameson's vision of historical sensibility (or the waning thereof) in the postmodern age of nostalgia. See his *Signatures of the Visible* (New York: Routledge, 1991).

18 John Nerone, "Social Memory and Professional History," *Communication*, no. 11 (1989): 89–104.

19 In another context, George Lipsitz (following Habermas) discusses how nostalgia works to legitimate consumerism on 1950s U.S. television. See his *Time Passages*, chapter 3.

20 About one-third of the student surveys named this character. In comparison, the second-largest group of stars/characters mentioned was an assortment of female newscasters who were named by about one-tenth of the students.

21 Herman Gray, "The Endless Side of Difference: Critical Television Studies, Television, and The Question of Race," *Critical Studies in Mass Communication* 10, no. 2 (June 1993): pp. 190–97.

22 Although I do not think it is possible to prove the relative importance of media versus education with the data I have, it is interesting that very few women students ever mentioned education as having any effect on their notion of women's history. One woman even stated "I'm trying to remember from high school history classes, CA [our department at the university] classes, [but] television programs make up a lot of my images truthfully." It is possible, of course, that women's history was marginalized in the classes this woman has taken, and in this respect this student's comment might reflect that marginalization as much as it reflects the relative importance of mass media over education in her more general sense of history.

Yesterday's Future, Tomorrow's Home

Everyone says the future is strange, but I have a feeling some things won't change.

General Motors, *Design for Dreaming* (1956)

We are all interested in the future, for that is where you and I are going to spend the rest of our lives.

Criswell, *Plan 9 from Outer Space* (1956)

✳ In the spring of 1999, I received an email from a program manager in strategic marketing at the Intel Corporation. He thanked me for writing *Make Room for TV* and informed me that he was using my study of television's entrance into American homes for his corporation's investigation of the way people use new digital technology in their domestic lives. He talked especially of my analysis of the way 1950s television was depicted as a center for family relationships, and he said his company was "perpetually interested in the 'Family Room'" for two reasons. First, he spoke of the "legendary Intel paranoia lest the TV usurp traditional PC functions," and second he wondered, "Is there some way to MAKE money in there?"[1]

I read this email with some shock and some ironic laughter. Although I was happy that my book had had an impact on corporate culture, I was nevertheless not so pleased to discover the way Intel was using it. While

I considered *Make Room for TV* in part a critique of the corporatization of everyday life, the corporate world obviously found it useful for exactly *that* purpose. In the end, I decided this was not so devastating, say, as the use of Einstein's science for nuclear destruction. Nevertheless, the email did disturb my sense of purpose in the world.

Apart from my own shaken ego, however, I decided that the email was symptomatic of a trend in the high-tech industry to apply a kind of reverse logic to the future. That trend was based not so much on the industry's newfound respect for cultural history as it was on its instrumental reasoning about the goal of history itself. That is, the Intel Corporation assumed that the best way to carve out a future for its company was to return to the middle-class home of the cold war past. With that in mind, Intel and numerous other high-tech companies search for ways to sell the public on new technologies by promoting them through the much older concept of the "home of tomorrow" and "progressive" family lifestyles circa 1955. Indeed, much of the current corporate wisdom on technological progress is steeped in a sense of nostalgia, not for yesterday per se but, more specifically, for yesterday's future.

That future, more precisely, is a future first imagined most prolifically in the 1920s and 1930s, and then expanded on and revised in the newly emerging electronic culture of cold war America. In the United States, the home of tomorrow was inspired in large part by the European avant-garde—in particular the Swiss Architect Le Corbusier, who famously pronounced, "The house is a machine for living in." By 1930, two distinct futuristic housing types had emerged on American soil. One version was based on an ideal of modern luxury and was associated early on with architect Richard Neutra and his 1929 Lovell House, which drew on the International Style. The other type was rooted in the ethos of mass production and was associated most famously with Buckminster Fuller, whose 1927 Dymaxion House was designed on the model of a navy ship, with factory-like efficiency, complete with an appliance-filled "service core." In both its upper-crust and mass-produced forms, the home of tomorrow was often the subject of women's home magazines, and it was displayed with great fanfare at fairs, exhibitions, and in middle-class department stores. Some housing companies even sold futuristic homes in ready-made inexpensive kits that could be built by the lay consumer. However, while American consumers were fascinated with futuristic homes, they did not eagerly embrace the avant-garde styles of client-built homes, nor did they necessarily want to live in the mass-produced homes of the future imagined by Fuller and others. For the most part, as Brian Horrigan suggests, "Americans did not want machines to live in; they wanted machines to live with."[2]

To be sure, companies specializing in electrical gadgets quickly understood the symbolic power of the home of tomorrow. Advertisers began to use the concept of the futuristic home as a way to sell a seemingly endless array of new and wondrous machines. During the 1930s, General Electric showcased its "magic home" at fairs and exhibitions. In 1934, Westinghouse chose Mansfield, Ohio, as the site for its Home of Tomorrow which functioned as a display venue for the company's line of household gizmos. By the 1940s, and after World War II, the home of tomorrow was most typically imagined as a technologically enhanced living space, chock full of "mechanical servants" that promised to liberate housewives from chores while also orchestrating daily activities ranging from home entertainment to waking the kids (Disneyland's GE-sponsored Carrousel of Progress pavilion is a prime example[3]). In this period as well, corporations put a new twist on the home of tomorrow by offering the more modestly defined kitchen of tomorrow. In 1943 and 1944, The Libby-Owens-Ford company promoted its Day After Tomorrow's Kitchen in department stores around the country. After the war, the kitchen of tomorrow continued to be a staple feature in home magazines. Disneyland's first home of the future, the Monsanto Home of 1957, contained an Atoms for Living Kitchen designed by Kelvinator.[4] The futuristic kitchen also served as a popular way of selling not just kitchen appliances but also other kinds of products. In 1956, General Motors produced a twenty-minute industrial ad titled *Design for Dreaming* that promoted its new fall cars by featuring a housewife who wanted to get out of her kitchen and into a new automobile. Nothing short of surreal, the ad shows the housewife dreaming of a high-tech, high-fashion lifestyle, complete with a magical kitchen (sponsored by Frigidaire) that instantly prepares any number of gourmet meals at her command. Thus liberated from domestic chores, the housewife is free to go to the GM Motorama car show where she not only chooses a car but also tries on fabulous designer clothes, takes part in a "dance of tomorrow," embarks on a romantic tryst, and finally takes off on the "highway of tomorrow" with a handsome dreamboat escort in an even dreamier Firebird 2. Within this context of a consumer-oriented technological sublime, it is easy to see how Vice Presi-

Despite the futuristic kitchen, "his wife Jane" still does the cooking in *The Jetsons*.

dent Richard Nixon could have imagined America's future as one huge kitchen of tomorrow in the now famous Nixon-Khrushchev "kitchen debate" of 1959.

While the cold war era home of tomorrow clearly drew on previous notions of technologically-enhanced lifestyles, new electronic technologies also helped to change the dominant image of tomorrow's home. With the proliferation of television, satellites, and computers, the home of tomorrow was not simply a model of machine-enhanced efficiency; it additionally came to be imagined as a sentient space. In other words, while Fuller designed the home of tomorrow as a factory-engineered ship with a "service core," in the postwar era that core became a brain that could electronically anticipate the needs of its residents. In fact, the home of tomorrow had become so smart that most public transactions could be accomplished indoors. In the early 1950s, television promised to fulfill a much older utopian dream (found, for example, in Edward Bellamy's 1898 *Looking Backward*) of networking the home to a web of public services. Today, at the dawn of the twenty-first century, the "smart home" promises to incorporate an electronic picture of the world that is not just representational but increasingly interactive.

Indeed, since its inception, and especially after World War II, the home of tomorrow has functioned not simply as a sign of technical progress but also as model through which we understand our relationship to private and public spheres in a media-saturated, technology-driven world. Paradoxically, in this respect, the home of tomorrow functions most typically as a deeply conservative structure that promises a version of technological progress based on nostalgic longings for privacy, property, and propriety. The General Motors epigraph with which I began this essay attests to this conservative vision of the future, as the housewife from *Design for Dreaming* assures us that despite all the push-button pleasures of her magical kitchen and space-age car she "has a feeling some things won't change." More generally, the home of tomorrow has historically looked backward. After 1940, most popular versions of futuristic homes were actually traditional in design—recalling Tudor, Spanish, and colonial architecture rather than the futuristic structures built by the likes of Neutra or Fuller. Indeed, the International Style of modernist architects was often the target of populist attacks (in the early 1950s, *House Beautiful* equated modernist design with Naziism and communism in an article titled "A Threat to the Next America"[5]). From this point of view, modernism was carefully reconfigured for popular middle-class tastes, transformed from the starkly "strange" designs of modernist architects to a more watered-down notion of newness that the furniture industry called "contemporary" design.[6] As a style, contemporary signals something new that is nevertheless modeled on traditional values of comfort and bourgeois display in the well-appointed private home.

But it isn't just the home itself that appeals to a romanticized notion of traditional bourgeois domesticity. Instead, the home of tomorrow is an insular design that fails to imagine a future for the community. Indeed, the home of tomorrow has historically been imagined as a kind of fetish space that typically appears disembodied from the surrounding town and city. Images of futuristic homes—whether those produced by modernist/postmodernist architects or those produced in more popular venues—almost never picture any neighbors who might actually reside next door. Although futuristic cities such as Le Corbusier's famous "city of to-morrow"[7] plotted utopian schemes for housing communities, as a building type the home of tomorrow has most typically been imagined as a self-sufficient and sentient space that satisfies all the needs of its residents.[8] At best, its sense of community is reduced to an aesthetization of "landscape," as architects search for ways to make the modern home fit into the grounds (or, in urban areas, the cityscapes) around it. Even historical variations on the "glass house," which blurs boundaries between inside and outside worlds, are more often based on theoretical problems of voyeurism, exhibitionism, and surveillance than on questions about community and social relations.[9]

In client-built homes, the media itself often provides the epistemological ground on which a sense of community is delivered into residential space. Beatriz Colomina traces the mediated domestic environment back to the modernist designs of Le Corbusier and his penchant for thinking of the home (and especially the window) as a kind of movie camera/projection screen that provided views of the outside world.[10] In postwar America the idea of the "media house" had realized itself in the mass-produced suburb, as Levittown, New York, became the first such community to offer homes complete with a built-in television set. Today's "new" virtual homes take the built-in concept to an extreme. Takahide Nozawa's 1991 design for his TV Garden is a graveled living space that is enclosed on all sides by 245 television screens. This kind of intentional play between nature and media similarly informs the design for Elizabeth Diller and Ricardo Scofidio's Slow House. This Long Island, New York, vacation house includes a rear picture window that captures a view of the landscape. Meanwhile a video camera mounted above the house depicts the same landscape digitally and transmits it back to a monitor suspended before the picture window. It will even digitally transmit the view back to the main residence in the city. Describing the Slow House, Terence Riley claims it speaks to the architects' "implicit recognition of the duality of the real and the virtual, emphasizing their relationship to consumption and possession." [11]

Meanwhile, in more speculative projects, other architects are trying to build virtual homes that turn mundane aspects of daily life into fantastic encounters with virtual reality (VR) entities. For example, in an attempt to demonstrate the impact of new technologies on the private home, *House Beautiful* sponsored Gisue Hariri and Mojgan Hariri's Digital House Project, whose liquid crystal walls provide surfaces and devices that interact with residents. Among the amenities, the Digital House contains a virtual chef from a favorite restaurant, who pops up in the kitchen to give residents cooking advice. A computer generation away from the earlier kitchen of tomorrow, the virtual chef promises not only to

Hariri and Hariri's Digital House comes with a "virtual chef" that gives cooking tips and keeps lonely residents company. (Copyright, Hariri and Hariri)

help with chores but also to provide companionship. And just in case the chef isn't enough, the home also features digital guests who appear in the living room. Taking this virtual visit in the other direction, Michael Trudgeon and Anthony Kitchener's Hyper House Pavilion 5 transmits a programmed message to neighbors on its electrochromic glass walls. According to Riley, such homes become " 'smart skins' that blur the distinction between the computer and architecture and perform various functions to assist or enhance daily living." [12]

From a historical perspective, I would argue, these "smart skinned" homes of tomorrow develop fantasies about media, mobility, and domesticity that I've previously discussed in relation to the cultural fantasies surrounding domestic architecture and portable television in the 1960s. [13] Just as 1960s advertisers promised consumers that portable TV would allow them to imaginatively liberate themselves from the mundane world of family life while also remaining in the safe space of their homes, these "smart skinned" homes negotiate a dual impulse for domesticity on the one hand and the escape from it on the other. According to Hariri and

Hariri, "In the Digital House, the comfort, safety, and stability of home can coexist with the possibility of flight."[14] In this sense, the home of tomorrow allows residents to have it both ways. Nostalgic appeals to domestic comfort and stability exist alongside a futuristic fantasy of liberation and escape.

To be sure, these client-built homes for the rich are the product of a deeply "theoretical" play with boundaries between privacy and publicness. Their merger of nature and technology is often distinctly ironic. Given this, such homes depend on what Pierre Bourdieu calls a particular taste "habitus" associated with degrees of cultural and economic capital.[15] In other words, the home's imagined residents presumably share the architect's aesthete disposition toward daily life—a disposition that delights in ironic twists on form and function, the mediated and natural environment, the social and the virtual, work and leisure, servant and master, art and kitsch, and so many other binaries that have informed homes of the future in the past. Yet while the houses described above are clearly "art houses" intended for the rich, the future of domesticity is (as it was in the past) also on the minds of corporations that want to sell gadgets to more middle-class and middle-brow taste publics.

Mimicking the futuristic model homes at worlds fairs and theme parks, Microsoft has recently built a model home in Silicon Valley that it uses to promote its notion of a completely sentient living space. Straight out of a postwar science fiction novel (although without the dystopian edge), the house knows when you want coffee, when you need to change a lightbulb, and when your kids are sneaking TV in the middle of the night. In a CNBC news report on New Year's Day 2000, Microsoft invited viewers into its futuristic mansion for a special glimpse of things to come. Filled with high-end contemporary furniture, the home looks oddly ordinary despite its extraordinary powers. In fact, apart from its millennial visions, this microchip home bears a striking resemblance to one in a 1955 issue of *House Beautiful* that was wired for the TV age. That home promised parents the ability to survey every nook and cranny of domestic activity while cameras also peered into the surrounding street, just in case anything "unusual" came by.[16] In the Microsoft house, this same enforcement of the "usual," the "mundane," and the "routine" is, paradoxically, what new technology ultimately promises. The future is a place where nothing changes.

In his 1995 bestseller book, *The Road Ahead,* Microsoft guru Bill Gates describes his own dream house, which was then being built in Seattle, Washington. Written with the obvious intent to persuade the reader to adopt his version of the future, Gates's book outlines his plan for a high-tech home that once again turns out to be a curious blend of nostalgia for the past and fantastic visions of tomorrow. In his chapter, "Plugged in at Home," Gates boasts of the unparalleled wonders of his fully computer-controlled dream house. "First thing, as you come in," he writes, "you'll be presented with an electronic pin to clip onto your clothes. The pin will connect you up to the electronic services of the house."[17] These services include an elaborate home theater system, Internet hookups everywhere, and computerized systems for lighting, climate control, security, and so forth. Meanwhile, each room contains information screens that display on demand a digital archive of famous paintings, historical photographs, music, and other such "data." In the ultimate move toward portability, entertainment and information will follow residents around the house as they move from room to room. Yet, despite these high-tech schemes, Gates nevertheless attempts to conserve a vision of home from the baby boom past. He continually reminds us that his home is above all to be a private, comfortable, relaxing, and pleasant space for the family and their guests. The dual desires for pleasure and comfort, he adds, "aren't very different from those of people who could afford adventurous houses in the past."[18] Through such rhetoric, Gates familiarizes new technologies; he appeals to the average reader by showing how computers will provide continuity with, as opposed to radical departures from, previous domestic lifestyles.

Gates also harkens back to the pastoral ideal as a way to root his futuristic dreams in something more familiar. He writes, "Like almost anybody building a house, I want mine to be in harmony with the land it sits on."[19] He promises that his house is built not only of "silicon and software" but also of natural materials like "wood . . . and stone."[20] At one point, he even recalls his unsuccessful plan to hide his wall of twenty-four video monitors behind wood-grained patterns that flash on the screens. Speaking about the house that Gates describes in *The Road Ahead*, architect Adi Shamir Zion comments, "Srangely enough, as the electronic technology becomes less dimensional, the architecture expresses nostalgia, not for the authenticity of material per se but for the look and feel of the 'natural.'"[21] Further critiquing Gates's house, Zion reminds us that despite its array of new technologies, "the Gates house reverts back to the pre-modern house."[22] More specifically, Zion claims that Gates's view of technology as an unobtrusive servant and loyal companion has much in common with the way the master viewed the servant class in the English country house. In other words, Gates's nostalgic return to nature is marked by hierarchies of social position and class privilege.

But, it isn't just nature to which Gates returns. Instead, his house is also built in memory of the homes of prior twentieth-century industrialists. In fact, Gates compares his house to that of newspaper magnate William Randolph Hearst, who, he tells us, also dreamed of a home of tomorrow when he built his San Simeon castle in 1925. As Gates puts it, "the technological innovations I have in mind are not really so different in spirit from those Hearst wanted in his."[23] Thus, whether in the guise of nature boy or industrial magnate, Gates writes about his dream house through nostalgic appeals to the past. In the end, the "road ahead" looks more and more like the "road behind."

This mixture of nostalgia and futurism also runs through discourses on sentient machines designed for the high-tech home. Technocopia.com, the Web site for *Home Automation Times,* offers news of domestic technologies designed to provide creature comforts associated with the middle-class domesticity of the cold war past. One such advertised product is the CareBot, which is made by Gecko Systems. Although now only in its "Model T stage," Gecko promises that in the future this "personal servant" will vacuum your rug, water your plants, serve you a beer, and even follow "junior around, playing games with him, answering his questions . . . reminding him to stay out of places he's not supposed to go." Clearly hoping to attract aging baby boomers, Gecko even promises that if you purchase a second CareBot it can be a companion for Grandma. "It reminds her when to take her medicine," "monitors her heartbeat," and "calls her doctor if there is a problem."[24] Even more recently, the Massachusetts-based iRobot Corporation released plans to market the first off-the-shelf Internet telerobot at the cost of $3,500. Like the Care-Bot, iRobot can do numerous domestic chores. As *Wired* magazine recently reported, it can "pester your kids, check up on sick pets," and provide "senior care" for your parents.[25] Moreover, because iRobot can be controlled through the Internet, it is possible to do all this at a distance, while at work, or away on travel.

Despite their futuristic promises, the Carebot and iRobot sound like wish-fulfillments of boomer-generation science fiction, recalling at once such lovable (and laughable) household servants as *Forbidden Planet*'s Robbie the Robot, *The Jetsons*'s Rosie, and Robot in *Lost in Space*.[26] (In fact, the article in *Wired* even begins by reminding readers of *The Jetsons*'s futuristic maid.) At another level, these robots stand in for a nostalgic urge to restore forms of human nurturing to contemporary households in which single moms, single dads, or two working parents simply don't have time to be full-time caretakers. They even alleviate the boomer generation's collective guilt about their aging parents (albeit replacing love with surveillance). These robots, in other words, are computer-powered versions of an *imaginary* 1950s housewife. They simulate the role of a full-time mother who lives in a suburban dream house and who looks after everyone's needs. Once again, the home of the future is a wish fulfillment of some idealized past.

This sense of a future without change is the reigning paradox at the heart of our contemporary high-tech world.[27] Speaking of postwar science fiction, Fredric Jameson claimed that the genre is no longer able to imagine utopia, but rather can only serve to "defamiliarize" the present.[28] The more instrumental promotional discourses of high-tech companies take this one step further, promising us that utopia is in fact that which is completely familiar, a constant procession of the digitally enhanced "same." Meanwhile, recent Hollywood films have deployed this strange mix of nostalgia and futurism in science fiction narratives that serve to reinforce this notion of a future without change. I am thinking especially of films like *The Truman Show, Pleasantville,* and (although somewhat differently) *The Matrix,* all of which revolve around issues of electronic media culture and its relationship to our contemporary sense of home, family, and social space. While all of these films present themselves as "critical dystopias" (or at least wary of the commodified futures of what William Gibson called the "Gernsback Continuum"[29]), they wind up not simply critiquing media and commodity culture, but also valorizing a nostalgic longing for the "real," which winds up being the white patriarchal "real" of the cold war past.

For example, Paramount's 1998 summer blockbuster *The Truman Show* announces itself as a biting critique of mass-produced suburbs and television. Directed by Peter Weir, with original music by Philip Glass, the film positions itself as an intellectual/art film that (in the tradition of the anti-Hollywood Hollywood movie) promises to attack tinsel town while still bringing in high box-office returns.[30] Set in contemporary America,

Truman Burbank is trapped in a false TV utopia with his dissimulating "retro" wife in *The Truman Show*.

The Truman Show nevertheless has a retro look, especially because it was partially shot on location in Seaside, Florida, a "new urban" planned community that on film looks like dreamland suburbia circa 1955.[31] Drawing on the literary convention of the false utopia, the film presents its lead character Truman Burbank (Jim Carrey) as a boyishly innocent, aging gen-Xer who has been manipulated by television—beyond his wildest imagination. Unbeknownst to Truman, his entire life, from birth to the present, has been produced and orchestrated by an evil TV producer, who presents "The Truman Show" nonstop, twenty-four hours a day on his money-grubbing global network. Truman's wife and his mother (who act like they are straight out of the 1950s), and even his long-lost and much-idealized college girlfriend, turn out to be cast members in the never-ending soap opera that is his life. Meanwhile, his tidy—and dazzlingly colorful—seaside community is an elaborate stage that is set inside a giant dome-shaped TV studio somewhere in Hollywood. Every time Truman tries to leave the town, he is stopped by a slew of narrative devices, including womanly wiles (his actress/wife seduces him into the bedroom), special effects (bad weather, fire), and brute force (hunting dogs, hired thugs). As the film goes on, Truman discovers that his doting wife and his mother are in reality evil manipulators working in cahoots with the

TV producer and are bent on hiding him from the truth of his made-for-TV life. Desperate to liberate himself from his existence, Truman dares to escape from the TV studio/town and reunite with his "college girlfriend" (who was fired from the show when she fell in true love with Truman and tried to fight the evil producer). Finally able to escape from his torturous TV-land, Truman enters the "real" world of Hollywood (and, given this ending, the film leaves open the ironic possibility that there is no exit from media culture after all).

In all of these ways, *The Truman Show* uses futuristic themes to present suburbia, TV, and women as interrelated forces of evil that collectively enslave Truman. In the process, the film inverts and considerably rewrites history. While the postwar suburb has historically been a racist and sexist living space that has been most oppressive for people of color and women in general, *The Truman Show* miraculously changes the terms of victimization. Now it is white men who suffer most from postwar suburbia and its electronic companion, television. In the end, the film returns to the misogynist trope of "momism," a popular term first coined in the 1940s by Philip Wylie, who saw women as part of a vast conspiracy to enslave and "emasculate" men. (And, as I have previously discussed, Wylie thought women were in cahoots with corporations, including broadcast companies, and that together they planned to annihilate masculinity by turning real men into henpecked "sissies.")[32] Moreover, in line with century-old notions of "true womanhood," the film retrieves a positive depiction of femininity, but only insofar as the good woman (here embodied by the college-girlfriend cast member who quits the show in protest) sacrifices her own self and her own acting career for the love of a man. Thus, although *The Truman Show* presents itself as a critique of commodity futurism, it winds up being more like a cold war era, liberal humanist plea for "man's liberation" from the deadening forces of coporatization, suburbs, women, and technology. (This plea also informs such 1950s sociological studies as *The Organization Man*, popular exposés like *The Crack in the Picture Window* and *The Split Level Trap*, humorous novels like *Mr. Blandings Builds His Dream House*, low-budget 1950s films such as *The Incredible Shrinking Man* and *The Invasion of the Body Snatchers*, and, perhaps more arguably, even the "new wave" science fiction of Philip K. Dick, whose *Time Out of Joint* presents a man caught in the false utopia of a 1950s mundane suburban home and who, in the end, discovers that suburbia is a hallucinatory memory trace of the cold war past that was dreamed up by a totalitarian government sometime in the postapocalyptic future.)

Fox's 1998 digital extravaganza *Pleasantville* is similarly about "man's liberation." Released a few months after *The Truman Show,* this film also offers itself as a critique of media culture and the suburbs, especially as they were imagined in the 1950s. The film begins in a contemporary American high school classroom, showing kids who have no future and expect even less. As one of these generation-Y classmates, the hero David (Tobey Maguire) turns out to have an equally depressing family life. He and his "valley girl" sister Jennifer (Reese Witherspoon) live in a broken family and have an estranged relationship with their single working mom. As an effect of this, David suffers from a state of arrested development. He's too shy to date girls, and instead spends his nights as a TV junkie who is obsessed with the fifties sitcom *Pleasantville.* The film establishes this TV as compensatory reality scenario in forcefully didactic terms; an early scene intercuts shots of David half-listening to his nagging mother with shots of the televised images of the 1950s sitcom family that David watches with fond absorption. In fact, David is so infatuated with the TV world of *Pleasantville* that, with the aid of a magical remote control and a "cosmic" TV repairman (played by cult sitcom favorite Don Knotts), he zaps himself and his sister into the black-and-white world of old TV. Now living their lives in Pleasantville, David and Jennifer find themselves in a nuclear family with a gray-toned mom and dad who are even less imaginative than Ozzie and Harriet Nelson.

Like *The Truman Show, Pleasantville* reveals the idealized world of television to be a false utopia that the hero must escape. Trapped in his TV sitcom prison, David spends the rest of the film fighting against his conformist—and bigoted—suburban neighbors. Increasingly over the course of the film, the sitcom characters begin to defect from the deadening black-and-white suburban trap of Pleasantville, instead finding love, passion, art, intellect, and sex. Those lucky enough to do so shed their gray-toned skins to emerge in full and vibrant color. But they pay a price. Afraid of the "colored" people, the gray-toned townsfolk strategize to purge them from Pleasantville. Meanwhile, David's formerly repressed sitcom mom has fallen in love with the local soda jerk and therefore has turned from a pale gray to a vibrantly colored woman. Making matters worse, her soda-jerk boyfriend is a closet artist whose colorful paintings and skin

Sitcom-junkie David is trapped in the TV time warp of *Pleasantville*.

also make him a target of the townsfolk. And finally, David himself finds true romance with a girl who also turns to color. As a result, David has to protect his mother, her boyfriend, and his girlfriend from the angry mob out to stone them. In the film's most extravagant set piece, David rushes to the soda store where the townsfolk throw rocks through the store's plate-glass windows. Huge colorful canvases—including a portrait of his mother—come crashing down. In the process of his heroic rescue, he bonds with his fifties mother, turns from gray skin tones to colored ones, and shields his girlfriend from the mob. Then, in a final climatic courtroom scene, David delivers a heroic defense of the town's colored people, finally convincing the gray-toned mob of their repressive ways. In a moment of harmonious resolution, everyone in the courtroom—including the most vicious conservative judge—turns from gray to color, so that everyone is now rendered the same. Thus having saved Pleasantville from its repressive past, David is finally able to escape from the sitcom world and return to his real-life nineties mom (with whom he is then able to bond).

Through these and other plot contortions the film enacts a series of reversals regarding both gender and race. Rather than escaping into a different future, the male hero instead fulfills his nostalgic longing for a "real" fifties-era full-time mom, while also rescuing her from the sexual repression of the suburban middle-class past. By bonding with his now fully sexualized full-time fifties mother, he is able first to experience his own sexuality and then to reconcile with his divorced, working mom in the present. A twist on the time-loop paradox of *Back to the Future* (1985), *Pleasantville* thus allows for a powerful Oedipal fantasy in which the boy witnesses the scene of his mother's sexual desire and then is able to give birth (or at least rebirth) to his own narcissistic ego. Meanwhile, his sister Jennifer sheds her oversexed, plastic, "valley girl" ways and develops into an intellectual, complete with nerdy glasses. She decides to stay in the fifties, where, we are somehow supposed to believe, women had more and better choices for self-actualization. (Jennifer's choice might also be read ironically as the film's final comment about the "no-future" state of teens in the 1990s. But even if read in this fashion, the film clearly resorts to a regressive solution.) Most strikingly in all of this, the white boy somehow emerges as the central hero in a story of women's liberation—rescuing his mom, sister, and girlfriend from the sexual repression and "occupation housewife" role of the 1950s past. *Pleasantville* thus restages women's liberation as a generational revolution in which young, white, "no-future" boys of the 1990s can retrace their pain in their mothers' suffering, magically restore the wrongs of the past, and rewrite their own future in the present.

Pleasantville also presents a not-too-veiled critique of 1950s suburban racism, but even here the critical edge is blunted by nostalgia. The film rewrites the history of suburban exclusion so that somehow the white boy and his white loved ones become the victims of prejudiced townsfolk who judge people on the color of their skin. It achieves this reversal by equating skin tone with sexual, emotional, and artistic repression. In other words, while *Pleasantville* uses skin color as the marker for prejudice, the actual history of racism and its institutional mechanisms is elided in favor of a pop-psychology lesson about sexual and creative repression. Indeed, by associating skin color with repression, the film becomes a textbook case of the racial dynamics of what Richard Dyer calls "white." [33] As Dyer suggests in his analysis of modern Western visual culture, if color signifies race then as the absence of color white has historically signified the absence of race. While this "unraced" status gives whites a sense of natural superiority—of neutrality and ordinariness—whiteness nevertheless also often signifies a sense of emptiness, a lack of passion, sexual repression and reproductive failure (as in the science fiction figure of the android), and even death (as in the horror film's zombie or vampire). Accordingly, Hollywood has often depicted color—and people of color—as the exotic "other" of white repression; color is that which whites desire but also must ultimately restrain. It is almost as if the screenwriters for *Pleasantville* read Dyer's work and then proceeded symptomatically—and even pathologically—to enact all the critical points he makes. By equating skin color with sexual, emotional, and artistic repression, the film is able to conclude that we can all indeed get along if everyone just gets in touch with their passions and lets it all hang out. Accordingly, *Pleasantville* achieves its happy ending by having David lead the townsfolk in a collective liberation of desire, which is visually depicted in the final courtroom scene as a collective colorization of their skin tone. Everyone in Pleasantville turns from a dingy gray to a variation on Crayola's "flesh." Ironically, then, while the film initially condemns the suburban sitcom universe for its inability to tolerate difference, it achieves closure by resorting to an image of community in which everyone is rendered exactly the same.

In the end, *Pleasantville* has science fiction both ways. On the one hand, it presents a popular critique of suburbia, television, and the repressive aspects of the 1950s family ideal; on the other—like *The Truman Show*—it does so in the service of depicting the white male hero as the ultimate victim of suburbs, women, and media culture. Moreover, in this case, it unites that message with the even more troubling proposition that it is white people who suffered most from suburban bigotry, and white men who somehow rescued us most heroically from the racist past.

While *The Truman Show* and *Pleasantville* use futuristic themes to rewrite the cold war past, Warner Bros.' 1999 release *The Matrix* presents a similar "male liberation" story about the digital, VR future. At first glance, the film seems to be part of the cyberpunk movement; even its title is derived from William Gibson's *Neuromancer* and the matrix he envisioned. In fact, in an early scene in the film the hero is shown with a copy of *Simulacra and Simulations* (which appropriately turns out to be a false cover for a hollowed-out book that contains the underground VR programs he sells). But, as the film progresses, its cyberpunk aura also turns out to be a false cover for a moral universe that has little in common with Gibsonesque cyberethics. Although, for example, *Neuromancer*'s hero (Case) is representative of a brand of cyborg subjectivity that thrives on being "plugged in" to the VR world, the hero in *Matrix* (Neo) is much more derived from liberal humanist science fiction as well as from humanist rejections of technology that pit "man against machines." Accordingly, the film revolves around a dystopian nightmare in which machines evolve into sentient beings and enslave all humans in a computer-generated reality. The machines plug humans into an intricately orchestrated virtual city, so real in fact that most people don't know there is a "natural" world outside. Instead, humans live in a semicomatose state, plugged into the matrix, while the sentient machines feed on them as an energy source.

The action of the film revolves around a kind of double rescue narrative. The film opens with "computerese" code messages filling the screen, as a female voice says, "Morpheus believes he is the one." The voice turns out to belong to a group of underground survivalists who rescue Neo (Keanu Reeves) from the matrix. Again, as with *The Truman Show* and *Pleasantville,* the film promises progressive themes because two strong female "warriors" and an African American man are the central characters in the rescue mission. In an early scene, Morpheus (Laurence Fishburne) informs Neo of their common struggle. He says, "You are a slave, Neo. Like everyone else you were born into bondage, born into a prison that you cannot smell or taste or touch. A prison for your mind." Like so much cold war era science fiction, this scene displaces race conflicts onto a war between man and machine, and in the process suggests that humanity is somehow united in its humanness. Assuming that the audience can actually believe that Keanu Reeves is a slave and that Laurence Fishburne can really say this with a straight face, the film then proceeds to reconfigure its white hero as the central protagonist in the "rescue" mission.

The rescue begins when Morpheus offers Neo a pill that transmits him (or, more accurately, his electronic nerve signal) through the telephone lines. Neo is thereby transported through the matrix into the world of machines. From there, he undergoes a rebirth, literally traveling through a water-filled canal and reemerging in Morpheus's hovercraft (a pirate ship from which he wages war on the machines). In the next scene, we learn that Morpheus has rescued Neo because he thinks Neo will be their savior. Sitting in a simulated "programmed" space that is composed of two stuffed chairs and an old TV set, Morpheus shows Neo how the machines took over. As images of Armageddon flash like reruns on the TV screen, Morpheus tells Neo, "As long as the Matrix exists the human race will never be free. After he [the savior] died the oracle prophesized his return and that his coming would hail the destruction of the matrix, end the war, bring freedom to our people." From there on, Neo is positioned as a Christ figure (albeit one with a great fashion sense). Meanwhile, Morpheus becomes his mentor, teaching him how to use his body and mind against the machines. In this way, the black man willingly names the savior as a white man. Complete with a Judas figure (a shipmate named Cypher), the story of the second coming ends with Neo triumphing over the machines, saving Morpheus (who is later called the "father"), and then taking his place as the savior of the human race.

The story also returns the action heroines back to their proper place. Switch (who is coded throughout the film as "butch") is killed, making way for Trinity (whose name is obviously in keeping with the religious theme) to form a couple with Neo. The machines collapse, choral music comes to a crescendo, Trinity and Neo kiss, and then in perfect classical symmetry the film ends where it began, with the "computerese" of the matrix. Going through the wires one more time, Neo returns to the virtual city to inform humans of the truth. As he delivers himself through the signal, he says, "I know that you're afraid. You're afraid of us. You're afraid of change. I don't know the future. I didn't come here to tell you how this is going to end. I am here to tell you how it's going to begin."

While the more cynical among us might see this open ending simply as a Hollywood strategy for a sequel, it also makes the white man the narrator of a creation myth, a position that Neo usurps from Trinity (who was the off-screen voice at the beginning of the film) and Morpheus (who narrated the story of Armageddon early on). In this way, not only the story but also the film's "ontological voice" is increasingly relayed from women and African Americans back to the authorial agency of the white hero. And note that during the film the question of who is telling the story of the future is key to the film's narrative structure. In one scene, a character known as the Oracle is given special power to predict whether or not Neo is really the savior. Hence, this character functions narratologically as a "predictor" of plot outcomes. Not coincidentally, I think, the Oracle is an African American woman who is depicted as a middle-aged housewife type who bakes cookies while she does her "black magic." In other words, the Oracle is aligned with femininity, domesticity, Africa, spiritualism, and the past, while Neo is aligned with masculinity, the postindustrial Western city, computers, and the future. In the end, we find the Oracle's predictions are only partially right, so that she is not a trustworthy nar-

Trapped and in love in *The Matrix*.

rator. Instead, Neo emerges as the white male voice of wisdom who, as in the biblical epic more generally, is the narrator of the "greatest story ever told."

On the positive side, films like *The Truman Show, Pleasantville,* and *The Matrix* do at least provoke audiences to think about sexism, racism, and multiculturalism, and they also ask us to consider our social relationships in a media-saturated, often alienating world. And to be fair, it is also true that all three stories encase their "male liberation" enlightenment fictions within a more secular irony that often negates the very message they seem to drive home. Just as *The Truman Show* ends paradoxically by depicting the "real" world to be Hollywood, California, *The Matrix*'s "heavy-handed" Christian metaphors are undercut by its playful "quoting" of Hong Kong action cinema and its self-reflexive "graphic comic book" feel that also serves as a coda for its "knock-em-out" ending. In the last shot, Neo appears in a phone booth, puts on his shades, and flies off like a cybernetic "black knight" Superman as Rage Against the Machine comes up full blast on the soundtrack. In this respect, my criticisms of the films

are not proposed simply in the spirit of hating Hollywood, nor am I suggesting that intellectuals have a special purchase on critical distance from
myth. Instead, my criticisms have to do with the way the films rewrite the
history of gender and race relations to inscribe white heroes as victims
of sexism and racial genocide and as central protagonists in the story of
women's liberation and Civil Rights. In this way, these fantastic visions
assure white men that they are still going to be the central subjects of
history, and that the basic paradigms of postwar patriarchy will be maintained no matter what else may happen. Meanwhile, the films' narrative
fascination with the mundane world of television and the emerging universe of computer-generated images revitalizes a century-old "male liberation" myth that consistently produces white men as both victims and
saviors of a technological nightmare and a media-saturated "inauthentic"
world. In the process, "reality" is restored, but only insofar as the "real"
contains a white man at its visionary core.

As with any particular texts of popular culture, these films should be
seen in relation to the wider social and discursive context in which they
take place. That context is comprised of a changing sexual division of
labor, of diasporic and multicultural populations, and of an increasingly
global culture. While cultural forms are obviously not direct reflections
of social relations, and while genre films are often about their own textu-
ality and generic histories, I think it would be foolish not to consider the
links between the fictional imagination and the social relations in which
these fictions circulate. One of the prime reasons we should consider the
links between popular culture and social forces is that the fantasies promoted in popular texts often become the material basis on which corporations such as Intel, Microsoft, and Sony—and even government organizations such as NASA—promote the future. As Constance Penley shows
in *NASA/TREK*, popular fiction and scientific engineering are intricately
"slashed" together in late capitalism.[34] Scientists, researchers, and corporate executives often get their ideas from popular fiction, and vice-versa.
A most striking example comes from my own university, which recently
joined forces with the military in an effort to make new VR training programs for soldiers. One of the people who attends the committee meetings
on this project told me that when a dean asked what the army wanted
from the university, the military representative said, "I want the Holi-
deck."

In the context of everyday technologies, we might similarly consider the reciprocity between fiction, science, corporate promotion, and, finally, our lived relations to all three. Today our discursive field is replete with predications about everyday life in the digital age of telecommunications. The home of tomorrow, with its promise of instant familiarity and sentient knowledge of all of our needs, should be seen in relation to the widespread cultural anxieties expressed in films and other popular media. Whether through the corporate discourse of prediction, or through fantastic Hollywood fictions, the promise of a future without change allows us to imagine tomorrow in ways that stave off the threat of difference in the present. Tomorrow's home—and the future more generally—turns out to be a digitally perfected version of a modern utopia, a future never realized, but now twice lived—at least within the cultural imagination.

Finding an alternate future is always a tricky problem. Prediction presupposes that people all have the same political stakes in creating new myths and new worlds. It presupposes as well that industrial giants like Intel and their own instrumental predictions for a technological future won't in any way affect our "pure" radical visions for a better world. Perhaps Donna Haraway said it best when she laid out her "ironic myth" of the cyborg—a myth that, I think, too many people have forgotten was posed precisely in the spirit of "irony." [35] Indeed, when Haraway said, "I would rather be a cyborg than a goddess," she was weighing two problematic icons for women, and deciding finally that by identifying with cyborgs we might get ourselves out of the Judeo-Christian myths that always lead women back to the Garden, back to nature, back to Trinity and Neo's final kiss, and away from our social relationships, which are intricately informed by our use of technology. The ironic playfulness of Haraway's "Cyborg Manifesto" has too literally become dogma. And, given her deconstruction of all binary oppositions as the basis of myth, it is no small irony that most discussions of new technologies return to a kind of either/or absolutism, one that embraces anything new, the other that reviles it.

Indeed, today, instead of irony we seem to be faced with two rather absurdly incompatible ethical mythologies on the technological future. As Kevin Robbins argues, one of these delights in the VR future to such an extent that it forgets that there is still a social reality that requires serious contemplation. As he suggests, too many VR enthusiasts think that we will somehow magically escape our bodies and (like the hero in *Quantum Leap*) take on new identities at will. He traces this brand of technological

utopianism not only in poststructuralist theories of VR and cyborg subjectivity, but also in more pragmatic thinkers such as Harold Rheingold,
who see VR as a possible new form of democratic community that can
counteract alienation in the real world. Robbins astutely points out that
even this more pragmatic view of cyberspace tends to pose it as a substitute for a degraded public sphere, rather than as a constructive solution to
real-world problems. Comparing cyberspace to Baudrillard's "synthetic
world" of Disneyland, Robbins argues:

> We might see virtual and network associations in the same light.
> There is the invocation of community, but not the production of
> society. There is 'groupmind,' but not social encounter. There is on-
> line communion, but there are no residents of hyperspace. This is
> another synthetic world, and here, too, history is frozen. What we
> have is the preservation through simulation of old forms of solidarity
> and community. In the end, not an alternative society, but an alter-
> native to society.[36]

This last point is especially important because with it Robbins highlights
the way present-day VR enthusiasts tend to recycle "age old" dreams of
utopian collectivity, rather than to imagine new social formations that
actually promote positive change. Along these lines, following Gerard
Raulet, he further argues that our current invocations of utopia through
cyberspace are rooted in a romantic dream of immediacy, transparency,
copresence, and commonality, which is to say a dream that denies difference and struggle in the social world. Critiquing cybervisionaries such as
Jaron Lanier, Timothy Leary, Brenda Laurel, and Michael Benedikt, Robbins challenges their "age old" dreams of transcendence, commonality,
and transparent identification with make-believe others. Instead, he asks
us to rethink the virtual world by considering it in terms of the "uses of
disorder" proposed by Richard Sennett in his discussion of urban life. Following Sennett, Robbins claims that a social system is viable only if it can
tolerate disorder, uncertainty, and even a level of fear. Thus, rather than
building a VR version of the bland, orderly "neutralized city" of Disneyland, Robbins argues that we need to conceptualize VR's possible worlds
by starting from the real-world social conflicts around us. "We must rec-
ognise that difference, asymmetry and conflict are constitutive features
of that world. Not community."[37] In the end, then, Robbins advocates a
sense of VR sociality based on a democratic working out of present-day

social antagonisms, rather than a nostalgic return to a utopian dream of collective sameness and commonsense.

If, as Robbins argues, the VR utopians simplistically imagine a utopian world of common interests, then conversely there is a second group of hasty thinkers who might be called the technological curmudgeons. The curmudgeons resort to the man versus machine logic of humanist myths about technology out of control. They reject cyberculture through everything from smug dismissiveness ("you are just reinventing the wheel") to hackneyed brands of phobic cultural conservatism ("our kids will be turned into sex-fiend maniacs"; "Big Brother will watch us"; and other exaggerated fears previously applied to novels, film, radio, music, comic books, and television). Although, of course, new technologies pose new social and cultural challenges, the curmudgeon's response is no more useful than the utopian's romantic immersion in a VR future. Somewhere between utopia and Armageddon lies something more material, more social, more concrete, which might be called the present.

The present is, of course, a notoriously difficult place to understand. In our contemporary world, the considerable confusion we feel about our own present gives way to two increasingly divergent analytical paths—history on the one hand, and prediction on the other. In the current intellectual climate there exists a kind of disconnection between the two. There are those people who call themselves historians of technologies, and those who position themselves as the new technology gurus. While the two types sometimes meet at conferences, the terms of engagement are typically only superficial. The historians (like me) get carted out to present colorful anecdotes about 1950s housewives decorating their TV sets or nineteenth-century kooks using x-rays to mutilate their hands, and that is usually the end of that. Meanwhile, the future is narrated by the new-technology crowd, many of whom are so steeped in enlightenment notions of "progress" and romantic dreams of community and transcendence on the Net that history seems only a dead weight bogging utopia down. Thinking about nostalgia and futurism as flip sides of the same coin might be one way of overcoming this unfortunate disconnection between the historians and the visionaries. It might also help both camps to understand the present moment, about which (whether we think so or not) we both ultimately speak. For, as Jameson suggests, science fiction and history are both representations of a present condition, they both tell us something about who we are now, where we want to go, and how we conceptualize the ways we got there.[38] Moreover, history and science fiction share the common project of "defamiliarizing" the present in ways that can open it up for change. It is in this spirit that I time-travel back through the media culture of postwar America. I'm hoping to find escape routes in the mediated past through which we might exit—not into some liberation myth of an enlightenment future, but rather back to the present where we might actually make a difference.

Notes

All transcriptions are my own.

1 Email from Mike S. Chartier to Lynn Spigel, 26 April 1999.

2 Brian Horrigan, "The Home of Tomorrow, 1927–1945," in *Imagining Tomorrow, History, Technology, and the American Future*, ed. Joseph J. Corn (Cambridge: MIT Press, 1986), p. 157.

3 First displayed at the New York World's Fair in 1964, the Carrousel of Progress became a central fixture in Disneyland in 1967. It replaced the earlier Monsanto Home of Tomorrow (a kind of futuristic structure built by MIT and poised at the gateway to Tomorrowland). The exhibit originally featured thirty-two Audio-Animatronics figures who sang "There's a Great Big Beautiful Tommorow," and demonstrated how the American family has benefited from electricity and appliances over the course of the twentieth century.

4 Designed by MIT, the Monsanto Home of Tomorrow stood at the gateway of Tomorrowland and resembled some kind of Martian vegetation, with huge window walls flanking out of its wings. In addition to its futuristic kitchen, it contained a slew of then high-tech machines, including push-button phones and lighting panels.

5 Elizabeth Gordon, "A Threat to the Next America," *House Beautiful*, April 1953.

6 In the 1950s, the furniture trade journal *Home Furnishings* was a forum for debates about the public response to modernism. The journal took a conservative attitude toward modernism, establishing a canon of contemporary design that was a softened version of the designs offered by modernist furnituremakers. Indeed, despite the fact that the 1950s saw various efforts to mainstream modern design (as was the case with MOMA's "Good Design" show), the popular response to modern design—in houses and in furniture—was often laced with skepticism.

7 Le Corbusier, *The City of To-Morrow and Its Planning* (New York: Payson and Clark, 1929). Le Corbusier's community ideal was one of individual "freedom through order." However, servants still labored in the homes of his ideal city. Note too that although Le Corbusier spoke of ideals of collectivity, it is debatable whether he actually strove to implement socialist political ideologies.

8 I am distinguishing the "home of tomorrow"—as an autonomous space of sentient technology—from utopian housing designs that have dealt with questions

of community and socialist living arrangements. Note that early on, social critics such as Lewis Mumford promoted ideals of community and criticized the more consumerist models of futuristic homes. See, for example, his "The Flaw in the Mechanical House," *New Republic* 67 (June 1931): 65–66. In the United States, this more community-oriented spirit manifest itself in New Deal housing programs, especially the Greenbelt Town Program. See Joseph L. Arnold, *The New Deal in the Suburbs: A History of the Greenbelt Town Program, 1933–1954* (Columbus: Ohio University Press, 1971); and Paul L. Conkin, *Tomorrow a New World: The New Deal Community Programs* (Ithaca, N.Y.: Cornell University Press, 1959). For more on issues of community with respect to feminist critique and design, see Delores Hayden, *The Grand Domestic Revolution* (Cambridge: MIT Press, 1981); and *Redesigning the American Dream: The Future of Housing, Work, and Family Life* (New York: Norton, 1984).

9 An interesting, if still problematic, exception to this is Michael Bell's as yet unbuilt Glass House @ 2° which was designed for a site in a low-income area in Houston's Fifth Ward. The house is designed to the specifications of a federally sponsored experimental housing program wherein money previously available for multifamily units would be granted in vouchers for the construction of private homes. As Terence Riley argues, the fact that Bell designed a glass house for a low-income neighborhood "intentionally underscores many of the ambiguities associated with this historically charged architectural type, which is typically identified with a certain level of sophisticated luxury." While glass homes have often been attacked for their assault on privacy, Bell asks, "Why should an invisible group of people choose to live behind walls rather than reveal their lives?" Despite the seemingly egalitarian impulse, it seems to me, this glass house for the poor has some obvious drawbacks, especially for its imagined occupants. Exhibiting poverty is not the same as exhibiting luxury, particularly when the people inside are more likely to be surveyed by everyone—from urban ethnographers to police—than are the upper classes. For a description of the house, see Terence Riley, *The Un-private House*, exhibition catalog for "The Un-private House" (New York: Museum of Modern Art, 1999), p. 64. For more on issues of voyeurism and exhibitionism in architecture, see Beatriz Colomina, *Privacy and Publicity: Modern Architecture as Mass Media* (Cambridge: MIT Press, 1996).

10 Beatriz Colomina, *Privacy and Publicity*. See also Beatriz Colomina, "The Media House," *Assemblage* 27 (1995): 55–66. Note that Colomina's main argument is not only about media in the house, but more centrally that the modern house has primarily been imagined through media (drawings, photography, magazines, ads, exhibitions, museum display, films, and now computers and VR).

11 Riley, *The Un-private House*, pp. 12–13.

12 Ibid., p. 13.

13 See my "Portable TV: Studies in Domestic Space Travels," this volume.

14 Cited in Riley, *The Un-private House*, p. 56.

15 Pierre Bourdieu, *Distinction: A Social Critique of the Judgment of Taste*, trans. Richard Nice (Cambridge: Harvard University Press, 1984).

16 *House Beautiful,* March 1955, p. 23.

17 Bill Gates, *The Road Ahead* (New York: Penguin, 1995), p. 250.

18 Ibid., 248.

19 Ibid., p. 247.

20 Ibid., p. 247.

21 Adi Shamir Zion, "New Modern: Architecture in the Age of Digital Technology," *Assemblage* 35 (1998): 67.

22 Ibid., p. 72.

23 Gates, *The Road Ahead,* p. 278. Ironically, given Gates's reputation, he distinguishes his house from Hearst's by calling Hearst Castle a "monument to excess," p. 248. In fact, throughout the chapter even while he is describing a mansion of untold costs, Gates continually takes a populist pose, speaking directly to the reader and implying that one day everyone can own this kind of home (at least if they purchase Microsoft products).

24 For a description of the CareBot, see Hillary Rettig, "Is There a Robot in Your Family's Future?" posted on the Web site Technocopia.com, 1999. Another notable development in robotics is Sony's AIBO, a sentient "entertainment robot" dog who, according to the Sony brochure, is capable of feeling "joy, sadness, anger, surprise, fear, and discontent." It can also exhibit a more complex range of emotions that its master/owner programs it to feel, and it comes with an AIBO performer kit and graphical user interface that enables the owner to train the dog to perform tricks. Since May 1999, in its initial six months on the U.S. and Japanese markets, AIBO sold out, so that Sony has now launched a new special edition, AIBO ERS-111. Currently, Sony has produced just ten thousand of these special edition dogs and is marketing them via the Internet and telephone in the United States, Japan, and Europe. See www.world.sony.com/aibo.

25 Erik Davis, "Telefriend: Meet iRobot, the Smartest Webcam on Wheels," *Wired,* September 2000, p. 274.

26 Perhaps, however, a more apt prototype would be the robot in Philip K. Dick's short story of 1952, "Nanny," in *The Book of Philip K. Dick* (New York: Daws Books, 1973), pp. 7–24. In this story Dick tells of a seemingly benevolent robot/ governess who is adored by the children in her charge. Unfortunately, the nanny turns out to be a war machine who is programmed not only for housekeeping but also for combat. Unable to repress her killing instincts, she sneaks out at night to fight the other nanny robots in the neighborhood. When she is destroyed by a bigger nanny robot, the children are inconsolable. Their father's only recourse is to buy a bigger, meaner, more expensive nanny who can better defend herself. Although Dick's tale was obviously fantastic, the sinister mix of domesticity and militarism that Dick envisioned is not too far off from the (artificial) life histories of the new domestic robots. For example, iRobot evolved largely from military urban-warfare robots, and the iRobot company went on to produce Hasbro's animatronic toy, My Real Baby Doll. Perhaps it is this mix of military warfare and innocent domesticity that makes such robots seem so uncanny.

27 A famous example of this paradox is Disneyland's Tomorrowland, whose future

is constantly in need of renewal. In 1959 and 1967, Disney refurbished this section of the park, adding elements that would update the obsolete future. Most recently in the 1990s, Disney has revamped this section of the park, tearing down portions of the cold war era tomorrow. Nevertheless, as a concept this new Tomorrowland functions less as a new future than a nostalgic memory of faith in the scientific future circa 1960. Clearly out of date with developments in the genre of science fiction (Disney, after all, can't really be the "happiest place on earth" if it admits the dystopian edge of contemporary cyberpunk fiction), Tomorrowland is an odd mix of new technologies and old utopian themes. So, too, in order to stave off the problem of an outdated future, Orlando's Disney World Tomorrowland (unveiled in 1995) is a retro-future that harkens back to the 1939 World's Fair future. This future is intentionally designed to be "kitsch" and fun. Finally, Euro-Disney built its Tomorrowland as a historical tribute to the "original" modern future imagined by Jules Verne and H. G. Wells at the end of the nineteenth century. For more on this, see Karal Ann Marling, ed., *Designing Disney's Theme Parks: The Architecture of Reassurance* (Montreal: Canadian Centre for Architecture, 1997), p. 140. On this topic, I am also indebted to Liza Trevino for her interesting examination of Tomorrowland in my science fiction seminar.

28 Fredric Jameson, "Progress versus Utopia; or, Can We Imagine the Future?" *Science-Fiction Studies* 9:27 (July 1982): 147–58.

29 William Gibson, "The Gernsback Continuum," in *Mirrorshades: The Cyberpunk Anthology*, ed. Bruce Sterling (New York: Arbor House, 1986), pp. 1–11.

30 Along these lines, it may be interesting to note that a few months before the film's release, a publicity person at Paramount phoned me and asked if I could give her names of scholars who study TV. She specifically said that she didn't want popular journalists' names, but serious scholars who might be able to give her ideas about TV, especially insofar as its impact on family life was concerned. She was also interested in having scholars comment on the film, and asked if I might let her prescreen the film to my students to see what they would think.

31 There is one major—and probably intentionally ironic—historical revision: the town includes a multicultural cast of middle-class neighbors.

32 Philip Wylie, *Generation of Vipers* (New York: Holt, Rinehart and Winston, 1941).

33 Richard Dyer, *White* (London: Routledge, 1997); see also his essay, "White," *Screen* 29 (fall 1988): 44–64.

34 Constance Penley, *NASA/TREK: Popular Science and Sex in America* (London: Verso, 1997).

35 Donna J. Haraway, "Manifesto for Cyborgs: Science, Technology, and Socialist Feminism in the 1980s," *Socialist Review* 80 (1985): 65–108.

36 Kevin Robbins, *Into the Image: Culture and Politics in the Field of Vision* (London: Routledge, 1996), p. 100.

37 Ibid., p. 101.

38 Fredric Jameson, "Nostalgia for the Present," in *Postmodernism, or, The Cultural Logic of Late Capitalism* (Durham, N.C.: Duke University Press, 1991), chapter 9.

Index

Lynn Spigel is Professor in the School of Cinema and Television
at the University of Southern California. She has written and
edited numerous books, including *Make Room for TV: Television
and the Family Ideal in Postwar America.*

*

Library of Congress Cataloging-in-Publication Data
Spigel, Lynn.
Welcome to the dreamhouse : popular media and postwar
suburbs / Lynn Spigel.
p. cm. — (Console-ing passions)
Includes bibliographical references and index.
ISBN 0-8223-2687-6 (alk. paper)
ISBN 0-8223-2696-5 (pbk. : alk. paper)
1. Television broadcasting—Social aspects—United States.
I. Title.   II. Series.
PN1992.6 .S663   2001
302.23′45′0973—dc21   00-045186

DATE DUE
